PRAISE FOR *AMERICAN CRUSADE*

"Seidel deftly guides us through some of the most explosive religious freedom cases of the last few decades. He shows how proponents of white Christian nationalism in the United States are refashioning the legal concept of 'religious freedom' into their preferred weapon for maintaining cultural supremacy. The implications of Seidel's razor-sharp work are clear: such weaponization of religious freedom harms us all. This book will soon become the go-to text helping Americans of any or no religious faith make sense of an ongoing crusade that is sure to reshape our society for generations to come."

—**Andrew L. Whitehead**, coauthor with Samuel L. Perry of
Taking America Back for God: Christian Nationalism in the United States

"Christian nationalism is real; and it threatens our democracy. But as Andrew Seidel documents, Christian nationalism is something more than an ideology or set of myths. It is also a richly funded and coordinated legal strategy that is transforming 'religious freedom' from a shield into weaponry—a sword to slash at one's cultural enemies and a battering ram to demolish the wall of separation between church and state. . . . Seidel minces no words about solutions. Confronting a legal system now weaponized for Christian nationalist goals requires serious court reform—and now."

—**Samuel L. Perry**, coauthor with Philip S. Gorski of
The Flag and the Cross: White Christian Nationalism and the Threat to Democracy

"*American Crusade* is a brilliant must-read for Americans. We are in the midst of a war on democracy by a Christian minority intent on inserting their beliefs into the Constitution and the law. For the theocrats, facts are often irrelevant, because the mission to impose their God justifies whatever means it takes. Seidel has marshaled the stories behind many aspects of this movement and pierced the taboo against putting religion in a bad light even when the religion has acted horribly toward others."

—**Marci A. Hamilton**, Fels Institute of Government Professor of Practice,
University of Pennsylvania, and Founder,
CEO, and Academic Director, CHILD USA

"It is hard to imagine a more necessary book at a more important time in our nation's history. . . . Seidel expertly navigates the symbiotic relationship between the evangelical right and the Supreme Court that has resulted in a weaponization of religious liberty ideals for a singular political purpose— to insulate white evangelical Christians from democratic governance. . . . *American Crusade* is a must-read for anyone hoping to understand our new political and cultural landscape."

—**Jessica Mason Pieklo**, Executive Editor of Rewire News Group
and coauthor with Robin Marty of *The End of* Roe v Wade:
Inside the Right's Plan to Destroy Legal Abortion

"Seidel writes a timely and poignant follow-up to his book *The Founding Myth* . . . making the depths of 'legalese' accessible and engaging. . . . Will stir controversy and debate and likely be on many readers' lists whether they agree or disagree with Seidel's arguments."

—*Library Journal*

"In this compelling account, Seidel weaves together seemingly disparate threads to demonstrate the modern-day perversion of true religious freedom. Instead of representing a shield against inequitable government overreaching, conservative Christians have turned 'religious liberty' into a sword in their efforts to recreate America as a Christian nation where Christians are privileged. Seidel's meticulous research and persuasive argument will convince all doubters about this troubling threat to our pluralistic, secular society."

—**Steven K. Green**, author of *Separating Church and State: A History*

"The Supreme Court's assault on *Roe v. Wade* was a gut punch to those of us who felt that our hard-won rights were secure. Just in time comes *American Crusade*, a brilliantly argued analysis of the methods and magnitude of the threat. Andrew Seidel carries Thomas Paine's torch to illuminate the danger to our most precious constitutional protections and human rights."

—**Ann Druyan**, author of *Cosmos: Possible Worlds*

"The Supreme Court is dismantling our secular state in favor of a Christian nation, Andrew Seidel shrewdly demonstrates in *American Crusade*. Seidel tells the real history of important religious freedom cases and exposes the powerful, monied network working to eliminate the last vestige of political neutrality that is supposed to lie at the heart of constitutional interpretation."

—**R. Laurence Moore**, coauthor with Isaac Kramnick of
The Godless Constitution: The Case Against Religious Correctness

"Andrew Seidel provides an insightful, deeply researched, and well-written account of how Christian zealots are using the term 'religious freedom' as a way to abrogate the rights of other Americans. Anyone who cares about the First Amendment—which should be everyone—must read this book."

—**Windsor Mann**, editor of *The Quotable Hitchens: From Alcohol to Zionism*

PRAISE FOR *THE FOUNDING MYTH*

"Brilliant, ambitious, well-researched, and compelling. . . . Seidel has written a masterful book. No one henceforth can attempt to discuss the claim that America was founded as, and is today, a Christian nation without seriously addressing his work."

—*Los Angeles Review of Books*

"Seidel, a constitutional attorney, provides a fervent takedown of Christian Nationalism in his furious debut. . . . His well-conceived arguments will spark conversations for those willing to listen."

—*Publishers Weekly*

"An indispensable book dismantling the idea that America was founded as a Christian nation."

—*GQ UK*

"[Seidel] demolishes the myth that America is based on scripture. . . . In this beautifully written book, he powerfully shows that Christian nationalists are arguing for a vision that is at odds with the essential nature of the Constitution and American government."

—**Erwin Chemerinsky**, Dean and Jesse H. Choper Distinguished Professor of Law, University of California, Berkeley, School of Law

"Andrew Seidel does a marvelous job debunking the 'Christian nation' myth. He reminds us that we're not a country founded on biblical principles and we should all be grateful for that. This book should be required reading for every member of Congress."

—**Hemant Mehta**, editor of *Friendly Atheist*, and author of *I Sold My Soul on eBay: Viewing Faith through an Atheist's Eyes*

"What if ['Judeo-Christian'] values are not only not the foundation of our country but are actually in conflict with America's bedrock principles? That is the stunning thesis of Seidel's new book—and it's one he backs up with ample evidence. This book is a game-changer. I can think of several politicians (and would-be politicians) who would greatly benefit from reading it."

—**Robert Boston**, Editor of *Church & State*, Americans United for Separation of Church and State, author of *Why the Religious Right Is Wrong About Separation of Church and State*

"At a time when too many religious and political figures trumpet the notion that the precepts of traditional Christianity were built into our national values, Seidel persuasively demonstrates that such an assertion is simply unfounded. This is an important insight that Americans of every political and religious stripe should understand and embrace."

—**Geoffrey R. Stone**, Edward H. Levi Distinguished Professor of Law, University of Chicago, and author of *Sex and the Constitution: Sex, Religion, and Law from America's Origins to the Twenty-First Century*

"With wit and brio, Seidel demolishes the Christian nationalist talking point that the United States was somehow founded on 'Judeo-Christian' principles (or on a list of nine or ten often offensive 'Commandments' allegedly delivered by a Near Eastern deity a few millennia ago). Along the way, his wide-ranging and well-researched narrative offers a much more inspiring vision of the American experiment than the bigoted exceptionalism of today's mythmakers."

—**Matthew Stewart**, author of *Nature's God: The Heretical Origins of the American Republic*

AMERICAN CRUSADE

How the Supreme Court Is Weaponizing RELIGIOUS FREEDOM

ANDREW L. SEIDEL

foreword by ERWIN CHEMERINSKY

UNION
SQUARE
&CO.

NEW YORK

**UNION
SQUARE
& CO.**

NEW YORK

UNION SQUARE & CO. and the distinctive Union Square & Co. logo are trademarks of
Sterling Publishing Co., Inc.

Union Square & Co., LLC, is a subsidiary of Sterling Publishing Co., Inc.

ISBN 978-1-4549-4392-1
ISBN 978-1-4549-4857-5 (e-book)

For information about custom editions, special sales, and premium purchases,
please contact specialsales@unionsquareandco.com.

Printed in the United States

2 4 6 8 10 9 7 5 3 1

unionsquareandco.com

Cover design by Igor Satanovsky
Interior design by Susan Welt and Gavin Motnyk

This book is dedicated to American Christian nationalists.
We're not coming for your rights, we're coming for your privilege.

* * *

"When liberty becomes license,
dictatorship is near."
—**Will and Ariel Durant**[1]

Contents

PART I

BATTLE PLANS, TARGETS, AND THE CALL TO ARMS

PART II

OPENING HOSTILITIES

PART III

THE ONSLAUGHT

Foreword

We should be scared. That is the message of Andrew Seidel's brilliant and chilling book detailing the dramatic changes in the current Supreme Court's approach to the religion clauses of the First Amendment. Because change in constitutional law generally happens incrementally, case by case, sometimes it is difficult to fully realize even radical changes until they have occurred. Seidel's book shows us that we are in the midst of the Court overruling decades of precedent and obliterating any semblance of a wall separating church and state.

How did we get here? Between 1960 and 2020, there were 32 years with a Republican president and 28 years with a Democratic president. But during that time, Republican presidents appointed 15 Supreme Court justices, while Democratic presidents appointed only eight. Put another way, President Donald Trump appointed three justices in his four years as president. But the prior three Democratic presidents—Jimmy Carter, Bill Clinton, and Barack Obama—served a combined 20 years in the White House, but appointed only four justices in those two decades.

Republican presidents have consistently, and especially in more recent years, appointed very conservative justices to please their political base. Above all, they have appointed individuals who would be perceived as sure votes to overrule *Roe v. Wade*.[1] They are, as Seidel explains, "crusaders" who want to dramatically change constitutional law. They reject the law that has been followed with regard to the religion clauses for decades. Their approach is not based on history or precedent, but on a conservative political ideology favored by the right wing.

There are two provisions in the First Amendment concerning religion: the Establishment Clause and the Free Exercise Clause. Seidel's book tells the story of how the law concerning both of these provisions is in the midst of profound change.

The First Amendment begins with the words, "Congress shall make no law respecting an establishment of religion." In 1947, when the Court first said that this provision also applies to state and local governments, all nine justices agreed that it is best understood through a metaphor coined by Thomas Jefferson, that there should be a wall separating church and state, and the Court said that it should be "high and impregnable."[2] Government should be secular; the place for religion is in people's lives, including their homes and places of worship.

There are many reasons for separating church and state.[3] Inevitably, there is coercion to participate when the government becomes aligned with a particular religion. Separating church and state allows all of us to feel that it is our government, something impossible when the government is supporting a particular religion. As James Madison long ago observed, it is just wrong for the government to tax people to support religions of others. Even from an originalist perspective, there is strong evidence that the founding generation wanted to make sure that the government was not involved in religious activities.

For decades, a majority of the justices on the Supreme Court, believed in the separation of church and state. But as Seidel shows, all six of the current conservative justices reject this and instead believe that the government violates the Establishment Clause only if it coerces religious participation. Under this view, little ever violates the Establishment Clause.

No longer are there restrictions on religious displays on government property. The Court's most recent decision about this, *American Legion v. American Humanist Association*, which Seidel discusses, upheld a 40-foot cross on public property at a busy intersection.[4] A majority of the justices were clear that they see no problems with religious symbols being prominently displayed by the government.

The conservative majority also sees no problem in overtly Christian prayers at government events. As Seidel explains, in *Town of Greece v. Galloway*, the Court upheld a practice where a town board invited Christian clergy for a long period of time to deliver invocations that almost always were explicitly Christian in their content.[5] There is no doubt that the current Court would not have imposed the limits on prayer in public schools and these decisions, too, may be reconsidered soon.

For decades, the Court limited the ability of the government to provide direct assistance to religious schools. Now, though, cases like

Trinity Lutheran Church v. Comer[6] and *Espinoza v. Montana Department of Revenue*[7]—each the focus of a chapter in Seidel's book—hold that the Free Exercise Clause *requires* that the government provide religious schools with the same aid that is given to private secular schools. It is an enormous shift from seeing the First Amendment as restricting government aid to religion to now the Court holding that the First Amendment obligates the government's subsidizing of religious education.

At the same time, the conservatives on the Court are moving to overrule decades of precedent concerning the Free Exercise Clause. In 1990, in *Employment Division v. Smith*, the Court held that generally people cannot get an exemption from a law on account of their religious beliefs.[8] Conservative Justice Antonin Scalia wrote for the Court and said that the Free Exercise Clause cannot be used to challenge a neutral law of general applicability no matter how much it burdens religion. In other words, if the law is neutral, in the sense that it was not motivated by a desire to interfere with religion, and if the law applies to everyone, there is no basis for a religious exemption from the law. *Employment Division v. Smith*, which Seidel covers in chapter 8, involved whether Native Americans could have an exemption from a state law prohibiting the consumption of peyote.

As Seidel explains, the Court got it right in *Smith*. In a society that is tremendously diverse with regard to religious beliefs, it is unwieldy and even dangerous to begin granting exceptions whenever someone has a religious objection. Besides, if exemptions based on religious beliefs are granted, then it will be necessary to define what is "religion" and to determine what is a sincerely held religious belief. Such determinations by courts are deeply problematic. And giving exceptions to laws for religious convictions, but not for secular ones should raise grave problems under the Establishment Clause.

But it seems clear that there is a majority on the current Court to overrule *Employment Division v. Smith*. In 2021, in *Fulton v. City of Philadelphia*—the subject of chapter 9—Justices Alito, Thomas, and Gorsuch expressly called for *Employment Division v. Smith* to be overruled.[9] Justice Barrett, joined by Justice Kavanaugh, expressed support for that view. Justice Barrett wrote, "In my view, the textual and structural arguments against *Smith* are more compelling."[10] But Barrett and Kavanaugh did not see a need to overrule *Smith* in that case.

Seidel shows the profound implications of overruling *Smith*. For example, businesses will have the constitutional right to violate laws that prohibit discrimination. Initially, this will be seen in cases where businesses, on account of the religious beliefs of their owners, want to refuse service or to employ gay, lesbian, and transgender individuals. But there is no reason why this would not also permit race and sex discrimination as well.

One cannot help but be afraid after reading Seidel's stunning book that explains all of this and what it will mean to have six justices committed to radical change with regard to religion and the Constitution. Soon before retiring from the Court, Justice Sandra Day O'Connor said: "By enforcing the [Religion] Clauses, we have kept religion a matter for the individual conscience, not for the prosecutor or bureaucrat. At a time when we see around the world the violent consequences of the assumption of religious authority by government, Americans may count themselves fortunate: Our regard for constitutional boundaries has protected us from similar travails, while allowing private religious exercise to flourish. . . . Those who would renegotiate the boundaries between church and state must therefore answer a difficult question: Why would we trade a system that has served us so well for one that has served others so poorly?"[11]

Why indeed? And that is the central point of this wonderful book.

—ERWIN CHEMERINSKY
May 2022

PUBLISHER'S NOTE:

This text was finalized in early June, about two weeks before the Supreme Court overturned *Roe v. Wade* and decided two major cases also mentioned by the author. To read the author's commentary on these important cases, please visit https://AndrewLSeidel.com/moreAC.

Introduction: Jesus Take the Wheel

"Those who would renegotiate the boundaries between
church and state must therefore answer a difficult question:
Why would we trade a system that has served us so well
for one that has served others so poorly?"

—Sandra Day O'Connor[1]

She "let go and let God take the wheel." That's what she told the police. Her eleven-year-old daughter was riding shotgun in her teal Ford Taurus. "Trials and tribulations" had plagued her like Job, and she believed it was time to "test her faith in God." So she "let her fear go and went for it." She blew through a red light at 120 mph, sliced the front off another car, careened backward off the road, toppled power lines, and ended up in a house. She reportedly told police "she did the right thing."[2] After all, nobody was hurt.

This wasn't the first time someone let Jesus take the wheel, nor the last. It's disturbingly common.[3] A Pennsylvania woman drove around for hours expecting a "calling from God." When the call finally came, she obeyed it and drove into oncoming traffic on Route 93.[4] The crash sent two people to the hospital, but "God took care of her by not letting her [get] injured," she told police. She had no remorse. Why would she? She was carrying out God's will. A Tennessee man flipped his truck five times when "Jesus was calling him and advised him to let go of the wheel," which he did. He also fled the scene, or, as he put it, left because he was "being called . . . to bow before someone."[5]

One woman deliberately rear-ended a line of cars at nearly 100 mph, causing a five-car pileup involving eighteen people and sending two to the hospital. When the police asked her why, she responded that "God told her to" and she "does whatever God tells her to do."[6]

I

A Florida man drove his Ferrari off a pier into thirty feet of water because "Jesus made me the smartest man on Earth and it's so hard to have this much responsibility," according to the police report.[7]

Some were fined. Some lost their licenses. Some were charged with crimes, including endangering a child and twelve counts of attempted murder. "Good," we might think. Let's hope they get some counseling, too. Letting Jesus drive is reckless behavior that kills or injures others, risks killing and injuring others, and destroys property.[8]

But hang on. What about their religious freedom?

In a day where millions of Americans believe religious freedom includes the right to risk the health and safety of others by worshipping in huge crowds without masks or vaccines during a pandemic, why is religious freedom not part of these news stories about Jesus taking the wheel? Where are the overfunded Christian legal outfits clamoring to vindicate the rights of these oppressed Christians who can't even drive on public roads the way their god intended? They'll take the case of a business that wants to violate civil rights laws and refuse LGBTQ customers all the way to the Supreme Court but not defend these prophets hearing directly from God? Why isn't this *the* culture war issue of our times?

Because it's absurd. And we understand that at a visceral level. The religious claim that Jesus will take the wheel is deadly. And the legal claim is ridiculous. There are laws against speeding, running red lights, and endangering children. If the driver doesn't want to comply with traffic laws, she doesn't get to drive; she loses her license. The same is true even if one's god is a bit of a backseat driver. Religious freedom isn't a license to drive recklessly.

This scenario is easy. But legally, it's the same as the cases we'll explore in this book, such as the Hobby Lobby case or the gay wedding cake case, or churches claiming that the Blood of Jesus will prevent the spread of a lethal pandemic. So why is it ridiculous to claim religious freedom to justify careening through a red light at 120 mph with your kid, but not to recklessly spread a lethal virus?

Along the religious freedom spectrum there are plenty of cases that seem easy, including in the other direction. In 1999, one federal court decided that two Muslim cops in Newark could grow their beards, as their sect of Islam required, even though department regulations said no. The regs sought a "professional and dignified image to the public," but seemed a bit arbitrary given the mustachioed chief.[9] Here too the result is obvious. Let them grow a beard, who cares? Nobody else is affected; nobody's rights are threatened by the religious exercise.

But a lot has changed since 1999. And even these seemingly innocent and easy cases are used to further a crusade against true religious liberty.

What Does Weaponizing Religious Freedom Mean?

The Book of Isaiah tells of a time when people "shall beat their swords into plowshares."[10] Repurposing weapons of war into implements of production, security, and stability is a lovely sentiment, but American Christians are proving the prophecy false. They're beating plowshares into swords. In particular, they're beating religious freedom into a sword. Turning a hallowed tool that protected conscience from government overreach—more of a shield than a farm implement—into a weapon. A network of faithful and well-funded activist groups are attempting to redefine and weaponize religious liberty. I'll call them "Crusaders" throughout this book. The Crusaders are perverting this constitutional protection to reshape it into a weapon to impose their religion on others.

The weapon is exclusive. You may wield it, if you're of the "right" religion. If you're a Christian or, really, if you're the right kind of a conservative Christian. Successfully forging this weapon will codify the receding privilege of this dwindling minority in the face of equality and demographic change. They'll become a special, favored class to which the laws do not apply.

But to do that, they have to redefine what religious freedom means for the average American, and judges have to agree to redraft a long-standing constitutional right. Quite a few are ready to do so.

Our Supreme Court is on the verge of consummating this contradictory notion of religious liberty and grafting it onto our Constitution. Unless we stop it and undo the damage done, the First Amendment will mean supremacy for conservative Christians and sanction for bigotry in the name of Jesus.

Our Constitution gives "to bigotry no sanction," wrote George Washington in a famous letter to the Touro Synagogue in Newport, Rhode Island.[11] Our first president toured the country in 1790 to shore up support for the new national government, unite the new country, and rally support for the constitutional amendments that would become the Bill of Rights, including the First Amendment. He visited the synagogue and wrote the congregation a letter condemning the idea that the government would simply tolerate religious minorities.[12] Toleration claims power, but does not exercise it. Thomas Paine put it like this a year later: "Toleration is not the *opposite* of intolerance, but is the *counterfeit* of it. Both are despotisms. The one assumes to itself the right of withholding liberty of conscience, and the other of granting it."[13] In her remarkable book, *Caste*, Isabel Wilkerson tells us, "It is not enough to be tolerant. You tolerate mosquitoes in the summer, a rattle in an engine, the gray slush that collects at the crosswalk in the winter. You tolerate what you would rather not have to deal with and wish would go away. It is no honor to be tolerated."[14]

Instead of toleration, Washington focused on individual rights, which the constitutional amendments set out to protect:

> The Citizens of the United States of America have a right to applaud themselves for having given to mankind examples of an enlarged and liberal policy: a policy worthy of imitation. All possess alike liberty of conscience and immunities of citizenship. It is now no more that toleration is spoken of, as if it was by the indulgence of one class of people, that another enjoyed the exercise of their inherent natural rights.[15]

The Crusaders, however, want to return to "tolerance." They want to go back to a time before the Constitution, when Christians were in charge of everything, unfettered by legal restraints, and when religious minorities and nonbelievers existed on sufferance.

The famous line from Washington's letter rejects this: "happily the Government of the United States . . . gives to bigotry no sanction, to persecution no assistance."

This understanding of religious freedom, which "requires only that they who live under its protection should demean themselves as good citizens," as Washington phrased it, is antithetical to claims that religious freedom allows one person to violate the rights of others. This version of religious freedom gives bigotry a sanction.

Can a business refuse to serve a gay couple in violation of civil rights laws because the owner is a conservative Christian? Can the government refuse to issue lawful licenses or documents to a gay couple because the issuing official is born-again? Can businesses and officials refuse to serve Black Americans because their personal god says so? Do Christian parents have a right to use the government's taxing power to fund their children's Christian schools? Can they do this even though our taxes already pay for an entire school system that's open to all? Can a city council ban certain religious practices in an effort to drive a church out of town? Can business owners thwart laws that grant employees' health-care rights because of what the owners' holy book supposedly dictates? Can government officials use state power and resources to spread Islam? What about Christianity? What about erecting and maintaining a 40-foot-tall Christian cross on government property? Can believers ignore rules that protect public health?

The answer to each question, posed in real cases, should be "no."

Legal questions of religious freedom are not always simple. They can be complicated and, more often, emotionally fraught. Especially when they involve children. But in their push to weaponize religious liberty, the Crusaders have misled and confounded many Americans about where we draw the legal lines for this founding American principle. While religious freedom cases may not raise simple questions, they're not very hard either.

Who Are the Crusaders?

The people and groups fighting to weaponize religious freedom are not formally affiliated under a single name or banner (other than the Christian flag[16]), but theirs is a holy war. A battle to privilege the few who believe in the correct version of the correct god, waged at the expense of those who do not. They're not conquering land, but it is a war of conquest. At the most basic level, they're seeking privilege. To codify supremacy.

The Crusaders' legal challenges are superficially about Christian crosses and veterans, or playgrounds, or private school vouchers, or bakeries and gay weddings—but really, they're about religious privilege. Often literally about privileging religion over nonreligion, Christianity over other religions, and the "right" kind of conservative Christian over other Christians. The Crusaders want to elevate Christian beliefs above the law and exempt Christians from the law, while disfavoring nonreligious and non-Christian citizens who are required to follow the law. Privilege and supremacy. Religious freedom could be their weapon to reclaim and entrench their dominant caste status. They can undo equality in the name of religious freedom.

We'll meet various Crusader groups as we discuss the cases, but there are commonalities. Usually, the group was started by a white Christian man, often one with early racist leanings and a professed homophobia. Quite a few groups, including the Alliance Defending Freedom, the Family Research Council, and First Liberty Institute, have early ties to James Dobson—an anti-gay white Christian with early racist and eugenics leanings.[17] Some were started with Koch brothers' seed money. Cash infusions from the DeVos empire are typical. The network is shadowy, complex, and vast, too much to fully cover in this book. Jane Mayer (*Dark Money*), Katherine Stewart (*The Power Worshippers*), and Jeff Sharlet (*The Family*) are excellent resources to get the curious started. But a taste of this small, wealthy, and opaque network is important because it has captured the Supreme Court. One Catholic couple, Ann and Neil Corkery, created the Wellspring Committee to funnel hundreds of millions into the fight for conservative Christian judges.[18] Ann is a self-professed member of Opus Dei, an uber-conservative wing of the Catholic Church that practices self-flagellation.[19] Using millions from the Koch brothers and their friends, the couple funded this "dark-money conduit, effectively laundering billionaire donations so no one would have to be accountable."[20] Wellspring, one of many such dark-money groups, partially funded two of the biggest players fighting to take over the court: the Judicial Crisis Network and the Federalist Society. Leonard Leo runs both.

Leo is universally recognized as *the* man who orchestrated the hostile takeover of the Supreme Court. A former employee described Leo's mission: "He figured out twenty years ago that conservatives had lost the culture war. Abortion, gay rights, contraception—conservatives didn't have a chance if public opinion prevailed. So they needed to stack the courts."[21]

The Judicial Crisis Network spent tens of millions to confirm Gorsuch, Kavanaugh, and Barrett, spreading misinformation about the court and the nominees.[22] Carrie Severino is listed as the sole employee on the JCN website[23] not because it's small, but because it's a shell and Leo runs the show: "JCN is Leonard Leo's PR organization—nothing more and nothing less."[24] Severino runs JCN for Leo, while her husband, Roger, worked in the Trump administration as a director in Health and Human Services. Tasked with enforcing anti-discrimination laws at HHS, Roger, who's virulently anti-LGBTQ, instead created a new Conscience and Religious Freedom Division with an eye toward allowing Christians to deny patients access to health care by claiming religious freedom.[25] Roger describes the couple as "serious Catholics."[26] He previously worked for two Crusaders: the Becket Fund for Religious Liberty and the Heritage Foundation, where he ran the DeVos Center for Religion and Civil Society (yes, that DeVos). Carrie clerked for Clarence Thomas, whose wife, Ginni, has deep ties with the Crusader network, including the shadowy Council for National Policy, the Heritage Foundation, and many others, *including those litigating cases before her husband.*[27] One of JCN's original founders is also a former Thomas clerk. She wrote other Thomas clerks that she and her friends "had been praying our knees off that January 6 would see light and truth being shed on what we believe in our hearts was likely a stolen election," that "Trump would be determined to be the legitimate winner," and that on that day she marched, and "prayed and shared another important message, 'Jesus saves.'"[28] John Eastman, the legal architect of the failed January 6 insurrection, who also tried to instigate a new wave of birtherism against Kamala Harris, is another former Thomas clerk; he weighed in on the listserv against the election result, too.[29] The network is highly religious, incestuous, and nepotistic.[30]

Leo began his takeover of the Supreme Court while at the Federalist Society and drove hard to get Roberts and then Alito installed, the rocks on which he would build his conservative supermajority. Leo and his network blocked Merrick Garland's nomination for nearly a year (with an anonymous $17 million donation to JCN, half of which was spent blocking Garland[31]). Leo also wrote the lists of potential Supreme Court nominees that Trump made public and from which Trump chose Gorsuch, then Kavanaugh, then Barrett.[32] The *Washington Post* estimated Leo raised $250 million for this judicial mission and his network between 2014 and 2017.[33]

Leo is a conservative Catholic and a member of the Knights of Malta, a Catholic order that traces its origins back to the Knights Hospitaller and the First Crusade. He's quite literally a Crusader. The Catholicism and reach of Leo's shadowy kingdom "seem ripped from the pages of a Dan Brown novel," as one journalist put it.[34] His "faith is paramount to him," said his former media director; when Leo travels, his staff finds the closest Catholic church so that Leo, like Clarence Thomas, can attend daily mass.[35] In 2007, George W. Bush appointed Leo as chairman of the US Commission on International Religious Freedom, where he was promptly sued for employment discrimination for terminating a Muslim, with other employees resigning in protest.[36] Leo was also involved in a group organized by Clarence Thomas's wife that opposed the "Ground Zero Mosque."[37] He even has his own highly rated law school, the acronymically challenged Antonin Scalia School of Law (ASSOL).

Yes, the Crusaders Are Christians

Some readers will—already have—reflexively countered some points with variations on a common theme: *They're not real Christians. True Christians don't X, Y, or Z. These people are fake Christians.* This argument is part of the problem. Inevitably, "such fundamentalisms will arise within the complex cultural systems that religions represent. Fundamentalism cannot be stamped out, and it is no use treating it as 'not really religious,'" explains Chrissy Stroop in an essay on this subject.[38] These Christians justify their beliefs with their bible, sermons, and church. Often, the messages they receive have a longer history and more biblical support than the newer, more inclusive strains of Christianity.

The "fake Christian" counter typically pops up when people feel personally attacked because they identify as a Christian or because they equate "Christian" with "good person." That myth, that to be a Christian is to be a good person, and vice versa, is persistent and problematic. Morality is independent of religion, and we must divorce these two concepts. Good people are good people. Christians are Christians. The two are not synonymous, and the more we link them, the more we encourage people to adopt the easy label rather than evaluate the behavior that makes a good person. The conflation of the two is one reason we've been so blind to this ongoing Crusade.

Put simply, Christians can be bigots, authoritarians, bad people. Most aren't. Many Christians fight for true religious freedom, including pro-choice pastors, nuns saving the environment, and the Unitarian minister arrested for giving food and water to immigrants coming across the southern border. Their religious freedom cases tend to be clearer and cleaner, and involve helping others, not harming them.[39] It's crucial for kind, empathetic, equality-minded Christians to stand up and fight against this Crusade, not just the theological label. Pretending that the Crusaders are not Christian doesn't solve the problem; it makes it insoluble.

The Weapon Is a Silver Bullet

There will never be enough privilege and power to satisfy the Crusaders. Even if the Crusaders successfully weaponize religious freedom, that's only the beginning. The power of this particular weapon is that it is a silver bullet. It can trump any law or rule or norm. Religion is a permission structure that grants people the moral justification for any action, however harmful; a weaponized religious freedom is the legal justification for those harmful acts.

Once religious freedom is weaponized, they'll carry it into every other legal fight. Public health measures and civil rights laws are two areas where religious freedom trumping good citizenship was once unthinkable but is quickly becoming the norm (see chapters 5, 11, and 16). And the license to harm others won't end with discriminating against LGBTQ citizens. Crusaders will use it to reestablish white supremacy—something that was made hauntingly clear in oral arguments at the Supreme Court (see chapter 5, pages 71–73 and 86–89). They'll also bring religious freedom into unexpected arenas, like the fight for voting rights.[40]

Even the absurd idea that people have a religious freedom right to violate traffic laws is conceivable. The Mississippi House passed the

"Jesus Take the Wheel" act in 2015, a law that would have allowed church-owned vehicles to transport busloads of people without the appropriate commercial license. Because why do you need a license to maneuver a 40-foot-long coach bus when Jesus is driving? The bill died, but the Crusade has gained ground.[41] The entire point of a weaponized religious freedom is that it is limitless.

A Hierarchy of Rights Enshrines Inequality

The Crusaders are reformulating our coequal, coextensive human rights into a hierarchy of rights. Some rights will be placed above others as more worthy of legal protection, with one right above them all: religious freedom. By placing atop the hierarchy of rights the free-exercise rights of conservative Christians, a demographic that is shrinking every day, they can act on those beliefs no matter what the cost to society, our secular government, or the rights of others.

This is easy to spot in the wild. One blatant example is Mississippi's "religious freedom" law, a law drafted by Crusaders. Governor Bryant signed the Protecting Freedom of Conscience from Government Discrimination Act in April 2016 (the state's third "religious freedom" law in as many years.[42]) The law doesn't defend freedom of conscience from government overreach; it singles out specific conservative Christian beliefs about sex for special legal recognition.

The second section of the bill lists all the "religious beliefs or moral convictions protected by this act" and, in its entirety, reads:

(a) Marriage is or should be recognized as the union of one man and one woman;

(b) Sexual relations are properly reserved to such a marriage; and

(c) Male (man) or female (woman) refer to an individual's immutable biological sex as objectively determined by anatomy and genetics at time of birth.[43]

The State of Mississippi examined the vast expanse of available theology and singled out three precepts from conservative Christianity for special protection. Never mind science, biology, or the beautiful complexities of human sexuality. This doesn't protect religious freedom; it codifies conservative Christian doctrine in the name of religious freedom. Not only does the Mississippi law prefer these beliefs to all others; it privileges actions inspired by the beliefs. Business owners, organizations, and even government officials who hold these special beliefs may deny marriage licenses, housing, foster care and adoption placement, and "marriage-related goods or services," like photography, baking, and floral arrangements, to anyone they feel has transgressed the sexual dictates of their god. It's easy to imagine what the reaction would have been if Islam or Hindu or Jewish beliefs were codified like this. Millions would suddenly muster to defend the wall of separation between state and church, and argue that the government has no power to legally recognize religious tenets.

When blocking the law, the lower court explained that it violated the separation of state and church as well as anti-discrimination principles. The law "violates both the guarantee of religious neutrality and the promise of equal protection of the laws." And yes, the law preferred conservative Christian beliefs: "The State has put its thumb on the scale to favor some religious beliefs over others."[44] The well-written decision surveys American law dating back to the colonial period, but in the end, the decision was simple. The law was unconstitutional because it "establishes an official preference for certain religious beliefs over others."[45] This is what a weaponized religious freedom does.

The lower federal court's analysis was spot on. The law is unconstitutional. But three Republican judges on the Fifth Circuit Court of Appeals—two appointed by George W. Bush and one by Reagan—overruled the lower court. Not on the merits, but on a jurisdictional issue that rendered the challenge impotent.[46] The law is still on the books today.[47]

This bill was not the brainchild of any elected representative of the people of Mississippi. It was written, promoted, and shepherded through the legislature by a Crusader we'll hear more about, the Alliance Defending Freedom. Formerly the Alliance Defense Fund, ADF has wormed its wealthy tentacles into every aspect of the Crusade. Not just here in the states, but also abroad.[48] Emails revealed ADF's widespread involvement with the Mississippi law, including handling legal challenges, drafting legislative language, and producing talking points and signing statements.[49] This law privileges conservative Christianity because that's ADF's goal.

This law is a stark warning of what the Crusade might look like if successful. A hierarchy of rights and a hierarchy of religions. The weaponized version of religious freedom replaces our egalitarian understanding of the concept with conservative Christian privilege. That right is the top of a pyramid. This "superright" (see chapter 9) then trumps other rights and others' rights. Religious freedom becomes a weapon—a shield beaten into a sword.

The Crusaders were explicit about their hierarchy. Mike Pompeo is a conservative Christian who yearns for the end times and said that politics is "a never-ending struggle . . . until the Rapture."[50] As Trump's Secretary of State, he slapped together the Commission on Unalienable Rights specifically to argue for this hierarchy. That commission produced a report, based in part on "biblical teachings," to argue that "foremost among the unalienable rights that government is established to secure, from the founders' point of view, are property rights and religious liberty." Religious freedom and property are raised up, "foremost," with other rights framed as lesser, "ad hoc rights," while still others, "abortion . . . same-sex marriage," were downgraded as "social and political controversies."[51] None of this is true, as hundreds of experts explained to Pompeo's commission repeatedly: "It is a fundamental tenet of human rights that all rights are universal and equal."[52] But the Crusaders' version of human rights is Christianity over humanity.

But Why the Crusade?

It's largely a backlash against equality realized. Christianity was once able to discriminate on the basis of race; now that's largely unthinkable. Christianity was once able to legally subjugate half the population. Christianity was once able to discriminate against LGBTQ people but now isn't. As more people realize rights due to them by virtue of being human, the sphere of religious imposition shrinks. The Crusade seeks to reclaim this lost ground.

Obamacare expanded equality by recognizing the reproductive rights of American women. Hobby Lobby's conservative white Christian owners fought against that expansion of rights under the guise of religious freedom.

The *Obergefell* decision expanded equality by recognizing the rights of LGBTQ citizens to marry. Masterpiece Cakeshop's conservative white Christian owner and a host of other businesses fought that expansion, claiming religious freedom.

Brown v. Board of Education expanded equality by recognizing the rights of Black Americans to equal access to public education, and in the name of religious freedom, Christians pushed for school choice and vouchers and segregation academies.

White Christian Americans facing equality act like martyrs suffering for their faith; they *feel* that these expansions violate their rights. But parity is not oppression. Equality, even when it means the erosion of privilege, is not discrimination. If you're given $100 that was stolen from someone else and the law demands that you give it back, you're not being robbed. Rather, justice has been achieved. To you, it may feel unjust to be forced to give up the money, especially if the law has not cared about the victim in the past or, worse, if the law had previously said that the victim wasn't human. It may feel doubly unfair if the law had, until recently, agreed with your religion. Slavemongers stole enslaved people's lives and complained about the unfairness of losing their property when the United States belatedly abolished slavery and recognized humans as humans. The only injustice would have been the continual refusal to do the latter. To fight against equality is to fight for supremacy.

Equality Is a Threat to Christianity as the Dominant Caste; Religious Freedom Is Their Answer

If we put all this together—the silver bullet, the hierarchy of rights, the fight against equality and for supremacy—the Crusade begins to look like a quest to find a holy grail that will reverse inexorable demographic trends. White Christian Americans' status as the dominant group is threatened, and when the dominant group or caste in society feels threatened or left behind by circumstances, it reacts or overreacts by seeking a way to retain that status.

Some political scientists credit *dominant group status threat* for Trump's 2016 electoral victory. Fearful White Christians aligned with the person claiming he'd bring back the America they knew, the America where they dominated all others. Diana Mutz, a leading proponent of this theory, argues that the 2016 election "was an effort by members of already dominant groups to assure their continued dominance and by those in an already powerful and wealthy country to assure its continued dominance."[53] In *Caste*, Wilkerson posits that the source of their discontent is the "end of an illusion, an awakening to the holes in the article of faith that an inherited, unspoken superiority, a natural deservedness over subordinated castes, would assure their place in the hierarchy. They had relied on this illusion, perhaps beyond the realm of consciousness and perhaps needed it more than any other group in a forbiddingly competitive society."[54] The disillusion strikes at their identity, and they choose to fight reality rather than diminish their self-image.[55] Fox News's success comes partly because the hosts tap into this fear, so that White Christians sitting comfortably on the couch safe at home feel threatened.[56]

Other researchers are finding evidence for the preservation of dominance as well, and it ties closely to Christian nationalism, the subject of my first book. A 2021 survey found that simply mentioning the fast-changing religious demographics in America elicited a threat response and triggered defensive political stances among Christians. Simply acknowledging shifting demographics created a feeling that their religious freedom was threatened and pushed them toward Christian nationalism and Donald Trump.[57] They conflate demographic loss with a threat to their freedom, which suggests that they fundamentally misunderstand religious liberty as privilege. That they believe freedom means enjoying the trappings of their dominant status.

Studies agree that "religious freedom" means something very different to White American Christians than it does to other Americans. One 2020 election study showed that voters who believed "religious freedom" was the most important issue and chose their 2020 presidential candidate accordingly also thought that the federal government should declare America a Christian nation.[58] These voters ranked religious freedom above the economy and abortion, *and* they want a Christian nation. As Sam Perry, one of the researchers, explained, it's "almost as if 'religious freedom' is code for 'Christian freedom.'"[59] The government aligning with one religion is the death of religious freedom; they see it as the definition of religious freedom. This is the essence of Christian nationalism and the antithesis of true religious freedom.

The Crusade is a quest to remake a protection into a weapon for maintaining a dominant group's status in the face of waning demographic power. This isn't a novel observation. "This legal offensive to elevate 'religious liberty' over other civic goals is coming even as the share of Americans who ascribe to no religious faith is steadily rising, and as white Christians have fallen to a minority share of the population," wrote Ronald Brownstein in *The Atlantic*.[60]

Religious freedom is a weapon for White Christian Americans to plant their crosses on public land, declaring it theirs, not ours.

For White Christian Americans to discriminate against lesser groups, lesser castes.

For White Christian Americans to remove their children from the public school system—integrated and diverse—and put them in private religious schools at taxpayer expense, forcing taxpayers to maintain two educational systems, one for everyone, the other for the waning dominant caste.

For White Christian Americans to deny bodily autonomy and reproductive freedom to people deemed subservient by their holy book.

For White Christian Americans to opt out of public health measures meant to protect everyone in a pandemic.

Most importantly, for this dominant caste to declare *unconstitutional* any failure to recognize any of these privileges. To declare that equality is hostility.

The expansion of equality and withering religious and racial hegemony is the contested territory in many religious freedom cases. This means that Christian privilege should be losing, not winning more often. In reality, we're not expanding rights or giving new rights; we are recognizing rights that have always existed under the law but were never enforced. We are affirming the humanity of our brothers and sisters and admitting that we've been wrong. As we realize the aspirational values implicit in "We the People," "equal justice under law," "all . . . are created equal," and other founding maxims, as we recognize that humans are human and worthy of rights, White Christian America is dying a slow demographic death and rebelling. They are raging against the dying of their privilege.

Author's Note: Jargon Be Damned

This book is not meant to be comprehensive. It's a warning that the First Amendment is being destroyed. In its place, Crusaders are forging a weapon to ensure their supremacy. This book will tell the real stories behind recent religious freedom cases to explain true religious freedom.

Sometimes we legal professionals get buried under legalese, procedure, judicial philosophies, and precedents. Sometimes we hide behind them. Often it's better just to cut through all that distraction and look at the core of a case or dispute. To go back to basics. I try to do that in these pages, and I write for everyone, avoiding legal jargon, case names, and even legal tests (compelling governmental interests, strict scrutiny, rational basis review). These tests can be manipulated by judges in a way that makes the search for intellectual or doctrinal consistency frustrating or futile. Focusing on the legal tests unnecessarily removes these cases from public understanding and also buys into the legitimacy of the inquiry. Focusing on court-created tests rather than underlying principles also buys into the myth of a court that, as Chief Justice John Roberts himself preached at his 2005 confirmation hearing, has one job: "to call balls and strikes."[1] Roberts and other judges don't do that. On politically charged and "culture war" issues, they're often manipulating the law and even the facts to reach a desired outcome. So we'll shun those myths and jargon in favor of foundational principles. These pages may not comport with the language our courts or the legal academy prefers, but that has the benefit of consistency, longevity, and, I hope, clarity.

This also means that we won't always be repeating the facts as stated by the Supreme Court, which often reverse-engineers decisions by emphasizing or ignoring certain facts, and even changing facts to fit their opinion. We'll dig deeper. I've interviewed the people involved in these cases and scoured archives and other records. We treat courts as arbiters of truth and justice, but they often fall very short of that.

I remember the indignation and shock I felt when I first experienced the Supreme Court altering material facts in a case. My friends at Americans United for Separation of Church and State, whom I now have the pleasure of working alongside, challenged the Christian prayers at city council meetings in the town of Greece, New York. Christian clergy delivered every single prayer for a decade.[2] I had been asked to write as a friend of the court (an *amicus* brief) when the case got to the Supreme Court.[3]

There's bad precedent on government prayer, which is unconstitutional by any reasonable legal principle, test, or standard. But in 1983, the court simply ignored all of that and reverse-engineered a politically palatable outcome—government-organized, government-led prayer is constitutional—using bad facts and flawed history. (I explored this in detail in *The Founding Myth*.)

Despite this bad precedent, Americans United brought a good challenge that both showed both (a) how faulty that 1983 decision was and (b) how it might succeed under the strange scheme the court fabricated. An important question under this backward scheme was *who was the audience for the prayers?* Were the prayers directed at the legislators themselves, or at the public? One reason such prayers are supposedly constitutional is that legislators aren't abusing state power to impose religion on everyone, just each other. In this town, the prayer giver used the podium from which citizens spoke to the council. Normally, the podium faced the semicircular dais on which the city council sat so that citizens could easily address councilmembers. It's a fairly typical setup. But in this town, as I noted in our brief citing numerous exhibits, when clergy came up to deliver the prayer, the city would turn the podium around to face the audience, not the members of the council.[4] The city went out of its way to direct prayers at citizens.

This was irrefutable factual proof that these prayers were not meant for the council members personally, but were imposed on citizens attending the meeting to hear about property taxes or restaurant licenses or kids' schools. People had to endure a Christian prayer imposed by their local government simply to participate in that government. The court altered this irrefutable fact: "The principal audience for these invocations is not, indeed, the public but lawmakers themselves, who may find that a moment of prayer or quiet reflection sets the mind to a higher purpose and thereby eases the task of governing," wrote Justice Anthony Kennedy in the 5–4 decision.[5] It may seem like a small thing, but the abnegation of reality by the highest court tasked with truth and justice is rather a big deal. The fact was inconvenient, so it was changed.

I asked Ayesha Khan, the AU attorney who litigated this case up to the high court, about this. "That was a complete distortion of the undisputed facts. It was unprincipled, results-driven decision-making by conservative activist judges. Pure activism," she said. "The justices twisted the facts and reality to suit their political agenda."[6] The fact was integral to the outcome in previously bungled cases, making the task of reverse-engineering here more difficult, so reality was simply altered. And now, for generations of law students and lawyers that read this case, that *is* reality.[7]

You must unshackle your mind from the belief that the Supreme Court is an impartial arbiter of truth and justice. The Crusade depends upon people believing this myth. McConnell, Trump, and Leo cheated and stole and packed the courts to put their collaborators in place not because they would administer justice evenhandedly, but because they wouldn't.

One final note. You'll notice that I often use exclusive language when talking about religion in this book. I write "churches" and "Christianity" rather than "houses of worship" or "religion." Yes. Because this Crusade is about privileging Christians. Occasionally, minorities will be swept into decisions benefiting Christians, but this Crusade is about Christian privilege. I won't help perpetuate the myth that this version of religious freedom is ecumenical.

PART I

BATTLE PLANS, TARGETS, AND THE CALL TO ARMS

1

Christian Legal Supremacy

"Let me never fall into the vulgar mistake of dreaming
that I am persecuted whenever I am contradicted."

—Ralph Waldo Emerson[1]

Domineque Ray was going to die. That was certain. Many believed he deserved death. Ray's crimes were horrible, the stuff of parents' nightmares. His appeals were virtually exhausted.

Two weeks before his scheduled death, the warden met with Ray and explained the execution step-by-step, including the fact that the prison chaplain—a Christian—would be present in the execution chamber.

Alabama law states that the prison chaplain—always a Christian—"*may* be present at an execution."[2] It also allows the condemned to have his own "spiritual advisor" present. The two are on the same list, equal under the law, but Alabama forced the Christian chaplain on everyone, no matter their religion, and excluded other advisors from the room.

Ray was a Muslim and wanted a fellow Muslim in the room. He also didn't want a Christian chaplain in the room. Ray's lawyers asked the courts to temporarily stay his execution long enough to sort this out—a short delay in the name of religious freedom.

The Eleventh Circuit Court of Appeals explained "the central constitutional problem" succinctly: "The state has regularly placed a Christian cleric in the execution room to minister to the needs of Christian inmates, but has refused to provide the same benefit to a devout Muslim and all other non-Christians." The three-judge panel (two Clinton and one Obama appointee[3]) then correctly held that Alabama's policy violated Ray's religious freedom: "If Ray were a Christian, he would have a profound benefit; because he is a Muslim, he is denied that benefit."[4] Clear, simple, correct.

The conservative bloc on the Supreme Court disagreed. In a two-paragraph opinion, the five justices said that Ray took too long to raise this religious freedom issue.[5] (Ray learned about the chaplain issue on Wednesday and his lawyers filed the religious freedom lawsuit on Monday.[6]) Ray would die on schedule. Chief Justice John Roberts and Justices Clarence Thomas, Samuel Alito, Neil Gorsuch, and Brett Kavanaugh were in such a rush to see Ray executed that they ignored the religious freedom of a dying man. Ray was a Black Muslim, not a white Christian. So unlike every Christian Alabama executes, Ray died without religious consolation. His imam was not in the room, nor was the Christian chaplain, a last-minute concession. Ray was pronounced dead about two hours after the justices issued their two paragraphs.[7]

Eighteen months later, Justice Alito delivered a keynote speech to Leonard Leo's Federalist Society and had the gall to lament the degradation of religious freedom: "It pains me to say this, but in certain quarters, religious liberty is fast becoming a disfavored right."[8] But for Alito, that feeling only seems to extend to Christians. Alito and his conservative cohort disfavor religious freedom when non-Christians seek to exercise it.

Judges are always skeptical of prisoners' religious freedom claims, but had Ray been a Christian criminal to be executed—had he not converted to Islam in prison—he'd have had spiritual comfort.[9] The court's failure to uphold religious freedom resulted in genuine inequality, trampling minority rights. Unbelievably, especially given Alito's later lip service, the court claimed that keeping to a schedule is more important than religious freedom.

The high court's conservative bloc read the First Amendment guarantee of religious freedom through the lens of Christian supremacy.

Just eight months before this religious freedom decision, the justices handed down the gay wedding cake case (see chapter 5). There, a bakery discriminated against a gay couple. The court claimed that the state was so hostile to the bakery that it had to throw out an entire civil rights case, giving the bakery a free pass for its bigotry. When a

Christian is facing off against the government, under "the Constitution's guarantee of free exercise, [the government] cannot impose regulations that are hostile to the religious beliefs of affected citizens. . . . The Free Exercise Clause bars even 'subtle departures from neutrality' on matters of religion."[10] But when a condemned minority tried to lean on that principle, it evaporated. It was suddenly so insubstantial that the conservative bloc could spare only two paragraphs, neither of which mention religious freedom, the First Amendment, or the Constitution. Ray took longer to die than will take you to read the opinion ignoring his religious freedom.

This is Christian supremacy. And this isn't an isolated example.

This court upheld the Muslim ban (see chapter 7). Before that, the justices ignored—literally did not examine—the constitutional principle that our secular government cannot fund religion when it held that Missouri *must* give taxpayer funds to a church because refusing to do so was religious discrimination (chapter 13). The court did this same thing in Montana, forcing the state to tax citizens for the benefit of Christian parents and Christian schools (chapter 14). We saw it again when the court allowed the government to spend hundreds of thousands of dollars displaying and maintaining a 40-foot concrete Christian cross on government property (chapter 12).

And it almost happened again a month after Ray's execution. But the backlash against Ray's execution had been furious, swift, and international;[11] the outcry was enough to change the outcome in a nearly identical Texas case.

Texas was set to execute Patrick Murphy, who had converted to Buddhism a decade earlier.[12] Texas gave Murphy a choice: he could have either "a Christian prison chaplain or no chaplain present."[13] Die with the state's preferred god or die alone. Murphy challenged this, claiming religious freedom, and his challenge received more attention because of Ray's loss. Murphy lost in the lower courts, which cited Ray's case.[14] But this time the Supreme Court stayed the execution (over Thomas, Alito, and Gorsuch's dissents). Kavanaugh wrote an opinion that backtracked on Ray's case, too late for Ray. But Kavanaugh also suggested that the state could "allow religious advisers only into the viewing room," not the death chamber.[15] So Texas banned prison chaplains and religious advisors from the execution chamber.[16] Alabama did too.

Those new bans were challenged. In February 2021, the court blocked Alabama's execution of Willie Smith, a Christian, because the state would not let his pastor in the execution chamber to provide consolation.[17] That September, the court stayed Texas from executing John Ramirez, a Baptist, who not only claimed a religious freedom right to have his pastor in the room, but also for that pastor to lay hands on him and pray out loud as the state kills him; it blocked the rule in Ramirez's case in March.[18] Christians are still favored. The Muslim lost and was killed with two paragraphs. But Christians thumping their Christianity receive full briefing and oral argument for their religious freedom. The Crusaders also came to their defense.[19]

Christians are litigating more religious freedom cases under this court and winning more than ever. That's not because this Supreme Court is vindicating religious freedom, but because it is dividing our nation along religious lines. It is on the path to make Christians a favored, privileged class and non-Christians second-class citizens.

2

The Court and the Crusade

"Deus vult! Deus vult! (God wills it! God wills it!)"

—**Pope Urban II**, as he launched
the first crusade in 1095[1]

Nothing so dramatic as the above quote marks the opening of Crusader hostilities on our Constitution. But the Roberts Court issued a clear call to arms in 2010. The Crusaders set up the cases, and the Supreme Court knocks them down. Together, they're weaponizing religious freedom as a constitutional right.

The story begins a decade earlier. John Roberts was appointed chief justice in 2005 by George W. Bush, who himself was appointed president by the Supreme Court in the 2000 decision *Bush v. Gore*. The impact of that decision is incalculable. The various "what if" scenarios are confusing, contradictory, and complicated by the legal remedies the parties sought and courts imposed. A full review and accounting of all 175,010 disputed Florida votes showed that more Floridians voted for Gore than Bush.[2]

I was a freshman at Tulane University and didn't grasp all the implications of the decision, but conservative politicians did. Chief Justice Rehnquist, Justice Antonin Scalia, and Justice Thomas readily abandoned their long-professed judicial and constitutional views to decide in favor of Bush.[3] It was naked partisanship. And it broke the court. "His colleagues' actions were so transparently, so crudely partisan that Souter thought he might not be able to serve with them anymore," wrote one court observer of Justice David Souter. "There were times when David Souter thought of *Bush v. Gore* and wept."[4] Shedding the skin of impartiality and nonpartisanship to claim a presidency is a bell that cannot be unrung. Certainly, it made clear to politicians who can read demographic trends that judges would be more important than ever in the future. Capturing judgeships could help maintain political power and even minority rule for a party shrinking demographically. (There's a good argument to be made that packing and capturing the judiciary began earlier. Others date it to the replacement of Thurgood Marshall with Clarence Thomas, an unqualified Republican operative credibly accused of sexual harassment, an accusation he denied.[5])

Bush v. Gore didn't just crystallize conservative thinking on capturing the judiciary; it helped them accomplish the goal. It's far easier to win a second presidential term than a first. Had Gore been president, who knows what would have happened in the 2004 election and who would have been president in 2005 when Chief Justice William Rehnquist died. But W. was and W. appointed John Roberts. This marked the first time the court had four Catholics (Roberts, Scalia, Kennedy, and Thomas). W. nominated the fifth, Sam Alito, a month after Roberts was confirmed.

Before Roberts, decisions involving religion and the Constitution were haphazard and reliably favored neither side. The court's twin decisions involving Ten Commandments displays exemplify this.[6] The decisions came down on the same day in June 2005, just months before Roberts was nominated. Both decisions were 5–4. The Ten Commandments monument at the capitol in Austin, Texas, was constitutional and allowed to remain. The Ten Commandments displays in two Kentucky courthouses were unconstitutional and had to be removed. Justice Stephen Breyer was incapable of consistency when deciding whether "I am the LORD your God, you shall have no other gods before me . . ." was a religious declaration or not. His indecisiveness and unwillingness to cause political offense made him the swing vote. The brace of cases illustrate a judicial failing, but also a judiciary that was up for grabs on those issues.

Before those June 2005 cases, the court had handed out wins and losses to everyone. In 2004, it held that religious freedom did not require the government to fund scholarships for students training to be pastors (7–2).[7] In 2000, it struck down organized prayer over the loudspeakers at public high school football games (6–3).[8] These were the last clear wins for state/church separation.[9]

But the court wasn't always adjudicating pure legal principles, and, especially in the five or so years before Roberts's appointment, that led to serious inconsistencies, as with the Ten Commandments monuments. Also in 2000, it allowed loans of taxpayer funds and government resources to flow to private religious schools in a confused split decision.[10] It allowed Ohio to use taxpayer money to pay for private religious education in 2002—the first time the court allowed vouchers and a devastating blow to public education (5–4).[11] The decisions upholding the wall of separation had stronger majorities, and the rationales for ignoring that wall were weak, confused, contradictory, and typically unable to win a majority of the justices, but not for long.

Three months after the twin Ten Commandments cases, John Roberts was the new chief justice. Everything changed. Roberts advocates for deeply conservative change, but *slowly*. That incrementalism has been a hallmark of his career. So after a slow transition and a post–Ten Commandments cases breather, in 2010 the Roberts Court started deciding a case involving the First Amendment religion clauses nearly every year. The Roberts Court has been demolishing the wall of separation between church and state one brick at a time ever since. As it is doing this, it's also altering the definition of religious freedom and, alarmingly, turning it against state/church separation. The Roberts Court has betrayed a founding American principle, often in the name of religious freedom. As author, Pulitzer Prize–winning *New York Times* journalist, and Yale law professor Linda Greenhouse put it, "A core project of today's Supreme Court under the leadership of Chief Justice John Roberts is to reorient the First Amendment's two religion clauses."[12]

The Roberts Court's 2010 call to arms was clear. The court approved a farcical fix for a monumental violation of the constitutional separation between government and religion. An 8-foot-tall Christian cross stood in the middle of more than 1.5 million acres of public land, the Mojave National Preserve. A retired National Park Service employee challenged the cross in court. Crusaders intervened (First Liberty Institute, then known as Liberty Law Institute.) This cross was the preeminent symbol of Christianity in the middle of government land, marking—like a conquistador's flag—land that belongs to We the

People for We the Christians. It was unconstitutional by any measure. Complying with the Constitution by removing it was seen as a threat to Christians, symbolic of their loss of dominant status. To ensure the cross stayed up, Congress transferred, out of sea of 1.5 million acres, the one acre of land under the cross to a private entity that would "maintain" the cross or lose the land. If the cross came down, the land reverted to the United States. This wasn't a solution to the constitutional violation, but a way to perpetuate the violation. That sham of a remedy was challenged because, like the cross, the land transfer itself had a religious purpose: to display *the* symbol of the Christian religion.

In a 5–4 decision, the Roberts Court approved the sham. This mockery signaled a willingness to accept the flimsiest of legal fictions over constitutional principle. More ominously, the Supreme Court agreed to accept that fiction because it could be employed *against* constitutional principles if the result privileged Christians. The message was unmistakable: Christianity first, the Constitution second, if at all.

The Crusaders heard the message, and the floodgates opened. They filed lawsuit after lawsuit, stoked fear of status loss, and raised millions. In 2011, the court allowed a voucher program to send taxpayer funds to religious schools by denying citizens' ability to challenge the program (5–4).[13] In 2012, it said that religious organizations can legally discriminate when hiring clergy and weaponized that against employees with no religious duties.[14] In 2014, it said that religious freedom can override the rights of other citizens (5–4) and upheld the Christian-only prayers the town of Greece, New York, imposed on citizens (5–4).[15] In 2017, the court forced taxpayers to fund a Lutheran children's ministry and church (7–2).[16] In 2018, it rediscovered a potent argument, hostility toward religion, and used it to let a business owner violate state civil rights laws and discriminate against protected classes of people (7–2).[17] That same year, after bemoaning hostility toward Christians in that case, it upheld Donald Trump's Muslim ban.[18] In 2019, it abandoned the need for a sham remedy and simply decided a massive Christian cross on government property didn't violate the constitutional separation between state and church (7–2).[19] In 2020, it continued to abandon pretense and said that taxpayers *must* fund religious schools (5–4), another betrayal of founding American principles.[20] Late that year and into the next, it also began striking down public health measures in the name of religious freedom.[21] In 2021, the court, using a phalanx of legalism and jargon, unanimously held that the Catholic Church can discriminate against a minority in the name of god while performing public functions, in a case similar to the gay wedding cake case.[22]

This run of religion cases is as remarkable as it is deliberate. Unlike other courts, which handle anything that gets filed, the Supreme Court chooses which cases to take. It typically rejects more than 97 percent of the cases that come its way.[23] The simple fact is that *this* Supreme Court *wants* to decide *these* cases.

If this seems impossible or unlikely or conspiratorial, know that conservatives have already succeeded in previous crusades. This is precisely what they did for the Second Amendment. In 1977, absolutists took over the National Rifle Association and converted an organization that advocated for firearm safety education and recreational shooting into a powerhouse focused exclusively on rewriting the Second Amendment into a personal, individual right to own a gun.[24] "The NRA's new leadership was dramatic, dogmatic and overtly ideological. For the first time, the organization formally embraced the idea that the sacred Second Amendment was at the heart of its concerns," explained Michael Waldman, a law professor who wrote a biography of the Second Amendment.[25] They sought to put their right to bear arms at the top of the hierarchy of rights, over the rights of the children at Sandy Hook and Robb Elementary schools to live. They pumped millions into the fight, funding legal scholarship, lobbying, litigation, and public relations campaigns. And they succeeded in 2008 when the Supreme Court finally held that the Second Amendment created "an individual right" to own a gun "unconnected with militia service."[26] They changed the culture and what the Constitution meant. But as Chief Justice Warren Berger once said: "The Second Amendment . . . has been the subject of one of the greatest pieces of fraud—I repeat the word 'fraud'—on the American public by special interest groups that I have ever seen in my lifetime."[27] The Crusade seeks to do the same with the First Amendment's protection of religious freedom. Except that it's happening much faster.

I began defending the wall of separation between state and church in 2011, just as the Roberts Court began destroying it in earnest. In another decade, it will be unrecognizable. This book will be a snapshot of the disaster, a frame frozen in time. Without massive institutional change, gravity and momentum will further destroy this founding American principle. But the primary weapon being used to dismantle that wall between state and church is a weaponized religious freedom. There are hundreds of cases at any given time being litigated in the courts—far too many to cover in a book. They are pushed by a phalanx of over-funded, Koch-backed crusading groups that have focused their energy on this singular issue because of its potential to change everything. Again, Linda Greenhouse gets it right. There are plenty of cases "making claims that would have been dismissed out of hand not too many years ago and that now have to be taken seriously by those of us worried about the growing threat that an increasingly weaponized free-exercise clause poses to civil society."[28]

The Supreme Court Didn't Just Call for the Crusade; It Joined In

It ought to be obvious by now, but still it must be plainly stated: The Supreme Court has been politicized. It openly crossed that Rubicon in *Bush v. Gore*. It has been packed—asymmetrically—as the Democrats ceded this ground to the extreme Christian wing of the Republican Party.

The new guiding principle of this new Supreme Court is not the Constitution or law, but simply this: Christianity wins. Sure, other religions will sometimes win, but if you're wagering on the outcome of a case, ignore the law and bet on conservative Christianity.

The Supreme Court is not the institution you learned about in high school. A court of justice that protects the powerless. A court that honors the words etched in stone on the facade of its own building: "Equal Justice Under Law." That myth is the true facade, and it brought us to this disastrous juncture. The Supreme Court is a deeply conservative and retrogressive institution, and has been for nearly all of its history. The bright spots, such as the Warren Court, were fleeting and led to political backlash and a retreating court.[29]

This is the court of *Plessy v. Ferguson*, of *Dred Scott* and fugitive slave laws, of trying to suffocate the New Deal in the cradle, of gutting the power of the 14th Amendment won with the blood of so many

Americans during the Civil War, of Japanese/internment camps, of Muslim bans, of billionaires and corporations and political gerrymandering and gutting voting rights.

The story of the Supreme Court is *Bush v. Gore*. It is a politicized body and packed with political activists. Three of the current justices worked for Bush on the *Bush v. Gore* litigation: Kavanaugh, Roberts, and Barrett. Helping assemble Bush's team of lawyers was Christian nationalist and deeply conservative Texas senator Ted Cruz: "I called John and asked him to help. Within hours, he was on a plane to Florida."[30] Roberts worked in the Reagan White House. So did Clarence Thomas. Scalia worked for Nixon and Ford. So did Rehnquist, and before that as an advisor to Barry Goldwater's campaign.[31] Kavanaugh worked in the Bush White House, married a Bush aide, and was on Ken Starr's team pursuing President Bill Clinton for crimes that seem tame after Trump's tenure. Kavanaugh even drafted parts of the final Starr Report. When Kavanaugh was credibly accused of sexual assault during his Supreme Court confirmation, he screamed at senators with undisguised loathing and uncontrolled anger. He promised partisan retribution on his political enemies, speaking of reaping "the whirlwind," suffering "consequences," saying that "what goes around comes around."[32]

The justices didn't just call for the Crusade; they're active participants. Leonard Leo, the powerbroker at the Federalist Society, selected them and supported or even forced their nominations through because their ideology aligned with the Crusade. Leo's job has been described as being "the monitor of the various nominees' ideological purity."[33] Roberts and Alito were both nominated in 2005, both members of Leo's Federalist Society, and Leo played a crucial role in their partisan nominations.[34] Clarence Thomas, a longtime friend of Leo's,[35] is a member of the group, too.[36] All told, Leo is responsible for the confirmation of Roberts, Alito, Gorsuch, Kavanaugh, and Barrett. That's six votes on the Supreme Court, and Leo chose five for their ideology, a Crusader ideology.

John Roberts

Roberts authored briefs in the first Bush's Department of Justice alongside Ken Starr, arguing that public schools can impose religion on children at graduation ceremonies and that Christian bible clubs can use public schools to organize.[37] He argued unsuccessfully for an entire rewrite of state/church separation jurisprudence, but he's done that on the bench.[38] He litigated those cases alongside Crusaders, including the American Center for Law & Justice, which would go to bat for Roberts during his nomination, especially when it came to issues of religion and the law.[39]

In private practice, Roberts represented Connelly School of the Holy Child, a Catholic school that wanted to construct a 30,000-square-foot. building in a residential neighborhood without going through the zoning process. Roberts wrote that when states exempt religion from secular requirements, it is *"invariably constitutional."*[40] This argument has been implemented in several decisions we'll look at in this book, perhaps culminating in the 2021 Philadelphia foster care case (chapter 16), an opinion that Roberts himself wrote.

As the *New York Times* explained, he always advocated the most conservative course in the Reagan White House, "taking positions even more conservative than his prominent superiors," "criticized court decisions that required a thick wall between church and state," defended school-imposed prayer, and supported transferring government resources to parochial schools.[41] All of these stances became part of the Crusade.

Roberts's Reagan White House memos are revealing. In one, he agreed that decisions like the 1980 Supreme Court decision striking down a Kentucky law requiring a Ten Commandments display in every public school classroom "betray a hostility to religion not demanded by the Constitution."[42] Labeling state/church separation as hostility toward religion instead of a basic constitutional guarantee that protects religious freedom is a hallmark of the Crusade and something Roberts incorporated into decisions furthering the Crusade, such as the Montana decision discussed in chapter 14.[43] Roberts himself appeared hostile to the ACLU on issues of law and religion,[44] and supported a constitutional amendment that would allow public schools to impose Christian prayer on schoolchildren.[45] He also lamented a 1985 Supreme Court decision that correctly struck down Alabama schools' minute of mandatory silence for "meditation or voluntary prayer."[46] Roberts wrote, "We still have an uphill battle to return prayer to schools." We. Battle. Return prayer to schools. This is the language of a Crusader.[47]

Samuel Alito

Alito was nominated a month after Roberts was confirmed. Alito pledged his fidelity to Crusader ideology early in his career. Asking for a promotion at the Reagan Department of Justice, he explained that his "deep interest in constitutional law [was] motivated in large part by disagreement with Warren Court decisions, particularly" upholding the separation of state and church.[48] He began, "I am and have always been a conservative," and ended with, "I am a life-long registered Republican" and "member of the Federalist Society." As his appellate judge record shows, he put this ideology into practice.[49]

After his Supreme Court nomination, Alito fearlessly told senators "he believed the court might have gone too far in separating church and state," and reportedly told Senator John Cornyn that the court's decisions give "the impression of hostility to religious speech and religious expression."[50] Again, framing the constitutional line drawn between state and church as hostility is a key argument for the attempt to weaponize religious freedom. Alito revived this hostility argument for the Crusade, and it has proven crucial in many cases, as we'll see. Alito spoke to a group of fellow Catholic lawyers, Advocati Christi, in 2017 and said, "It is up to all of us to evangelize our fellow Americans about the issue of religious freedom."[51]

Antonin Scalia

Before Neil Gorsuch, there was Antonin Scalia. Scalia and Leo were "longtime friends." Joan Biskupic writes that "traditional Catholicism was integral to Scalia's identity" and quotes Leo on the fervent faith they shared: "It's pretty clear to me that [Scalia] believes the Catholic Church is the one true Church."[52] Scalia believed in a literal devil and a dead Constitution, "dead, dead, dead."[53] He was the kind of judge Leo wanted.[54] When Scalia died with nearly a year left in Barack Obama's administration, the Republicans refused to even consider any replacement, a gross departure that politicized the court and effectively changed its size. Leo raised millions of anonymous dollars opposing Obama's nominee,[55] before he and Trump finally replaced Scalia, fourteen months after his death, with Neil Gorsuch.

Neil Gorsuch

Before he was a judge, Gorsuch penned an opinion piece for the *National Review* attacking "American progressives" and "liberals" and their "overweening addiction" to "constitutional lawsuits" to "[effect] their social agenda on everything from gay marriage . . . to the use of vouchers for private-school education."[56] The article doesn't mention the lawsuits conservatives coordinated to, for instance, redefine the Second Amendment. Gorsuch's crusading tendencies were a bit less obvious until he was on the bench, but Leo presumably knew who he was picking. Before joining the high court, Gorsuch dissented in a case involving government displays of 12-foot memorial crosses stamped with state insignia along highways, and argued that it was a "biased presumption" to say that state Christian crosses amount to the state endorsing Christianity.[57] That was just seven months after the 2010 *Deus vult*. He also dissented in a case striking down a Ten Commandments monument at a county courthouse because the Ten Commandments, which begin "I AM the LORD thy God, you shall have no other gods before me," might actually "convey a secular moral message" and their influence on American law is "undeniable."[58] (*The Founding Myth* disposes of this claim.) He also helped Hobby Lobby's anti-contraception case while on the bench.

Brett Kavanaugh

Kavanaugh's crusading bona fides were clearer, plus he and Leo are "longtime personal friends."[59] Kavanaugh's fellow appellate judges described him as "affable but unyielding," a man who would "rarely, if ever, change his mind," and "a great colleague except in the cases where it mattered."[60] In other words, he was an ideological hardliner. As a lawyer, Kavanaugh fought to uphold a Florida program that sent taxpayer money to private religious schools.[61] Kavanaugh coauthored a Supreme Court brief for the New Jersey affiliate of James Dobson's Focus on the Family, which argued that students should be able to use loudspeakers at public school football games to broadcast prayers.[62] In it, Kavanaugh attacked people who supported the First Amendment and state/church separation as "absolutist," "hostile to religion in any form," advocating for an "Orwellian world," and seeking "the full extermination of private religious speech from the public schools" and "to cleanse public schools throughout the country of private religious speech."[63] Kavanaugh argued that if the justices decided the case in favor of the people suing (Catholic and Mormon students and their families), Christians would be relegated "to bottom-of-the-barrel status in our society—below socialists and Nazis and Klan members and panhandlers and ideological and political advocacy groups of all stripes." This is the Crusader mentality—Christians must be privileged and allowed to impose their religion on everyone using government power and resources; anything less is discrimination and inequality.

Crusaders (American Center for Law & Justice) orchestrated the school prayer defense alongside Texas Attorney General John Cornyn.[64] As a senator two decades later, Cornyn shepherded Kavanaugh's crippled nomination through to a confirmation after he was credibly accused of sexual assault. Kavanaugh and Cornyn lost when the court struck down the prayers in a 2000 decision, possibly the last unequivocal victory for state/church separation at the United States Supreme Court.[65]

THOMAS AND BARRETT WE'LL HEAR MORE ABOUT LATER. (This says nothing about the dozens, perhaps hundreds, of lesser federal judges chosen and placed by this same network for their ideological fidelity. Something like one-third of George W. Bush's nominees were members of Leo's group.)[66]

It's one thing for a liberal lawyer to rant about the court, but data doesn't lie. In the religious freedom context, our courts are politically captured. Stanford Constitutional Law Center fellow and NYU Law adjunct professor Zalman Rothschild looked at challenges to pandemic-related public health measures that restricted religious gatherings.[67] The results are shocking. As we'll see later, these cases were easy, and all should have come down in favor of public health—the right to worship does not include the right to infect others or risk their lives. Rothschild found that every judge (100 percent) appointed by

Democratic presidents sided with the public health orders and against the religious challengers seeking a right to risk other peoples' lives. That's the right call, and consistent with over a century of Supreme Court precedent. But only one-third (34 percent) of judges appointed by Republican presidents sided with public health measures. Even more striking, only 18 percent of Trump judges voted to uphold measures.

Tellingly, other legal challenges to public health orders, including challenges based on other First Amendment rights like free speech and free assembly, were uniformly rejected by judges across the political spectrum (again, showing that the correct decision was to let those public health orders stand.)[68] That's the hierarchy laid bare: religious freedom above other constitutional rights. We've seen a "cataclysmic change," Rothschild writes, "the politicization of religious freedom has infiltrated every level of the federal judiciary."

In the past, partisanship existed in some areas of law but not really for religious freedom cases.[69] After the court's 2010 *Deus vult*, that began to shift. From the mid-2010s through when the pandemic hit, explains Rothschild, "the unprecedented number of constitutional free exercise cases brought in such a condensed span of time forced that partisanship into sharp relief." That's the Crusade.

Two studies of religion cases from 1947 through mid-2020 revealed similar trends. Political ideology affected the outcome, but the religion of judges themselves also played a significant role.[70] Before the Reagan era, Catholic and Protestant justices were more likely than Jewish justices to favor religion when deciding cases. But beginning in the early 1980s, Catholic justices began favoring religious parties more, about twelve times more, than Protestant justices. The court is now majority Catholic. The latest numbers show that *Christians* are more likely to win with this court than ever before.

Before the courts were packed, the court ruled in favor of religion about half the time.[71] But that massively shifted under Roberts. From that baseline of about half, "in the Roberts Court, the win rate jumps to 81 percent."[72] This is not a pro-religion, but a pro-Christian shift: "in the Warren court, *no* plaintiff was affiliated with a mainstream Christian religion; thus, all of the pro-religion outcomes benefited minority or dissenting religious groups."[73] Religious freedom was once a shield to protect minorities, but "by the time we reach the Roberts Court, eight mainstream Christian plaintiffs win six of their cases."[74] The researchers also examined whether a given ruling favored not just Christian parties but mainstream Christian organizations, practices, or values. In the earlier cases of the Warren court, mainstream Christianity was favored in 44 percent of cases; under Roberts, it nearly doubled, up to 85 percent.

The researchers suggest that "one way to think about this pattern is that the Roberts Court extended the Warren court's protections for minority religions so as to encompass majority religions as well," but this book will show that this trend showcases privilege, not equality.

3

Drawing Lines

"Thus, the Amendment embraces two concepts—freedom
to believe and freedom to act.
The first is absolute but, in the nature of things, the second cannot be.
Conduct remains subject to regulation for the protection of society."[1]

—**Supreme Court, 1940**

The law is lines. Lines between permissible and not, between legal and illegal. Most of the time, it's clear where the lines must curve and meander. Murder and Jesus taking the wheel on that side. Growing a slightly longer beard and not standing for the Pledge of Allegiance on this side. To understand religious freedom, we must understand three basic lines. First, we distinguish between belief and action. Your right to believe is absolute; your right to act on that belief is not. Second, we draw a line between actions that can and should be regulated, even if religiously motivated, and those that shouldn't. If your action harms someone else or impacts their rights, it can be regulated, regardless of religious motivation. Third, we draw a line between government power and personal religion; you don't get to use the machinery of the state to amplify or impose your religion.

These lines cut through the maze of religious freedom cases and provide clear solutions to issues that are often much simpler than the Crusaders and the court make out.

Line #1: Action vs. Belief

Religious freedom is first and foremost about a free mind. The Supreme Court has said so in its more lucid moments.[2] Religious freedom protects our right to think freely.

Freedom of thought is embodied, but unnamed, in the First Amendment. It's the one unlimited right we possess. All of our other rights are limited. You have free speech, but slander and libel can get you into trouble. You have a privacy right in your home and belongings, but the government can intrude with a warrant. Even overly expansive Second Amendment rights are limited in obvious ways: you cannot carry a gun into the Supreme Court building or on an airplane. Rights are limited. The free exercise of religion included. An unrestrained right to religious freedom is a weaponized religious freedom.

Imagine that you hear your god telling you to kill your child as a sacrificial offering. There's a voice, and you're *sure* that it's this god speaking to you. He talks to people all the time in the bible. You were raised on those biblical stories, constantly told that they were part of the ultimate truth. You know he's commanded this of some of the most important people in the bible. God demands that Abraham murder his son Isaac in Genesis 22 (one of the stories the three big monotheistic religions agree on). The Israelite general Jephthah's battle plan to defeat the Ammonites consisted of sacrificing his daughter in Judges 11. And then of course, the big one, John 3:16, "For God so loved the world that he gave his only son." The central plotline in the Christian bible is your god sacrificing his only son. In your solipsism, you believe he's demanding the same from you. Sincerely. Without question.

Does religious freedom give you a license to kill your child?

Of course not. Just as obviously then, religious freedom is limited.

But why? If a parent believes a god commands child sacrifice, why can't they act on it?

Partly because belief and action are not the same. Parents can *believe* that a god is telling them to kill their children. They are even free to worship such a god (though I'd call that a bit of a red flag). But they are not free *to act* on the belief. The civil law can intervene and stop or punish them. Freedom of belief is unlimited; freedom of action is limited.

This example is extreme, but clear. Professor Micah Schwartzman drily observed, "At the bottom of every slippery slope involving religious liberty is human sacrifice."[3] (He adds, "Human sacrifice is protected as long as it is actuarial."[4]) And while the hypothetical seems absurd, it's not unthinkable. In early 2021, I debated a Christian apologist and asked a version of this hypothetical. My opponent admitted that "yes, absolutely" he would kill his child if his god asked.[5] Parents murder their children at a god's behest with startling regularity. An Oklahoma mother drowned her seventeen-month-old because "God told me to do it."[6] A "devout Christian woman" from Tyler, Texas, bludgeoned her children with a rock, killing two, because "God had told her to" and she wanted to be closer to the Lord.[7] In Plano, Texas, a woman dismembered and killed her eleven-month-old because her god told her to: "I want to give the baby to God," she said. The first officer to arrive on the scene testified that she would randomly smile and say, "Thank you, God," and "Praise God."[8]

Stories like this are so distressingly common that *The Onion* mocked our pious former vice president with the headline, "Mike Pence Disappointed God Has Never Asked Him to Kill One of Own Children."[9] It was so believable and widely shared that Snopes had to debunk the story.[10]

The bible is more violent than many followers of the good book realize. Those better versed might wonder why these horrible reports are so mercifully infrequent. First, nearly every believer is better than their holy book. Christians are more moral than the bible. Second, parents who murder their children have other mental issues that react lethally with their deeply held religious beliefs and the dangerous permission structure those beliefs create. Finally, our law punishes those who murder, even if they kill in the name of god. The law can punish god-mandated infanticide because the right to exercise one's religion— the right to act on religious beliefs—is not unlimited.

We are free to believe anything. We can believe in talking snakes and donkeys, vicarious redemption through human sacrifice, eternal torture for people who believe differently, or that thoughts and prayers are more effective than modern medicine. But when your religion tells you to sacrifice your child or pick a pocket or break a leg, the government can step in and say no. And this is where we draw a second line.

Line #2: The Rights of Others
So at some point the government can limit religiously motivated actions. The question is, where? The answer here is also simple: where

the rights of others begin. Your right to swing your religion ends where the rights of others begin. It may end sooner in some cases, but without doubt, it ends there. That's where we've always drawn the line.

At about the time that Thomas Paine was writing in *The American Crisis*, "These are the times that try men's souls," Thomas Jefferson was musing on this line and wrote, "It is unlawful in the ordinary course of things or in a private house to murder a child. It should not be permitted any sect then to sacrifice children."[11] The Supreme Court also used the human sacrifice example nearly 150 years ago and made the point more clearly.[12] First, the court explained, "Laws are made for the government of actions, and while they cannot interfere with mere religious belief and opinions, they may with practices." That's Line #1. Then, the court raised and dismissed the human sacrifice hypothetical in one sentence: "Suppose one believed that human sacrifices were a necessary part of religious worship; would it be seriously contended that the civil government under which he lived could not interfere to prevent a sacrifice?" The court can't even imagine someone making the argument.

This has been our understanding of religious freedom since the founding. This is a simple, discernable starting point: your religion is not a license to violate the rights of others. Ever. It may be that the government must burden religious acts in additional cases—Jefferson and the Supreme Court thought so—but this is an inviolable line.

The human sacrifice example is useful not because we draw the line between life or death, but rather because another human's rights are being violated. Child sacrifice is a most extreme example, but the principle protects lesser rights as well.

According to a Vatican insider, Pope John Paul II whipped himself to get closer to Jesus.[13] The pope's right to inflict pain to get closer to his god ends with him. Unless you're asked, keep your whips to yourself. Again, what seems outlandish is sadly real. One Indiana mother, an evangelical Christian, beat her seven-year-old son so severely that authorities cataloged more than thirty-five bruises on his little body, including "one curved bruise on his cheek in the shape of a hook on a coat hanger." An observant teacher notified the police, who arrested and charged the mother. The mother argued that the religious freedom law that Mike Pence signed as governor (amid a wave of other such bills, including Mississippi's), gave her the "right to discipline her children in accordance with her beliefs." She cited Proverbs 13—spare the rod, spoil the child—and claimed that her religious beliefs mandated this action. "I was worried for my son's salvation with God after he dies," she said in court documents. "I decided to punish my son to . . . help him learn how to behave as God would want him to." Citing religious freedom as a defense, she pled guilty to lesser charges, and got probation.[14] Weaponized religious freedom looks an awful lot like a coat hanger.

The violation of another's rights need not be physical. Imagine that a pair of Mormons, who believe they have a divine mandate to convert people, come to your door. "My name is Elder Price, and I would like to share with you the most amazing book," says one. You politely ask them to leave. They refuse. Or let's say you wake one morning, pour a mug of coffee, and walk out in your bathrobe to enjoy your backyard only to find someone preaching to thirty people scattered about your bird feeders and tulip beds. You tell them to leave and threaten to call the cops, but preacher-man says, "God told me this is holy ground and we have to worship here." Not only that, the site is so holy that five acolytes must constantly attend it. Do their religious freedom rights trump your property rights? Of course not. (Again, not as far-fetched as it seems. In April 2021, a Florida couple invited family and friends to a 16,000-square-foot mansion for their dream wedding weekend. They didn't own the property or bother to rent it because "it was God's plan that the couple marry there." Police escorted the revelers away.[15])

The second line we are drawing cuts two ways, but not always as clearly. Religious actions that don't impact others are less problematic. Jehovah's Witnesses famously and bravely challenged laws requiring them to recite the Pledge of Allegiance. They took their case all the way to the Supreme Court. Twice. Their right to opt out of a forced, performative pledge didn't harm anyone or anything. Let's let them do it.

His gods say he must do peyote to commune with them, but possessing and taking peyote is a crime. Her god commands her to kill her child, but murder is illegal. The difference in our reactions to these two claims comes not just in the severity of the crime, but in its impact on others. This is Line #2.

This line enshrines equality and tumbles the hierarchy of rights the Crusaders are building. Without this line, my religious freedom can trump your rights to life, liberty—anything. Without Line #2, your rights are subordinate to my religion. That means you are *not* free to live your life, unless it's within the parameters of my god. This is the weapon I'm warning about.

Americans understand, at a visceral level, that your freedom must end where mine begins. Nearly 90 percent of the country agrees that "everyone is free to follow their religious beliefs and practices in their personal lives, provided it does not cause harm to others," according to the Public Religion Research Institute.[16] That is a fine summation of Line #2 and an overwhelming consensus for America, 2021. (When was the last time you saw Americans agree in such numbers? And the survey was conducted within two week of the January 6 insurrection). There's an old legal adage: "Your right to swing your fist ends where my nose begins." Your right to swing your whip, coat hanger, prophecy, or holy book ends where my rights begin, too.

Line #3: State and Church

The third line ensures that people do not use government power or resources to swing their religion. Extending the reach of one's religion with governmental power is not part of religious freedom, is specifically prohibited in our Constitution, and violates the religious freedom of every other citizen.

Citizens are free to pray all they want. That's religious freedom. They can even pray on public property. That's religious freedom, too. But they don't get to broadcast the prayer over a government PA system.

This line protects religious freedom. Every one of us gives up a few rights, a little bit of personal liberty and sovereignty, in return for living in a civilized society governed by laws. Our government has no religion to exercise. It is an abuse of power for officials to promote or impose their religion with that power. People holding public office are free to worship and preach and promote their god and holy book in their personal capacity, but not in their official capacity. *Mr.* Johnson might pray every night, but *Sheriff* Johnson should not be leading prayers at staff meetings or with prisoners—that is an abuse of power.

This abuse of public power is sadly common. We decry similar power abuses when politicians abuse official power to line their pockets, or sexually harass staff, or benefit partisan political campaigns. But when the abuse of power promotes Christianity, people are silent.

Every American has a right to a secular government as a matter of personal religious liberty. In a case striking down school-organized prayer at a public school graduation, several justices explained that mixing government and religion is "a threat to free government" because it excludes a class of people as unfavored. The case was decided before the courts were broken and the Crusaders were powerful, but some were involved, and they lost: "A government cannot be premised on the belief that all persons are created equal when it asserts that God prefers some."[17]

Religious freedom prevents the entire government from promoting religion. The Crusaders understand this when government power is promoting another god. Crusaders don't want non-Christian beliefs anywhere near their government. In *Taking America Back for God*, Andrew Whitehead and Sam Perry show that while Christian nationalists pay lip service to religious liberty, they "drew a distinct line, however, at whether these same people [non-Christians] should be allowed to bring their sincerely held beliefs into the public sphere in order to influence civil society."[18]

The data are backed up with decades of bigotry. During the first Hindu prayer in the US Senate, in 2007, self-identified "Christians and patriots" in the gallery screamed, "This is an abomination!"[19] No one had interrupted the thousands of Christian prayers that had come before. The American Family Association objected, too. AFA founder and Methodist minister Dan Wildmon explained: "We're not opposed to the ability of people to worship their own gods or god, but when it comes to our civil government . . . it's always been the recognition of the God of the Bible. Every religion is not equal. That's my belief. That's logic."[20] Actually, that's Christian supremacy. When the first Hindu prayer was said in the House, Tony Perkins's Family Research Council, Crusaders originally affiliated with James Dobson's Focus on the Family, responded:

Our nation is drifting from its Judeo-Christian roots. . . . "Tolerance" and "diversity" have replaced the 10 Commandments. . . . It has become necessary to "celebrate" non-Christian religions—even in the halls of Congress. . . . Our founders expected that Christianity—and no other religion—would receive support from the government.[21]

Government support is precisely the problem. Using government power for religious ends violates everyone's religious freedom; it's just that when it's your religion, you tend not to care. When it's not your god, the breach of Line #3 becomes rather obvious.

The Crusaders understand Line #3—that's why they want to destroy it. The Crusade seeks to codify Christian privilege, to enshrine the idea that "every religion is not equal," as Wildmon put it. Christians are more equal than others. The separation of state and church guarantees equality, so it's a barrier to the privilege the Crusaders seek.

A MULTITUDE OF HISTORICAL COUNTEREXAMPLES seem to contradict these lines. For much of American history, "We the People" and "all . . . are created equal" were aspirational ideals, at best. The counterexamples exist not because we drew these lines in different places, but because historically women and racial minorities were considered chattel, not humans worthy of human rights. Religion often provided the permission structure for that subjugation. As Frederick Douglass explained, "I should regard being the slave of a religious master the greatest calamity that could befall me. For of all slaveholders with whom I have ever met, religious slaveholders are the worst. I have ever found them the meanest and basest, the most cruel and cowardly, of all others. It was my unhappy lot not only to belong to a religious slaveholder, but to live in a community of such religionists."[22] (See *The Founding Myth* for more on religion's relationship to slavery, women's rights, and god-given rights.)

W. E. B. Du Bois's haunting line "the Negro church antedates the Negro home" reminds us that Black Americans were granted a measure of religious freedom before other rights and for ulterior motives.[23] For instance, "slave bibles" often omitted the Exodus story, lest slaves think of fleeing their bondage.[24] Women fared little better, so suffragist leaders like Lucretia Mott and Elizabeth Cady Stanton rewrote the entire bible. *The Women's Bible* rectified biblical immorality on slavery and women's rights because "No reform has ever been started but the Bible, falsely interpreted, has opposed it," as Stanton once wrote.[25] The failure was in not recognizing our shared humanity and, to a lesser extent, not enforcing the lines, especially Line #3. The lines would have worked, but we lacked the collective courage and moral fiber to heed them.

These three commonsense lines are what the Crusaders are seeking to obliterate as they weaponize religious freedom. They are claiming the right to act on any religious belief, no matter what the harm to others, and to abuse government power to extend the reach of those actions.

Origins of the Lines

Where do the lines come from? Especially Line #2, sometimes called the third-party harm principle? We're going to answer that question because scholars and Supreme Court justices have asked. In one of Amy Coney Barrett's first Supreme Court oral arguments—her first religion case, first First Amendment case, essentially her first case that would impact that national conversation in any way—she asked this bad question. She asked about Line #2: "This third-party harm principle, the principle that religious beliefs can never give a believer the right to harm a third-party even slightly. I'm wondering if you agree with that and, if so, if you could tell me where in law the principle comes from."[26]

That's an easy one.

The original, unamended US Constitution draws these three lines. But not explicitly enough for some of the founding generation, so they amended it to include specific rights—a Bill of Rights—that lay out these boundaries even more clearly.

The American experiment written into the Constitution was bold for a few reasons and woefully anti-democratic (Electoral College, Senate) and inhumane (the Three-Fifths Clause) for others. But in Philadelphia in 1787, the framers came close to getting religious freedom right. Most wanted to protect the religious freedom of everyone, not just Christians. "They meant to comprehend, within the mantle of its protection, the Jew and the Gentile, the Christian and Mahometan, the Hindoo and infidel of every denomination," Jefferson later wrote of the law that became the forerunner of the First Amendment, explaining why the legislature refused to dedicate the law to Jesus Christ.[27] Certainly not every founder agreed that this was or should be the ideal, but it's the argument that won the day and led the founders to one of their truly revolutionary decisions.

They decided that the best protection for true religious liberty is a secular government. There is no freedom *of* religion without a government that is free *from* religion.

Nowadays lawyers, scholars, and judges often situate state/church separation in the First Amendment because so much of the litigation stems from its two religion clauses. Worse, some situate the right only in the first clause of the First Amendment. Roberts and the Crusaders have turned the clauses against each other, as if two parts of the same carefully crafted sentence are fundamentally contradictory. That's wrong. Had there been no First Amendment, we would still have Line #3. This separation of state and church is woven into the fabric of our Constitution. It can be clearly seen in at least four structural aspects of the Constitution, as I discuss in *The Founding Myth*.

First, the Constitution is both secular and godless by design.[28] Second, the first words, "We the People," are a philosophical declaration that government draws its power from the consent of the governed, not from a deity.[29] Third, the emphatic religious test ban in Article VI was the only mention of religion in the original document: "**No religious Test shall ever be required** as a Qualification to any Office or public Trust under the United States." Each of these was innovative, but a fourth aspect of the Constitution also draws these lines. The Constitution created a government of limited powers that could only exercise powers expressly enumerated in the document or implied by those enumerations.[30] We ceded some personal liberty in return for safety, stability, justice, etc. Some rights were given over in this limited fashion to imbue the government with power; some were not.[31] We the People never ceded or granted to the government power over the mind, over conscience. (Line #1).

Alexander Hamilton compared the king of Great Britain's powers to the limited powers of the president, listing checks on presidential power. Hamilton drove his final point home with a rare exclamation mark: "The one has no particle of spiritual jurisdiction; the other is the supreme head and governor of the national church!"[32] (Line #3).

Crucially, this doesn't mean that the government has no power over religion and religious acts: we instituted the government to, in part, prohibit murder, even religiously motivated murder. We instituted the government, in part, to protect property rights, even if people think your backyard is holy ground. Even when people claim religious freedom, the government can still regulate action to accomplish its goals and exercise its limited power. We the People gave the government no particle of power on matters of conscience or belief. Nor could we. Most of the founders thought it was impossible to grant power over the mind to the government.[33] (Line #1). Belief is unlimited, but, again, action is not. This is but another way of saying, as Jefferson would in the famous Danbury Baptists letter, that "The legislative powers of government reach actions only and not opinions." (Lines #1 and #2).

This wasn't a power vacuum, but a prohibition. And they weren't done.

To further limit the government and protect the people's rights, the first Congress proposed constitutional amendments, including the First Amendment:

> Congress shall make no law respecting an establishment of religion, or prohibiting the free exercise thereof; or abridging the freedom of speech, or of the press; or the right of the people peaceably to assemble, and to petition the government for a redress of grievances.[34]

Those six rights—a secular government, free exercise of religion, free speech, free press, assembly, and petitioning the government, all seeking to protect the freedom of thought—draw the lines.

Line #2, the line Amy Barrett was most concerned with, was almost assumed as a given. James Madison, the father of that First Amendment, wrote a friend about how Congress "deviated from the strict principle" in Line #3 when it hired chaplains and when presidents declared fast days. In the same letter, he explained Line #2, which "has always been a favorite principle with me," that religion is only immune "from civil jurisdiction . . . *where it does not trespass on private rights or the public peace."*[35] The right to swing your religion ends where the rights of others begin.

Put more simply, Line #2 is enshrined by equality, an aspirational ideal America hasn't fully realized. Barrett's question about the origin of third-party harm assumes Christian supremacy. Why ought any right be a license to *harm* others, to violate their rights? Inconvenience, annoy, anger, frustrate others—sure, all of that. But why would free speech or freedom of the press or free exercise of religion be a license to trample another's right to bodily autonomy or to be free of discrimination in a place of public accommodation? The better question is not where the concept of third-party harm originates, but why the right to religion should ever extend beyond the individual, let alone in a way that violates the rights of another? It shouldn't. The question is not "why can't religious freedom harm others," but rather, "why on earth do you think it can?" Why, for example, would believing in the pious utility of self-flagellation give you dominion over the body of others?

To permit this is to subjugate non-adherents' rights. That may be the aim of the Crusade, but these constitutional lines exist to prevent precisely that.

Our government "gives to bigotry no sanction" but that first requires believers to "demean themselves as good citizens." (Washington uses "demean" here in the sense "to conduct or behave [oneself] usually in a proper manner," not in the sense of diminishing oneself.[36]) Religious freedom was never an absolute right; it was always subordinate to law, rules, regulations, rights of others—to being a "good citizen." To enjoy the rights protected in the Constitution, one must first cede a bit of sovereignty and comport themselves as a good citizen; only *then* may they exercise their religious freedom.

WE OFTEN DEBATE THESE FIGHTS AS "RELIGIOUS EXEMPTIONS," religion exempting itself from the law. But that's not quite right. Religion and government are two different systems of law. In the American Experiment, one is mandatory, the other is voluntary. Civil law, which all must follow, and religious law, which people can adopt or not. The two systems are separate, though bound to collide. If voluntary religious law can always exempt a person from the mandatory civil law, that mandatory law would eventually cease to exist, replaced by religious law. "To permit this would be to make the professed doctrines of religious belief superior to the law of the land, and in effect to permit every citizen to become a law unto himself. Government could exist only in name under such circumstances," explained the Supreme Court 150 years ago.[37] People can add rules for their personal behavior if they so desire, but they must follow the baseline. If your religion demands more of you and that additional burden doesn't conflict with the law, you may do more. If your religion demands more of you and it does conflict with the law (kill your kid, whip your friend, trespass), you must follow the law.

Believers must find the courage of their religious convictions and accept the consequences for acting on their beliefs. The faithful are supposed to be, well, faithful. Religious freedom cases often arise because believers lack this courage. Is the believer bearing the burden of their religious belief or are they asking others to bear that burden? Is the believer accepting the costs of the belief, or are they trying to pass those costs along with religious freedom? If your god doesn't like birth control, don't take it. It your god thinks marrying a person of the same sex is sinful, don't marry someone of the same sex. If your religion demands private religious education for your children, you and your church pay for it. Religious freedom does not mean burdening others with your religion; it means freely burdening yourself.

Devout Christians should be leaning into the consequences of their religion. The Trump administration pointed to the bible to justify ripping children from their parents' arms at the southern border.[38] "I would cite you to the Apostle Paul and his clear and wise command in Romans 13, to obey the laws of the government because God has ordained them for the purpose of order," said then Attorney General Jeff Sessions.[39] Sarah Huckabee Sanders, Trump's Press Secretary, agreed. "It's very biblical to enforce the law," she said.[40] A biblical mandate to heed the civil law was to be obeyed when the burden fell on brown families crossing the southern border. But when White American Christians wanted to disobey the law, Sessions joined the Crusade to exempt them from the laws, even using the Department of Justice to weaponize religious freedom across the federal government. He created the Religious Liberty Task Force and issued a twenty-five-page memo that redefined the "principles of religious liberty." Sessions consulted with Alliance Defending Freedom, the Crusaders responsible for Mississippi's religious freedom law (see pages 10–12), on that memo and spoke at an ADF conference.[41]

The Crusaders are cowards, lacking the courage of their loudly confessed religious convictions. American Christians' own religion tells them to expect tribulations, not government and law bending to their every whim and fancy. Impending persecution is one of the few points on which all four gospels agree. American Christians preach, expect, and even yearn for persecution. The fabricated "War on Christmas," the *God's Not Dead* movies (which have financial ties to the Crusaders), the Left Behind books, and Fox News feed this persecution complex.[42] About half the country—and three-quarters of Republicans—think American Christians face persecution.[43] According to the Public Religion Research Institute, "White evangelicals are the only major religious group in which a majority say Christians face a lot of discrimination" and are also the only group that thinks American Christians face more discrimination than Muslims.[44] I'd be the first to stand alongside my Christian comrades if the government were persecuting them, but that's not happening.

Christians must find the courage to bear the costs of their beliefs, especially their bigotry. Each year, Crusaders at the Family Research Council bestow the "Cost of Discipleship Award." In 2015, a county clerk in Kentucky received the award. She reveled in what she mistook for persecution but was simply Line #3.[45]

4

Drawing Lines:
Bigotry in Kentucky

(*Davis v. Ermold*)

"Let's not be naive, we're not talking about a simple political battle; it
is a destructive pretension against the plan of God. We are not talking
about a mere bill, but rather a machination of the Father of Lies that
seeks to confuse and deceive the children of God."

—Pope Francis (then Cardinal Bergoglio)
in a 2010 letter to nuns in his home country,
Argentina, after it legalized gay marriage[1]

The Crusade's most celebrated defender of "biblical marriage"
was the thrice-divorced, four-times married clerk of Rowan
County, Kentucky. George Wallace stood in the schoolhouse
door to block equality in 1963. Kim Davis stood in the courthouse
door to block equality in 2015.[2]

Davis's stand provides a clear example of all three of the lines. One
that the courts got right. The Supreme Court correctly decided that
two consenting adults could marry, even if they are both of the same
sex, on a Friday in late June 2015. Roberts read his angry dissent from
the bench, the first and only time he's done so. That Monday, Davis
announced that, "based on her Christian beliefs," she would not issue
any marriage licenses.[3]

Video of Davis denying a gay couple a license went viral. Davis
had already denied other couples, so David Ermold and David Moore
recorded their encounter. "The Davids," as they were affectionately

dubbed, had been together for seventeen years and owned a house in the county. Davis refused to issue their and other lawful licenses and ended up in court defending her bigotry against numerous couples. She lost, repeatedly, at every turn, and even ended up in jail for refusing to comply with court orders.[4]

DAVIS BECAME COUNTY CLERK after winning a primary by twenty-three votes and amid accusations of nepotism.[5] Her mother had occupied the office for nearly forty years, and Davis was her deputy for twenty-five.[6] She already had a history of abusing her county connections and government power to cross Line #3, imposing religion on a captive audience at the county jail with a bible study and "often offer[ing] her prayers" to people who came into the clerk's office to conduct government business.[7]

There's no zeal like that of the recent convert (see chapter 9, page 127). Davis was a born-again Apostolic Pentecostal Christian.[8] Apostolic Pentecostals speak in tongues, faith-heal, and believe the bible is inerrant. Davis converted to this brand of Christianity right about the time the Solid Rock Apostolic Church opened, about four years before she rose to infamy.[9]

Less than six months after taking her oath of office to uphold the law and Constitution, Davis began wielding official power to impose biblical law on Rowan County. Davis's response to marriage equality was right from the segregationist playbook (see chapter 15). If *they* can get married, then nobody is getting married. This was the response to desegregation. Close the schools. Close the pools. Shut it all down. Davis was following the racist playbook. She ordered her deputies to refuse to issue licenses, too. (Fox News's Megyn Kelly later referred to this burn-the-house-down mentality as "the equal treatment you were giving."[10])

One obvious issue with this strategy is that if this county clerk can deny lawful licenses, then so can other county clerks. It's not hard to envision all 120 Kentucky counties on that bigotry bandwagon. This shows the hollowness of the "just go somewhere else" arguments—if denials are permitted, there would be nowhere else to go.

Issuing such licenses was one of the clerk's duties. If a clerk cannot do her job, the solution is to resign, not take away everyone else's rights. The violation of LGBTQ people's rights is clear. They were denied the ability to marry. The Supreme Court had vindicated this right just days earlier.

Dan Canon is a Louisville law professor and the lead counsel for the plaintiffs who won that case at the Supreme Court. Canon also represented several couples against Kim Davis. Canon suspects "that if she had had counsel who really cared about anything other than publicity . . . we might have been able to come up with a creative solution to the license issue."[11] But Crusaders often take advantage of the credulous. "Liberty Counsel turned it into a circus," said Canon. Liberty Counsel espouses Christian supremacy more openly than other Crusaders.[12] It bills itself as a Christian "ministry" with a "Christian mission."[13] It also claims to fight for religious freedom but means something else: it "advances religious freedom by advocating, supporting advancing and defending the good news about Jesus Christ."[14] Mat and Anita Staver run the outfit, designated a hate group by the Southern Poverty Law Center.[15] Liberty Counsel represented the Kentucky counties in the 2005 Ten Commandments case and lost, costing the taxpayers hundreds of thousands of dollars, even though "Staver stated that the battle is costing Pulaski taxpayers 'zero' dollars, since Liberty Counsel is working 'pro bono.'"[16]

Staver absurdly likened Davis to Jews in Nazi Germany.[17] She seemed to agree. When Megyn Kelly asked Davis on Fox News if she was a villain or heroine, Davis responded that it "depends on if you love God or not which side I'm on," then said she was simply "someone that God is using."[18] Humble suggestions of being an instrument of god aside, this was a minor civil servant abusing what little power she had to impose her religion on everyone, transgressing all three lines.

Line #1

Kim Davis is and was free to believe whatever she wanted about marriage: that it's only for people of the opposite sex or people of the same race or anything else. There was no coercion on her right to believe. County clerks are elected to do certain jobs, including issuing marriage licenses. People in all manner of work do things they disagree with or would rather not do. That's why we call it "work." None of the county clerk duties forced Davis to change her belief. She was still, like everyone else who works, perfectly able to hold any belief about her job. She was free to believe marriage was between one man and one woman. There's no Line #1 issue here.

Line #2

But that religious belief is not a license to act. Davis acted on her belief to deny the rights of others. This cannot be permitted, even in the name of god. Davis was free to believe such things about marriage and practice such beliefs in her own marriage but was not free to impose those beliefs on others and impact their rights. The Davids had the right to marry, guaranteed by the Constitution, and a county clerk had no power or freedom to deny them that right.

Line #3

At one point, as the litigation was nearly exhausted and courts had repeatedly ordered Davis to issue marriage licenses and she had consistently refused, the Davids asked her, "Under whose authority are you not issuing licenses?" Davis responded, "Under God's authority."[19] That's incorrect. County clerk is a government office, created and empowered by the people, not a god. It has "no particle of spiritual jurisdiction" and no religious power. It is a secular office set up to perform secular functions.

A government official denied the right of families to exist outside of Christianity's heteronormative construct using the machinery of the state. This wasn't just one person trespassing on another's backyard, but one person abusing the power of a public office to deny people their rights.

Davis's inept attorneys argued for the supremacy of biblical law because Davis swore an oath that ended, "so help me God."[20] That's not an argument for transgressing Line #3, but it is a great argument for dropping that language from our oaths of office (see *The Founding Myth*, chapter 23).

In the end, the best proof that Davis was discriminating in her government position as clerk, not as a private citizen, is that Rowan County paid the American Civil Liberties Union and Canon's $224,000 in legal fees. As a private citizen, she had no power to do anything with marriage licenses. Davis was not prevented from exercising her religious belief. She was prevented from imposing her religious belief, using a government office and government power to do so.

Kim Davis's Line #3 problem is relatively clear. Others require slightly more examination. For instance, a public high school football coach in Washington State prayed on the fifty-yard line after games. He only had access to the field because of his position as a coach. He used that government platform and power for prayers intended to influence students. This also violates Line #3 because he was using the power of a public position to extend the reach of his personal religion. He was free to pray. He could have bowed his head at any time and said a little prayer on the sideline inconspicuously to himself. The school even attempted to accommodate his prayers in a way that wouldn't have violated the rights of students. But he wanted to exercise the power of a government position to showcase his Christianity to students under his care. No other adult was free to walk onto the field and pray; he was there because of his role in the public school, and no aspect of that role was religious. He refused to stop abusing his power, so the school district put him on paid leave. He chose to sue the school district instead of reapplying for the $5,304 per year contract. Every court sided with the school district, relying on decades of precedent. But a Crusader kept his case alive, and the Supreme Court, which was packed since he first brought his case in 2015, is set to rule in his favor as this book went to press.[21] Jesus himself condemns performative public prayer as hypocrisy in the Sermon on the Mount: "When you pray, don't be like the hypocrites who love to pray publicly . . . where everyone can see them."[22] So much for being true to "God's Word."

In a conversation about Kim Davis, Salman Rushdie identified the "classic trope of the religious bigot . . . while they are denying people their rights, they claim their rights are being denied. While they are persecuting people, they claim to be persecuted. While they're behaving colossally offensively, they claim to be the offended party. It's an upside-down world."[23]

Davis claimed persecution, that her rights were violated. But which ones? She was able to worship on Sundays, study the bible on Wednesdays, pray every day, get divorced three times, marry four times, and have two children out of wedlock, an outdated phrase.[24] She was invited on national television to spout her bigotry. National figures rushed to her defense. They hosted rallies and wrote op-eds in her favor.[25] The most-watched "news" channel breathlessly supported her fight. People thought she was "a hero," as one woman told the *New York Times*, adding that Davis was "standing strong against the gays. And I agree with her. The Bible says husband and wife. Not two women, and not two stupid men."[26]

Still, Davis was insistent: "I never imagined a day like this would come, where I would be asked to violate a central teaching of Scripture and of Jesus Himself regarding marriage. To issue a marriage license which conflicts with God's definition of marriage, with my name affixed to the certificate, would violate my conscience."[27] But she wasn't actually asked "to violate" anything.

This raises a helpful question we can ask in these cases. If the court decides against the person claiming religious freedom, what's the worst that will happen? Here, nothing. Davis was not asked to marry in violation of her faith. If Davis was against same-sex marriage, then she shouldn't marry someone of the same sex. Davis was against others getting married. She wanted her version of biblical law imposed on others.

The issue of her name appearing on the certificate was minor. Eventually, all clerks' names were removed from the marriage licenses, the easy solution Dan Canon envisioned at the outset. If her convictions were really as strong as she claimed, she would have simply quit her job. "Kim Davis's convictions were not so strong that she'd quit her $80,000 a year job," Canon pointed out. She didn't want that; she wanted the gay couples to bear the cost of her religious conviction. She was pious when her actions impacted others, when it took away their rights. She was pious right up until the point when it affected her.

If her god refuses to let her do her job, that's on her and her god. The government and the rest of the citizenry need not be involved and cannot be affected.

"MY CONSCIENCE WILL NOT ALLOW ME TO ISSUE A LICENSE for a same-sex couple because I know that God ordained marriage from the very foundation of this world to be between a man and a woman," claimed Davis.[28] But that is not quite true. The bible is remarkably unclear about marriage.

"For me," said one of the Davids when they finally married, "this is our blessing from God . . . and they can't take that away from us."[29] He believed his god blessed same-sex marriage.

Who's right, Davis or the Davids? Does it matter? Courts nearly always uncritically accept every religious claim of anyone arguing religious freedom. Courts never examine the truth or coherence of a belief, and typically refuse to question the sincerity of the belief, though this is permissible (and, as mentioned earlier, regularly done to prisoners).

This abstemious policy might make sense in a case where a religious exemption has no impact on anyone else. But religious justifications for impacting another's rights should be treated with more skepticism, not more deference, if only because the bible is rarely clear on any point and can be cited to justify nearly any position. "With God," says the book of Matthew, "all things are possible."[30] But that god cannot even defeat "chariots of iron."[31] It's a book that preaches an eye for an eye, but also turning the other cheek.[32] The Ten Commandments tell us to honor our parents, while Jesus said that he will not have anyone as a disciple who "does not hate father and mother, wife and children, brothers and sisters."[33]

"Biblical marriage" is all over the place. Polygyny was the norm in most of the stories (polygamy means having multiple spouses, but the bible is a patriarchal book that tells only of multiple wives, polygyny). David, a king appointed by the biblical god and a "man after God's own heart," had at least eight wives.[34] Solomon, David's son and divinely appointed successor, had 700 wives.[35] Jacob, Esau, Gideon, and other biblical heroes had multiple wives or openly cavorted with concubines. Polygyny and concubinage were entwined like so many writhing limbs. Incestuous marriage is also common. Jacob marries a pair of sisters. Isaac marries his cousin Rebekah. The gruesome story of Lot and his two daughters and their progeny smacks of the father raping his daughters, not the drunken reverse-seduction portrayed (see *The Founding Myth*, chapter 15).

Abraham, the father of the three dominant monotheisms, married his half-sister Sarah and pimped her out to an Egyptian pharaoh and a Philistine king. The biblical god ordered Abraham to sacrifice the offspring of that incestuous marriage, Isaac, giving us our easy line-drawing example. Abraham also married his sister-wife's slave, Hagar, and they had children together.

Other biblical marriages that might actually fit the definition of one man and one woman are immoral: the widow forced to marry her brother-in-law, the kidnapped woman forced to marry her kidnapper, the slave given a wife, and the rape victim forced to marry her rapist.[36] When Moses conquered his promised land, he often slaughtered every inhabitant, "but all the young girls who have not known a man by sleeping with him, keep alive for yourselves," he commanded his soldiers. They were "booty" and "spoils," tens of thousands of human beings forced into sexual slavery.[37] The soldiers could choose to marry them or not, depending on how well the chattel pleased the men who had slaughtered their family and friends.[38] Legal marriage requires consent, but biblical marriage is conquest.

When the main biblical characters finally move away from polygyny, the writers move them to the opposite extreme. Jesus and some of his disciples never married, a happy state Paul wished on all disciples.[39] This has led many—from serious scholars to satirists—to assume that Jesus and his unmarried male disciples enjoyed the "sin" this Kentucky clerk loathed.[40]

Amid all this polygynous licentiousness and incest and forced marriages and rape and prudish chastity, does the bible say that marriage is between a man and a woman? Not really. The big gotcha comes when Jesus is condemning divorce, not speaking of who can marry whom.[41] One must either assume Jesus would have naturally excluded same-sex marriages from the definition of marriage, or that such relations were included in acts Jesus implicitly condemned. Both are fair assumptions, if only because Jesus says he came to uphold the law of the Hebrew bible, every jot and tittle, and that book does not mince words about homosexuality—it's an "abomination."

It's not. The bible is wrong. Regardless, what an old book claims a god said two or three millennia ago cannot be an excuse to rob an American of their rights today. The Supreme Court never officially weighed in on Davis's religious freedom argument, but a question in her case—could Davis be liable for damages for the denial or was she immune from such lawsuits?—did reach the high court. As Barrett was careening toward confirmation in early October 2020, the court refused to take up Davis's cause. Attached to that refusal, Thomas penned a four-page screed against marriage equality, joined by Alito, that seemed like another *Deus vult*. Give us this judge and we'll give you back marriage, Thomas seemed to say.[42] They stated, quite plainly, that they would use religious freedom to overturn or at least under-cut marriage equality: "By choosing to privilege a novel constitutional right over the religious liberty interests explicitly protected in the First Amendment, and by doing so undemocratically, the Court has created a problem that only it can fix." Davis was simply "a public official with traditional Christian values." Barrett's confirmation three weeks later marked three Trump justices added to the Supreme Court since Davis denied that first marriage license, since the court upheld mar-riage equality. The change in personnel was meant to change the law. And it might. They now have the votes to undo marriage equality.[43]

Plenty of cases involving marriage equality and religious freedom claims are churning through the courts. Some, such as those involving gay wedding cakes, are actually civil rights cases repackaged by Cru-saders as religious freedom to further their bigotry and, like Davis, to recast the bigot as the victim.

5

It Was Never about a Cake

*(Masterpiece Cakeshop v. Colorado
Civil Rights Commission)*

"Jesus was a carpenter. I don't think he
would have made a bed for their wedding."[1]

—**Jack Phillips**, Masterpiece Cakeshop owner

Charlie Craig and Dave Mullins decided to get married after two years together. Months before their wedding, they arrived at Masterpiece Cakeshop to taste some cakes and design their own. The owner greeted them warmly, and they sat to peruse photos of custom cakes baked for other customers. When the owner realized that Charlie and Dave were planning their own wedding, to each other, the atmosphere seemed to darken. Gone were the smiles and warmth. He informed them that he wouldn't sell *them* a wedding cake. As Dave and Charlie told me, "We never got a chance to ask for anything, this all happened so fast. It felt like forever in the moment, but we just sat down, he asked who the cake was for, we said it was for us, and he immediately said he wouldn't make a cake for our same sex wedding."[2] That forever moment was "a gigantic, yawning, pregnant pause."

Charlie and Dave left the bakery, feeling humiliated, hurt, and marginalized. Charlie's mom happened to be in town, and choosing the cake was "the one moment where she got to be involved in the whole process."[3] The couple had already selected the other vendors, and none had "raised an eyebrow about the fact that we were gay." She later recounted the scene in an interview: "We went into that store happy.

We left broken."[4] Charlie recalls, "She didn't really understand what was happening right away, so there was this extra layer of embarrassment because we had to explain to her that [the bakery owner] understood perfectly well what we asked for, *that* is why it's happening."[5]

"We were all upset," Charlie said, admitting he broke down in tears in the car. This kind of discrimination can be damaging. "I grew up in a small town in Wyoming, and it just wasn't okay to be gay," Charlie explained. He was bullied and struggling to be true to himself in the shadow of a hideous murder. Matthew Shephard, a twenty-one-year-old gay man attending the University of Wyoming, in Laramie (which Charlie would also attend), was abducted, tortured, beaten, robbed, tied to a fence, set on fire, and left to die. He died after six days of agony. The vicious murder helped launch a movement against homophobia and eventually led to a federal hate crimes law, but at the time, it also sent a chilling message. "To protect myself and my family," said Charlie, "and even protect Dave later on, I was just really closed off about it. I didn't announce to everybody that I was gay all the time, to protect myself and the people around me." Being gay is, in a way, constantly coming out of the closet, he explains. Most of the time, a person controls if and how to do that. That control allows for self-care and sensitivity to the once-constant threat of violence. But in the bakery, that choice was impossible. It's not that Charlie planned to hide who he was, simply that he was particularly exposed and without a lifelong defense. "There was no way in this situation that I could hide the fact that I was gay because I was getting a cake for Dave and I, and so it was a really vulnerable moment for me." It was in that vulnerable moment that Christian love struck.

The owner explained his side on *The View*: "I don't believe that Jesus would have made a cake if he had been a baker."[6] "Christ . . . wouldn't make the cake," he said in another interview,[7] adding, "I believe that the bible clearly teaches that marriage is between one man and one woman" and "I don't believe [Jesus] would have because that would have contradicted the rest of the biblical teaching." Why bigotry? Because god.

What happened is as important as what didn't happen. The baker is a for-profit business organized and operating under the laws of the state, not an individual person. The bakery wasn't for worshipping or praying. Nor was the couple asking the bakery or its employees to participate in a wedding. At the time the business rejected the couple, they were planning a small wedding in Provincetown, Massachusetts, a small family affair for their "nearest and dearest," to be followed by "a big, giant party with everybody" when they got back home.[8] "The phrase 'wedding cake' for us was always off, it was the cake for the reception," the couple tell me. But then, that's most wedding cakes.

We know what happened—and what didn't—because way back at the beginning of the case, the parties actually agreed on certain important facts. These undisputed facts tell the same story I just recounted: "The whole conversation between Phillips and [Charlie and David] was very brief, with no discussion between the parties about what the cake would look like."[9]

The refusal was not because of what they wanted on their cake—they never even discussed the design—but because they were gay. The only new piece of information that bakery had between acceptance and rejection was that two men were the couple getting married. They didn't discuss the decoration, the color, the artistry, or flavor. As Charlie had said, "We never got a chance to ask for anything."[10]

Charlie and David signed their legal complaint hours before their wedding in Provincetown. The complaint notified the Colorado Civil Rights Commission, the state administrative body that enforced the Colorado Anti-Discrimination Act (CADA), about what happened.[11] CADA is a series of laws that prevent discrimination in employment, housing, advertising, and against people with disabilities—it's Colorado's version of the Civil Rights Act. Federal and state civil rights statutes are why businesses can't put up signs declaring "No Jews" or "No Blacks" or "No Irish" or implement discriminatory policies.

Charlie and Dave brought their case, with the help of the ACLU, to the commission and the commission agreed with Charlie and David that this bakery had broken the law when it discriminated against them because of their sexual orientation. The bakery made it easy, "aver[ring] that its standard business practice is to deny service to same-sex couples based on religious beliefs."[12] The business discriminated against a class of people Colorado law protects, just as so many businesses before it had discriminated against Black Americans. The commission ordered the business to stop discriminating against "same-sex couples by refusing to sell them wedding cakes or any product [it] would sell to heterosexual couples," train its staff, and inform the commission about its progress with compliance.[13]

Sadly, this was just another business discriminating against a minority simply because of who they were.

How Civil Rights Laws Work

That made the case ordinary. Hundreds of similar cases are brought before state and federal civil rights agencies each year. State agencies like the Colorado Civil Rights Commission exist because the cases are so important and plentiful. But most people don't seem to understand how the laws work. The basic idea is simple—don't discriminate. But how does that function legally? Who can't discriminate? When? Where? And why can a business put up a sign that says, "No shirt, no shoes, no service," but not "No Jews"?

Civil rights laws operate in basically the same way. They list groups of people who are protected. Then they list businesses, services, and the like that cannot exclude those people. The groups of people are known as "protected classes." Colorado's Anti-Discrimination Act protected several classes: "disability, race, creed, color, sex, sexual orientation, marital status, national origin, or ancestry." That's more than federal civil rights laws. These protected classes are statutory, established by law, and legislators may give additional groups protection if they choose. These laws establish clear legal rights, which is why Line #2 is the central issue in these cases: religion is not a license to violate other people's rights, including rights established by civil rights laws.

As Charlie and Dave's case moved through the courts and up to the Supreme Court, the widespread unfamiliarity with civil rights laws bred thousands of bad "gotcha" analogies (Nazis and Jewish bakeries, bacon and kosher delis, KKK customers in Black-owned businesses). Any good analogy here must have (1) a protected class that's actually protected under the law, (2) a place of public accommodation, and (3) a service that is being provided to others but denied to people in the protected class.

Many of the analogies didn't involve protected classes. "Imagine a Jewish baker being required to put a swastika on a cake," wrote the editorial board of the *Chicago Tribune*.[14] Nazis aren't a protected class, so businesses can discriminate against them. Bigots aren't protected by civil rights laws. Nor is political affiliation. There's an unintentional bigotry in this analogy. "Why all of a sudden do gays get compared to Nazis and the KKK?" asked Dave.[15]

Other analogies failed to include places of public accommodation. This means a public business, something that is meant to be open to the public. Your house does not count. Civil rights laws don't require you to host a gay wedding in your backyard.

Finally, other analogies failed to understand a third requirement—the service aspect. *If* a business provides a service, it must provide it to members of protected classes. Civil rights laws do not tell businesses what they must sell, only that if the business sells a certain product, it cannot refuse to sell it to certain classes of people. For instance, if you don't bake wedding cakes for any customers, you don't have to start when a couple, gay or straight, asks. The government *can't* force a kosher deli to serve bacon because it never served bacon. The government *can* tell a kosher deli that it must sell a pastrami on rye to people in protected classes.

That's how these laws work, with one caveat. They always exclude any "place that is principally used for religious purposes," as the Colorado statute phrases it, from the definition of a "place of public accommodation." So no church, synagogue, mosque, or other house of worship need worry about "the gays" kicking down their doors and forcing homophobic preachers to pronounce their marriage vows. Businesses organized and protected under the laws of the state have other rules to follow.

Charlie and Dave's case was typical of this genre, but it was made special, a cause célèbre, by Crusaders who saw an opportunity: the Alliance Defending Freedom (ADF).

God's Warriors

ADF skillfully manipulated and distorted the narrative of the case. Instead of a loving couple being victimized by a bigoted business owner, the narrative flipped into "the gays" and the big bad govern-ment coercing a poor, persecuted Christian artist. Many people still know the bakery's name, but not the names of the couple that suffered the discrimination.

Weaponizing religious freedom is ADF's principal mission. It was created to entrench homophobia and anti-LGBTQ bigotry, and quickly decided religious freedom was the best tool for that. This is best captured by a simple fact: Alan Sears, who ran ADF for its first twenty-five years, coauthored a book entitled *The Homosexual Agenda: Exposing the Principal Threat to Religious Freedom Today*. The title says it all. Using "religious freedom" to oppose LGBTQ rights and equal-ity. When Dave rhetorically asked, "Why all of a sudden do gays get compared to Nazis?" it's because this is a page out of ADF's playbook.

In *The Homosexual Agenda*, Sears wrote that the "radical homosex-ual activist community has adopted many of the tactics used in Nazi Germany."[16] Sears likened his fight to overturn marriage equality to Lincoln's fight to abolish slavery, an analogy as historically flawed as it is narcissistic and deluded.[17] Sears retired in 2017, after it was clear the Crusaders had captured the Supreme Court and would eventually succeed. Michael Farris, who founded the Homeschool Legal Defense Association and Patrick Henry College "to shelter homeschool gradu-ates and funnel them into Republican politics," now runs ADF.[18]

ADF is one of the youngest and one of the biggest Crusaders. A group of televangelists and radio preachers—many of them Christian nationalists, such as D. James Kennedy and James Dobson—founded the Alliance Defense Fund, as it was originally known, in 1993 to undermine the work of the ACLU. Sears's *Homosexual Agenda* shows something of an obsession with the ACLU. ADF's total annual revenue exceeded $60 million in 2019.[19] Homophobia and bigotry are baked into the ethos of ADF, and the Southern Poverty Law Center classifies ADF as a hate group.[20] ADF litigated many of the cases in this book, including the government prayer case, where the court reimagined the facts (see Author's Note); churches challenging public health orders (chapter 11); the companion case to Hobby Lobby (chapter 10); and the Missouri children's ministry case (chapter 13).[21]

ADF works to alter public perception, to cast American Christians as a poor minority besieged by culture and persecuted by the government because, as ADF's website explained, "It is not enough to just win cases; we must change the culture."[22] ADF is so serious about changing the culture that it got into the Christian movie business, teaming up with the makers of the lucrative, risible, and shockingly bigoted *God's Not Dead* movies. A list of "real life" ADF cases appears in the credits in an attempt to further a Christian persecution narrative.[23] This case and the Hobby Lobby case both appear.

ADF is also trying to change the legal profession by training young lawyers to "engage the legal culture."[24] ADF claims to have trained nearly 2,500 lawyers through its legal fellowships.[25] With the fellowships, ADF "seeks to recover the robust Christendomic theology of the third, fourth, and fifth centuries."[26] Author Rob Boston always believed that the Crusaders sought to "take us back to 1950. Turns out I was off by about 1,500 years."[27]

That yearning to return to the days when Christians first seized full political power and unified their church with the state stayed on the ADF website from at least 2010 until mid-2014—the *Deus vult* era—during which a future Supreme Court justice lectured ADF fellows several times. Amy Coney Barrett was a paid ADF teacher from 2011 to 2016, delivering lectures to ADF legal fellows for a couple of grand.[28] During her Supreme Court confirmation hearing, Barrett disingenuously claimed she was "not aware" of "ADF's decades-long efforts to recriminalize homosexuality." At best, speaking to a group that advocates for criminalizing homosexuality and sterilizing transgender people shows poor judgment; lying about it would be worse.[29] Evidence suggests Barrett's relationship with ADF was much closer than she disclosed.[30] The day after the Senate voted to confirm Barrett, ADF crowed: "Newly confirmed Justice Amy Coney Barrett will hear an ADF case later this term."[31] Barrett didn't recuse herself from that case and decided in favor of ADF.

ADF's influential tendrils have burrowed deep into the government. Josh Hawley, a Christian nationalist US senator from Missouri, helped push Amy Barrett through the Senate Judiciary Committee.

Like Barrett, he was on ADF's fellowship faculty.[32] As attorney general, Jeff Sessions visited ADF's headquarters and consulted with it on a massive "religious liberty" memo he imposed on the DOJ. Trump made an attorney in ADF's allied network, Noel Francisco, solicitor general.[33] Francisco then had the United States wade into the cake case on the bakery's side when it reached the Supreme Court, an extraordinary step, even participating in the oral argument himself.[34]

It may be impossible to understand just how devastating that was. "When I was reading their brief to the Supreme Court," Charlie tells me, "it didn't say 'the Trump administration.' It said, 'The United States of America,' and that was just a really awful feeling. To read those words, that the United States of America does not believe Dave and I have equal rights."[35]

ADF tainted almost everyone's understanding of reality with a comprehensive and expensive media strategy, but the ACLU outlawyered ADF at every step. ADF offered two big legal arguments. (1) Free speech: the government can't compel a person to craft a message in support of gay marriage. (2) Religious freedom: the government can't compel a person to act against their religious beliefs. But these arguments depend on what actually happened that day at the bakery. Judges and law professors are fond of hypotheticals, but cases are about reality and impact real lives.

Accompanying these arguments was a massive dodge—a business refusing to serve people—but ADF substituted a person for that corporation. We'll look at that distinction first, then free speech, then religious freedom.

Bakery or Baker?

The Alliance Defending Freedom was remarkably successful at conflating the corporation with its owner, who comes off as gentle and soft-spoken on camera. Soft-spoken bigotry is still bigotry, and the bakery was still a business. A business, in a business mall, the Mission Trace Shopping Center, alongside Freaky's Smoke Shop & Tattoo VIII, Mojo Massage, Vapergate, a Pizza Hut, an H&R Block, and other businesses. It's open to the public and, like other businesses, sells products. Not just cakes for special occasions, but T-shirts, candles, cookies, cinnamon rolls, banana bread, coffee, and mugs. If you buy a mug, you get a free coffee.

The bakery is a legal entity organized under Colorado law, which protects the individuals behind the business from personal liability. If a cake gives fifty people food poisoning, the bakery can be sued, but not the owner personally. The business may have to fork over some cash, but the owner's personal assets are protected. The business could borrow heavily and fail spectacularly, consumed by debt, but the shareholders and owners aren't personally liable for those debts.[36]

This separation is fundamental to American business. Before the Crusade, the Supreme Court called it "a general principle of corporate law deeply ingrained in our economic and legal systems" and even this court would probably agree with that principle outside the religious freedom context.[37] Thirty corporate law professors explained, "This separation is not an ancillary part of corporate law and governance. It is instead the *sine qua non* of the wealth-creating legal innovation of the corporate form."[38] It's difficult to overstate how important this separation is.

The massive benefits of forming a legal corporation come with some burdens, including obeying laws meant for corporations and places of public accommodation, rather than for individual citizens. Jack Phillips had enjoyed the protections of this corporate separation, the "corporate veil," for twenty years. Masterpiece Cakeshop Incorporated was founded as a corporation in 1992, with two shareholders and a four-person board of directors, to operate a "retail bakery."[39] During this litigation, it reorganized several times. Phillips may personally believe that Jesus wouldn't make a cake for a gay couple, but in 2017, a few months before the Supreme Court heard oral arguments, the bakery reorganized as a limited liability company that didn't even list Phillips on the paperwork.[40]

Philips used the laws of the state of Colorado to create a legal entity that was deliberately and completely distinct from him as an individual. He then sought to use that creation to discriminate in the name of his personal god. The state may prevent entities created under its laws from being used for such an end. If Charlie and Dave had knocked on the door of Phillips's house and said, "Hey, we hear you bake cakes. Would you make one for our wedding?" Phillips could've said no without consequence. But Phillips didn't say no; Masterpiece Cakeshop Incorporated said no.

Imagine a world in which this was not the case, in which for-profit companies could exempt themselves from rules and regulations because an employee or shareholder or owner or operator or employee disagrees with the rules. Guaranteed religious exemptions in a competitive marketplace would launch a race to the bottom as every business decided which rules to follow or not.

How long would it take oil companies to realize that, simply by claiming to adhere to this or that religion, they no longer have to comply with environmental regulations? And before you shrug this off as unlikely, recall that Representative John Shimkus (R-IL) once claimed that global climate change might be happening, but we don't need to worry about it because God promised Noah he wouldn't flood the earth again.[41] The "Evangelical Declaration on Global Warming" states four beliefs and four denials of belief, including "We deny that carbon dioxide . . . is a pollutant."[42] How hard would it be for a company to adopt this religious declaration as a sincere religious belief?

Want to test your drugs on animals? The biblical god gave man "dominion over the fish of the sea, and over the fowl of the air, and over the cattle, and over all the earth, and over every creeping thing that creepeth upon the earth" (Genesis 1:26).

Want to keep women out of management positions? The Christian god permits no woman to "teach or . . . assume authority over a man; she must be quiet" (1 Timothy 2:12).

When I wrote about this race to the bottom after the Hobby Lobby decision in 2014, I worried that "racism, sexism, and homophobia all have biblical and religious support for any company to avoid complying with all that burdensome equality legislation." These fears aren't hypothetical, but real cases. In 1990, a Christian school paid male employees 25 percent more than females, using a "head of household salary supplement" because "the Bible clearly teaches that the husband is the head of the house, head of the wife, head of the family." The school also underpaid support staff for years. The school argued that it didn't have to comply with wage laws because its pay scale was based on "a sincerely held belief derived from the Bible."[43] The court rejected this argument in 1990, partly using Line #2.[44]

In another case, a religious nonprofit funded its proselytizing ministry with commercial businesses, including gas stations, retail clothing and grocery stores, farms, construction companies, a record-keeping company, a motel, and candy companies. To keep costs down, the businesses employed workers, "most of whom were drug addicts, derelicts, or criminals before their conversion and rehabilitation," but didn't pay the workers a salary, instead giving them "food, clothing, shelter, and other benefits."[45] The businesses had a sizable edge over secular competitors because they didn't pay employees, let alone pay them fairly. The Supreme Court rejected the argument in 1983.[46]

In Colorado, the court would depart from this precedent and bring us closer to that imaginary world by simply ignoring the bedrock principle of American corporate law.

Free Speech

The parties' agreed-upon facts destroy the free speech arguments. The bakery didn't reject a "message," but people. It didn't refuse to design a specific cake because of what that cake communicated; it refused to design any cake *for them*.

The first judge found that "the undisputed evidence is that Phillips categorically refused to prepare a cake for [Charlie and Dave's] same-sex wedding before there was any discussion about what that cake would look like. Phillips was not asked to apply any message or symbol to the cake, or to construct the cake in any fashion that could be reasonably understood as advocating same-sex marriage." The bakery had no idea about their potential design, only who they were. "For all Phillips knew at the time," explained the judge, the couple "might have wanted a nondescript cake that would have been suitable for consumption at any wedding." The free speech claim was "specious."[47]

It's also specious in another respect: "What kind of a cake is gay?'" the couple asked me. It's a good point. What's the difference between a gay wedding cake and a straight wedding cake? If given a lineup of twenty cakes, could you sort them into gay and straight? The three-tiered white wedding cake with the word "Congratulations," is that one gay or not? Charlie and Dave didn't want a rainbow cake; they wanted a minimalist cake, probably three tiers of white cake that incorporated red and teal, their wedding colors. In the end, that's pretty much what they got. It was only after they were discriminated against that they added a single rainbow layer under the icing.

There's an argument to be made that cakes are expressive speech, but Justice Sonia Sotomayor disposed of this nicely in oral argument, "The primary purpose of a food of any kind is to be eaten. Now, some people might love the aesthetic appeal of a special dessert, and look at it for a very long time, but in the end its only purpose is to be eaten."[48] I love the *Great British Bake Off* more than the next person, but, I agree, cakes are food meant to be eaten.

At oral argument, much of the free speech discussion centered on hypotheticals involving chefs, makeup artists, sandwich artists, jewelers, hair stylists, hotel chefs, and more. Hypotheticals about denying service to the KKK were popular. There was even a hypo about a cake celebrating Kristallnacht. These analogies were shockingly bad for the three reasons explained above, but were still trotted out by the nation's top jurists.

Interestingly, the bakery admitted, under questioning from Justice Elena Kagan, that a hair stylist is "absolutely not" engaging in "expression or protected speech," and neither are the makeup artist, tailor, or, most tellingly, the chef.[49] "Bakers are speaking, but chefs aren't" was the sum of the Crusader's free speech argument.

Charlie mentioned another curious moment during oral argument that undermines the free speech claim: "They asked if Jack Phillips would give us an already made cake, a pre-made cake." There were quite a few such exchanges, and the Crusader repeatedly said things like, "In the context of a pre-made cake . . . Mr. Phillips is happy to sell anything in his store." But Charlie told me that he was watching Phillips, not the justices, and "while that was happening, Phillips was shaking his head 'no.'"

Between oral-argument admissions and the undisputed facts, it would have been almost impossible for the court to decide the case in the bakery's favor on free speech grounds. So instead, the Court decided the case on religious freedom, but probably not how you remember.

Hostility toward Religion

The Supreme Court should have reiterated Line #2 in this case. Sorry, bakery, your owner's religion does not trump the rights of others. Done.

Instead, it invented some hostility *against* a bigoted bakery. Essentially, it gave the bakery a "get out of jail free" card. It didn't fully weaponize religious freedom. This was before Kavanaugh and Barrett, when Kennedy was still the swing vote. Reading between the lines of Kennedy's 7–2 opinion, it sounds like the court was looking for a way out of deciding a case that initially seemed to involve simpler issues. The justices held that the Colorado Civil Rights Commission said mean things about the religion of the man who runs the bakery. The court claimed this "hostility" tainted the entire civil rights case against the bakery, and so the court threw it all out. In doing so, it ratified the bakery's overt hostility toward LGBTQ people.

Hostility toward religion was barely mentioned by the parties, let alone argued as a central pillar of the case. In 345 pages of briefing from the principal parties and the United States, it was an afterthought: maybe eleven paragraphs and one footnote mention hostility.[50] In the eighty-seven minutes of oral argument, hostility toward religion came up during a brief exchange between Justice Kennedy that, though short, is in hindsight revealing because Kennedy tipped his hand.[51] This exchange was noteworthy, but "unexpected," even for conservative observers.[52] Kennedy mentioned a single quote by one commissioner that he actually misattributed to a different commissioner, inadvertently confessing to the esoteric nature of the comment.[53] It was so unimportant he couldn't get the name right. Hostility was barely mentioned in the briefing and misattributed in the oral argument because the hostility wasn't real. We were witnessing its creation.

In the opinion Kennedy wrote:

> The neutral and respectful consideration to which Phillips was entitled was compromised here, however. The Civil Rights Commission's treatment of his case has some elements of a clear and

impermissible hostility toward the sincere religious beliefs that motivated his objection.[54]

That's a harsh accusation to level at any official, but especially those charged with protecting civil rights and eradicating discrimination. That's career-ending criticism. And it was unfounded.

Kennedy manufactured this hostility from three pieces of evidence: two commissioners' statements that he mangled and fragmented, and a homophobic troll.

1. Commissioner Rice's Statement

Kennedy focused primarily on one statement by Commissioner Diann Rice (which he misattributed to another commissioner in oral argument). Rice's comment came after the case was over. The commission had written its final order two months before, the bakery had responded, and notice of appeal was already filed. The commissioners had considered the merits and were just deciding whether or not to stay their final order. They had already rejected the bakery's arguments three separate times and voted unanimously against the stay.

The case was over. The commission's work was done. But Kennedy claimed that the entire case against the bakery had to be thrown out because the commission was so hostile to Christianity *during the case* that the bakery couldn't have received a fair hearing. But Rice's comment was, quite literally, the last substantive comment in that hearing and therefore the Commission's inquiry. She said:

> Freedom of religion and religion has been used to justify all kinds of discrimination throughout history, whether it be slavery, whether it be the holocaust, whether it be—I mean, we—we can list hundreds of situations where freedom of religion has been used to justify discrimination. And to me it is one of the most despicable pieces of rhetoric that people can use to—to use their religion to hurt others. So that's just my personal point of view.[55]

Kennedy's retelling truncated Rice's quote to exclude the final sentence, "So that's just my personal point of view."

Kennedy took umbrage at Rice's words, "To describe a man's faith as 'one of the most despicable pieces of rhetoric that people can use' is to disparage his religion in at least two distinct ways: by describing it as despicable, and also by characterizing it as merely rhetorical— something insubstantial and even insincere." Rice later told me that Kennedy's rendering of her words was wrong "on many levels."[56] But I think it's a deliberate misreading. Rice was arguing for Line #2, a line the Supreme Court upheld *until this Crusade.*

When Justice Alito delivered the keynote address to Leo's Federal- ist Society, he mentioned not only the Masterpiece Cakeshop case, but also singled out Rice's statement for additional opprobrium.[57]

As a college freshman at George Washington University, Rice and her friends went to a civil rights march on the Mall. The young Rice heard Martin Luther King Jr.'s "I Have a Dream" speech. Rice tells me, "His speech gave me chills" and "is what led me to where I am and my beliefs." Since then, "people's rights have always been at the core of my beliefs."

Rice comes across as a thoughtful, careful public servant, con- cerned with the rule of law and human rights, nothing like the bigot of Kennedy's opinion, "I believe to my core that every person should be allowed their faith and their beliefs, and far be it for me to criticize . . . but I will always believe it's wrong to use your religion or beliefs to hurt or discriminate against someone else." That's Line #2. She believes in freedom and equality, but that necessarily means one person's religion cannot trump another person's rights.

I asked Rice about being the Supreme Court's scapegoat. "I was very disappointed and hurt at the time," she said, but she also had perspec- tive. Throughout our conversation, she touched on the hurt and anger over Kennedy "twisting" her words, but her overriding feeling was frus- tration that this might've hurt civil rights: "I really regret that the work of the Civil Rights Commission was hurt. That's my biggest regret." She worried that Kennedy's decision "made the entire Civil Rights Division take a step back and say, 'maybe we can't fight this battle.'"

It also shattered some illusions she had about the court, which many Americans still have: "It hurts. It made me somewhat angry. It made me realize that I've wanted the Supreme Court to be that one place, that one pillar in our democracy that is above politics, where the decisions are made on the basis of law and precedent. . . . I thought that they left their political biases behind. . . . I question that every day now."[58]

Rice's statements are, of course, true. And they're true to the extent she was talking explicitly about religion rather than religious freedom. Half of Americans who opposed same-sex marriage in 2012 justified that stance by citing their religion or the bible.[59] Religion *has been* used to justify slavery and murder. More to the point, the bakery in this case was claiming a right to discriminate *based in religious freedom.* Religiously motivated bigotry was one of the issues the commission had to decide *because the bakery made it an issue.*

Judicial bodies routinely declare that bigotry and discrimination are wrong, "abhorrent," "odious," or even "despicable."[60] Many Supreme Court justices have said so. Kennedy himself, in an opinion penned during the previous term, said, via quote, that racial discrimination is "odious in all aspects" and "especially pernicious in the administration of justice."[61] But saying that such bigotry is motivated by religion, even when true and the bigot himself is claiming so, is apparently a bridge too far.

2. Commissioner Jairam's Statement

Kennedy also constructed hostility from another statement at an earlier meeting:

> One commissioner suggested that Phillips can believe "what he wants to believe," but cannot act on his religious beliefs "if he decides to do business in the state." A few moments later, the commissioner restated the same position: "If a businessman wants to do business in the state and he's got an issue with the—the law's impacting his personal belief system, he needs to look at being able to compromise."[62]

Kennedy suggested different interpretations were possible, but chose to read these as "inappropriate and dismissive comments showing lack of due consideration for Phillips' free exercise rights and the dilemma he faced."

This is so disingenuous as to be dishonest. Commissioner Raju Jairam was restating Lines #1 and #2 in the first sentence Kennedy mangled. The transcript actually reads, "I don't think the act necessarily prevents Mr. Phillips from believing what he wants to believe. And—but if he decides to do business in the state, he's got to follow [inaudible]."[63]

In the second sentence, Jairam was trying to quote a concurring opinion in the New Mexico Supreme Court's *Elane Photography* case, in which the court said a photography business cannot discriminate against LGBTQ couples. The Supreme Court refused to hear that same case three years before it accepted Charlie and Dave's case. Justice Ruth Bader Ginsburg cites this same case in her Hobby Lobby dissent.[64] Jairam explicitly invoked the court decision these same justices allowed to stand:

> And I believe the—it was best said by the judges in the New Mexico case, where the laws are here just to protect individuals from humiliation and dignitary harm. . . . I'm referring to the comments made by Justice [Bosson] in that case. And essentially he was saying that if a businessman wants to do business in the state and he's got an issue with the—the law's impacting his personal belief system, he needs to look at being able to compromise. And I think it was very well said by that judge.[65]

This thoughtful public servant was not offering an off-the-cuff opinion, but trying to decide a nearly identical case by referring to the opinion of top jurists in a similar case that the Supreme Court let stand. This is how public officials should behave.

The judicial passage to which Commissioner Jairam was referring is eloquent on the necessity of Line #2:

> At its heart, this case teaches that at some point in our lives all of us must compromise, if only a little, to accommodate the contrasting values of others. A multicultural, pluralistic society, one of our nation's strengths, demands no less. The [owners of the photography business] are free to think, to say, to believe, as

they wish; they may pray to the God of their choice and follow those commandments in their personal lives wherever they lead. The Constitution protects the [owners] in that respect and much more. But there is a price, one that we all have to pay somewhere in our civic life.

In the smaller, more focused world of the marketplace, of commerce, of public accommodation, the [owners] have to channel their conduct, not their beliefs, so as to leave space for other Americans who believe something different. That compromise is part of the glue that holds us together as a nation, the tolerance that lubricates the varied moving parts of us as a people.[66]

This is accurate, well-stated, and, for a legal opinion, somewhat moving—it's certainly not hostile toward religion. To say, as Kennedy did, that paraphrasing this opinion shows "a lack of due consideration" for the baker's religion is a lie. Six fellow justices assented to that lie.

Raju Jairam "grew up in the Hindu faith" in Madras among Muslims and had a Zoroastrian mentor. He went to Irish Catholic school, then a Syrian Christian school, then a Jesuit college for a time, and an engineering school, before coming to the states for graduate school. He told me that he served on the commission to "give back to the community." Our conversation revealed a thoughtful, measured man, neither Democrat nor Republican, a small businessman, a caring person trying to do the right thing. "I was sick when I saw what they [the justices] said" about him; "That was not pleasant." When I ask how it feels knowing that, because of this opinion, his name will be remembered in this way, he responds that it is, in a word, "appalling." He even hoped that the court might "revisit this decision and set the record straight"—clear his name, as it were. After reading Kennedy's opinion, Jairam tells me, "I think I decided it correctly."[67]

Largely because of these two statements, Kennedy wrote, "Phillips' religious objection was not considered with the neutrality that the Free Exercise Clause requires." This is not only wrong, but absurd. At worst, religious bigotry was called out in mild and truthful terms, and only because the bakery made it an issue, and only after the case was decided. Kennedy took issue with the tone. Then White House press secretary Sarah Huckabee Sanders was, for once, actually not far off the mark when she said: "The Supreme Court rightly concluded that the Colorado Civil Rights Commission failed to show tolerance and respect for [the bakery's] religious beliefs."[68] Or, to quote Kennedy, "This sentiment is inappropriate."[69] This was about tone and propriety, not the law. Basically, the commission was mean.

The decision elevates delicate Christian sensibilities over the civil rights of citizens. To offend Christianity, even in the slightest manner, is to be hostile to religion in a way that violates the Constitution.

3. The Troll

A "victim" offered Kennedy the final piece of evidence for the commission's hostility toward Christianity.[70] In internet slang, a "troll" is an attention seeker who traffics in inflammatory rhetoric to antagonize and sow chaos and discord. As Supreme Court author and journalist Ian Millhiser pointed out, to defend Masterpiece Cakeshop Incorporated, a troll visited other Colorado bakeries and demanded custom cakes with homophobic imagery and bible verses.[71] For instance, "an image of two groomsmen, holding hands in front of a cross, with a red *X* over the image" and decorated with bible verses:

God hates sin. Psalm 45:7

Homosexuality is a detestable sin. Leviticus 18:2

The troll filed three cases; all three recount him asking for Leviticus 18:2, which says, "Give the following instructions to the people of Israel. I am the LORD your God." The troll can't even get his own biblical bigotry right; he meant Leviticus 18:22, "Do not practice homosexuality, having sex with another man as with a woman. It is a detestable sin."

The troll's delicious biblical illiteracy and inattention to detail are fitting. He's a young-earth creationist who founded Jesus camps (42,000 campers claimed[72]) and gave Christians "biblically correct" tours of zoos and science and history museums. He agreed that inclusive public schools "are whorehouses" and said, "We need to burn 'em down." Not just that, but that earlier generations of Americans would, if alive today, "tear the bricks out of the walls" and "use the bricks to stone the apostates."[73] This was Kennedy's counterbalance for the commission's "inappropriate" tone.

The troll targeted bakeries he identified as gay-friendly. Each bakery listened to the troll's design request. Unlike Masterpiece Cakeshop Incorporated, none kicked the troll out when they realized he was a Christian. Each bakery employed Christians and regularly prepared custom, Christian-themed, and bible cakes for anyone; but all refused to make bigotry cakes for anyone, including this troll.

The gleeful troll brought his three cases to the Colorado Civil Rights Commission, which found no discrimination. The law requires businesses to treat people from protected classes as they would treat any other customer. The bakeries the troll visited treated everyone equally—"we don't sell these kinds of cakes to anyone." Masterpiece Cakeshop Incorporated refused to treat LGBTQ people equally—"we don't sell these kinds of cakes *to you*." Remember, the government cannot force kosher delis to sell bacon, but if they sell bacon, they must sell it to everyone. These bakeries were refusing that kind of cake to anyone, as opposed to refusing to sell wedding cakes to a protected class.

More obviously, civil rights laws are meant to stop discrimination. They outlaw discrimination primarily, but are also intended to protect businesses that refuse to discriminate. Bigots once demanded businesses discriminate or face boycotts or worse—common KKK tactics before such laws existed.

Masterpiece Cakeshop made "a lot of money" selling wedding cakes, six-figures annually off about 200 to 250 wedding cakes of about $500 each.[74] The bakery tried to get around "selling wedding cakes but not to gays" by later arguing that it would sell Charlie and David a bland, undecorated cake, just not a custom cake. Or sell them "birthday cakes, shower cakes, sell you cookies and brownies, I just don't make cakes for same-sex weddings."[75] But from a legal standpoint, even if that were factually true, we settled the "separate but equal" stupidity a few decades ago. Separate isn't equal; it's discrimination.

Like a drowning man thrown a lifeline, Kennedy seized on the troll, the creationist who wants to stone apostates and "the gays" and burn down public schools, as evidence of hostility against Christians. "Another indication of hostility is the difference in treatment between Phillips' case and the cases of other bakers who objected to a requested cake on the basis of conscience and prevailed before the Commission," he wrote.[76]

This exposed the raging hypocrisy at the center of the opinion. Kennedy pointed to the explicit religious bigotry of that troll, who wanted to proclaim that "homosexuality is a detestable sin," to justify his decision, while also arguing in that decision that it's hostile to religion to point out that bigotry in the name of god exists. Kennedy disproved his own argument.

Religious Freedom and Civil Rights Laws

In Charlie and Dave's case, the justices all agreed that civil rights laws are perfectly valid and legitimate. It's "unexceptional that Colorado law can protect gay persons."[77] Nevertheless, a larger conversation wedges itself into arguments about whether religion should be a license to discriminate. Its basic thrust is that civil rights laws are wrong, though it's rarely phrased so candidly. Instead, the argument usually sounds something like: "Why not just get another cake at another store?"; "You don't want a bigot baking your cake anyway"; "Just go somewhere else!"; or sometimes, "The free market punishes bigots with less business."

Understanding the history and success of civil rights laws is crucial to understanding why these arguments are wrong. Martin Luther King Jr. explained in a letter to his fellow clergymen, penned on scraps of paper and smuggled out of the Birmingham jail by his lawyers, the harm that these laws guard against.[78] King listed injustices Black people had endured, such as being forced "to sleep night after night in the uncomfortable corners of your automobile because no motel will accept you." And being constantly humiliated "by nagging signs reading 'white' and 'colored.'"[79] Another outrage spoke to every parent:

> When you suddenly find your tongue twisted and your speech stammering as you seek to explain to your six year old daughter

why she can't go to the public amusement park that has just been advertised on television, and see tears welling up in her eyes when she is told that Funtown is closed to colored children, and see ominous clouds of inferiority beginning to form in her little mental sky.

The harm is not just denying a motel room or amusement park or cake, but also denying a person's humanity. The incalculable damage of implanting that heinous sense of inferiority in a child's impressionable mind is the real and enduring harm. That the harm is mental and difficult to quantify makes it no less real.

The physical denial is harmful too. Sleeping in a car, as King was forced to do, may not seem risky but is during a Wisconsin winter or in a state where the KKK roamed the night. And what if it weren't being denied entry to Funtown, but groceries—food or baby formula? Or gas? Or medical care? "Just go somewhere else" might not meet the exigencies or even be possible. Before the Civil Rights Act, entire towns denied services to Black people. The KKK firebombed businesses that dared to treat Blacks equally. Successful Black businesses were also targeted. Rampaging whites killed and jailed Black citizens in the Tulsa Massacre of 1921 and then targeted the thriving Black business community known as Black Wall Street, burning down forty city blocks.

Widespread denials of service could happen again. In early 2016, Georgia legislators proposed a new "religious freedom" law that would weaponize religious freedom just like Mississippi's law (see pages 10–12).[80] CNN visited a small Georgia town and interviewed all five of the florists who admitted that they would refuse to serve LGBTQ people if given legal sanction.[81] These could easily be gas stations. Or grocery stores. Or doctors refusing to treat children because of who their parents are. These are real examples.[82] What if the next town is the same? And the town after that? (After civil rights groups organized pressure from businesses such as the NFL, Coca-Cola, and film and television studios, Governor Nathan Deal vetoed the Georgia bill.)

Without these laws, discrimination thrives, and the Supreme Court's utter failure to do the right thing in this case also led to more discrimination.

Dr. Netta Barak-Corren documented a substantial increase in discrimination against LGBTQ people in the wake of this bad decision.[83] Her team contacted more than 1,000 wedding vendors (photographers, bakers, florists, etc.) four different times: pretending to be part of a same-sex couple before and after the decision, and pretending to be part of an opposite-sex couple before and after the decision.

The court's "decision seems to have exposed same-sex couples to heightened risk of discrimination." It emboldened discrimination evenly across conservative/liberal and rural/suburban/urban divides. But the "discriminatory effect of the decision was significantly more pronounced in counties with relatively more religious congregations per capita." The Supreme Court undermined a civil rights law, and that caused "a meaningful increase in discrimination" against LGBTQ people, "even among vendors that provided this service before the decision."[84] In other words, before the decision, some vendors would have served LGBTQ couples, but they would have refused after the decision.

Enforcing civil rights laws works.

The market, on the other hand, failed because market solutions assume that people make rational, rather than emotional, decisions. We don't. One major political party has consistently convinced about half the electorate to vote against its own economic self-interest.

The market allowed discrimination for centuries. People were sold in that same market for centuries. Later, non-market actors, like the KKK, added costs to market actors, disincentivizing equality with death and destruction. While we were waiting for common decency to infuse itself into the market, an entire class of people were, quite literally, second-class citizens. Without these laws, we'd still be waiting.

Markets also reward bigotry. The reward mechanism is disputed, but exists. Chick-Fil-A capitalized on its owners' bigotry. It became a "hub for the anti-same-sex marriage brigade," and eating there became its own form of activism, leading to long lines and huge profits.[85] Bigotry also brought notoriety and customers to Masterpiece Cakeshop Incorporated. Media profiles often included anecdotes about customers shopping to express their support for homophobia; it "happens all the time," said the co-owner.[86] People organized fundraisers. One pulled in

more than $300,000 and continues to take donations.[87] Another raised
$75,000.[88] The company's legal team worked for free (fundraising on
the narrative was more lucrative). The bakery owner sold the rights for
his book.[89] A free, unrestricted market, populated by irrational, emotional consumers and producers, is incapable of solving every problem,
including discrimination against a stigmatized minority.[90]

Finally, there is the freedom argument against civil rights laws.
Two months after King was jailed in Birmingham, President John F.
Kennedy delivered a televised address on civil rights. He wanted a law
to guarantee "all Americans the right to be served in facilities which
are open to the public—hotels, restaurants, theaters, retail stores, and
similar establishments."[91] That law would be the Civil Rights Act of
1964. Kennedy was assassinated five months after this address.

The Civil Rights Act went into effect in July, and by October, the
Supreme Court was hearing oral argument in a case challenging the
law. The owner of the Heart of Atlanta Motel was a virulent segregationist and an attorney, so he argued the case himself: "The fundamental question, I submit, is whether or not Congress has the power to
take away the liberty of an individual to run his business as he sees fit
in the selection and choice of his customers."[92] Sound familiar?

The racist motelier rooted his liberty argument in the Thirteenth
and Fourteenth Amendments. The unanimous court batted away the
arguments with a restrained contempt that I find pleasing: "It would
be highly ironical to use the guarantee of due process—a guarantee
which plays so important a part in the Fourteenth Amendment, an
amendment adopted with the predominant aim of protecting Negroes
from discrimination—in order to strip Congress of power to protect
Negroes from discrimination."[93] Recall that the same businesses that
yearn for freedom are taking advantage of many laws and regulations
that protect them from financial and legal liability when they breach
a contract or a human finger ends up in a customer's food, a disturbingly common occurrence.[94] Strings can and should be attached to
these protections.

Perhaps the most grotesque iteration of this freedom argument is
that "forced" equality amounts to "involuntary servitude" that violates
the Thirteenth Amendment. Slavery. The Thirteenth Amendment

abolished slavery and involuntary servitude. Attached to the contemptuous sentence batting down the motelier's Fourteenth Amendment freedom argument is a derisive footnote explaining that the motel's Thirteenth Amendment argument "is so insubstantial that it requires no further discussion."[95] Crusaders actually made this same argument to the court more than fifty years later in the cake case. The Foundation for Moral Law, disgraced and twice-removed judge Roy Moore's outfit, argued that "Phillips has been subjected to involuntary servitude."[96]

Religious Freedom and Race

In the months after the Civil Rights Act took effect, Anne Newman, Sharon Neal, and John Mungin went for barbeque at Maurice's Piggie Park, a barbeque chain in South Carolina. The details aren't as clear as in Charlie and David's case, but are clear enough. The restaurant was the kind of place where you pull in, park, and a server comes out to the car to take your order. When Anne, Sharon, and John stopped by, the server saw they were Black and "went back into the building without taking their order or saying anything to them." A second server did the same, although "white customers were being served."[97] The lower court opinion ends the story there, but John Mungin, also a Black minister, told *Slate* fifty years later that someone at Piggie Park "put a pistol to my head" to make them leave.[98]

If true, Maurice Bessinger may have wielded the gun. He owned the chain and was president of the local chapter of the National Association for the Preservation of White People, founded to "fight for the restoration of legal segregation" and "to boycott any Merchant, Manufacturer or Industry who fosters racial integration" (making so-called market solutions impossible).[99]

Bessinger was known to proclaim, "God gave slaves to whites" and believed South Carolina's "biblical slavery" was a kind form of owning human beings.[100] He was "a devout Baptist," "supported missionaries abroad," and thought highly of himself because of his Christianity: "I'm just a fair man. I want to be known as a hard-working, Christian man that loves God and wants to further God's work."[101] His restaurants sold Confederate flags and other racist paraphernalia, including the "Biblical View of Slavery," a pamphlet written by a Baptist minister who argued that slavery is not evil because the bible permits it.[102] Through the early 2010s, his franchises flew Confederate flags, and the corporate offices featured a massive, building-length sign that read, CHRIST IS THE ANSWER.[103] If you're wondering about the barbecue, don't. Louisiana food writer Rien Fertel visited and wrote, "I have eaten plenty of bad barbecue in my life: microwaved mystery meat; pork doused with vegetable oil to remoisten stale grub, pork the taste and color of cigarette ash. Maurice Bessinger's barbeque was not the worst bite I've ever chewed, but it ranks mighty low."[104]

Piggie Park refused to serve Anne Newman, Sharon Neal, and John Mungin because Bessinger believed that "serv[ing] members of the Negro race . . . would violate his sacred religious beliefs." Bessinger argued to the Supreme Court that the Civil Rights Act was invalid because it "contravenes the will of God" and interfered with the "free exercise of his religion." This is the same argument Masterpiece Cakeshop Incorporated made against the Colorado civil rights law.

The religious freedom argument was so ridiculous that the Supreme Court in 1968 laughed it off in a footnote. "This is not even a borderline case," wrote the court, adding that Bessinger's defenses were "patently frivolous."[105] This was true even though Bessinger opened a Christian mission "in Piggie Park Headquarters," "became a lay preacher and started directing a Bible Study."[106] No court involved in the case, at any stage, countenanced the religiously motivated discrimination, however well-entrenched. Line #2 was clear. There was no religious right to violate others' rights.

Like Masterpiece Cakeshop's owner, stories about Piggie Park BBQ and its owner abound. The brave Black women and man who challenged the law are all but written out of the story. Anne Newman, who worked for the South Carolina NAACP at the time, is given one line in most stories and typically is just identified as a minister's wife, if she appears at all. Her husband, Isaac DeQuincey Newman, is rarely identified as NAACP field secretary at the time or the first Black state senator in South Carolina after Reconstruction and a civil rights icon in the state. Sharon Neal and John Mungin are mentioned even less. The 2017 *Slate* interview with Mungin talking of the gun to his head is an outlier. Court documents say little more than that they were denied service on two separate days. As far as I can tell, their stories of this world-changing Supreme Court win have never been told.[107]

The Masterpiece and Piggie Park cases are conjoined—inseparable. The media focus on the bigot, rather than the victims, is one similarity. Another is that there is no way to say that discrimination is legal and acceptable in one case and not the other. If a homophobic god can grant a license to discriminate against LGBTQ people despite civil rights laws, then a racist god can do the same against Black and brown Americans.

The Crusaders tried, desperately, to distinguish discriminating against one stigmatized minority from discriminating against the other, but they failed. Utterly and repeatedly. I think this failure may be why the court (pre-Kavanaugh) didn't fully dive into the weaponized religious-freedom abyss. During oral argument, none of the justices or the bakery's attorneys could draw a satisfactory line that would allow anti-LGBTQ discrimination but not racial discrimination.[108]

Interracial marriage was outlawed in many states—laws justified with Christianity (see *The Founding Myth*, chapter 19)—until the Supreme Court struck them down in 1967.[109] During the Masterpiece oral argument, after some excellent questioning on the Piggie Park case from Justice Sotomayor, Justice Kagan asked the Crusader about interracial marriage:

JUSTICE KAGAN: Same case or not the same case, if your client instead objected to an interracial marriage?

CRUSADER: Very different case in that context.

JUSTICE KAGAN: Not the same. How about if he objected to an interreligious [marriage]?

CRUSADER: Similar case, assuming that the objection is to—

JUSTICE KAGAN: Similar to what?

CRUSADER: Similar to Mr. Phillips [bakery owner]. That would be protected . . .

JUSTICE KAGAN: You're just saying race is different?

CRUSADER: I'm saying yes . . . I think race is different.[110]

The Crusader's clumsy attempts to distinguish the indistinguishable boiled down to the bare assertion that "race is different." Noel Francisco, Trump's Crusader-affiliated solicitor general, put race in a "different category" and offered the same conclusion without substantive support: "I think that race is particularly unique."[111]

This failure to distinguish racial and homophobic discrimination is predictable. It's impossible to draw a logical or consistent line between discrimination against one protected class (race) and another (sexual orientation) because once religiously motivated discrimination is permitted, the line has already been drawn in the wrong place. Line #2 was the appropriate line in this case: your religion is not a right to violate the rights of others. Instead of drawing the line between night and day, the Crusaders tried to draw the line between shades of benighted bigotry.

Racial discrimination *is* different in one sense: it is now reviled by most Americans. That shift in public opinion is due in no small part because civil rights laws mandated equal treatment. Justice Sotomayor explained this to the bakery at the end of oral argument: "America's reaction to mixed marriages and to race didn't change on its own. It changed because we had public accommodation laws that forced people to do things that many claimed were against their expressive rights and against their religious rights."[112] Those laws work.

Once discrimination is permitted in the name of one's god in some cases, the constitutional Rubicon has been crossed, and nothing makes sense. The most remarkable aspect of the cake case was how easy it should have been for the court to decide and how miserably Kennedy and six other justices failed to uphold Line #2.

CHIEF JUSTICE ROBERTS MAY HAVE INADVERTENTLY OFFERED some insight into why the justices may have decided the case with manufactured hostility: they were *personally* affronted. They, perhaps, felt hostility toward their religious sentiments on LGBTQ equality. Roberts acknowledged during oral argument that "the racial analogy obviously is very compelling," but objected to "decent and honorable" religious bigots who oppose LGBTQ equality, perhaps like himself, being lumped in with religious bigots who oppose racial equality.[113] Roberts was deeply opposed to the court's 2015 marriage-equality decision and even read his dissent from the bench—the only time he's done that in a decade and a half on the court. He began that diatribe, "From the dawn of human history until a few years ago for every people known to have populated this planet, marriage was defined as the union of a man and a woman. . . . for any civilization at anytime at anyplace in the world," which is as untrue as it is sweeping.[114] His anger was palpable: "Just who do we think we are?" Roberts asked his fellow justices.[115]

While Roberts might object, the reality is that religion motivates racism and homophobia. A year after the cake decision, Boone's Camp Event Hall, a Mississippi wedding venue, refused to rent to an interracial couple. "We don't do gay weddings or mixed race, because of our Christian race—I mean, our Christian belief," said the owner.[116] As the story exploded, the owner reversed course. Christianity motivates both anti-Black and anti-LGBTQ bigotry, and the Christian justices seemed personally affronted by this fact. Had the court gone whole hog and allowed discrimination in the name of religious freedom, we would have seen more Boone's Camps.

What's the worst that would have happened had the court decided against the bakery? The bakery owner wasn't forced to marry a man. He wasn't asked to officiate a wedding. In fact, as a religious individual, he wasn't asked to do anything; a business organized under Colorado law and open to the public was asked to do what it has done for thousands of couples and provide a cake for a reception. The owner was still able to go to church and worship as he saw fit. He could still read and study his bible. He could still condemn homosexuality as an abomination and justify that bigotry with Jesus's carpentry.

The case was not the win the Crusaders wanted, but it was a win, and their legions of followers were emboldened. Their zeal has only grown since Brett Kavanaugh and Amy Coney Barrett, mercenaries plucked from their own ranks, were dumped on the court. They're not going to be content with winning a license to discriminate. They're coming for marriage equality, for Charlie and David's marriage.

"When all of this really got crazier and crazier," explained Dave, "we just decided that we were always a team and that we were always going to put ourselves first in this process."[117] They learned to communicate better and while under media scrutiny: "We'd have to be able to read the other's body language or eyes or pick up on certain words." They developed a language of silent hand signals they could use while holding hands. In the moments before oral argument, Charlie felt anxious and panicky. In the court, everyone except the arguing lawyers are packed tightly together on benches, including Charlie and Dave. "I thought I was going to have a panic attack," Charlie recalled. But Dave was there. On the television show *Arrested Development*, each character has a taunting chicken dance they use to mock their fellow family members, none of them remotely resembling a chicken. Dave "whispered in my ear 'everybody's chicken dance' and made me laugh and . . . I was able to carry on and not have a full-blown panic attack in the middle of the Supreme Court." A story that is all the more endearing if you watch any of these dances.

From communicating with the eyes, certain words, and hand signals, to simply putting their team first and growing as a couple, "a lot of that was really beautiful," mused Charlie. Bigotry is meant to break, but Charlie and David fought back and found beauty in the struggle. There are cases in which hostility toward religion is a serious concern, as we'll see in the next chapter, but they are vanishingly rare against Christians in the United States. This should go down as one of the court's worst decisions: cowardly, mendacious, and ratifying bigotry in the name of god.

★

PART II

OPENING
HOSTILITIES

6

Hostility in Hialeah

(*Church of the Lukumi Babalu Aye v. City of Hialeah*)

"Ignorance, allied with power, is the
most ferocious enemy justice can have."

—**James Baldwin**, *No Name in the Street* (1972)[1]

The Constitution envisions religious freedom as a protection for
minorities, not a weapon to maintain privilege. But as we've
just seen, the Supreme Court has been reversing this basic concept using hostility.

A trio of cases shows the evolution of hostility in religious freedom
cases. Before the court was captured and corrupted, it decided a case
out of Hialeah, Florida, that vindicated the rights of a minority religion that the local government was deliberately suppressing. The court
rescued the religious minority. This 1993 decision is now the textbook
case of a government body crushing religious freedom by targeting a
minority religion. We'll look at that case in this chapter. Then, just
before Brett Kavanaugh's appointment bent the arc of justice toward
the Crusade, it upheld Trump's Muslim ban, despite clear hostility.
We'll look at that in the next chapter. Finally, at about the same time as
the Muslim ban, the court manufactured hostility toward a Christian
in the cake case we explored in the last chapter.

In each case, governmental hostility toward religion was a central and decisive issue. But this kind of hostility is remarkably rare,
as Kennedy observed in his opening line of the Hialeah case. In fact,

that 1993 decision was the first time the court used hostility to *decide* a case, though it had discussed the idea regularly.[2] The hostility was genuine, directed against a minority, and properly struck down. But after the court was packed, that changed. In the Muslim ban case, the hostility was genuine, directed against a minority, and improperly upheld. In the cake case, the hostility was manufactured by the court, supposedly directed against a Christian, and improperly struck down. At some point under the Roberts regime, the court redefined "hostility" to advance the Crusade.

This evolution and the court's increasing reliance on hostility to decide religious freedom issues is one of convenience, not principle. Hostility is now a pretextual hook to reverse-engineer results. When hostility exists against non-Christians, as in the Muslim ban, the court does nothing. When hostility doesn't exist against conservative Christians, the court manufactures it to privilege their bigotry. "Christianity wins" is the guiding principle.

These three cases show the court forging a weapon, not a natural evolution. Since, the court has been using this lesser version of hostility to aid the Crusade, in at least eight important cases. In none was the hostility genuine.

So it's useful to see what genuine hostility toward religion looks like.

Hostility Looks like This

"What can we do to prevent the Church from opening?" the city council president asked, voicing the angry crowd's feelings at a mob-like emergency meeting of the Hialeah City Council on a hot June night in 1987.[3]

The mayor and city council, police department, citizens, and their god were united against the church. The Hialeah Police Department testified that the government should "not permit this Church to exist." The audience cheered when a city councilor mentioned that Cuba jailed "people . . . for practicing this religion." Another councilman cited biblical law—what "the Bible says" and what "the Bible allows"—to argue his point. A third member of the council said that this church and its religion "are in violation of everything this country stands for."

The council wasn't all talk; it considered a resolution which the city attorney described as a declaration that "this community will not tolerate religious practices which are abhorrent to its citizens." The mob joined in. One townsperson claimed the country would "regress into paganism" if the city council allowed the church to worship, while another claimed that "the city would not please God."[4]

The hated church had just leased an old car dealership and begun preparing the building for religious services. Before this, the church had been largely unorganized and underground. It didn't have a power structure or central house of worship but was practiced in houses and at small gatherings. Ernesto Pichardo wanted to bring his religion into the open. As he readied the property, service providers—water, trash, electrical—stalled, and the city delayed inspections and final occupancy permits.[5] The June meeting of the mob came about two weeks after the church applied for several permits and failed the city's inspection.

Already this is beyond the trumped-up hostility the bakery supposedly endured in the cake case. But it gets worse.

Beginning at that rancorous meeting and through late summer the council adopted new resolutions and ordinances that targeted this church.

Why? Because this was a Santeria church that practiced animal sacrifice.

Santeria, which means "way of the saints," has a long history entwined with colonialism and Catholicism. Santeria mixes the gods, saints, beliefs, and rituals of people ripped from their homes in the Yoruba nations in West Africa by slavers with the Catholicism that Spanish and Portuguese conquistadores and colonists brought to the Caribbean centuries ago. The blend matured on the island of Cuba, but the 1959 revolution caused an island exodus; Cubans fled the Castro regime, many to Florida, bringing their religion with them.

Santeria rites include singing, dancing, and drumming, but also possession by spirits, acting as a medium, divination, and animal sacrifice. Animal sacrifice has different purposes: an offering to the gods, healing (the sickness is transferred to the sacrificial animal and then killed off), and marking major life events. The victims typically include birds, guinea pigs, turtles, and even pigs.[6]

Spilling blood to appease the gods scared Hialeah Christians, who seemed not to realize it is central to their religion as well. Animal sacrifice is common in the bible. Everyone remembers the animals going onto the ark two by two, but in the story, the biblical god also tells Noah to pack seven additional pairs of "clean" animals on the ark.[7] Noah's first post-deluge act is to build an altar and sacrifice and burn every "clean" animal. It's this sacrifice that convinces Yahweh not to rain down another genocide: "And when the Lord smelled the pleasing odor" of burning flesh, he said "I will never again curse the ground because of humankind."[8] The biblical god's tastes mature in what Christians call the New Testament: "It is not possible that the blood of bulls and of goats should take away sins."[9] Jesus is meant to be the final sacrificial lamb: "He is the atoning sacrifice for our sins, and not only for ours but also for the sins of the whole world."[10] This is what the ubiquitous John 3:16 verse signifies, too. According to Christianity, after Jesus, no more animal sacrifice was needed. So the Hialeah City Council banned it.

The council wanted to ban the church outright, "What can we do to prevent the Church from opening?" The "furious crowd booed and jeered" assistant city attorney Richard Gross for correctly advising the council that it couldn't ban the Santeria church outright and "could be held personally liable if they" did.[11] So, instead, the council passed new ordinances that targeted this specific minority religion, the regulatory boundaries of which encompassed only this particular religious ritual.[12]

First, it passed a resolution that declared "certain" religious "practices . . . inconsistent with public morals, peace or safety" and an ordinance that incorporated an already-existing state law punishing animal cruelty, specifically naming its "great concern over . . . animal sacrifices."[13]

Next, the city asked the Florida attorney general if the incorporated animal cruelty law allowed a city to target *religious* animal sacrifice. It did. The state law "prohibits the sacrificial killing of animals other than for the primary purpose of food consumption" and that therefore "a municipality may adopt an ordinance prohibiting the religious sacrifice of animals," said the AG.[14]

With that green light, the council passed a resolution declaring its "great concern" over "ritualistic animal sacrifices" and ordinances that targeted "religious practices," "animal sacrifice," and "ritualistic animal sacrifice." The second ordinance prohibited possessing animals for sacrifice. The third made it a crime "to sacrifice any animal." Both were riddled with odd and broad exemptions that whittled away who and what the laws applied to—not the hunter, not euthanasia for terminally sick pets, not the exterminator and his mice, not fishing, not medical experimentation. Only Santerians were left.

The fourth and final rule didn't specifically mention animal sacrifice; instead, it prohibited slaughtering animals anywhere other than a slaughterhouse. The rules carved out an exception for kosher slaughter, giving one religion a statutory exemption, but not the other.

The exemption-riddled rules created bizarre and obvious contradictions.[15]

Governments can legitimately be concerned about animal cruelty, and should be. Governments can also regulate slaughterhouses and public health. But Hialeah wasn't protecting animals or concerned with public health. It wanted to suppress non-Christians. The rules that supposedly stopped animal cruelty and regulated public health instead only prohibited acts *when motivated by a particular religious belief.* They included only religiously motivated conduct and excluded identical conduct when motivated for nonreligious reasons. But "the animal is equally dead whether killed in a ritual or ceremony or killed otherwise," explained the church's attorney.[16] The rules created a "religious gerrymander." Animal cruelty and public health were pretexts; the true aim was to prohibit one form of religious worship. This is what the First Amendment forbids: "shall make no law . . . prohibiting the free exercise" of religion.[17] The Supreme Court held that gerrymander unconstitutional.[18]

Simple Religious Freedom Inquiry

Hialeah targeted religiously motivated acts only, not identical acts when done for nonreligious reasons. Remember, the law can step in against religiously motivated action at some point, Line #1. The question is where? It can *always* step in when another person's rights are violated, Line #2. But this case presents a rare and different inquiry: Can the law step in against *only* religiously motivated action?

No, because this would mean the law has no issue with the underlying act, only the religion. It's fairly easy to show the problems with this by analogy. The human sacrifice analogy to the Santeria case would be a law that allowed child murder, but not when commanded by the biblical god. The nonsensical law doesn't ameliorate the harm—children will be murdered; it only suppresses religion. Its only purpose is suppression of religion, and it's therefore indeed hostile to religion.

Now, however, Crusaders and their justices on the court have decided that hostility means something different: that no law can *touch* an action motivated by Christian beliefs. That is, any broad, neutral law (such as a criminal law against murder) that sweeps in religiously motivated action must be struck down or Christians granted an exemption. But laws targeting *only* religion are very different from laws that regulate behavior that happens to include some religiously motivated behavior.

Thomas Jefferson actually explained this distinction back in 1776 using animal slaughter and child sacrifice as examples. If the law allows the slaughter of animals, it must allow the same for religious reasons. Jefferson wrote that whatever is lawful for a citizen "cannot be forbidden to him for religious uses." He continued, saying that whatever is harmful "and therefore prohibited by the laws, ought not to be permitted to churches in their sacred rites. For instance, it is unlawful in the ordinary course of things or in a private house to murder a child. It should not be permitted any sect then to sacrifice children." He said the same of animal sacrifice, but with a caveat. It's lawful "to kill calves or lambs. They may therefore be religiously sacrificed, but if the good of the state required a temporary suspension of killing lambs, as during a siege, sacrifices of them may then be rightfully suspended also,"[19] an important caveat for religious freedom in pandemics.

So the government *could* regulate, for instance, animal slaughter and disposal in the name of public health. But the government cannot regulate *only* religiously motivated animal slaughter and disposal because, even if it claims public health as a justification, targeting only religion shows that justification to be pretextual.

Hialeah cited public health to justify its religious gerrymander. Evidence proffered included a resident who had supposedly lived "next door to Santeria for 7 years" and spoke of nights "filled with horror: drums beating and animals crying. I witnessed throat-cutting. . . . The madman danced around the animals." She added, "AIDS is transmitted by blood. Santeria, as I told you, engages in the drinking and exchanging of blood." Then the final dose of fear: "there could be blood on their hands. Under their nails. And your gracious waiter may be a Santeria practitioner who drank blood the previous evening."[20] If there's a hint of a public health concern in there, it's too hard to spot amid the bigotry. The city did better when it argued that sacrificial carcasses presented a public health risk. The Santeria church insisted that it always cleanly disposed of animal remains, but one local cemetery complained of people dropping sacrificial carcasses "over the fence or they leave it on a grave. Every day we send an employee to clean up. We throw away the dead animals."[21] That could be problematic but is dealt with by addressing disposal. If food waste is littering city streets, you ban littering, not eating.

As it turned out, the public health concerns were unfounded. Two years after the case, the *Los Angeles Times* reported that sacrificial animals with their throats slit turn up in public, "but," says Hialeah Mayor Raul Martinez, 'from time to time we find animal carcasses next to palm trees. We pick it up and discard it, and that's that.'"[22]

LINE #3 MAY BE THE BEST PROTECTION for true religious freedom in this case. The attempt to suppress Santeria was at least partly rooted Christian privilege and supremacy.

City councilors "were suddenly professing their Christianity," noted one scholar who studied the case.[23] Local churches, "including Baptist, evangelical, Jehovah's Witnesses," opposed the Santeria church.[24] A local reverend proclaimed that, if "we allow . . . a satanic, Satan-worshipping church in this city . . . the blessing, the prosperous blessing of God over this city could just turn into a dark cloud, because instead of a blessing this will bring a curse upon the city."[25] The Hialeah Police Department's chaplain testified about sin, the worship of "demons," and said that the government "need[s] to be helping people and sharing with them the truth that is found in Jesus Christ."[26] The chaplain (a position that's a Line #3 problem itself) added, "Nations that are controlled by this system of religion are in darkness, and the Bible says that these things are an abomination to the Lord."[27]

The townsfolk certainly saw this as spiritual warfare. They picketed. JESUS UP, SATAN DOWN, NO SATANIC CHURCH IN OUR HIALEAH, and HIALEAH FOR JESUS, said signs, some with bilingual bigotry. Another photo of the protest shows a pastor and deacon praying over and laying hands on passersby, who they "felt called on to save."[28]

There was almost an official declaration of war from the Catholic Church. These anti-Santeria meetings and ordinances came as the Miami area prepared for a papal visit. The Miami Archdiocese was "trying to root [Santeria] out" of its South Florida adherents and promised to oppose a Santeria church "on religious principles."[29] The archbishop said as much in an interview, published after the pitchforks-and-torches city council meeting and before Pope John Paul II's visit. (That archbishop was later "criticized for covering up clergy abuse. . . . In one [law]suit, a former altar boy claimed the archbishop coerced him to stay silent about alleged sexual abuse by a priest at a group home for troubled boys," according to the *Washington Post*.[30]) The official position of the archdiocese was that Santeria created deep "concerns" and might require a "purification of the faith."[31]

This wasn't just government hostility toward one religion; it was religiously motivated hostility toward *another* religion. The city was abusing its secular power, acting like a Christian government "purifying the faith," as it were. That violates Line #3 and was reason enough to strike down the ordinances.

THIS CASE IS THE TEXTBOOK EXAMPLE of government hostility toward religion. Literally. It's in most constitutional law texts.[32] It was as if the extreme hypotheticals we debated in law school came to life.[33] But the open hostility in this case is rare in modern Supreme Court history. This is "far from a representative free exercise case," observed Justice Souter in his concurrence.[34] The first sentence of Kennedy's majority opinion agrees: "The principle that government may not enact laws that suppress religious belief or practice is so well understood that few violations are recorded in our opinions." Such hostility is scarce now. Yes, we see anti-Semitism and anti-Muslim bigotry and violence, but rarely manifested legislatively like this. (Trump's Muslim ban is the exception that proves the rule; see next chapter).

The hostility was so open and virulent and atypical that I wondered whether something else might have been going on. There were two major forces acting behind the scenes in this case. One motivated the Supreme Court; the other motivated the Hialeah City Council.

Congress Pressures the Court

Beyond legal principle, the court had a compelling reason, going to the very heart of the court as an institution, for deciding any religious freedom case strongly and decisively in favor of a religious minority.

Congress was challenging the court's sovereignty when the justices heard this case. We'll hear more about this in chapter 9, but in 1990 the court decided that drug counselors who were fired from their private employer for doing drugs couldn't collect unemployment benefits, even if they took the drugs for religious reasons. That decision was framed as an attack on religious freedom and caused a massive backlash. The Religious Freedom Restoration Act was introduced on March 11, 1993, and passed the House on May 11, a few months after oral argument and exactly one month before the court handed down the Santeria decision on June 11. The RFRA would take effect five months later.[35] Congress openly explained that the RFRA was intended to overturn the Supreme Court's interpretation of the First Amendment in the 1990 drug counselor case. The Court may have wanted a strong religious freedom decision to send a message to Congress that it didn't need to interfere—all was well.[36]

The court's Santeria opinion seemed to send this message. It focused on criteria the court laid out in the drug counselor case. Some justices attacked that case outright. Constitutional law scholar Kenneth Karst posited that, had the chronology been flipped, the court would have let the Santeria ordinances stand and struck down the rule in the drug counselor case.[37] In other words, it was political pressure, not legal principle that guided the justices. Supreme Court justices bowing to political pressure is not without historical precedent, the most famous being "the switch in time that saved nine." (In 1937, after a conservative bloc on the court had been striking down FDR's popular New Deal legislation in a series of 5–4 decisions and FDR threatened to expand the court in response, one conservative justice switched sides to save a minimum-wage law, the New Deal, and the nine-justice court.) It's as if the justices in the Santeria case were waving Congress off. Congress enacted RFRA anyway (see chapter 9).

Hialeah Motivations: Money and Politics

It's at least possible that the city's initial motivations were banal and eternal: political and pecuniary profit. Local politicians targeted the Santerians not because they wanted to open *a* church, but that they had leased *that specific property* to open a church. When we pull back the curtain, the scene looks like a Carl Hiaasen novel: bribery, corrupt Florida politicians, an upcoming election, and a pugilistic mayor.[38]

Hialeah was a corrupt town. One councilman had just been removed on corruption charges.[39] The mayor, Raul Martinez, testified in that case just months before the Santeria fracas,[40] and he ran the city "like a Chicago ward boss," said the *Washington Post* under the headline "Florida Corruption Probes Proliferate."[41] Martinez was Hialeah's mayor for nearly a quarter century. In 1999, the 6 foot 3 inch, 250-pound Martinez "pummel[ed] a young butcher who," who was "protest[ing] the Coast Guard's treatment of six Cuban rafters."[42] Martinez was indicted in 1990, and the jury found him "guilty of racketeering and extortion in the sale of his votes and influence on zoning matters in return for about $1 million in cash or property from developers."[43] But after six years, multiple appeals, three trials, and a few hung juries, the charges were dropped.

Martinez's legal tribulations overlapped with the Santeria case, which was in the trial court by 1988 and at the Supreme Court by 1992. During that period, Martinez eked out an electoral victory by 273 votes in a city of 200,000.[44] His opponent in that race—in each of the four mayoral races from 1987 to 1994—was Nilo Juri. Juri had a "blood feud" with the mayor and was good friends with the owner of the property that the Santeria church leased.[45]

The mayor wanted that property, which he'd quietly included in a new redevelopment plan that would have significantly increased its value. But the property owner[46] was also a developer and wanted to retain it until it was rezoned and cash in. Still, hoping for a million-dollar payday, the mayor tried to buy the land for a pittance. The owner refused, so the mayor vetoed zoning changes that the owner wanted. The owner then leased the property to the unsuspecting Santeria church, maliciously, some locals thought, as revenge against the mayor.[47] The church unknowingly walked into Mayor Martinez's multimillion-dollar redevelopment deal and scooped up the lot he wanted.

The city councilman who had been helping the property owner try to rezone the property had been indicted, removed from the council, and would go to prison for extorting $15,000 to rezone the same property.[48] To fill that vacant city council seat, "one of the Mayor's employees in his real estate firm was appointed."[49] Other councilors had just seen a colleague jailed for trying to rezone that property on the sly, for aiding the owner instead of the mayor. That could be substantial motivation to shut down *anyone* that leased the property, not just the church.

The church learned all of this two weeks after leasing the lot. A reporter told the church that the new city council member, the mayor's real estate crony, "was going to bring up the issue of [the church] and present a number of legal violations"[50] at the next meeting. That meeting would devolve into a mob scene.

There were also political incentives. Campaigning in local elections was well underway when the anti-Santeria hostility broke in June. Voters would hit the polls in early November. Later that summer, Mayor Martinez claimed, "The move to open the church is politically motivated . . . is calculated to embarrass him in the upcoming re-election," which the church denied.[51] Pamphlets warning of the "satanic church" were left at neighborhood homes, alongside other political pamphlets.[52] One pastor of a local Protestant church with a large Cuban American congregation explicitly tied the council's votes on the Santeria-suppression ordinances to the upcoming election; "who voted for what or against what" that night would be crucial to voters' decisions.[53] This could explain why the council stretched the anti-Santeria measures over months. The week before the election, an incumbent city councilman running for reelection listed "introducing an ordinance that outlaws animal sacrifice in the city's first Santeria church" as the second of three top accomplishments.[54]

One final, curious piece of evidence suggests that something other than religious hostility motivated the attacks. These hostile government officials had family members who practiced Santeria and maybe even dabbled themselves. "Many of the most vociferous opponents on the council had strong . . . ties" to Santeria, writes Professor Fred Frohock, a scholar who interviewed many of the parties. Frohock discovered that the city councilor "who proposed two out of the three later ordinances against [the church] had a wife who was a member of the religion. The Mayor's father was a member."[55] Frohock kept digging and found that all city councilors were linked to Santeria "in some way through family ties, business associates, close friends."[56] Rumor held that Mayor Martinez himself dabbled in Santeria, a rumor the church founder, Ernesto Pichardo, believed.[57] In fact, Pichardo viewed the entire controversy as "politically motivated and having little to do with one religion," according to another scholar.[58] So the two primary movers in this case each thought the other side was politically motivated.

The more we look beyond the court's opinion, the more it seems like hostility toward a minority religion, not public health, was the pretext and that it was intended to cover up political and financial misdealings. There's a certain low cunning if that's true and if it was deliberate. A local government violating the First Amendment is not a criminal inquiry, but extortion and corruption are.

We've been asking, in these cases, what's the worst that would happen? If the court failed to vindicate the claimed religious right in this case, the church would have been legislated out of existence, legally suppressed. Whatever the motivation for the local government, that outcome required a judicial solution. Governments can legislate in ways that impact religion, but they cannot target and legislate a religion out of existence.

Sadly, the Santeria church's Supreme Court victory was hollow. The church never opened the building on the property it leased along the Miami River, at the busy intersection at Fifth Street and

Okeechobee Road, settling instead for a small storefront three blocks away.[59] It operated there from 1987, when the case began, until it closed permanently in 1999. The prized lot at the center of this case remained vacant for years.[60] In 2017, thirty years after the church first leased the property, a 100,000-square-foot Public Storage facility opened. It's worth over $7 million and, according to records, was part of a $63,000,000 property deal in 2019.[61] No word on whether Martinez, who remained mayor until 2005, profited.

This is a seminal case in religious freedom largely because it is so easy and clear. If the facts are as Justice Kennedy recounted in his opinion—and that's how history will remember them—the council deliberately targeted the church and tried to run it out of town. The government hostility is perhaps less clear given the political campaigns, corruption, shady real estate deals, blood feuds, and congressional pressure on the Supreme Court. Even in the cleanest religious freedom case in Supreme Court history, there is more to the story. It seems at least possible that the hostility against the religion was pretextual and the real reasons for targeting the church were more pedestrian. That would explain why there are virtually no other modern cases that featured such open, vitriolic hostility towards a minority religion. Until Trump.

7

The Muslim Ban

(*Trump v. Hawaii*)

QUESTION: "What is the most prominent lie that
the American public is being propagandized
with in regards to national security in your opinion?"

DONALD TRUMP: "One of the lies, I think, is that fact that Muslims
can come in but other people can't; Christians can't come
into this country but Muslims can. . . . Muslims can
come in but Christians can't. And the Muslims aren't
in danger and the Christians are."

—Iowa National Security Action Summit, May 16, 2015,
Point of Grace Church, Waukee, Iowa[1]

Until the Santeria case, the court had never actually decided that the government was hostile toward religion.[2] It had discussed the Constitution preventing "hostility" toward religion occasionally since 1844 and regularly since the mid-twentieth century.[3] After all that talk, those "years of hostility to religion playing a substantive and recurring role in First Amendment jurisprudence," the Santeria case is the first time that it actually happened, wrote Professor Mark Satta.[4] That's how rare this hostility is.

It was just as rare in the two decades after the Santeria case. The court only cited the case to support a substantive decision twice, *defending* Line #3 both times. Once in 1997 to overturn the Religious Freedom Restoration Act as it applied to the states, and then again just before Roberts took over the court, rejecting a 2004 challenge brought by a Crusader, to say that *not* publicly funding theology scholarships wasn't hostility.[5] Not paying to train ministers is not the same as legislating a church out of existence. In both cases, the court disagreed with Christians seeking privilege by arguing religious freedom; hostility wasn't an issue. So the Santeria case was originally decided to vindicate the rights of a minority and then used twice to curb Christian privilege and defend Line #3.

It remains rare, but in 2016, the crusading justices rediscovered the power of claiming government hostility toward religion. The court's newfound fascination with hostility is not just the power to win media and public opinion by claiming something is anti-religion, but also the lack of history. There's only one precedent to bind the Crusade, the Santeria case. Unlike Line #3, which has countless cases in a long precedential line, hostility was putty in the justices' hands, shaped and exploited to further the Crusade.

The argument was powerful, but real cases were vanishingly rare. Until Justice Alito wrote a 2016 opinion in *Stormans, Inc. v. Wiesman* that began, "This case is an ominous sign."[6] The owners of a pharmacy didn't want to dispense certain contraceptives because they believed that their god didn't like those particular drugs. That refusal violated state law (pharmacies are heavily regulated, and refusing to dispense prescriptions for nonmedical reasons is a concern. Even so, religious *pharmacists* had an opt out, and *pharmacies* had to promptly get patients their medicine.[7]) Two Crusaders, the Alliance Defending Freedom and the Becket Fund, took the case to the Supreme Court, which declined to hear their case over Alito's written objection. He cited the Santeria case nearly twenty times, arguing that "it is hard not to view [the State's] actions as exhibiting hostility toward religious objections."[8]

Roberts and Thomas agreed with Alito, but it takes four justices to hear a case, and the other potential vote, Scalia, died as the court was waiting for the state's brief.

Alito's opinion suggested a drastically lower bar for what constitutes hostility toward religion, from the Hialeah mob and targeted suppression down to a state rule that balances the needs of patients with pious pharmacists' complaints. He also flipped that hostility, so that instead of protecting a minority attacked by Christians abusing their civil power, it privileged conservative Christians ideologically aligned with Alito and the Crusade. Since then, the reshaped Supreme Court has applied Alito's reimagined hostility while citing the real hostility in the Santeria case. It's done so in majority opinions involving Christians' religious freedom nearly every year, including at least nine crucial cases that furthered the Crusade.[9]

First, to let churches access the public purse (see chapter 13). Then, to let a Christian-owned business get away with discrimination against LGBTQ people (chapter 5). Then, to uphold a massive government-maintained Christian cross (chapter 12).[10] Next, to open the public treasury for Christian schools (chapter 14). In multiple cases, to let churches exempt themselves from public health orders meant to stop a deadly pandemic (chapter 11).

And, for slightly modified reasons, to let Catholic foster care charities discriminate against LGBTQ people (chapter 16).[11]

The court cited the Santeria hostility twice in twenty-three years, both times to curb Christian privilege, and then Alito's overhauled hostility nine times in five years, each time to privilege Christians. This court *wants* to redefine religious freedom and understands the power in claiming hostility to do so.

TRUMP CAMPAIGNED ON A MUSLIM BAN. "Donald J. Trump is calling for a total and complete shutdown of Muslims entering the United States until our country's representatives can figure out what is going on," declared his campaign.[12] Criticized for this open bigotry, Trump doubled down, tweeting, "That's right, we need a TRAVEL BAN for certain DANGEROUS countries, not some politically correct term that won't help us protect our people!"[13] He later amended his rhetoric slightly, a strictly political shift he explained.[14] In the debates, Trump said, "The Muslim ban still stands," but admitted that it got a rhetorical makeover, "It's called extreme vetting."[15] "We're having problems with the Muslims, and we're having problems with Muslims coming into the country," Trump claimed, adding later, "They want sharia law."[16] Even as the Supreme Court considered challenges to the Muslim ban, Trump was unrepentant, "There's nothing to apologize for."[17]

A week after taking office, Trump implemented the Muslim ban with an executive order that banned citizens from seven countries from entering the United States: Iran, Iraq, Libya, Somalia, Sudan, Syria, and Yemen. All Muslim majority countries. The order even barred refugees from those countries, but with an exception for religious minorities—Christians. The Muslim ban banned Muslims, but also favored Christians. This is just like the religious gerrymander in the Santeria case: exempt the "good" religions suppress the "scary" minorities.

This "Protecting the Nation from Foreign Terrorist Entry into the United States" order was enjoined two days later. Lawsuits and injunctions piled up. It was repeatedly challenged and struck down, and then rewritten after about five weeks. Same result: lawsuits and injunctions. Then, in September 2017, Trump signed Muslim ban 3.0, which limited travel from eight countries: Chad, Iran, Libya, North Korea, Somalia, Syria, Venezuela, and Yemen. Including North Korea and Venezuela was a clumsy and conspicuous attempt to diffuse the anti-Muslim bigotry that motivated the order—to camouflage a religious gerrymander. None of the orders included Egypt or Saudi Arabia, countries where most of the foreign terrorists that actually attacked this country came from, but where Trump also had significant personal financial interests.[18] So, ban 3.0 favored Christians and maliciously targeted Muslims, but with some clumsy camouflage, and not in a way that might hinder terrorism or the Trump family's ability to borrow money. The Supreme Court heard oral argument on ban 3.0 in April 2018, just two months before it released the opinion in the cake case.

Restricting people's movement because of which god they worship or which holy book they revere is a threat to religious freedom; it's genuine hostility. It's also a slippery slope. The federal government can regulate interstate travel as well as immigration, and if it can prevent people from coming into the country on the basis of religion, can it stop religious minorities crossing state lines? Why can't it force them to live in certain areas, perhaps with badges to clearly mark their status? Outlandish, but remember Trump's team talked of a "Muslim registry," and Trump himself refused to disavow the internment camps for Japanese Americans in camps during World War II, one of the most shameful episodes in American and Supreme Court history.[19]

This was a serious violation of religious freedom and actual, real hostility directed at a minority with the full force of the US government. The Alliance Defending Freedom's president, Michael Farris, said, "The test of religious freedom is whether you're willing to stand up for the religious freedom of those that you disagree with theologically."[20] If so, the Crusaders failed. None defended the religious freedom of Muslims.[21] Jay Sekulow's American Center for Law & Justice sent briefs to the Supreme Court arguing *for* the ban. Two of the biggest, ADF and Becket Fund, filed briefs that claimed to support neither side, an inexplicable approach to such a clear threat to religious freedom, unless their understanding of religious freedom centers on Christian privilege. Both dodged the media, a telling change of strategy that left a "deafening silence."[22] Both ostensibly impartial briefs actually argued *for* the ban. The Becket Fund wrote, "Proper Free Exercise analysis would focus on the facts conserning [*sic*] specific plaintiffs,"[23] essentially arguing that every individual wishing to immigrate must litigate their own religious freedom challenge to the ban separately. ADF's duplicity and Christian supremacy was even more stark. The same ADF attorney that argued the cake case wrote the milquetoast brief. ADF argued that the lower court "engaged in impermissible psychoanalysis of the President's heart of hearts" and that "courts are not empowered to sift unofficial and passing comments in search of evidence discrediting officials' heart of hearts," which is precisely how ADF's client, the bigoted bakery, dodged justice.[24]

The Crusaders defended a ban that Trump repeatedly confessed targeted adherents of a non-Christian faith. Their hypocrisy is eloquent. Their mission is not to defend religious freedom, but to privilege Christianity.

The court upheld the Muslim ban in a 5–4 opinion released three weeks after the cake case. The cases are similar in time and argument, but the outcomes are contradictory. A manufactured hostility that, at worst, amounted to an inappropriate tone was enough to pollute an entire civil rights process that had already concluded, and thereby allow discrimination against an LGBTQ couple to stand. Bigotry spoken, tweeted, repeated, and defended was not enough to taint a ban that required multiple iterations to even begin to appear unbiased on its face, and this open hostility was insufficient for the same court to strike down discrimination against a stigmatized religious minority.

Chief Justice Roberts wrote the Muslim ban opinion and argued that, while there seemed to be bias, the court must accept the other reasons Trump claimed for the ban "because there is persuasive evidence that the entry suspension has a legitimate grounding in national security concerns, quite apart from any religious hostility, we must accept that independent justification."[25] In the face of Trump's clearly and oft-repeated bigotry and hostility, which started long before he had any national security clearance, briefings, or intelligence, Roberts clung to the fact that the text of the ban itself "says nothing about religion."[26] And that court could not infer that banning immigration from five Muslim-majority countries (by Muslim ban 3.0) was hostile toward religion because it wasn't a ban on immigration from all Muslim-majority countries: "the policy covers just 8 percent of the world's Muslim population," and some were security threats.[27] Other than that, Roberts, Kennedy, and the other justices who had clutched their pearls at the tone of a commissioner in the cake case, didn't mention hostility at all. Apparently, it's not hostility unless it's directed at Christians.

Justice Sotomayor refuted this in her brilliant dissent and was joined by Ruth Bader Ginsburg; they showed the ban's hostility: "The full record paints a far more harrowing picture" than Roberts recounted; the ban "was motivated by hostility and animus toward the Muslim faith."[28] Sotomayor expressly called out the conservative majority's hypocrisy: "The Court recently found less pervasive official expressions of hostility and the failure to disavow them to be constitutionally significant." She adds that the majority "utterly fails to address" the facts showing hostility. As to the government's sham national security camouflage, Sotomayor properly invoked the Santeria case, arguing that the "Government's asserted national-security rationale reveals that the Proclamation is nothing more than a 'religious gerrymander,'" and cited the infamous Japanese internment case, which offered "stark parallels" and warned of "uphold[ing] the Government's actions based on a barren invocation of national security."

Kennedy wrote the Santeria decision and the cake decision and a short, sad concurrence in the Muslim ban case. His progression from the Santeria decision in 1993 to the bakery and ban cases twenty-five years later mirrors the court's shift. Religious liberty was once a shield to protect hated and stigmatized religious minorities from the hostility of the majority. But now, for this court, it's a cudgel to advance conservative Christianity.

We'll pick up the threads of fabricated hostility again, but first we need to examine the last case, the final barrier, that stands between the Crusaders and a fully weaponized religious freedom.

8

It Was Never about the Drugs

(*Employment Division v. Smith*)

"They were fired because they were drug counselors . . . at a
drug and alcohol treatment center."

—**Oregon Attorney General David B. Frohnmayer**, during the
oral argument of *Employment Division*, November 6, 1989[1]

The court wrote such a strong definitive opinion in the Santeria
case partially to repulse congressional pressure. That stemmed
from a 1990 opinion in which the court strongly and correctly
defended Line #1 and Line #2. In that 1990 case, the court explained
that religious believers (non-Christians, in this case) must comply with
secular laws, even if those laws don't agree with the requirements of
their personal gods. It's an uncontroversial conclusion, but the opinion
stands as precedent between the Crusaders and a weaponized religious
freedom. The opinion has been attacked, maligned—all but overturned. Even though it's basically correct.

The fight to overturn the 1990 precedent made for strange
bedfellows: Crusaders favoring unemployment compensation for
hallucinogenic drug users and vilifying an opinion by notorious arch-
conservative Justice Antonin Scalia, a hero of theirs in every other
respect, aligned with liberals disparaging the opinion because Scalia
doled out bigotry and ethnocentrism with his characteristic venom.
Liberals and conservatives united against the court to pass a new federal superstatute reinterpreting religious freedom. That law gave Crusaders the road map for weaponizing religious freedom. Given how
loathed this case is and the myths built around it, it's critical that we

understand exactly what happened. Only then can we see what the court got right and wrong.

RELIGIONS LOVE DRUGS. Wine is the blood of Christ for some. Rastafarians smoke marijuana to elevate their consciousness. Aztecs ate mushrooms, and Incas chewed coca leaves. And some Native Americans take peyote. That peyote rite became the focus of this Supreme Court case, but the case was never really about religion or the rite; it was about unemployment benefits. More specifically, whether a private drug counseling organization can fire drug counselors who do drugs in violation of the organization's policy. Obviously, it can. But does religious freedom require the state to pay unemployment benefits to private drug counselors who took drugs and were therefore fired for cause? That uncontroversial proposition—drug counselors can't do drugs and keep their jobs—lay at the heart of the Supreme Court case, but was lost in Scalia's opinion, the backlash, and new law that backlash spawned.

The drug counselors were Galen Black and Al Smith, alcoholics in recovery, who wanted to help others recover. Both got jobs with the Douglas County Council on Alcohol and Drug Abuse Prevention and Treatment, a mouthful known as "ADAPT."[2] Despite the name, it wasn't a government agency. ADAPT is a private drug rehabilitation organization in Oregon, a 501(c)(3).[3]

ADAPT's treatment philosophy was that alcoholism and drug addiction are continuing diseases that require total abstention. Any alcohol or nonprescription drug use, however minor, was grounds for an employee's dismissal.[4] Both men knew about the policy when they were hired. Each signed a copy of the rules on drug use.[5] Smith knew that ADAPT considered peyote a drug.[6]

Smith was a member of the Klamath tribe, a Native American. Black was white, not a Native American, as nearly every retelling of this case suggests. Both were affiliated with the Native American Church, but neither were full members,[7] so when Black asked Smith about taking peyote, he sent Black to the church to ask around.[8] Black went, talked with a leader, and ate peyote in a ceremony.[9] That was about a year after he began working as an addiction counselor.

ADAPT suspended Black.[10] A counselor at the VA hospital evaluated Black during his suspension and recommended intensive personal counseling or a residential inpatient care facility for alcohol and drug abuse.[11] Black refused. Because of the drug use, his refusal of treatment, his alcoholism, and, most importantly, his position as a drug counselor at a private facility with an abstinence policy that he had signed, Black was fired. Fired for cause—drug counselors can't do drugs.

Like ADAPT, Smith initially thought of peyote as a drug: "To me peyote is a drug. I'm not about to jeopardize my sobriety."[12] But after trying peyote in 1979, before working at ADAPT, he reevaluated and began to think peyote could potentially help addicts and alcoholics. After Black's initial suspension, Smith discussed peyote with ADAPT's executive director, who reminded Smith that any drug use, including peyote, was against ADAPT policy. The men recall the meeting very differently. According to the executive director, Smith left "furious," but recommitted to ADAPT's strict drug use policy.[13] Smith instead remembers ADAPT issuing a challenge to his religion. "I can't go to church?" he remembers thinking.[14]

The next months were tense for the Native American community, which was worried about Black, the white interloper, suing for "racist discrimination," as he was threatening to do, or taking a religious freedom case featuring their sacred rite. Black's VA counselor had corresponding concerns and thought Black's sudden fascination with the Native American religion was "extreme" and "indicat[ed] a tendency toward obsessive-compulsiveness."[15]

About six months after Black was fired, Smith received an envelope full of eagle feathers—an invitation to a peyote ceremony. He met with ADAPT's executive director, explained that he planned to take peyote that weekend, and took peyote.[16] The following Monday, Smith told ADAPT that he had taken peyote and, after declining to resign, was fired.[17]

Two drug counselors, who knowingly took drugs against the policy of their employer, a drug rehabilitation facility, were fired for using drugs.

I LIKE AL SMITH AND I LOVE HIS "FUCK YOU" STAND against his employer. He was fighting for his identity, one of many such stands he'd taken in his life. Smith got himself sober on January 15, 1957, and stayed sober until his death on November 19, 2014, at ninety-five. "Al Smith, like Native America, has refused to vanish. Drinking didn't kill him; neither did tuberculosis nor the army nor the federal penitentiary," wrote Garrett Epps, whose book on this case is invaluable.[18] The Catholic boarding and Bureau of Indian Affairs schools that were meant to "civilize" and "Christianize savages" didn't break or kill him, though they proved lethal to thousands.[19] Al Smith rebelled and escaped.[20] There's an element of this history in ADAPT's abstinence rules. The US suppressed Native American religions to "Christianize" and civilize them, as historian Patricia Nelson Limerick detailed. This included suppressing "old heathenish dances," "medicine men," "heathenish rites," and "traditional healing ceremonies."[21]

Smith took a principled stand against ADAPT's rules. He argued that peyote was acceptable within the parameters of ADAPT's abstemious recovery, partly because it was religious and partly because it wasn't a drug that compromised sobriety. He thought it might even be a recovery tool that could help alcoholics, especially Native Americans. This remarkable man made an admirable stand. He argued, and ADAPT didn't agree. At least, not then. (After this case ended and ADAPT's executive director left for private practice, he agreed: "The reality is that there are a lot of people with alcohol and drug problems who recover in all sorts of different ways, not just abstinence."[22]) Smith's stand is admirable. But admiration does not create a constitutional right.

Black, a less sympathetic figure, has been written out of the story or rewritten as a devout Native American, rather than an obsessive-compulsive white guy. But his case went to the Supreme Court too.

When Galen Black was fired, he asked Oregon for unemployment compensation. The Employment Appeals Board denied the benefits because Black was fired for misconduct—drug counselors can't do drugs. Smith was denied benefits for the same reason.

That's harsh. America's social safety net is callous, often deliberately so at Christianity's urging, as we'll explore in chapter 16. The focus on why people need help rather than the need is somewhat cruel. Politicians are possessed by "fears of malingering or deceit," as the court once phrased it.[23] That, and a healthy dose of racism.[24] Extending benefits to everyone who's unemployed, whatever the reason, is more humane; but under the harsh system, the denial of benefits was proper because they were fired for cause.

Black and Smith each independently appealed to the Oregon Supreme Court. Then to the US Supreme Court, which combined their cases, accepted review, and issued a long opinion that sent the cases back down for additional findings, including whether or not sacramental peyote use was illegal. The US Supreme Court also seems to have regretted taking the case. Scalia even said, "Had we known that, we wouldn't have granted cert in the case."[25] It kicked the case back down to the Oregon Supreme Court, which said that peyote use violates Oregon criminal law and there is no religious exception. The combined case then went back to the US Supreme Court.

The complicated undulations confused a rather simple issue. The question was whether the state could deny workers unemployment benefits because they were fired for misconduct. For there to be a religious freedom question under the Constitution, there must be a government action that burdens religion. There was no government burden on the drug counselors' religion. None.

When they first accepted the job, the government wasn't involved. The government didn't force them to decide between a paycheck and religion; Black and Smith decided when they accepted the job. They willingly compromised their religious beliefs. When they were fired, both were unburdened by the employer's religiously restrictive policy. That freedom wouldn't change whether they get unemployment benefits or not. In other words, by the time they asked the state for unemployment benefits, there was no burden on their religion, no matter how that request was handled.

There was no state burden on their religion regardless of whether or not religious peyote use was illegal, because the benefits denial was tied to their work as drug counselors, not to criminal law. Whatever the criminal law said, they would still have been fired for cause.

The only possible burden from the state came from the "for cause" aspect of the unemployment benefits scheme. But that then shifts the question back to the employer. It was the employer's policy, and it was legitimate. A drug counseling organization with rules about drug counselors doing drugs, which the men agreed to, is not a state burden on their religion. This is a privately imposed burden willingly accepted in return for a paycheck.

The men weren't powerless, though. Either could have sued ADAPT. Black would have had a hard time arguing racial discrimination, but not Smith. Both could have sued for religious discrimination. Instead, they chose not to challenge their firing. Smith didn't argue "that ADAPT had no right to fire him; this is not a wrongful discharge claim" and "does not challenge the employer's decision to fire Al Smith, only the state's denial of unemployment benefits," as the lower court explained.[26]

Black and Smith were fired because of the nature of their jobs, not the religious ritual they engaged in. Religious freedom was not an issue. The central point of the case is that they were ineligible for unemployment benefits because they were fired for misconduct. Drug counselors can't do drugs. ADAPT had rules and policies: no alcohol or drug use by employees. And anyone, regardless of their religion or reason for doing drugs or the legality of the drugs, would also have been fired.

Imagine another scenario: these two men, self-described alcoholics in recovery, get drunk. Alcohol is legal. They broke no law, but transgressed the employers' rules—rules they agreed to and which are central to the organization's mission. They refuse treatment and get fired. They don't have a right to unemployment benefits because a right to alcohol is spelled out in the Twenty-first Amendment. It's harsh, but not a constitutional violation. ADAPT "would have taken the same action had the claimant consumed wine at a Catholic ceremony or any drug anywhere. It would be the same result," noted a lower court.[27]

The central issue was the nature of their employment, not their religion or the legality of peyote. Justice Harry Blackmun, who dissented in the final opinion, asked Oregon's attorney general, "Mr. Attorney General, why were these people fired?" The Oregon AG responded,

"They were fired because they were drug counselors . . . at a drug and alcohol treatment center."[28]

> BLACKMUN: So they were fired because they violated the employer's policy.
> OREGON: That is right.
> BLACKMUN: They were not fired because the use of peyote was illegal.
> OREGON: That is correct.

Oregon explained that, under its law, illegal conduct was not necessarily enough to fire them, but that violating a valid job-related requirement was. The criminal laws around peyote and any possible religious exemptions to those laws were a massive distraction. (Oregon exempted religious uses of peyote from the criminal statutes after the case, but that would not have changed anything in this case.[29]) Nevertheless, the Supreme Court asked the Oregon Supreme Court to rule on the illegality of peyote and religious uses, and extensively discussed it in the final opinion. The unnecessary, arrogant challenge Scalia issued at the end of the opinion, which caused massive backlash, stemmed from this irrelevant query.

What the Court Got Right

The majority opinion reached the correct outcome and clearly explained Lines #1 and #2. There is a distinction between belief and action: "The free exercise of religion means, first and foremost, the right to believe and profess whatever religious doctrine one desires," Scalia wrote of Line #1.[30] To make this point, Scalia quoted Thomas Jefferson's letter to the Danbury Baptists: "The legislative powers of the government reach actions only, and not opinions." That's Line #2, and it's from the very same letter the Supreme Court first quoted in 1878 and which gives us the useful metaphor for Line #3: "wall of separation between church & state." Favorably quoting that letter is reason enough for the Crusaders to target this opinion for destruction, but the opinion also reinforces the boundaries of all three lines. If religious freedom is to be weaponized, this case must fall.

The opinion reiterates that there cannot be a right for religion to be exempt from any law that conflicts with the religion. This is particularly important when the laws are broad, neutral, and generally applicable—that is, when the laws do not target religious worship, as in the Santeria or Muslim ban cases. Traffic laws apply to everyone, even to people who want to let Jesus drive; they don't target solely these believers.

Not only did the court defend Line #2, it explained that even when another person's rights are *not* violated, a religious freedom right may not exist. The opinion explains with an analogy to taxes and freedom of the press, another hallowed First Amendment right. Taxes don't prohibit the free exercise of religion of "citizens who believe support of organized government to be sinful,"[31] any more than the taxes on the book you are holding abridged the "freedom . . . of the press." It simply cannot be the case that a religious command is automatically exempted from the civil law: "Any society adopting such a system would be courting anarchy, but that danger increases in direct proportion to the society's diversity of religious beliefs, and its determination to coerce or suppress none of them." That's correct. Automatic exemptions for every believer would be untenable, especially in America. "Precisely because 'we are a cosmopolitan nation made up of people of almost every conceivable religious preference,' and precisely because we value and protect that religious divergence, we cannot afford the luxury of deeming presumptively invalid, as applied to the religious objector, every regulation of conduct that does not protect an interest of the highest order."[32] All correct.

The court then listed some of its many cases that rejected automatic exemptions for any religious objection. Under the automatic exemption theory, it would have had to grant religious freedom exemptions from paying taxes, manslaughter and child neglect laws, traffic laws, minimum wage laws, child labor laws, environmental protection laws, and laws providing for equality of opportunity, among others. Scalia even included "compulsory vaccination laws" as an obvious and clear instance in which religion gets no exemption (this is a measure of the court's extreme ideological shift and the success of Leo). Scalia summed it up like this, quoting an opinion from more than a century earlier: "To make an individual's obligation to obey such a law contingent upon the law's coincidence with his religious beliefs, except where the State's interest is 'compelling'—permitting him, by virtue of his beliefs, 'to become a law unto himself,'—contradicts both constitutional tradition and common sense." He's correct.

This case has become a target for the Crusaders because of what it got right. But it became a target for liberals because of what it got wrong.

What the Court Got Wrong

Scalia didn't need to defend the two lines in this case because religious freedom was irrelevant; the only issue was the nature of the men's employment. The court should have simply explained that it is within a drug counseling facility's power to discharge drug counselors who use drugs. Especially when that is a policy the drug counselors have signed. Such discharges are necessarily "for cause," are unrelated to the sanctity or illegality of the drugs, but are related to the ability of the drug counselor to counsel addicts. The court could've explained this empathetically in an opinion that put the blame where it belonged: on ADAPT and the state's draconian unemployment requirements.

But Scalia was temperamentally incapable of writing such an opinion. Instead, the court used the irrelevant illegality of peyote to distinguish this case from previous religious unemployment decisions that extended unemployment benefits to minor Christian sects, which proved to be a mistake.

Really, the court erred by letting Scalia write the opinion and focusing on the irrelevant question of whether religious peyote use was illegal or not. Those two errors were like a match that set alight a swirling mix of explosive ingredients.

Explosive Ingredient #1

As they often do, the justices considered issues outside Smith and Black's case. It was never about the drugs; the justices had been worried about a runaway train. Scalia expressed that regret at oral argument—"Had we known that, we wouldn't have granted cert in the case"[33]—when he realized the case was not quite the opportunity to stop the runaway train he'd first believed. Earlier cases, including the unemployment-religion cases mentioned in the next chapter (see pages 129–30) were about to undo the lines the court defended here. The defense was unnecessary in this particular case, but not, thought the justices, in the jurisprudence more broadly. One scholar who delved deeply into the private papers of the justices observed that, for over a decade before this case was decided, they were preoccupied with "whether the Court would put the brakes on this constitutional runaway train."[34] That is, would the court make it clear that the obligation to obey the civil law is not contingent on its coincidence with religious beliefs? Would it hold the lines? So the court was stretching outside the facts of the case to put the brakes on that train— mandatory exemptions for believers from any and every law. To stave off lawlessness. And it chose the worst possible engineer.

Explosive Ingredient #2

Scalia often wrote dissents and usually with an acid pen. He'd be near the middle of today's wretchedly conservative court, but during his time, Scalia was on the fringe. Again, this is a mark of the court's capture, not shifting legal thought. Scalia's conservative views were unpopular, and his infamous claim "My Constitution is . . . dead,"[35] adding "it's dead, dead, dead,"[36] on another occasion, found little support. His consistent inability to persuade his fellow justices to accept his fringe views led to venomous dissents. Scalia admitted that "he writes with the verve and panache he does in part to ensure that his opinions are included in constitutional law casebooks, where they will influence the next generation of lawyers and legal scholars."[37] His flamboyant invective—everything from "pure applesauce" to "jiggerypokery"— drew the popular media's focus, increasing his influence.[38]

Scalia was also a bigot. His guiding judicial philosophy, originalism, is inherently bigoted. Originalism freezes the meaning of laws and our Constitution in the time they were first passed—at a time when women, Blacks, LGBTQ people, Native Americans, nonbelievers, and others were not considered humans worthy of rights and were at the mercy of white Christian men like Scalia. Scalia's bigotry worked its way into his decisions, speeches, and writings.[39]

Explosive Ingredient #3

The United States has a long, evil history of abusing Native Americans. And the Supreme Court itself had just added a fresh wound to this litany of abuse. After the court agreed to review the drug counselor cases but before issuing a final decision, it handed another loss to Native American religions, which, like the peyote case, also led to congressional legislation rebuffing the judiciary.[40] The US Forest Service was considering paving a new, six-mile-long road through the Chimney Rock area of the Six Rivers National Forest in northwestern California and harvesting virgin timber in that roadless tract.[41] The area is sacred to the local tribes, which use it for religious worship.[42] As required by federal law, the USFS commissioned a study of the project's environmental impact, which found that the entire area "is significant as an integral and indispensable part of Indian religious conceptualization and practice" and that any road "would cause serious and irreparable damage to the sacred areas."[43] The report recommended not building the road. USFS decided to build it anyway, and log or clear-cut more than 700 million board feet of timber.[44] Native Americans and environmental groups challenged that decision.

The Supreme Court okayed the road. It wrongly said that this local, nuanced, highly studied, and individualized government action—building a road through virgin wilderness, selected from one of many plans—was no different from a universal and neutral law that requires every single citizen to have a Social Security number, even if their religion said otherwise.[45] There's nothing universal about the individualized roadbuilding/logging project. Their religion depended on this wilderness remaining wild. They can't just build or find another sacred wilderness. The government would have made their exercise of religion impossible.[46] The court was fine with that.

The court's decision was also entirely unnecessary because Congress stepped in and saved the area by creating the Siskiyou Wilderness five years before the court got the case. (Once again, the Court's eagerness to decide an issue it need not have decided led to a bad decision.)

Had the court demurred, public opinion wouldn't have been primed to see its First Amendment maneuvering as racist and ethnocentric.

The Supreme Court's first decision in Smith and Black's case came just a week after the wilderness opinion. The cases were still linked in the public mind when the Supreme Court handed down the final decision on the drug counselors two years later.[47]

These ingredients created a heightened danger of the court "enshrining an ethnocentric view . . . of what constitutes religion in the United States," as Smith and Black's lawyer warned during oral argument.[48] This danger, paired with Scalia's bigotry and arrogance, detonated a religious freedom firestorm.

The Explosion

The court held the lines, but it didn't need to. And Scalia couldn't limit himself to those lines or to a civil, conciliating, or empathetic opinion. He almost made it. But in the last substantive paragraph before the conclusion, Scalia basically told all minorities "too bad." He noted that some states exempted religious use of peyote from criminal laws, which didn't matter, and then, in a phrase that would come to symbolize the case and would lead to a massive national push for a superstatute privileging religion, Scalia wrote:

> It may fairly be said that leaving accommodation to the political process will place at a relative disadvantage those religious practices that are not widely engaged in; but that *unavoidable consequence of democratic government must be preferred* to a system in which each conscience is a law unto itself or in which judges weigh the social importance of all laws against the centrality of all religious beliefs.[49]

Exemptions for religions must come from the democratic process, and minorities should expect to lose, is how this has been read. The *New York Times*, *Chicago Tribune*, *Los Angeles Times*, and a host of legal scholars quoted the passage.[50] Members of Congress often quoted the phrase when they debated "restoring" religious freedom with legislation to undo Scalia's opinion, which even the most obtuse observer could have predicted when reading the words "unavoidable consequence of democratic government."[51]

It's a harsh sentence delivered by a powerful white Christian man to a sympathetic Native American (and another now portrayed as such). The phrase "unavoidable consequence of democratic government" from Scalia's pen consummated liberal fears of an ethnocentric First Amendment.

Liberals loathe this decision because it suggests that all religious minorities are second-class citizens under the First Amendment. It also reinforced an image of a court hostile to Native Americans. And because Scalia wrote those words, not another justice, the Christian supremacy and ethnocentrism were more palpable. It's hard to think Scalia, a Catholic who believed in the literal devil, would have decided this case the same way had it been two Catholics fired for taking communion wine (which ADAPT said it would have done).

Crusaders loathe this decision for different reasons. In fact, the Crusaders of today are fighting to overturn the decision precisely because it fails to do what liberals at the time were so worried about: it fails to enshrine Christian supremacy in the First Amendment. Scalia's defense of the lines has proven to be the major roadblock to that goal.

The Crusaders mounted their assault on this precedent because of what it got right. Liberals attacked it for the racism they rightly read in Scalia's words. But on the issue of religious freedom, everyone was aligned against the high court.

AL SMITH CONTINUED TO FIGHT for Native American rights his whole life. Galen Black is alive and is being used by First Liberty Institute as a pawn to further the Crusade. The institute filed a brief with the Supreme Court representing Black in the Philadelphia case we'll cover in chapter 16, and had him do the same in a case the institute itself is litigating about the prayer-pushing football coach discussed in chapter 4 (see page 55). In each, Black argues for Christian privilege.

★

9

Restoring Christian Supremacy

(The Religious Freedom Restoration Act of 1993)

"I do not think we have to discriminate against anyone
to protect the faith-based community."

—Georgia Governor Nathan Deal, when vetoing a state RFRA[1]

In stopping the runaway train, the court put itself squarely on the tracks.

Scalia's "tough shit, minorities" passage united liberals and conservatives. They asked Congress to do what Scalia dared: pass legislation giving religion the unworkable blanket exemption.

Congress obliged Scalia with a new "superstatute," the Religious Freedom Restoration Act.[2] RFRA remade religious freedom and ordered the court to interpret religious freedom protections differently from then on. The political rhetoric surrounding RFRA made it clear that the entire purpose was to undo this Supreme Court decision, to correct Scalia's wrong. Congressional supporters mentioned the Supreme Court countless times during the RFRA debate. "Our religious rights have been under siege. In 1990, a single Supreme Court decision abolished the standard that protects religious freedom in this country," said one representative.[3] "The Supreme Court's decision three years ago transformed a most hallowed liberty into a mundane concept with little more status than a fishing license," said a forty-year veteran of the House, attacking "the sorry legacy of the Court's view of this matter."[4] When Senator Joe Biden introduced RFRA in the

Senate, he said that the drug counselor decision "will erode religious freedom."[5] Senate Judiciary Committee Chairman Biden also invoked the decision in his opening remarks at the Supreme Court confirmation hearing for David Souter, as did others.[6]

Well-intentioned though some legislators were, RFRA became the fulcrum with which Crusaders would seek to reshape our understanding of religious freedom in the First Amendment. They'd redefine religious freedom as a concept under the statute (RFRA) first, then under the Constitution (the First Amendment).

By its own terms, the Religious Freedom Restoration Act didn't redefine but rather *restored* religious freedom to a gold standard the court supposedly abandoned in the drug counselor case. In "restoring" that standard, Congress advanced Christian supremacy, if inadvertently. This could have been avoided with more careful attention to Line #3. But the mistake is also inexcusable given the clear problems with RFRA. First, RFRA cuts across every single law past, present, and future—hence "superstatute." That effectively makes RFRA a constitutional amendment passed outside the required amendment procedure. Second, RFRA violates the separation of powers because Congress ordered the Supreme Court to interpret a constitutional protection in a certain way, a role that the Constitution reserves for the courts. Third, RFRA privileges believers compared to everyone else, crossing Line #3.[7]

Then there is the flawed standard RFRA sought to restore—an "aberration," as one leading scholar put it. The oddity was based on a few cases decided in favor of minor Christian sects in the narrow context of unemployment benefits, into which the drug counselor case and its explosive elements also fell. These cases were the runaway train the justices were worried about. In these earlier cases, the court was careful to say that "there is no absolute constitutional right to unemployment benefits [for] all persons whose religious convictions are the cause of their unemployment."[8] On three separate occasions, however, it granted benefits after framing their denial as the state forcing employees to choose between fidelity to religious belief and work. We only need to look at the first case in this niche area of religious freedom because the subsequent cases were based on it.

That 1963 case is not the gold standard for determining how the Constitution solves conflicts between religion and the law—it's fool's gold. A preexisting constitutional violation of Line #3 taints the entire case. Christian supremacy written into the law and ignored by the court: mandatory Sunday closing laws. So RFRA "restores" a standard that forced every citizen to honor the Christian god because of an old law that was openly hostile to non-Christians and obliterated Line #3.

ADELE SHERBERT BECAME A SEVENTH-DAY ADVENTIST about two years before the conflict between her new religion and her employer boiled over. Sherbert had worked for thirty-five years at Spartan Mills, a textile mill in Spartanburg, South Carolina.[9] The textile industry was struggling to compete with imports, so mills, seeking competitive edge, mandated six-day weeks, up from five.[10] That meant Saturday shifts because state law closed all manufacturing on Sundays to honor the "Lord's Day." But the Seventh-day Adventists observe the sabbath on Saturday. Sherbert missed six successive Saturdays and was fired. She found other work, but nothing that let her worship and rest on Saturdays (150 other Seventh-day Adventists had no problem finding work[11]). She was denied unemployment because she was fired for misconduct—she missed work.[12]

The Supreme Court's opinion in Sherbert's case is short. The denial of benefits forced "her to choose between following the precepts of her religion and forfeiting benefits, on the one hand, and abandoning one of the precepts of her religion in order to accept work, on the other hand."[13] The court flubbed Lines #1 and #2. Those obvious errors made the case an "aberration," according to Professor John Ely, who taught at Yale, Harvard, and Stanford law schools, and was the fourth-most cited American legal scholar.[14]

But the real problem was the Lord's Day. South Carolina imposed one version of Christianity on all its citizens, and courts repeatedly upheld this constitutional violation. Had the state not imposed this holy commandment on Sherbert or her employer, she could have worked the six-day week. This violation of Line #3 got her fired.

Emperor Constantine probably selected Sunday as the Christian day of rest, partly to distinguish the new Christian religion from the

Jewish sabbath and partly to make it easier for the pagans to convert by keeping the same holy day on which they had worshipped the sun, or so the story goes.[15] It's a fascinating historical rabbit hole and a religious dispute to this day. But the state of South Carolina imposed that religious edict on all citizens and made "it unlawful for an employer to require or permit an employee, especially a woman, to work in a mercantile or manufacturing establishment on Sunday."[16]

South Carolina's Sabbath laws[17] had been repeatedly challenged and upheld by the state's courts, which brushed off arguments about the laws forcing non-Christians "to observe the Christian Sabbath."[18] South Carolina courts invariably rejected these challenges by citing an 1846 case, the first such challenge these courts rejected. Mr. S. A. Benjamin, a Jewish merchant who sold one pair of gloves on Sunday, was fined $40 for violating the Sunday closing law.[19] Benjamin argued that this law violated his religious freedom. He lost. The court obliterated Line #3 in an opinion that's a favorite of today's Christian nationalists.[20]

Judge John O'Neall, later chief justice of South Carolina's highest court, penned the decision against Benjamin. O'Neall often used the power he possessed to influence people to convert to Christianity. He owned about 150 slaves and published *The Negro Law of South Carolina*, in which he argued against a law prohibiting slaves from learning to read, because "As Christians, how can we Justify it, that a slave is not to be permitted to read the Bible? . . . The best slaves in the State, are those who can and do read the Scriptures."[21] O'Neall was president of the Newberry Baptist Bible Society and the Bible Board of the Baptist State Convention, and, as a young boy, he memorized chapter and verse.[22]

O'Neall's opinion in Benjamin's Sabbath challenge is breathtaking for its willingness to legislate his personal Christianity and admit that Sunday closing laws impose Christianity on everyone. O'Neall declares that "the Christian religion is part of the common law of South Carolina!"[23] His opinion reads like a religious text: "Christianity robed in light, and descending as the dove upon our ancestors."[24] O'Neall upheld the Sunday closing law to uphold biblical law: "It is simply an Ordinance for the better observance of the Lord's day."[25] He continued, "The Lord's day, the day of the Resurrection, is to us, who are called Christians, the day of rest after finishing a new creation. It is the day of the first visible triumph over death, hell and the grave! It was the birth day of the believer in Christ." O'Neall defended Sunday closing laws on theological grounds, and he imposed that theology on everyone because he wrongly thought that Christianity is the law. It was legally wrong, morally reprehensible, and unconstitutional in that O'Neall abused civil power to impose his personal religion on everyone. O'Neall's opinion shows precisely why Sunday closing laws should be struck down. Instead, such a law was effectively adopted by the Supreme Court via Sherbert's case, and then by Congress via RFRA in 1993.

The Supreme Court got this right on other occasions. In 1985, it invalidated a Connecticut law requiring employers to give employees their Sabbath off because the statute "arms Sabbath observers with an absolute and unqualified right not to work on whatever day they designate as their Sabbath," which imposes their religion on the employer and other employees, and "this unyielding weighting in favor of Sabbath observers over all other interests contravenes a fundamental principle of the Religion Clauses."[26] This isn't precisely the same as a mandatory Sunday closing law but shows the path the court should have taken to avoid the problem in Sherbert's case.

The Supreme Court's failure to deal with Sunday closing laws was the true problem with Adele Sherbert's case. The court even recognized the problem: "Significantly South Carolina expressly saves the Sunday worshipper from having to make the kind of choice which we here hold infringes the Sabbatarian's religious liberty."[27] But for that law, Sherbert could have worked six days.[28] Professors Marci Hamilton and Leslie Griffin explain, "If the Court had struck down Sunday mandatory closings, Sherbert would never have been unemployed for her Saturday adherence. The law would have applied equally to Saturday and Sunday Sabbath worshippers, as it should."[29] Her willingness to work on a day most might want off would have been *more* valuable to her employer; the Christian law got her fired. And that is effectively *state* discrimination against a religious minority in a way the drug counselor case is not. The state burden on Sherbert's religion from the Line #3 violation is real. The Supreme Court recognized "the religious discrimination which South Carolina's general statutory scheme necessarily effects," but utterly failed to redress it.[30]

This is what RFRA restored: religious discrimination and Christian supremacy.

THE JUSTICES FRAMED THE UNEMPLOYMENT BENEFITS CASES as a forced choice: The government forcing unemployed believers to choose between a government benefit and their religion. But the Sunday closing law is what got Sherbert fired. The drug counselors, however, had already made that choice when they took the job. When they were fired, they were surely worse off, but that was not, as Scalia mistakenly thought, because of the nature of a democratic society, but because of the demands of their gods.

Having personal convictions is hard. Having the courage of those convictions is harder. It's up to believers to shoulder their personal religious burdens. If they can force others to bear that burden by claiming religious freedom, then that protection has become a weapon.

The court's forced-choice framing also implicates Line #3. Effectively, believers are asking us to pay them to have the courage of their convictions. That expectation is interesting, especially in Supreme Court litigation, in which recent converts are overrepresented. Sherbert had converted just a couple years before the case. Another recent Seventh-day Adventist convert won at the Supreme Court in 1987, relying on Sherbert's case.[31] The drug counselor case started similarly—Galen Black, a white guy with obsessive-compulsive tendencies diving into a Native American religion. Kim Davis, too. The zeal of the convert spurred their fights,[32] but at least some were, presumably, of the majority caste, accustomed to legal favor and privileges of a loosely enforced Line #3, not the disadvantages.[33] They fought like members of the privileged caste expecting the law to bend to their religion.

Line #3 means the government cannot pay people to worship. I'd chip in a few bucks to help out Al Smith, and I wish our safety nets were more just and forgiving, but had he won, the government would be required to use its taxing power to take our money and give it to someone *because* they were religious. The fired-for-cause rule meant that any other drug counselor fired for doing drugs wouldn't get unemployment benefits, only the pious peyote users. Justices John Marshall Harlan and Byron White denounced this in Sherbert's case: "The State, in other words, must single out for financial assistance those whose behavior is religiously motivated, even though it denies such assistance to others whose identical behavior (in this case, inability to work on Saturdays) is not religiously motivated."[34] Chief Justice Rehnquist dissented with this same observation in a similar case, finding it absurd that a state could be "constitutionally required to provide direct financial assistance to a person solely on the basis of his religious beliefs."[35] This amounts to paying believers to exercise those religious beliefs; it's no different than paying them to go to church. That is unconstitutional. Instead, we must ask them to have the courage of their convictions.

As they had for much of North American history, Crusaders used and abused Native Americans. They took advantage of liberal sentiment against the ethnocentric Supreme Court opinions in Native American cases to build up sentiment for expansive, transgressive religious freedom. They allied with equality-minded lawyers, scholars, and Native Americans to pass a law enshrining their privileged vision, RFRA. A slew of state versions of RFRA followed, beginning in the mid-1990s. Scholars characterized these as uncontroversial, bipartisan, nonideological efforts until 2010—until the Supreme Court called for the Crusade—when the sinister possibilities in these laws began emerging.[36] Republican-controlled states continued to pass more RFRAs, including Texas and Arkansas, and the Mississippi and Indiana laws we met earlier. By 2013, liberals, progressives, and equality activists were fighting, often successfully, an all-out war against these religious freedom bills and laws.

Like thankful pilgrims begging assistance only to turn around and slaughter their neighbors, the Crusaders had weaponized the restored vision of religious freedom liberals helped realize and turned it against them. By 2014, desperately working to obstruct our first Black president and women from getting reproductive health care, the Crusaders finally pushed RFRA beyond what the liberals understood and intended in the Hobby Lobby case.

PART III

THE ONSLAUGHT

10

The War on Women
●
(*Burwell v. Hobby Lobby Stores*)

"What's at stake in a decision like this—and in a debate
like this—is women's basic humanity."

—**Jessica Valenti**, feminist author[1]

The Crusaders' strategy for the Religious Freedom Restoration
Act was simple and cunning. Weaponizing religious freedom
under RFRA, then under the First Amendment. Redefining
religious freedom under RFRA would be easier than altering the First
Amendment to the Constitution because RFRA was basically a blank
slate that privileged religion. The strategy was to pick off the easier
target and then migrate that version of religious freedom to the First
Amendment.

Twenty years after Congress passed RFRA, the Crusaders accomplished step one in the Hobby Lobby case; they rewrote Line #2
under RFRA.

Justices Alito, Scalia, Thomas, Kennedy, and Roberts—five Catholic men—decided that billionaires could use the legal structure of a
multibillion-dollar corporation to impose their religion on the employees of that company, effectively robbing the employees of their right to
preventative health care.

The Patient Protection and Affordable Care Act, known as the
ACA or Obamacare, required large employers (50+ employees) to provide health insurance to their employees.

To implement that law, the Obama administration promulgated new regulations that required health insurance plans to cover essential health-care services at no cost to the patient, including important preventative health care like wellness visits, contraceptive counseling, and HPV screening. Those regulations became known, somewhat misleadingly, as the "contraceptive mandate," and they expanded health care for Americans. Crusaders targeted the administrative rules. All told, over 100 lawsuits were eventually filed against this benefit.[2] The Becket Fund filed a slew of lawsuits,[3] as did the Alliance Defending Freedom. These two Crusaders brought the cases that would be combined in the Hobby Lobby decision.

There were two big exceptions to the contraceptive mandate. First, the regulations exempted churches and other religious groups.[4] Sensibly, the religious exemption did not extend to for-profit companies.

Second, any employer could pay taxes in lieu of providing employees health insurance. The taxes ensured that the cost of covering its employees' health care wasn't passed on to taxpayers.[5] Though, at $2,000 per employee per year, the tax was significantly less health coverage, which was about $4,000 to $12,000 a year.[6] If the employer provided health insurance but that insurance didn't meet the coverage requirements, it paid higher taxes ($100 per employee per day or $36,500 per employee per year).[7] As we will see on the following pages, Hobby Lobby could've saved money and adhered to its owners' medieval beliefs by simply paying the taxes and not providing health insurance.

The Motivation: Misogyny

The Crusaders don't view women's reproductive health as health care. They believe that birth control is for "sluts." Mike Huckabee preached to the Republican National Committee that the mandate existed because "the women of America . . . cannot control their libido," though he tried to hang that slander on Democrats.[8] Crusaders seem to imagine—quite vividly, one expects—pill-popping women wantonly coupling. The stultified religious objection is that contraception comes between women and the natural consequences of their actions—between women and the Crusaders' god. Abortion and contraception rob this particular god of his ability to punish harlots with motherhood. God's impotent wrath and the frustrated consequences, tellingly, never apply to the women's partner, a tradition well-established in the bible itself.[9] Patriarchy and reproductive rights are inversely related.

Racism also motivated the attempt to damage the landmark legislation of America's first Black president and him in the process. "Obamacare" itself began as a slur on the ACA, a racist dog whistle, according to data.[10] When wrapped in religious freedom, racism and misogyny are sufficiently disguised to enter mainstream discourse, but righteous blowhards like Huckabee tend to say the quiet part out loud. Rush Limbaugh said it the loudest.

The radio host and commentator, a known bigot, abused a thirty-year-old Georgetown law student for testifying before Congress about whether religious organizations should be exempt from ACA contraceptive coverage regulations and to what extent.[11] Sandra Fluke refuted the Crusaders' assumption that all women who take birth control are "sluts." She understandably opted not to lay bare her personal medical history, but explained that people take birth control for many reasons beyond sex, including a friend who has "to take prescription birth control to stop cysts from growing on her ovaries."[12] About 1.5 million Americans, including one-third of teens, use birth control pills exclusively for non-contraceptive purposes, and only 42 percent took those pills exclusively for preventing pregnancy.[13] (And yes, people can, should, and do take it to enjoy sex. It's a brilliant invention.)

Simply by stating reality, Fluke threatened the "slut" assumption. So Limbaugh crucified her. Viciously. He hurled so much invective that her testimony was lost in the tumult. And that was the point. Limbaugh attacked Fluke as "a slut," "a prostitute," "who wants to be paid to have sex," who's "having so much sex she can't afford the contraception," and who wants "the taxpayers to pay her to have sex."[14]

Limbaugh resumed hostilities the next day. He called women who want contraception "feminazis" and said, "If we are going to pay for your contraceptives, and thus pay for you to have sex, we want something for it . . . we want you to post the videos online so we can all watch."[15] (President Trump awarded Limbaugh the Presidential Medal of Freedom in 2020.) Mitt Romney tried to be more circumspect when he said of Limbaugh, "It's not the language I would have used."[16] But as Maureen Dowd asked in the *New York Times*, "Is there a right way to call a woman a slut?"[17]

Limbaugh bared his own misogyny, but also showed the true colors of the religious freedom challenge to contraception. This fight was part of a war on women, and religious freedom was simply a new weapon in that war. One Texas state representative with the apt name Wayne Christian told the *Texas Tribune*, "Of course it's a war on birth control, abortion, everything."[18]

The Crusaders don't see women as full people worthy or capable of self-determination. Women shouldn't have agency over their body or reproduction—men should. Catholic bishops and Christian billionaires should. Writing for *The Guardian*, Jessica Valenti explained, "What's at stake in a decision like this—and in a debate like this—is women's basic humanity, of which sexuality is an integral part. Yes, contraception is about health, and women often need birth control for medical reasons—but we also need it for sex, and that's just fine."[19] Five Catholic men infantilized women and robbed them of their agency in the Hobby Lobby decision. Noticeably absent from the decision, Supreme Court journalist Dahlia Lithwick explained, was "the very notion of the woman herself as moral circuit breaker, as an agent of her own ethical choices and preferences, whose decision to obtain an IUD, or a condom, or a morning-after pill is a fully autonomous moral choice that supplants the spiritual choices of her employer."[20] While women fought for that basic recognition of their humanity, the Crusaders opposed them.

Misogyny and racism motivated the attack on the ACA, and then the attack was justified morally with religion and legally with religious freedom.

The Challenge: Religious Freedom

The Green family is among the 100 richest Americans, worth over $4 billion. "We're Christians, and we run our business on Christian principles,"[21] wrote David Green, patriarch of the family that controls the Hobby Lobby chain, in a 2012 *USA Today* op-ed. That op-ed also announced that this for-profit S subchapter corporation, owned by several layers of legal trusts which Green controlled, not only believed that Jesus Christ is Lord and Savior, but also that this corporation was suing in federal court over the contraceptive mandate.

David Green comes from a family of Christian preachers.[22] His Christianity is not what one might call humble: "For me, I want to know that I have affected people for eternity. . . . I believe once someone knows Christ as their personal savior, I've affected eternity. I matter 10 billion years from now."[23] Green's three adult children run the Hobby Lobby empire. Steve Green, the second son, is the CEO of Hobby Lobby Stores, Inc. He's also the driving and economic force behind the desperately overdone Museum of the Bible in DC.[24]

The Greens use their wealth and power to proselytize. Hobby Lobby buys annual Fourth of July ads that misleadingly alter and edit quotes from the founding era in a disingenuous attempt to prove that America is a Christian nation. Despite repeated debunkings and corrections, the Greens insist on publishing the misleading edits anyway.[25] Bearing false witness perhaps, but not illegal. Nor is using the Museum of the Bible to push the Greens' particular brand of Christianity under a thin veneer of scholarship and ecumenicalism. The gift shop hawks Steve Green's *Faith in America*. The book's cover features one of Hobby Lobby's deliberately misleading July 4 ads. The book is full of these misleading quotations and is mostly Green recounting a conversation with the Christian propagandist David Barton. The museum is similarly misleading. It's also plagued with legal troubles, which Alison Frankel summarized for Reuters: "In 2017, Hobby Lobby paid $3 million and forfeited more than 140 ancient artifacts to resolve US Justice Department allegations that the pieces were illegally imported into the United States. In March 2020, the museum disclosed that its Dead Sea Scroll fragments were modern forgeries. Then in May 2020, the museum sent more than 13,000 artifacts back to Iraq and Egypt after determining their provenance was questionable."[26]

Other Green efforts were also questionable, like the bible curriculum the Greens tried to roll out in public schools in Mustang, Oklahoma.[27] The Greens developed the bible class with some of the same scholars who would later join the Museum of the Bible. The class didn't teach the bible as literature but preached the bible as objective truth. The curriculum didn't educate children about religion; it indoctrinated them in the Greens' version of conservative Christianity. The Greens even sought to circumvent open-meeting laws meant to ensure the school board's transparency to smuggle the curriculum into the schools.[28] Working for the Freedom From Religion Foundation alongside the ACLU and Americans United, I was able to stop this curriculum, a clear violation of Line #3. The Greens took it overseas to implement in countries that don't separate state and church.[29]

So when the Greens sued in September 2012 over the contraceptive mandate (which they tellingly referred to as the "preventative care mandate" in their lawsuit[30]), this wasn't the first or last time they would use wealth and power to impose Christianity on others. Nor was it the first time the Greens had been involved with the Crusaders. The Crusaders are a broad, if shadowy, front. They receive massive funding from the National Christian Charitable Foundation and other wells of dark money. The largest funder of that foundation traced back to Hobby Lobby.[31]

The network is so well-funded and vast that the Crusaders can craft virtually any case they like. So when Justice Sotomayor posed a difficult hypothetical to Hobby Lobby's lawyer about how courts could possibly determine the religious belief of a corporation and added as an aside, "Just assume not a business like yours—you picked great plaintiffs, but let's assume," everyone laughed, but it's also true. The Crusaders pick their plaintiffs and the cases they want to go to the Supreme Court, not vice versa.

One of the most effective Crusaders is the Becket Fund for Religious Liberty, which brought the Hobby Lobby case. The Becket Fund is named after Archbishop of Canterbury Thomas à Becket, because, in its retelling, he "stood resolutely at the intersection of church and state."[32] Tom Becket is lionized today and sainted for his martyrdom at the hands of England's Henry II. Less well remembered is why he and Henry were feuding in the first place. (In Britain, he seems to be remembered more honestly. One national poll ranked him the second-worst Briton ever, behind Jack the Ripper and ahead of King John, Henry II's son.[33]) To overstate the case only slightly, in addition to a question of missing funds, Henry thought one law should apply to everyone and that churchmen who, say, murdered someone, should be tried in civil courts. The church, led by Becket, refused, demanding that ecclesiastical courts try "criminous clerks"—churchmen accused of any crime. He wanted one law for the Catholic clergy and a different, stricter law for everyone else. In other words, Becket was fighting for religious privilege. There is no record of Henry uttering the infamous line "Will no one rid me of this turbulent [or meddlesome or troublesome] priest?" but he must have expressed some frustration because four knights murdered Becket in Canterbury Cathedral.[34] To the extent Becket died for a principle, it wasn't for religious freedom, but for religious privilege. The Becket Fund fights for that privilege today.

Becket's founder, Kevin "Seamus" Hasson, has a theology degree from Notre Dame and wrote the Christian nationalist book *Believers, Thinkers, and Founders: How We Came to Be One Nation Under God.* Becket fights for taxpayer-funded religious schools, for government-organized and -led prayers, and against marriage equality and contraception. Becket even fought to keep a Christian prayer banner displayed in a public school.[35] It recently funded a $1.6 million Religious Liberty Clinic at Stanford Law School.[36]

Among the Crusaders, the Becket Fund is better at diversifying its clientele to include non-Christians, but it is still preoccupied with weaponizing religious freedom. One former employee explained that the ecumenicalism was self-interested and also that Leonard Leo, the court packer, saved Becket twice by tapping his shadowy network for massive cash infusions.[37] Becket awarded Leo its Canterbury Medal in 2017 for being a "stalwart defender of religious liberty."[38] So one of the most successful and active Crusaders is intimately involved in the network that packed the Supreme Court with justices that decide their cases.

When Becket and the Greens crafted Hobby Lobby's challenge, they had allies on the Supreme Court. It was the first Supreme Court in American history without a Protestant: six Catholics and three Jews.[39] The five Catholic men were all nominated by Republicans, and most had worked in Republican administrations.[40] Alito wrote the controlling opinion. Becket's founder, Hasson, worked for Alito in Reagan's Justice Department (the job Alito got by writing that he opposed decisions separating state and church, has "always been a conservative" and "a life-long registered Republican").[41]

It's remarkable that the five Catholic men comprised the majority, though remarking on it is frowned upon because it suggests that their religious beliefs tainted their decision. But we know it does, that it did and should reject this courtesy, which only protects the Crusaders (see chapter 1).

The Hobby Lobby decision is a nightmare for a number of reasons, but, above all, it was the first time the Crusading court violated Line #2. Alito's awful, illogical opinion turned religious freedom into a cudgel of misogyny, violating the rights of every Hobby Lobby employee in the name of their employers' god. Samuel Alito beat the plowshare into a sword.

Alito's opinion is so poor that correcting it could be a standalone book, but here are five major failings that go to the religious freedom aspects of his opinion.

1. Religion Trumps Reality

The bible never discusses contraception. Or abortion. They're not condemned in the various versions of the Ten Commandments. Or in the 613 *mitzvot*. Sure, the biblical god commands Adam and Eve to "be fruitful and multiply," but we can multiply with a measure of reproductive choice. The two aren't mutually exclusive the way Christianity and women's rights seem to be. Despite this lack of a biblical mandate, the Greens believe their god opposes abortion.

In the first court filing, the Greens admitted that they had "no religious objection to providing coverage for non-abortion-causing contraceptive drugs and devices."[42] The case could have ended there. The Greens challenged a few specific contraceptive drugs that *don't* cause abortions, but which they *wrongly* believed caused abortions—a belief unequivocally refuted by science, medicine, and reality.

A truly impressive collection of doctors and medical professionals signed a brief addressing one question: Are the drugs Hobby Lobby objects to, in fact, abortifacients? No, was the unequivocal answer, "The scientific evidence confirms that the FDA-approved forms of emergency contraception are not abortifacients."[43] *Preventing* pregnancy is not the same as *terminating* pregnancy. The medical professionals' brief clearly explained the difference. Contraceptives prevent pregnancy; abortifacients terminate a pregnancy. The brief explained the science. The drugs "function by inhibiting or postponing ovulation; they do not prevent fertilization or implantation."

The doctors and scientists spoke, and the Catholic men on the high court ignored them—and reality—because the Greens professed a religious belief—that these forms of contraception, which are not abortifacients, are abortifacients.

Alito accepted, virtually without comment, this erroneous belief about science and medicine as true. "If the owners comply with the HHS mandate, they *believe* they will be facilitating abortions," he wrote.[44] With that, the Supreme Court elevated an unsupported, unscientific religious belief to an unassailable perch, ignoring the evidence-based, scientific, medical fact. Alternate facts trumped science and reality.

It was as if the Greens premised their case on a religious belief that the earth is flat, or that water is composed of carbon, rather than hydrogen and oxygen, and the court agreed. Even worse, Alito isn't simply rewarding false religious beliefs; he's giving beliefs that are held in spite of all evidence to the contrary special legal protection under the law. *Truth matters less than the fervency with which a belief is held,* which leads to rather perverse incentives.

Normally, the wrongness of a religious belief doesn't matter because Line #2 ensures that the belief only impacts the believer. Courts blindly accepting the truth of a religious belief is a standard rule, perhaps even a good rule when the impacts of the unexamined belief don't extend beyond the individual believer—that is, as long as Line #2 is intact. "While the truth of a belief is not open to question," the rule states, "there remains the significant question whether it is truly held."[45] The courts might look at the sincerity of a belief, not the content. But if courts are going to pretend that Line #2 doesn't exist and allow religious beliefs to harm or impact others, then courts must also examine the objective truth of a belief. You may believe that your god is telling you to sacrifice your child, and the court can accept that as true *so long as it defends the rights of everyone else against that belief.* If, however, the court accepts that belief as true and subjugates the rights of others to that belief, the religious freedom has been weaponized. Alito did just that.

The end of this inevitable road is worrisome and has profound implications for our right to contraception, especially in light of the leaked opinion overturning *Roe v. Wade* (see pages 153–54). Because if it can be argued or legally claimed that birth control causes abortion even when it prevents pregnancy, after *Roe v. Wade* is overturned and reproductive freedom is a memory, the road to blocking access to contraception is cleared. That has always been the next step, as some of us have been saying for a long time. The Crusaders aren't hiding this agenda.[46] Joyce Meyer Ministries argued in a brief that the "contraceptive services mandate violates freedom of opinion" because it encourages "female sexual activity without risk of pregnancy." The contraceptives and counseling "ensure that more and more women do not get pregnant unless . . . they want to."[47] That's a fairly clear call for forced pregnancy. It's less slouching toward Gilead than barreling at full throttle, Jesus at the wheel.

2. Hobby Lobby's Hypocrisy

Hobby Lobby's hypocrisy was given a free pass because, in America, to criticize or question religion is seen as vulgar and wrong.

The rule just stated—that courts cannot examine the truth of a religious belief, only its sincerity—is born partly of the American cultural taboo against criticizing religion or suggesting that it's factually mistaken or morally insincere. Yet American history gives plenty of examples of just that. My favorite date to Prohibition, which was foisted on the country largely by Christian temperance groups. The Volstead Act exempted sacramental wines and liquors, and an insincere American piety exploded. One Jewish congregation grew overnight from 180 to 1,000 families.[48] Catholic clergy and Jewish rabbis essentially became bootleggers under the legal fiction that they were providing sacramental wine to their newly pious flock.

Unfortunately, the judicial refusal to probe the truth of a belief is nearly always accompanied by an uncritical acceptance of its sincerity. So Hobby Lobby's blatant hypocrisy didn't matter in court. Alito pointed out that "no one has disputed the sincerity of [Hobby Lobby's] religious beliefs." None of the justices asked Hobby Lobby why, if it was so crucial to the owners' religion, the company voluntarily covered these same drugs before the lawsuit? The Greens claimed that "coverage of these drugs was not included knowingly or deliberately," but that doesn't explain why the company invested more than $73 million in the drug companies that manufacture these un-Christian drugs and "intrauterine birth control devices, emergency contraceptive pills and drugs *used in abortion procedures*."[49] Or why the company imports most of what it sells (perhaps 90 percent[50]) from China, a country that has suppressed Christianity and has abortion policies that had fellow Christians criticizing the Greens for sending American dollars there. Nor how a for-profit, billion-dollar empire comports with the Christian duty Jesus expressed: "If you want to be perfect, go, sell your possessions and give to the poor, and you will have treasure in heaven. Then come, follow me."[51]

The Greens' sincerity should have been questioned. And even if the Greens were sincere, how do we know Hobby Lobby Stores, Inc, which is not a person but a corporate entity dedicated to making money, actually cares about contraception? Hobby Lobby's transparent hypocrisy was legally irrelevant. Had its sincerity been challenged—a near impossibility, given the taboo just mentioned—Alito would almost certainly have admonished the government for doing so and declared that it cannot require consistency from believers on religious freedom claims.

3. When "Choice" Matters

There's hypocrisy in Alito's obtuse reasoning too. The Supreme Court has used the "true private choice" of individuals to cut off possible state/church violations. For instance, a decision chain featuring private choices cuts off the constitutional problem with Line #3 when the government funds a neo-voucher scheme, even if 96 percent of the money goes to religious schools.[52] Taxpayer funds are flowing to a religious purpose, which is a clear violation of the First Amendment, but the court pretended that private choice severed the chain and therefore the violation (see chapter 16).[53]

However, when it came to the religious objection of a family who owned "various trusts"[54] that owned a corporation that employed individuals, the court ignored the individuals' choice. Alito held that the Green family's religion was "substantially burdened," despite a causal chain replete with individual choices:

1. Science and reality clearly show Drug X prevents pregnancy; it does not cause abortions.

2. G believes that Drug X causes abortions (not a religious belief).

3. G believes his god is against abortions (a religious belief).

4. G controls several distinct legal entities, including Trusts T and V.

5. Trusts T and V own controlling shares in a corporation with limited liability, Company H.

6. Company H buys health insurance plans for employees, as required by law.

7. Federal rules require the plan to cover certain medical services.

8. H hires Employee B at one of its stores.

9. B goes to her doctor for a regular checkup.

10. Dr. C recommends and prescribes Drug X for B.

11. B fills the prescription for X at Pharmacy Y.

12. The insurance plan pays Pharmacy Y for Drug X.

13. Y gives X to B.

14. B personally chooses to take X.

15. B takes X.

16. B does not get pregnant.

17. Therefore, A's religion is violated.

One would think an employee exercising private choice in consultation with her doctor would sever the chain. But, as with the Greens' religious objections, intellectual consistency is not required when, like Alito, you make the rules up as you go.

4. There Was No Burden on the Greens' Religion

This causal chain also shows no government burden on the Greens' religion, a prerequisite for a religious freedom case. Even if we ignore the chain, and the fact that corporations have no religion, no burden existed. The Greens claimed the burden was paying out taxes to exercise their religion, but its company was actually saving money. Recall that businesses could opt out of the contraceptive mandate by paying more taxes. Assuming conservatively that Hobby Lobby paid $5,000 for health plans annually per employee, it had three options:

1. Pay $26 million/year in taxes and not provide health insurance.

2. Pay about $45 million/year for health insurance that meets the legal requirements.

3. Pay $520 million/year ($475 million/year in taxes, plus the cost in option 2) for health insurance that doesn't meet the coverage requirements.

The company could have saved millions with option one.

We don't know the exact numbers because Hobby Lobby never provided them.[55] That failure should have tanked the case because the company was required to prove that a burden on its religion existed, but Alito allowed the Greens to simply assert that the company would have to pay taxes as a burden when it might have actually been saving money by paying the taxes rather than buying health insurance.

To circumvent this problem, the company argued that the Greens' religion also required the company to provide health care to its employees.[56] Justice Ruth Bader Ginsburg asked, "Covering their employees for health care, that is not a religious tenet, right?" "No, it actually is," Hobby Lobby responded.[57] (That tenet evaporated during a pandemic.[58])

Moreover, the Greens, who have religious beliefs, would not have paid any additional taxes because the Greens are separate from their corporation, which has no religious beliefs. Hobby Lobby Stores, Inc. would've paid the taxes, and Hobby Lobby would've saved money.

In the end, the court shifted that burden from the billion-dollar corporation to 13,000 employees. So the cost of the billionaire Greens practicing their religion is borne by their low-wage employees. Just like Jesus would have wanted.

5. Alito Rewrote the Lines

Hobby Lobby wrongly claimed that the contraceptive mandate compelled Christians to act in a way that violated their faith. But recall our lines:

Line #1: With the contraception mandate in place, the Greens still have an unburdened, unlimited right to believe whatever counterfactual tenets they choose.

Line #2: The mandate applies to companies with more than fifty employees, not billionaires. The Greens aren't acting; corporations and trusts are. Corporations are created specifically to protect their creators from the consequences of the corporation's actions. There would be no corporations, no corporate law, if not for the principle that corporations are separate from people. *This separation is the entire purpose of corporations.* The Greens don't even own Hobby Lobby Stores, Inc; "they own and operate" the company "through various trusts."[59] A series of trusts protects the family and likely shields them from considerable tax liability, and then another layer of protection is added through the corporate structure. They rake in billions without personal risk. To ignore that and declare Christians exempt from this corporate shield is to rewrite American corporate law, which Alito did.

The central "question that RFRA presents," according to Justice Alito, is "whether the HHS mandate imposes a substantial burden on the ability of the objecting parties to conduct business in accordance with *their religious beliefs.*"[60] (Alito's emphasis.) This is absolutely wrong. Citizens possess a *limited* right to exercise their religion, Line #2, not to "conduct business" through a corporation owned by trusts in which they have an interest and then to pass their religion through those layers of legal armor to trample the rights of their employees.[61] This is not religious freedom.

Alito attempted to distract us from this massive rewrite of corporate law with talk of "closely-held corporations," which means that more than 50 percent of the corporation's stock is controlled by a few people.[62] Mars, Uber, and Koch Industries are all "closely held corporations," each with billions in revenue and tens of thousands of employees. Something like 90 percent of all American companies are "closely held." The same goes for the "family owned" rhetoric. Walmart is a family-owned business, even though it's the largest company in the world by revenue and number of people employed. These are meaningless distractions.

Whatever the court had decided, the Greens personally would've been able to go to church, to pray, to worship, oppose abortions and contraception, and not get abortions or use contraception. They didn't pay anything. The soulless corporation did.

The Dissent

The women on the court dissented. As did the non-Christians. *Hobby Lobby* is a sexist, majoritarian decision. The first thing Ruth Bader Ginsburg points out in her brilliant dissent was the "startling breadth" of the decision. Anticipating the Crusaders' strategy, she heads off arguments that this case means anything for religious freedom under the First Amendment: "The Court does not pretend that the First Amendment's Free Exercise Clause demands religion-based accommodations so extreme, for our decisions leave no doubt on that score."[63] She saw where the Crusaders wanted to take RFRA.

Ginsburg, Sotomayor, Breyer, and Kagan slammed Alito for departing from Line #2; "our decisions leave no doubt" that religious freedom cannot be wielded to impose religion on others. They highlighted cases spanning more than five decades where state and federal courts got Line #2 right, rejecting the Greens' argument.[64] The Supreme Court refused to let devout Christians discriminate against Black Americans in the Piggie Park barbeque case.[65] The Minnesota Supreme Court rebuffed born-again Christian business-owners who refused, in violation of employment discrimination laws, to hire someone "living with but not married to a person of the opposite sex," "a young, single woman working without her father's consent or a married woman working without her husband's consent," or any person "antagonistic to the Bible," including "fornicators and homosexuals."[66] And the New Mexico Supreme Court decision against a photography company that refused "to photograph a lesbian couple's commitment ceremony" because the bible told them to.[67] (Which a certain civil rights commissioner in Colorado would quote to a bakery and which Kennedy would declare was hostility.) Each time, the courts held Line #2, refusing to allow religious freedom claims to violate the rights of others. Religion is not a license to harm, the dissenters reminded Alito.

Ginsburg also discussed a 1982 Supreme Court case decided under the First Amendment that Alito unconvincingly addressed.[68] An Amish carpenter objected, on religious grounds, to paying or withholding Social Security taxes. The court rejected the religious freedom challenge because to accept it and to give the carpenter an exemption would be to "impose the employer's religious faith on the employees."[69] It would violate Line #2. That was not permissible under the First Amendment, but Alito held that it was under RFRA.

The dissent laid the groundwork for undoing this awful decision, both for a future Supreme Court free of partisan hackery or Congress, which could repeal RFRA tomorrow. The shadow of that repeal is why the Crusaders are still fighting to graft this weaponized version of religious freedom onto the First Amendment.

Ever since the Hobby Lobby decision warped RFRA beyond what the strange coalition that created it intended, a campaign to repeal RFRA has been growing.[70] Bills have been proposed to ensure that it cannot be used as a tool to discriminate, including the Do No Harm Act,[71] which takes its name from the principle embodied in Line #2. If Congress repealed RFRA tomorrow, court decisions based on RFRA, including this one, would be meaningless. However, if the Crusaders can successfully transfer RFRA's rewritten religious freedom to the First Amendment, then their weapon is the Constitution itself. This is the terrifying aspect of the Crusade that Americans fail to grasp. Once the Supreme Court weaponizes religious freedom in the First Amendment, undoing that harm will require massive court expansion and reform—which we need anyway—or a constitutional amendment to alter the sacrosanct text of the First Amendment. Neither is easy. The final grafting of this bastardized religious freedom onto the First Amendment has not fully taken.

For a self-proclaimed family of deep faith, there is something deeply profane about the Hobby Lobby lawsuit. The Greens took the hallowed right and brought it down, through RFRA, to hawking trifles. One American conservative writer hoping for a Hobby Lobby win put it like this: "On the rare occasion that I enter the store, even amid the Chinese mass-produced crosses and the piped-in Christian music, under the endless fluorescent lighting and displays carefully managed to optimize impulse buying, I am hardly moved to a state of piety, prayer, and thanksgiving."[72] Millions of young Americans, millions of women, millions of empathetic people looked at the Greens' Christianity and rejected it. For all their desire to impact eternity, the Greens drove Americans away from their god.

The Postscript

There's a rather long postscript to the Hobby Lobby case. Recall that the contraceptive mandate exempted religious orders and churches.

This exemption wasn't enough for the churches. They demanded more. They all but demanded that their employees not get contraception.

The church exemption created a Line #2 problem; the same problem with many argued-for religious exemptions. The church exemption is a civil law that effectively imposed religious law on employees. For instance, imagine that the local Catholic diocese hires an accountant, a young Catholic woman it would inevitably label a bookkeeper. The exemption would apply to the diocese. If the diocese were *not* exempt, the bookkeeper would have a statutory right to no-cost birth control. She could and, given all the data, likely would exercise that right.[73] However, the exemption takes away her right to cost-free contraception. So the exemption is a civil law that allows employers to impose religious fiat on employees. Without some additional move by the government, this was not an exemption, but a weapon.

To solve this Line #2 problem, the government required insurance companies to bridge the gap in contraceptive coverage for employees of exempt religious entities at no cost to those religious employers. The federal government would even reimburse the insurance company. Religious employers don't provide the coverage, but patients get the coverage. It seemed a workable compromise for all.

But the insurance company and government needed to know which religious employers took the exemption. So the government asked religious employers to fill out five blanks on a form and submit it:[74]

1. Entity name

2. Name of individual filling out the form

3. Mailing address

4. Signature

5. Date

That's it.

Religious orders and religious schools, such as Notre Dame and Wheaton, filed dozens of lawsuits claiming that this form burdened their religious freedom.[75] One federal judge explained "the novelty of Notre Dame's claim—not for the exemption, which it has, but for the right to have it without having to ask for it."[76] Even this description is too generous because religious organizations didn't have to ask for the exemption; they simply had to tell the government that they were taking it. And they didn't even have to use the form, which states, "Alternatively, an eligible organization may also provide notice to the Secretary of Health and Human Services."

The real objection was to "*any* system in which their employees gain an entitlement to contraceptive coverage from third parties," explained Solicitor General Donald Verrilli in yet another challenge to the form, one brought by priests.[77]

On the National Day of Prayer in 2017, Trump singled out a group of nuns in a Rose Garden speech after he signed an executive order "promoting . . . religious liberty." "We know all too well," Trump began, "the attacks against the Little Sisters of the Poor," and then he spontaneously invited the nuns up on stage: "Come on up here, Sister, come on up."[78] Trump placed the nuns, impoverished by personal choice, on stage with megachurch preachers Jack Graham and Paula White, skillfully exploiting the mascots for the cameras. Before this presidential recognition of their suffering, the Crusaders had paraded the Little Sisters of the Poor at every opportunity. Photos of the nuns descending the steps of the Supreme Court in their gray habits, smiling and waving as if on a homecoming float, became de rigueur for most publications. They were the perfect Crusader mascots for the war on contraception, women's rights, and health care: pious women the media was incapable of criticizing. The Catholic nuns had Catholic friends on the court. Parroting Trump, Alito trotted out "the protracted campaign against the Little Sisters of the Poor" in his 2020 speech to the Federalist Society, saying that the nuns "have been under unrelenting attack for the better part of a decade."[79]

What were the "attacks" Trump and Alito mentioned? The five-blank form, which these nuns challenged as a burden on their religious freedom. Name, name, address, date, sign. *That* was a burden, they argued to judge after judge for nine years. The Supreme Court initially seemed set to rule on the form when Justice Scalia died and

Mitch McConnell refused to consider his legitimately name replacement, so the court punted.[80] Then the Trump administration killed the notification requirement and automatically exempted any religious organization, or even an organization that had a "moral" objection to providing health care to employees. The careful ACA compromise was sabotaged, and perhaps 126,000 people lost contraceptive coverage when the Supreme Court upheld the changes in 2020.[81] Ruth Bader Ginsburg and Sonia Sotomayor began their dissent by reasserting Line #2 and then wrote, "Today, for the first time, the Court casts totally aside countervailing rights and interests in its zeal to secure religious rights to the nth degree."[82]

The nuns argued a five-blank form was a substantial burden on their religion. Compare that to how courts have decided what constitutes a burden on the right to an abortion. In 1992, the Supreme Court upheld the right to an abortion, but said that the government could regulate it so long as there was no "undue burden" on the right. (At the time, Samuel Alito was an appellate judge on the court that heard that case before it got to the Supreme Court. He wrote a dissent that made him something of a star for the anti-abortion crowd.)[83]

An "undue burden" on the right to an abortion certainly sounds like a lower bar than a "substantial burden" on religious freedom, but judges have proven hypocritical. Forcing people to drive hundreds of miles to a clinic, often multiple times, because the others were shut down by deliberate overregulation; or forcing the patient to hear a legislature-prescribed sermon; or inflicting, as 27 states do,[84] medically unnecessary ultrasounds are not *undue* burdens on the rights of these patients, but nuns filling out five blanks on a form is supposedly a *substantial* burden on their religious freedom. The flagrant hypocrisy shows that many jurists aren't guided by legal principle.

Religion, or perhaps Christian nationalism, seemed more like the court's guiding principle for overturning *Roe v. Wade* and abolishing reproductive freedom. This became suddenly clear to many observers when, as this book went to press in May 2022, the draft opinion overturning *Roe* leaked. Journalist Eleanor Clift wrote "there's no more pretending that religion doesn't play a role," while Sarah Posner called it "the crowning achievement of a Christian nationalist movement," and Jennifer Rubin correctly observed that it is meant "to impose a particular set of Christian views on the entire country."[85]

Sixteen days before Ruth Bader Ginsburg died, the Supreme Court scheduled a conference on the case that ended the reproductive freedom of 170 million Americans. Ginsburg died on September 19, 2020, and the conference—set for September 29—that would decide whether the high court would hear this pivotal case was postponed. And then postponed again. It's easy to imagine that the justices were waiting to see what would happen with the election and any possible new justice before taking the case. After delaying and rescheduling more than twenty times, the Supreme Court accepted a case out of Mississippi orchestrated specifically to weaken *Roe v. Wade*.[86] The challenge was certain to succeed once Amy Coney Barrett replaced RBG. She proved pivotal in the fall of 2021, when the court allowed a Texas law that instituted mob rule over the womb to take effect, essentially banning all abortions in the state two weeks after a missed period and enforcing that rule with a bounty system and cash rewards of no less than $10,000.[87] Mississippi was so confident after Barrett's conformation that it actually overhauled its argument, making it more extreme. In its initial petition, Mississippi focused on restrictions on abortion before viability. But after Barrett was confirmed, Mississippi changed its substantive argument into an all-out assault on reproductive freedom as a concept and asked the court to overturn *Roe v Wade*.[88] Christian nationalist preacher and Trump acolyte Robert Jeffress discussed the case on Fox News, explaining "the deal": "We're gonna see now what the justices do and if they uphold their part of the deal."[89] Trump and McConnell put Barrett on the court, and the court finally ends *Roe*. That was the deal.

The draft opinion that consummated that deal and overturned *Roe* was what was leaked. Justice Alito authored the draft, which appeared to have the support of Justices Thomas, Gorsuch, Kavanaugh, and Barrett. Those five justices could make it the law of the land. This draft is extreme and absolutist, the language aggressive and abrasive. It's utterly uncompromising, while cutting broadly across much of our understanding of the law. It sought to overturn *Roe v. Wade*. But the end of *Roe* is also just the beginning.

The Crusaders won't be satisfied until abortion and contraception are outlawed across the United States. Alito's draft opinion paid lip service to the idea of returning these issues to the states and to the people. The court could have decided a case like this at virtually any time, but waited until after it had completely gutted the Voting Rights Act in *Shelby County* (2013) and *Brnovich* (2020) and after it had upheld partisan gerrymandering in *Rucho v. Common Cause* (2019). Those decisions protect the power of the conservative white Christians who would otherwise be subsumed in a demographic tide that would keep them out of office for good. The measures empower the shrinking demographic that's raging against the dying of its privilege—that wants to resurrect long dead bans on contraception (*Griswold v. Connecticut*, 1965) and gay marriage (*Obergefell v. Hodges*, 2015). That wants to criminalize being gay (*Lawrence v. Texas*, 2003). Alito's opinion reads like a hit list, with rights and decisions that have helped ensure equality for BIPOC, women, and LGBTQ people as the targets. The Crusaders will not stop until conservative white Christian men are a special, privileged class and everyone else sits in the second-class cars. In short, they want a Christian nation.

And that's also why they have targeted Line #3. Line #3 has prevented religious extremists from realizing their Christian nationalist dream and has been a major roadblock for opponents of reproductive rights because it forces them to talk about abortion in unfamiliar and secular terms. Alito didn't mention religion or religious freedom, but his draft opinion began and ended with religion. Some will disagree because Alito phrases it as "morality," but that's the point: he's forced to adopt euphemisms for imposing his conservative Christianity on us all.

For a brief, clear moment during the oral argument, Justice Sotomayor cut through all the pretense and asked Mississippi: "How is your interest anything but a religious view?"[90] The state fumbled for an answer. Like the Mississippi religious freedom law we saw earlier on, its abortion ban enshrines the beliefs of conservative Christians. So does Alito's draft opinion.

The draft shows us the America that Justice Alito and four other justices want. Even if it's diluted in the backlash to the leak or some behind the scenes horse trading, this is still the future they want. They

want their conservative strain of religious belief to trump the reproductive freedom of half the population.

It's a bleak future. The war on women is really about *con*ception,
not *contra*ception. They're coming for contraception, yes, but forced
conception lies at the end of bans on abortion and contraception.
Remember, Joyce Meyer Ministries said the quiet part out loud: contraceptives ensure that "women do not get pregnant unless . . . they
want to."[91] Instead, they'll get pregnant when the biblical god wants
them to or, more accurately, when old white men say that god wants
them to.

11

Religious Freedom Is Killing Us

(The Covid Cases)

"I will send a plague among you."

—The biblical god, Leviticus 26:25

"I'm covered in Jesus's blood," the Ohio churchgoer told CNN. "No," she wasn't worried about contracting Covid or infecting other people at the grocery store, Walmart, or Home Depot, all of which she admitted, on camera, to visiting. She wasn't worried, she said, while wearing her seat belt, because of "Jesus's blood."[1] Her interview went viral online. I don't know if she went viral in the other sense, but the governor said the virus spread "like wildfire" in Ohio churches.

The full clip shows another worshipper using the same language. "The blood of Jesus cures every disease," she said.[2] That sort of unanimity is no coincidence. The day CNN interviewed the churchgoers leaving Solid Rock Church in Lebanon, Ohio, Pastor Lawrence Bishop II preached "The Sickness and the Cure." Video shows church musicians encouraging the maskless worshippers to sing along: "Come on . . . open up your mouth." After twenty minutes of singing, they passed the collection plates, and Bishop asked the congregation to cheer and shout, to "raise the roof for the King of Kings. . . . Hallelujah for the blood of Jesus."[3]

The blood of Jesus was the message. Bishop mentioned the "blood" some thirty-six times in the fifty-two-minute sermon. He attacked the media and the health department: "Here's one message I have for the health department. None of us are sick. . . . We are covered in the blood of Jesus. . . . None of us are dying. None of us are on our deathbeds. I got news for ya, we not gonna be dying either. Because Psalm 91:7 said 'a thousand might fall at your side and ten thousand at your right hand, but it shall not come near you.' We got the blood of Jesus to cover us."[4]

His followers took the message to heart and regurgitated it on CNN. Bishop quoted Psalm 91:6 accurately and with proper context: "You will not fear . . . the pestilence that stalks in the darkness, nor the plague that destroys at midday," reads the verse. His biblical exegesis was accurate, but also deadly. And it was preached more widely than we realize.

Greg Locke, the preacher who burned my first book, *The Founding Myth*, with a blow torch, vowed early in the pandemic never to close Global Vision Bible Church and became more extreme as the pandemic wore on.[5] In one anti-masking tirade at Dunkin' Donuts, Locke screamed at staff, "I'm going to take these work boots, and I'm going to kick your teeth down your throat."[6] By July, Locke believed himself an American revolutionary, proclaiming "We will not shut down church services. We will not social distance at church. We will not require masks. . . . We will not bow. #IndependenceDay #NoMask."[7]

Locke eventually banned masks at his services and railed against vaccines. He encouraged his followers to join him on January 5, 2021, at a Trump rally in Washington, DC, on the eve of the January 6 insurrection. At the rally, Locke preached Christian nationalism and "thank[ed] God" for the Proud Boys, a group "that we can lock shields [with], and we can come shoulder-to-shoulder with . . . to fight, and if need be, lay down our life for this nation."[8]

Mainstream preachers joined in. Robert Jeffress of First Baptist Dallas supported Trump before the primaries and joined Trump's Evangelical Advisory Board alongside Paula White, James Dobson, and others.[9] In his Christian nationalist "Freedom Sunday" celebration, which Vice President Mike Pence and HUD Secretary Ben Carson attended on July 4, 2020, Jeffress claimed that sin was more lethal than Covid: "See, the problem is we have all inherited a virus, Dr. Carson, a virus that is even more deadly than the coronavirus. It's the virus of sin; we're all born with that virus."[10] The church had an outbreak just before the MAGA service,[11] and it's never been explained what, if any, spread may have resulted from the event. One expert from Johns Hopkins called the church's coronavirus response "appalling."[12]

This theology, preached in too many American churches, was best summed up by a street preacher as Covid first pummeled the supply chain: "You need Jesus more than you need toilet paper! You can clean your butt, but who's gonna clean your sin? Toilet paper can't wash away your sins."[13] These churches believe that they're more important than grocery stores or hospitals because sin is an illness that condemns one to an eternity of hell. Sure, doctors and nurses are on the front lines fighting Covid, but have they considered saving souls? This goes to the heart of these churches' existence. They believe they are more important—more essential—than everything else.

That belief, that "essential" label, would reshape religious freedom law.

THE CORONAVIRUS SEEMS TO HAUNT CHURCHES. Worship services are actually designed to be super-spreader events—to spread the religion, spread the word, spread the good news—but the air that carries those words also carries suspended, virus-laden droplets. When the coronavirus was searching for a foothold in the United States, churches provided. By April 1, the health board in Sacramento County, which is one of the twenty-five most populous counties in the country, traced *one-third of all coronavirus cases* to churches.[14] Bethany Slavic Missionary Church, a Pentecostal church at the geographic center of the county with a history of anti-gay rhetoric, was an epicenter of "more than six dozen confirmed cases" by early April 2020.[15]

"It spread like wildfire. Wildfire," said Ohio governor Mike DeWine, explaining how one worshipper infected 53 other people at his church (primary spread), some of whom spread the virus to at least 38 others (secondary spread), for a total of 91 known cases traced back to a single infected worshipper at a single service. Patient Zero infected one worshipper who brought the virus home and infected his thirty-one-year-old wife and four kids, ranging from one to eleven years old.[16] There were also several documented cases of tertiary spread, worshippers taking the virus home to family members who then spread it to coworkers.[17]

County health officials in Mecklenburg, North Carolina, tracked 12 deaths and 213 cases to a worship celebration at the United House of Prayer for All People, an evangelical Christian church that refers to its leaders as "Daddy."[18] That one cluster spread to perhaps seven other states, including California and New York. Overall, religious gatherings were responsible for at least 211 clusters across North Carolina, fueling nearly 3,000 cases (more than any other category except schools and meatpacking businesses) and 44 deaths (higher than everything except independent living facilities).[19]

This story was repeated endlessly, even after the vaccine was available. The Peoples Church in Salem, Oregon, sued the government over public health measures, and the pastor vowed to never stop holding in-person services. Months later, that pastor and his wife were hospitalized, and the church was the epicenter of one of the worst outbreaks in the state, infecting at least 87 people at a time when cases in the state were rapidly declining.[20]

In a pandemic, the choice to worship communally is not an individual choice. Worship can spread the virus to people who cross paths with that worshipper, and then people who encounter them. The choice can put immense pressure on the local health-care system, too, affecting not only other infected people or people who simply need help, but our frontline workers. It is a selfish choice with a widespread impact. That didn't concern the newest Supreme Court justice.

Amy Coney Barrett was a conservative Notre Dame professor when Trump made her an appeals court judge. Three years later she was on the Supreme Court, ready to aid the Crusade. Senator Feinstein was inelegant, but not wrong when she said the "dogma lives loudly within" Barrett. Barrett's personal religious beliefs matter, but not as much as her pattern of saying that Catholicism should take precedence when it collides with professional responsibilities.

When judicial nominees have said that their faith trumps their oath of office, senators must ask about those beliefs.[21] Plenty of Catholics agree.[22] In 1957, William Brennan was asked about his Catholicism during his Supreme Court confirmation hearing and gave an excellent answer: "I took my oath as unreservedly as you did . . . there isn't any obligation of our faith superior to that. . . . What shall control me is the oath that I took to support the Constitution and laws of the United States." *Of course* one can be religious and a judge. But when judges don that robe, they must be a judge first and set their personal religion aside—the Constitution comes first.[23] Barrett disagreed. She criticized Brennan's answer: "We do not defend this position as the proper response for a Catholic judge to take with respect to abortion or the death penalty." Barrett recommended that judges "conform their own behavior to the Church's standard" and declined later to repudiate this recommendation.[24]

That was the first red flag. Barrett also added her name to a Catholic anti-abortion group's 2006 letter that said, "It's time to put an end to the barbaric legacy of *Roe v. Wade* and restore laws that protect the lives of unborn children."[25] In 2015, she signed a letter from "Catholic women" to the "Synod Fathers in Christ" that expressed the authors' "fidelity to and gratitude for the doctrines of the Catholic Church, and our confidence in the Synod of Bishops as it strives to strengthen the Church's evangelizing mission."[26] The letter raised a number of topics Barrett will or has ruled on, including reproductive justice and LGBTQ equality. In 2006, Barrett told law students at the Notre Dame Law school commencement that a "legal career is but a means to an end . . . and that end is building the Kingdom of God."[27]

Barrett belongs to a charismatic Catholic group called People of Praise that takes the "Kingdom of God" language literally.[28] Former members call it "a cult."[29] The group labeled women "handmaids," including Barrett's mother, and teaches that "a married woman is . . . under her husband's authority. . . . He is, in fact, her personal pastoral head. Whatever she does requires at least his tacit approval."[30] Members take an oath, which the group calls a covenant (as in an unbreakable pact with god): "We agree to obey the direction of the Holy Spirit manifested in and through these ministries in full harmony with the church."[31]

Barrett's letters, articles, and speeches and her membership in a *Handmaid's Tale*–type order are a pattern that points to a belief about whether her fidelity to her order and religion trump her oath of office. That pattern was clear to any observer, and we know Leo was watching especially closely, as "the monitor of . . . ideological purity."[32]

Trump's reception for Barrett at the White House was as much a religious event as it was political. It also became a "super-spreader event," in the words of Dr. Anthony Fauci, and infected Trump himself. The Trump administration didn't require basic precautions like masks or contact tracing, though both would have been easy, given White House security.[33] Among the two hundred attendees were top Crusaders, including representatives from the Alliance Defending Freedom, the Becket Fund, First Liberty, Leo's network, and more.[34] Perhaps fifty people[35] tested positive as a result, including pastors,[36] Donald and Melania Trump,[37] and Senators Mike Lee and Thom Tillis, both of whom sat on the Senate Judiciary Committee and attended Barrett's hearings in person despite their infection. (Former Trump White House chief of staff Mark Meadows disclosed in his book, released in December 2021, that Trump tested positive shortly after the super-spreader event, leading some to wonder whether he was patient zero. Trump was hospitalized with Covid a week later.[38])

The Barrett super-spreader event marks a directional shift in American religious freedom law. Before Barrett, indeed for about at least a century before Barrett was on the court, there was little doubt that the government had broad powers to fight a pandemic, including in ways that may inconvenience people and curtail freedom. This is Line #2. Your religious freedom is not a license to violate the rights of others, including by spreading lethal viruses. In 1905, the Supreme Court upheld mandatory vaccines because "real liberty for all could not exist" if someone was allowed to act "regardless of the injury that may be done to others."[39] In 1944, the court explained that "the right to practice religion freely does not include liberty to expose the community or the child to communicable disease or the latter to ill health or death."[40] One federal judge summed up the centuries of law quite nicely by invoking a famous phrase used by Justice Robert Jackson in a 1949 First Amendment case: "The Constitution is not a suicide pact. The First Amendment may not be used to make it one."[41]

Even in the few months before Barrett, the court twice refused churches' attempts to declare themselves immune from public health measures meant to fight Covid. Both times, Roberts had been unwilling to agree with his fellow conservatives.[42] The four other conservatives—Thomas, Alito, Gorsuch, and Kavanaugh—were eager to give Christians weekly super-spreader passes. To the extent this evinced a rift between Roberts and the other conservatives, it was about how to implement the conservative agenda—about methodology, not ideology. Roberts wants slow change to preserve the legitimacy of the court because that is the only currency the court has. An unpopular court cannot enforce its opinions or stave off congressional interference, i.e., adding new seats to rebalance the court. Roberts wants to implement the conservative agenda incrementally, not so rapidly as to be self-defeating. The death of Ruth Bader Ginsburg and the imposition of Barrett tipped that balance, with five votes for rapid conservative change, not Roberts's incremental approach. (Interestingly, the five eager conservatives received an object lesson in Roberts's incrementalism when they badly bungled the Texas abortion law, SB 8, which instituted mob rule over the womb. The backlash to the court after it indefensibly allowed that law to go into effect seems to have taught Kavanaugh and Barrett the effectiveness in Roberts's politically savvy, incremental approach.)

The radical shift in American law was an unsigned midnight ruling on the eve of Thanksgiving on the court's shadow docket: a fifteen-paragraph, 5–4 decision in which Barrett flipped the court. Shadow docket cases aren't meant to alter substantive law, but simply to deal with emergency issues as established law dictates. The opinion came on, what was at the time, the peak of the worst seven-day average for new coronavirus cases, the fourth-worst day for Covid overall (183,000 new cases), and the worst single day for deaths since May 7, when the initial wave swept the country.[43] The Roman Catholic Diocese of Brooklyn and an orthodox Jewish organization, Agudath Israel of America, challenged a public health order, claiming it violated their religious freedom by discriminating against houses of worship.[44] The Crusaders were behind this attack, too. The diocese was represented by Rudy Giuliani's former deputy mayor, and Agudath by the Becket Fund. Other Crusaders brought and would bring many similar challenges.

The New York public health order that the Crusaders and Catholic Church challenged as a violation of religious freedom actually treated religious worship more favorably compared to similar events.

But for the newly remade Supreme Court, if *any* events or organizations were treated more favorably than churches, even if they had *no* risk factors or if people depended on them to survive, that differential treatment was discrimination. Remember, the dominant caste sees equality as hostility.

Discrimination is measured by looking at whether similar things receive equal treatment. Walking, biking, driving a car, driving a semitruck, and flying are all modes of transportation, but the government doesn't discriminate against pilots or truckers because they're regulated differently than pedestrians or drivers; the risk posed by each is different. And religious worship poses some unique risks of spreading Covid.

Sadly, many of the reasons people love church are the very things that help the virus spread. Everyone arrives and leaves church at basically the same time, filing in and out of the building in a scrum. Hugs, handshakes, and other welcome customs ignore social distancing.[45] Taking communion—it's right there in the name: communal, community, shared food and drink. Shared bathrooms, busy before and after the service. Singing and praying aloud. Often in older buildings built with no air flow or retrofitted ventilation systems. In such conditions, social distancing and masks are not enough. "Our churches have followed protocols—masks, go in one door and out the other, social distancing, and still people have tested positive," one Methodist bishop in Louisiana told the *New York Times*.[46]

So worship is not like going to the store for the food staples one needs to survive. Or even to the liquor store. Or dropping your car or bike off for repairs. Or visiting the bank for a quick transaction so you can afford to eat or pay rent. Or even visiting a lawyer to get a last will and testament drawn up during uncertain times. All comparisons that drew the justices' ire. In those scenarios, people are in and out in a matter of minutes, and they are moving about, not sitting in one shared, droplet-laden airspace. They come and go randomly, spread out over a sixteen- or even twenty-four-hour day and not in big crowds twice a day. Worship services are more like watching a movie or play in a theater, or attending an indoor sporting event or concert, or even a lecture.[47]

When the pandemic first hit, New York shut everything down. The "PAUSE" initiative ended every in-person gathering "of any size for any reason." Grocery stores, hospitals, and some other "essential" entities stayed open in-person with masking and social distancing. Churches—the buildings themselves—could remain open to the public, but no gatherings were permitted, even for worship.

This contained the spread. But as New York began to reopen, the virus took hold again, and New York shifted its strategy to focus on areas about to have an outbreak, instead of total shutdowns.[48] When a cluster of positive tests flared up, heightened restrictions immediately went into place for that geographic area (a red zone), and restrictions faded in progressive zones expanding from the center of the hotspot (orange and then yellow zones). This prevented the clusters from growing and spreading.

The goal was to shut down in-person contact in red zones entirely, except at the essential places. Restaurants were closed for in-person dining. Schools were immediately closed.[49] But churches were actually favored, allowed to open with occupancy limits of ten in red zones and twenty-five in orange, while comparable activities—plays, indoor sporting events, casinos, bowling alleys, movie theaters, gyms, and more—were closed completely in both zones. In-person gatherings in yellow zones were limited to twenty-five people, while houses of worship could fill up to 50 percent of maximum occupancy. So the Christian Cultural Center in Brooklyn, which can hold 13,000 people, could have had 6,500 worship in a yellow zone, compared to nonreligious gatherings limited to twenty-five people.

Churches were favored, but the five Covid justices decided that these favorable rules "strike at the very heart of the First Amendment's guarantee of religious liberty."[50] Their rationale was thin. The controlling opinion is short and irrational. More than anything else, churches, Crusaders, and the justices seemed offended that churches weren't labeled "essential."

"Some governors have deemed liquor stores and abortion clinics as essential but have left out churches and other houses of worship. It's not right. So I'm correcting this injustice and calling houses of worship essential," Trump complained from the podium in the White House briefing room. He then declared "houses of worship—churches, synagogue, and mosques—as essential places that provide *essential* services."[51] In 130 or so seconds, Trump said "essential" eight times.

The declaration had absolutely no legal effect, though the CDC issued slightly updated guidelines for houses of worship.[52] It was a quintessentially Trumpian move: bombast, repetition, and a trivial action added for later exaggeration. Like a mama bird feeding her chicks, Trump ground up the grievances of his base and regurgitated the mix back to them. The Crusaders cheered Trump for defending religious liberty.[53]

The court's midnight decision striking down New York's public health measure is disturbingly similar to Trump's pandering. Gorsuch's longer, concurring opinion reads like a man pissed that churches weren't labeled "essential," an emotion he manifested with scare quotes:

> Religious institutions have made plain that they stand ready, able, and willing to follow all the safety precautions required of "essential" businesses and perhaps more besides. The only explanation for treating religious places differently seems to be a judgment that what happens there just isn't as "essential" as what happens in secular spaces. Indeed, the Governor is remarkably frank about this: In his judgment laundry and liquor, travel and tools, are all "essential" while traditional religious exercises are not. That is exactly the kind of discrimination the First Amendment forbids.[54]

If the "essential" designation had been a different word, I wonder whether churches would have rebelled against public health measures. What if the label had been something boring like "infrastructure-related" and "infrastructure-unrelated"? Better yet, "basic" and "higher." Grocery stores and hospitals meet basic needs, and churches meet a higher need. Public policy, especially in an emergency like a pandemic, shouldn't have to worry about tone or offending religion.

This ought to be plainly stated: religion is not essential. People don't die if they stop worshipping. We need food, water, and air. We need clothing and shelter and medicine and an income to purchase these necessities. We don't need to worship a god in person, in a particular place, every week (especially, one would think, if that god is truly everywhere). It's nice to have community, religious or not, but its absence will not kill us (though in a pandemic, community might prove fatal). We crave explanations and certainty and community, things the religion can bring, even if falsely. But we don't *need* it.

The government is "downplaying the role that religion plays in the lives of Americans and suggesting it's more important to go to the gym than to go to church," said one Crusader spokesperson.[55] In the Ohio church that was covered in the blood of Jesus, Pastor Bishop praised proclamations by Florida and Texas governors that "church is considered an essential business"[56] and covetously noted that Home Depot and Planned Parenthood were open. In a way, the court was adopting this theology to interpret the law. That's a problem under Line #3, but the real problem here is Line #2.

The Ohio worshipper coated in the gore of her savior didn't just visit her church. She was all over town. Churches spread the virus around the community. Churches weren't asking the Supreme Court for a right to worship; they were asking for a right to risk everyone's health and safety. They're demanding a right to put more strain on doctors, nurses, and frontline workers—to burden a hospital and medical system at maximum capacity. They're wielding religious freedom not just to violate the rights of another citizen, but to claim supremacy over everyone. My god says this, so you have to die. Functionally, this is little different than the human sacrifice or Jesus-take-the-wheel examples. Worse, as many more could die from the reckless believer. This is why we have Line #2.

The court was not blind to this problem, so it simply rewrote reality. The state showed over and over that public health was threatened without these measures, and our highest court chose to ignore that impact:

> It has not been shown that granting the applications will harm the public. As noted, the State has not claimed that attendance at the

applicants' services has resulted in the spread of the disease. And the State has not shown that public health would be imperiled if less restrictive measures were imposed.[57]

This is a lie. Gorsuch doubled down in his concurrence: "No apparent reason exists why people may not gather, subject to identical restrictions, in churches or synagogues." We know the virus rampages through religious services, and the justices were given countless examples and studies showing this, but they ripped apart Line #2 anyway. And they lied to do it.

Americans died because of this opinion. Amy Coney Barrett, Clarence Thomas, Samuel Alito, Neil Gorsuch, and Brett Kavanaugh rewrote religious freedom and helped spread a lethal virus. Their lawless opinion killed Americans. The decision emboldened Crusaders and further politicized public health measures, killing even more. But the court wasn't done.

IN FEBRUARY 2021, THREE MONTHS AFTER THE COURT struck down New York's public health orders, the first case of the more deadly, more transmissible Delta variant was detected. On Friday, February 5, in a pair of shadow docket decisions issued near midnight, the court struck down some of California's public health measures.[58] But neither the court nor the virus were done. By April, Covid cases were rising again, and though down from its mid-January high, the virus was raging.[59] California had thousands of cases and a hundred deaths daily. In another midnight ruling on the shadow docket, the five Covid justices again rewrote the First Amendment in an unsigned, nine-paragraph opinion.[60]

California had implemented a responsive rule meant to maximize freedom and limit virus transmission by adjusting public health measures according to infection rates.

Depending on infection rates, one of four tiers of policies applied to an area. In-home gatherings were either banned or limited to a percentage of capacity or, for private homes, limited to three households. Importantly, this applied to all gatherings in private homes, whatever their purpose. Secular gathering in a private home? Three households.

Religious gathering in a private home? Three households. Everyone was treated equally.

But to Crusaders, equality is persecution. A pastor in Santa Clara had been meeting once a week with eight to ten people for an in-home bible study. He challenged the measure because studying the bible in person is more important than other people's lives. A woman who hosted a rotating bible study with six couples every two weeks also challenged the rule. Both claimed the rule violated their religious freedom.

A three-judge panel—two W. appointees and a Trump appointee—held 2–1 that the rule was valid because it treated religion fairly and equally.[61] But Christian privilege, not equality, is the goal for the Covid justices. They went out of their way to decide this case when they didn't need to. By the time it got to the Supreme Court, even on the expedited shadow docket, California had announced a new rule that would take effect in a few days and would allow these bible studies. Perhaps before their next scheduled meetings.

But this court *wants* to decide these cases. So, ignoring procedure and judicial principle, they jumped in with a midnight ruling just six days (five, really, given how late the decision dropped) before the new rule took effect.

The decision is even thinner than the New York opinion. But still, it rewrote the law to privilege Christians. The opinion boils down to two things. First, if there is an exemption anywhere in any law for anything, then Christians also get an exemption. Second, this first rule holds true even if the exemption has nothing to do with religion.

The opinion means that laws must be perfectly universal if the court is to consider them nondiscriminatory toward Christians. Maybe the law exempts students with a disability—well, now believers get exemption from education rules. Maybe there's an exemption in pharmaceutical law based on, say, regional differences in a disease—well, now pharmacists can deny women birth control. Let's say Title VII of the Civil Rights Act, which prohibits employment discrimination based on race, color, and religion, exempts certain businesses from the law because of their size. (It does.) Then Christians also get exemptions from the Civil Rights Act, meaning employment discrimination is now legal for Hobby Lobby, MyPillow, or any other business that says, "God told me to."

If this sounds crazy to you, it is. The idea that a single exemption to any law necessitates every religious exemption to that same law has been roundly rejected in the legal academy as: "unprincipled and bizarre," an "untenable proposition that would make every religious objector 'a law unto himself,'" "an almost insurmountable barrier to regulation," and "intellectually incoherent," among other things.[62] It's impossible to overstate this shift in our law. Professor Jim Oleske, an expert in this area, called this the "most important free exercise decision since 1990," meaning since the drug counselor case.[63]

Steven Vladeck, a law professor and leading expert on the court's use of the shadow docket, noted at the time that this April 2021 "ruling was the seventh time since October [2020] that the justices have issued an emergency injunction—all of which have blocked Covid restrictions in blue states on religious exercise grounds. Before these rulings, the court had gone five years without issuing a single injunction pending appeal."[64] In four years, Trump's administration made forty-one requests on the shadow docket and won twenty-eight. Only eight requests were filed in the sixteen previous years spanning the two terms of both George W. Bush and Barack Obama, and they only won four.[65] By the end of Trump's term, the shadow docket looked like collusion between Trump justices and the Trump administration to advance the Crusade. Of all the entities that brought shadow docket cases, only two groups won: the Trump administration and churches.[66] Between August 2020 and July 2021, the court sided with ten out of ten churches challenging public health measures amid the coronavirus pandemic.[67] This perfectly encapsulates the court placing religious freedom at the top of a hierarchy of rights. Christianity wins; everyone else loses.

In these Covid cases, the court created the hierarchy of rights. Religious freedom is the most important right, sitting atop the other rights and the rights of others. Whatever the law gives to anyone, it must also give to every religious claimant. Christians are special and, yes, favored, but in elevating Christianity to a special, first class, the Supreme Court has made other Americans second-class citizens.

The court changed law that has been settled for centuries. The Constitution didn't change, only the court's personnel did. This is why they stole seats and packed the court. Not to put impartial jurists on the bench, but partisan activists.[68] This was the point.

12

Deus Vult Revisited

(*American Legion v. American Humanist Association,* the Bladensburg Cross Case)

"A mammoth cross, a likeness of the Cross of Calvary,
as described in the Bible, will be built at the
beginning of the highway at Bladensburg."
—*Washington Times*, May 25, 1919[1]

The Crusade was launched with a *Deus vult* and a Christian cross in the middle of the desert. Nine years later, the justices advanced the Crusade by rewriting the First Amendment and obliterating Line #3 in a case involving a Christian cross just five miles down the road from the Supreme Court.

The gray-and-salmon concrete is discolored and cracked. Rust, exposed rebar, and a protective tarp underscore decades of neglect.[2] On the banks of the Anacostia River in Bladensburg, Maryland, in the middle of a traffic island—an almond-shaped plot of land bounded by three busy, two-lane roads—the forty-foot-tall Christian cross is crumbling.

From above, the intersection's arcing, crisscrossing, one-way roads and stoplights look like a triangular Celtic knot, with the cross marooned, alone, and unreachable on one of the islands. The closest parking lot is the pawn shop. Pedestrians must then risk at least two busy lanes, littered with cars and garbage. No sidewalk or crosswalk bridges the rivers of traffic to the island that appears to have been claimed for Christ. Few people visit the island, let alone read the explanatory plaques listing forty-nine individuals who died in World War I. Plaques obscured by untended, overgrown bushes.[3]

The cross dominates the space, towering above the streetlights and signs. An American flag on a diminutive pole shrinks in the cross's shadow, a submissive afterthought. A few other memorials are scattered around—not within—the busy intersection. The cross stands alone. Inaccessible, yet conspicuous. Ensuring that contact with the cross is fleeting, but the impression is indelible: *This is Christian territory.*[4]

The cross has been Christian since fundraising began in 1918. "Trusting in God," donors signed a "contribution" pledge that highlighted "the way of godliness, justice, and liberty," and concluded, "With our motto, 'One God, One Country, and One Flag,' we contribute to this memorial cross."[5] One local report detailed a "mammoth cross, a likeness of the Cross of Calvary, as described in the Bible."[6] But interest in the project ended with the war. The American Legion took over the failed project *and the land.*[7] This simple fact is likely why the cross wasn't viewed as constitutionally problematic when it was finally built (three years after the transfer) and why it was unchallenged. Erecting a massive Christian cross on *private* property doesn't violate Line #3.

The cross was dedicated in 1925 while the cross and land still belonged to the Legion. The ceremony included only Christian prayers, Christian chaplains, and Christian songs—one a hymn that tells of a cross raising the singers "nearer, my God, to thee." The Daughters of the Confederacy joined the parade, and one state representative said the cross is "symbolic of Calvary." For a time, the Legion organized regular Christian prayers, memorial services, and even Sunday worship services at the cross. These faded with time as traffic spread around the island.[8]

Though there's some disagreement about the timeline, the cross became a Line #3 problem in 1961 when the American Legion disclaimed all interest in the land and it was unequivocally back under state control.[9] Additional Line #3 problems arose in 1985, when the government taxed citizens and spent $100,000 partially rehabilitating the cross (about $250,000 today).[10] The government also claimed, without much evidence, that it "rededicated"[11] the cross in 1985, though the alleged rededication featured Christian prayer.[12] By 2001, the

Christian cross supposedly represented *all* Americans who sacrificed their lives for this country.

In 2011, the American Humanist Association, on behalf of local citizens, explained the Line #3 problems to the state commission that manages the intersection and asked for a solution.[13] The year before this complaint, the Ninth Circuit declared a 43-foot cross that dominates a San Diego hilltop unconstitutional under Line #3.[14] The same thing happened with 12-foot-tall roadside crosses along Utah highways that the Tenth Circuit declared unconstitutional over the objections of a judge named Neil Gorsuch.[15] The decisions in these cases, which had been in court for years, came just after the Roberts Court called for the Crusade, but before it had gathered momentum. The Supreme Court decided AHA's challenge to the cross in 2019, long after the Crusade was underway.

A government display of a Christian cross is not about the free exercise of religion. Our government has no religion to exercise because of Line #3. The attack on state/church separation is crucial to the Crusade's success. "Line #3 doesn't apply to *us*" is a core Crusader argument. So the Crusaders framed this as a religious freedom fight.[16] For instance, one senior contributor at *The Federalist* argued that "continued acts of iconoclasm would erode religious freedom."[17] This is the dominant caste seeing equality and loss of unconstitutional privilege as a threat. More importantly, Crusaders are trying to weaponize religious freedom in a way that allows them to use the machinery of the state to promote Christianity. That's the unspoken, underlying question in the case: Does religious freedom include the right to use government power to promote and impose that religion on others? The court said yes.

BEFORE THE ROBERTS COURT'S *Deus vult* almost right up until this case was filed, no final decision in any federal court had allowed the government to maintain and display a Christian cross on government land. (About six months after this case was filed, the Second Circuit upheld the display of the "9/11 cross." The wisdom of that legal challenge aside, I'm mystified by the reverence for this particular cross, which consists of the intersection of two I beams. There must have been literally thousands of such intersections in the Trade Center. This is how skyscrapers are built. To find one intact seems thoroughly unremarkable. But humans are pattern-seeking animals with a penchant for spotting Jesus in toast and other edibles, so perhaps the fault lies with me.) The federal appeals court examining this cross stuck to this just precedent holding that "the display and maintenance of the Cross violates" the First Amendment.[18]

The Bladensburg cross was the perfect case for Crusaders to change that precedent. It was old. It was undoubtedly Christian, but they could argue that it represented everyone. There were questions about private ownership and government land. Most importantly, it was accessible to the Washington, DC, media, ensuring far more coverage of the case than a cross in the middle of the desert. Nina Totenberg of NPR drove to the cross for a report.[19] More media meant more Christian outrage at the attempt to equalize their privilege. The cross is so close to the court that it's easy to imagine the justices detouring on their commute to take a look, an opportunity rarely afforded them in their cases.

By the time the case reached the Supreme Court, many veterans and veterans groups opposed the cross. To them, the cross embodied the inherent inequality in letting a violation of Line #3 stand. For instance, the Jewish War Veterans of the United States of America, the oldest active national veterans organization in America, explained to the court that at least some of the 2,000 Jewish Marylanders who served in World War I and some of the 3,500 Jews who died in that war might have come from the Bladensburg area, and that the cross is "a memorial to religious-based exclusion."[20]

The Freedom From Religion Foundation and other secular organizations—including a secular military group—argued that there are many atheists in foxholes.[21] One 2019 report showed that there are more atheists and agnostics on active duty in the military than Jews, Muslims, and Mormons combined, and that the "nones" were the second largest "sect" in the military, ahead of Catholics and Protestants, but after "nondenominational" Christians.[22] One quarter of FFRF's 35,000+ members are active-duty military or veterans. This monument omits or denigrates their service and sacrifice.

Sixteen high-ranking veterans and military officials, including generals with impressive résumés (one had a Nobel Peace Prize) argued that the cross is exclusionary and that dividing soldiers along religious lines is a threat to national security because it threatens unit cohesion: "Religious preference, harassment, and discrimination are examples of the kinds of divisiveness that can threaten military functions, and . . . nothing is more important to military functioning than internal cohesion."[23]

The problem with these arguments is that the Crusaders are gunning for Christian supremacy and privilege. They *want* a weapon to enforce their dominant status. Excluding non-Christians is precisely what the Crusaders sought.

Pulling the strings on the other side was the same Crusader that was involved in the 2010 cross case, the case that precipitated this Crusade: First Liberty Institute.

First Liberty Institute has had many names—First Liberty, Liberty Institute, Liberty Legal Institute—but it's Kelly Shackleford's child.[24] In 2001, the organization brought in $565,000.[25] Back then Liberty Legal Institute was the legal arm of the Free Market Foundation, an affiliate of Focus on the Family, James Dobson's outfit. The Institute gobbled up its mother—IRS number and all.[26] The 2019 financials show an income of more than $14 million.[27]

In churches around the country, Shackleford often tells a less-than-humble creation story.[28] The Institute aims to "promote Judeo-Christian values"[29] and fearmongers about "wealthy institutions . . . spending enormous sums of money per year to destroy your religious liberty and scrub references to God from the public square."[30] Shackleford used the cross in the Mojave Desert case in 2010 to shed other conservative causes, not because he cared less for those, but because weaponizing religious liberty has become the key to unlocking them all.

The Institute wants Christian supremacy. It's fought to keep evolution *out* of public schools, and bible classes, Jesus portraits, and school-imposed prayer *in* public schools.[31] Like other Crusaders, the Institute wraps this supremacy in religious freedom, which the average American understands as equality. To build the perception that it's fighting for equality rather than supremacy, the Institute seeks stories that it can blow out of proportion and bend into the Christian persecution narrative. It delays and drags out cases for years to continue to fundraise and push the persecution message, like the praying football coach mentioned on page 55 in chapter 4.[32] One federal appellate judge, a George W. Bush appointee who was confirmed 93–0 in the Senate, wrote that the Institute had "spun" a "siren song of a deceitful narrative of this case" and that the Institute's claims that the coach was being persecuted by the school district for saying silent private prayers by himself "is false."[33] Such an opinion would make an honest lawyer hide in shame, but the Institute appealed to the Supreme Court and doubled down on the "deceitful narrative" of "brief, quiet prayer by himself."[34] And why not? The conservative justices have proven themselves amenable to alternative facts. The coach even up and moved to Florida in March 2020, right in the middle of litigation and a full eighteen months before the Institute asked the Supreme Court to take up the case.[35] Because the Institute and coach asked for limited relief that doesn't include damages, his move mooted the case, and the Institute had a duty to inform the courts that the case was moot.[36] The Institute did no such thing, and the move was only discovered after the Supreme Court agreed to hear the case.

THE COURT ALLOWED THE CROSS TO STAND BY A 7–2 VOTE. Only Justices Ginsburg and Sotomayor got it right. Justice Alito wrote the main opinion. Though seven justices voted to uphold the cross, there was mass disagreement about why, with six different opinions.

Surprising many, Justices Breyer and Kagan, both Jewish, concurred in the result and upheld the cross. Kagan's vote ought not to have surprised; nine years earlier, as solicitor general she defended the Mojave cross, the cross that launched the Crusade.[37] Breyer wrote their opinion, and he argued that the forty-foot-tall Christian cross "cannot reasonably be understood as a government effort to favor a particular religious sect or to promote religion over Nonreligion."[38] It cannot reasonably be understood as anything else. Breyer also argued that there's "no single formula" for determining when a government action crosses Line #3. Breyer prefers to decide each case based on feel and perception, then reverse-engineer to that result. He's proved this repeatedly, most notably with the dual Ten Commandments cases in 2005, his version of Solomonic wisdom and splitting the baby.

The conservative justices disagreed vigorously about what new standard should replace Line #3. A fruitless, shortsighted disagreement because Line #3 is the only standard that works, something humanity discovered after centuries of oppression and bloodshed, and which became obvious at oral argument.

I was in the packed courtroom for that argument. This was my first time seeing Kavanaugh on the high bench, and it was jarring. A man credibly accused before the nation's highest deliberative body of assaulting a woman calmly questioned a young female attorney with that same entitlement he showed in his hearing, if not the rage and threats ("the whole country will reap the whirlwind"). Another man credibly accused of sexual harassment, Thomas, sat a few seats away, manifestly uninterested.

As I waited in line with the other members of the Supreme Court bar, a few Institute lawyers were gleefully and loudly chatting about the New Jersey church repair case I was litigating (see chapter 13, pages 195–96) and how it would "rip open" government coffers for churches. During the oral argument, the Institute suggested a standard that would strike down a government act that coerces or "prohibits tangible interference with religious liberty." When pressed by Ginsburg for an example of something that would violate this proposed coercion standard, the Institute said, taxing citizens three pence to pay preachers. And yet, a few months later in the Montana case, the Institute argued for precisely this kind of coercion, saying the state *must* tax citizens to fund religious schools (see chapter 14).[39]

Under more questioning about this new coercion standard, the Institute's lawyer copped to another long-standing constitutional violation, one the court has relied on to ignore Line #3. "'In God we trust,' certainly promotes religion, endorses religion, no question about it," the Institute lawyer said.[40] He then tried to connect that promotion and endorsement to religious freedom: "It's not an effort to proselytize. The free exercise—" But Justice Kagan interrupted him with questions about whether "In Jesus Christ we trust" would be coercive. His responses were an indistinct mess. This was a terrible argument delivered by an experienced lawyer, Michael Carvin, a partner from Jones Day, the world's fifth-largest law firm, who spent thirty-five years at the Department of Justice and had argued ten Supreme Court cases by that time. Carvin had an impossible task. The problem is, there's no way to draw the lines the Institute wanted because Line #3 already includes coercion. Any time the government places the might of We the People behind a religious question or a religious issue, it is inherently coercive. It divides people along religious lines, alienating some, favoring others, and coerces all of the people into adopting and endorsing a religious message with which they may or may not agree. A once-personal religious issue is now made relevant to one's civic standing. The weight of We the People bearing down on one citizen with a religious message is, and can only be, coercive.

The Institute concluded its oral argument with a final desperate point that seemed directed at Alito: hostility. "If you ban sectarian symbols, then you are necessarily banning all religious symbols, which evinces hostility" that conflicts with religious freedom. Of course, the court isn't going to ban religious symbols. Nobody asked for that, and the people and everyone on both sides of this case, myself included, would condemn the government for doing so.

Since it was the Crusaders' final point, we should ask, what's the worst that would have happened if the court had done the right thing and declared this cross unconstitutional? A crumbling, neglected cross would have needed a new home. The town and the American Legion had failed to maintain the cross, so it may not have survived the move, but it wasn't going to survive without another massive infusion of government cash anyway. (Another $100,000 has been budgeted.[41]) In its place, the government could put up a war memorial that actually honors all our heroes, not just Christians. Individual crosses would still appear as individual grave markers when Christian veterans and service members chose them from the seventy possibilities. But enormous Christian crosses that the government chooses to represent the sacrifice of Jewish, Hindu, Sikh, Muslim, atheists, agnostics, nonreligious, and every other non-Christian soldier would have been as impermissible as they are tasteless and exclusionary.

Unfortunately, Alito and six other justices chose Christian supremacy and justified it with hypocrisy, hostility, and history.

1. Hypocrisy

The court said that this massive Christian cross, "symbolic of Calvary," was a secular symbol. The Institute, founded to "promote Judeo-Christian values," argued that this wasn't a Christian cross, but a "cross-shaped memorial."[42] For principled believers who hold their faith above political power, this is blasphemy. The Baptist Joint Committee's brief argued as much, that a court declaring a Christian cross to be a secular monument is tantamount to the government "desacraliz[ing] the most sacred symbol of Christianity."[43] Line #3 would normally prevent this, but the opinion also obliterates Line #3. Imagine for a moment if the courts had declared that John 3:16 or praying the rosary were secular. The Crusaders would have had a collective stroke, and rightfully so.

But the Crusaders argued this "secular symbol" with a wink and a nod. Courts have upheld other religious establishments in this manner, including "In God We Trust" as a motto and "under God" in the pledge, which are no longer religious because "any religious freight the words may have been meant to carry originally has long since been lost."[44] These have "lost through rote repetition any significant religious content."[45] The Institute actually admitted this hypocrisy during oral argument—"In God we Trust certainly promotes religion, endorses religion, no question about it."

Everyone knew the cross was *the* symbol of Christianity. But those who professed to be the most devout were willing to lie so that the cross could remain. This cross isn't a monument to fallen soldiers; it's a monument to Christian hypocrisy.

A second aspect of this hypocrisy is that, for Alito, a Christian monument built of concrete and cast in bronze can change meanings if the shift morphs a constitutional violation into something constitutionally permissible. But later, the justices would take the opposite stance and strike down a founding American principle—not taxing citizens to build churches or teach religion—as bigoted from the beginning, even though they clearly are not now (see chapter 14). Founding American principles guaranteeing religious freedom are forever bigoted, while Christian monuments become secular.

2. Hostility

Alito returned to his favorite religious freedom argument: hostility. He invoked the French Reign of Terror to describe Line #3, used loaded language like "scrubbing," "militant . . . regimes," "aggressively hostile." Alito declared that enforcing the Constitution—his job—is hostile to religious freedom, "A government that roams the land, tearing down monuments with religious symbolism and scrubbing away any reference to the divine will strike many as aggressively hostile to religion. Militantly secular regimes have carried out such projects in the past."[46] Again, we see the dominant caste's fear of equality manifested as accusations of hostility and persecution.

If Alito is truly afraid of a tyrannical majority using the government to impose their anti-religion on religious citizens, we have a ward against such fears: Line #3, which he shelved in this case. Instead, Alito held that if a government-maintained religious symbol sits on government property long enough, it attains "familiarity and historical significance" in the "local community."[47] Once it passes some vague temporal milestone, removing the symbol—that is, correcting a constitutional violation—"may evidence hostility to religion."

Importantly, *Alito's hostility argument admits that the cross is unconstitutional*. If removing the cross is hostile to religion, then displaying the cross promotes religion. By claiming religious hostility, Alito is admitting that the cross is religious, not secular, refuting his first argument. It's a fatal catch-22 that none of these justices addressed.

Alito's argument is also inherently unjust and deeply dangerous. He excuses a towering violation because curing it would be hostile to the violator: "You broke the rules. But enforcing the rules against you would be hostile to you, so you get away with it." Alito incentivized rule-breaking. This is almost exactly what the court held in the gay wedding cake case (see chapter 5). And in the follow-up case in Philadelphia (see chapter 16).

Imagine where we would be if the court always took this approach with other constitutional amendments:

"Sorry, ladies, enforcing your right to vote under the Nineteenth Amendment would seem hostile to men who prefer the 'familiarity' of male politicians."

"Segregation has attained 'familiarity and historical significance' in the 'local community'; to cure it now just because it violates the Equal Protection Clause might appear hostile to white people."

This is as ridiculous as it is dangerous.

Alito summed up his fearmongering and hostility at oral argument with a dramatic hypothetical about all the other government crosses: "assuming for the sake of argument . . . we say you got to take down all of the crosses, what message does that send when people see that on TV, they see crosses all over the country being knocked down?" The hypothetical drove Alito, Gorsuch, and Breyer to distraction, spending nearly a quarter of the challengers' time on that question alone—"if you win, tear them down," said Breyer. But for that matter, what message does women voting send? Or different races going to the same school? It sends a message of equality, not supremacy. So, too, here.

The message would be that the Constitution comes first. That our government does not belong to one religion or to the Christians, but to We the People. That our government cannot divide people by religion. It cannot exclude non-Christians who fought and died for their country. It cannot honor only those who are of the "right" religion. The message it would send is that a secular government is the only true guarantee for religious freedom. Perhaps most importantly, it would tell this country that rule of law is supreme.

If you disagree with my framing of this movement as a Crusade, this case leaves you with very little. At best, you're left with a cowardly court. Afraid that Americans might be upset with the court or even think it hostile for upholding the Constitution, the court failed to uphold the Constitution. At best, seven justices were afraid to order the cross removed. That fear, in a nation with a church on practically every other street corner and with crosses dominating the landscape, is cowardly. Or it's something more deliberate.

3. History

Alito carefully curated a few moments from American history to justify his opinion and the cross. He elevated bad history over legal principle. This revisionist history was intended to show that America has always been a Christian nation. This is precisely why I wrote *The Founding Myth*. Alito's historical missteps are corrected in that book. I won't recapitulate all those arguments here, but two are worth highlighting because they are so bad and thoroughly debunked that it helps show the dishonesty of Alito's opinion.

He claimed that "the Ten Commandments . . . have historical significance as one of the foundations of our legal system." Chapters 13–22 of *The Founding Myth* debunk this. Alito also wrote about how "religion and morality" were mentioned in George Washington's Farewell Address and the Northwest Ordinance. This is such a common myth I debunked it in chapter 2. The quoted language actually proves that the founders did *not* turn to religious principles when crafting our Constitution, contradicting Alito's invocation of the history. None of Alito's poor history is worthy of a Supreme Court opinion. But distorted history is central to the Crusade.

I'm trying to avoid legalese in this book, but this case requires a short discussion of the *Lemon* test because the court threw out five decades of precedent. The *Lemon* test is named after the landmark decision in *Lemon v. Kurtzman* in 1971 (see also page 220). The court surveyed all the Line #3 cases it had decided and synthesized a simple three-part test to determine whether the government action crossed that line. Does the challenged government action: (1) have a secular purpose, (2) have a primary effect that neither advances nor inhibits religion, and (3) foster excessive government entanglement with religion? If the government action fails any one of these three prongs, it violates the Constitution. That's the *Lemon* test.

This test was strong precedent, older than *Roe v. Wade*, and issued in an 8–1 decision built on all the court's earlier cases. But because the

Lemon test enforced Line #3, it was a barrier to the Crusade and under siege for years. In this opinion, the court crucified the *Lemon* test on the Bladensburg cross.[48]

THE COURT DEFENDED A SYMBOL OF, AND OPENLY ADVANCED, Christian supremacy. Alito laid out a road map to preserve these monuments to Christianity's cultural dominance and privilege: "As our society becomes more and more religiously diverse, a community may preserve such monuments, symbols, and practices for the sake of their historical significance or their place in a common cultural heritage." The subtext is clear: as Christians lose their majority and their privilege, fallacious claims of hostility and history will allow them to preserve their privilege, even unconstitutional privilege.

For a court that loves unearthing hostility toward Christians, it again missed the same hostility against non-Christians. The Christian cross cannot—does not—represent Jews, Hindus, Muslims, Buddhists, Sikhs, atheists, agnostics, pagans, non-Christians, and even Christians who interpret the bible differently. Those service people are not simply ignored, but blacklisted. What could be more hostile than honoring those who are of the correct religion, and excluding everyone else?

13

Targeting Children, Taxing Everyone

(*Trinity Lutheran Church v. Comer*)

"When a Religion is good, I conceive that it will support itself; and,
when it cannot support itself, and God does not take care to support,
so that its Professors are oblig'd to call for the help of the Civil Power
it is a sign, I apprehend, of its being a bad one."[1]

—Benjamin Franklin

American Christianity isn't meekly accepting its demographic decline. It spends a lot of time and money trying to keep children in the faith. Or convert them. This is a deliberate strategy, rather like Big Tobacco: get 'em while they're young.

The "Christian number cruncher" George Barna is an evangelical, a well-known pollster, and author of a book about evangelizing children entitled *Transforming Children into Spiritual Champions: Why Children Should Be Your Church's #1 Priority*.[2] After looking at the data and market research, Barna shifted his ministry from adults to children because "if people do not embrace Jesus Christ as their Savior before they reach their teenage years, the chance of their doing so at all is slim."[3]

There are entire ministries that target children in the "4/14 window." According to some studies these evangelizers treat as gospel, perhaps 85 percent of people select their lifelong religion between the ages of four and fourteen. This is "[God's] battle for the little ones," wrote Luis Bush, one of the top missionary strategists. Public schools present a serious problem for the strategy, explains Bush: "Secular education does not enlighten, rather it dims one's grasp of the 'real reality' rooted in the truth of scripture."[4]

They target children in this conceptual window with precision. "The missionaries I encountered were aiming at little kids, and they seemed to agree that public schools were where the action is,"[5] wrote Katherine Stewart, who investigated and exposed the child evangelism movement in her book *The Good News Club*. Public schools are seen as a problem. Education and pluralism have long been viewed as the enemies of American Christianity, especially after public school desegregation.

The next three chapters explore how the Crusade blends with this long-running attack on public education, with religious freedom the chosen weapon and nexus between the two. The siege against our public schools had gained some ground, but the Crusade accelerated that march, beginning in 2017 with a Missouri ministry.

MANY CHURCHES AND SECTS HAVE CHILDCARE and school networks that help keep kids in the faith and win new converts. Trinity Lutheran Church in Columbia, Missouri, identified three "child ministries": Children's Sunday School, the Trinity Lutheran Child Learning Center, and the Good Shepherd Lutheran School.[6] From age two through eighth grade, kids could be kept in this "network of national Lutheran school's [*sic*] preparing children to be Christian citizens." The church is very clear and open: these are ministries to make and retain Christians.

The Child Learning Center "is a ministry of Trinity Lutheran Church."[7] Promotional images feature silhouettes of young children praying and appeared on the center's website, social media, the cover of the parent-teacher handbook, and a banner on the playground fence. A fence that was always gated and locked, according to Geoff Blackwell, an attorney who works at American Atheists and whose grandparents lived a block away. Only kids in the church daycare could ever access it. Blackwell told me, "The church didn't intend this to be a community benefit. Nobody was going to steal the equipment, they put the fence up to keep people out."[8]

This particular "ministry" served "young children ages 2½ years . . . through Pre-K" and "incorporates daily religion" and worship.[9] Church members receive priority enrollment and a discount, but this is a ministry and meant to proselytize: "The center also provides an opportunity for the congregation to witness the Gospel of the Lord Jesus Christ through the enrollment of non-member residents," explained the church.[10]

It was a rich mission field: 90 percent of the kids who attended the childcare ministry didn't attend the church.[11] The church used "preaching, teaching, worship, witness, service, and fellowship according to the Word of God" to carry out its mission "to make disciples," quoting Jesus's command to spread his gospel, known as the Great Commission in Matthew 28.[12]

This Christian ministry, dedicated to propagating this particular brand of Christianity, wanted state money. When the Missouri Department of Natural Resources wouldn't contribute to the ministry, the church sued.

Missouri DNR charged disposal fees to clean up nearly 20 million illegally dumped tires and recycle them into something useful, including rubberizing running tracks, walking trails, and playground surfaces. The point of the program is not actually to make playgrounds safer, but to get rid of the plague of tires, which are unsightly and a public health problem.[13] As part of this program, Missouri's DNR awarded grants of up to $30,000 to purchase recycled scrap tires to rubberize tracks, trails, and playgrounds. The program was successful, reusing 16 million scrap tires (nearly 9,000 tons) in its first decade.[14]

The program doled out taxpayer money for the "scrap tire material, installation (by vendor) and delivery costs only."[15] And there was never a shortage of grant applicants. The church wanted $20,000 of taxpayer funds to renovate its ministerial playground.[16] Taxing citizens to fund a ministry was one of the original problems Line #3 was meant to solve, so the church's request ran smack into a founding American principle.

The framers declared a new universal truth: that every citizen had a right to a secular government. Line #3. For the first time, secular law and civil government could not be employed to impose, advance, or fund religion. No more government-enforced tithing. The church couldn't tax citizens, and the government couldn't tax citizens on the churches' behalf. Instead, for the first time ever, churches were required to rely on voluntary support. This financial freedom is a crucial aspect of Line #3.

"Sinful and tyrannical"—that's how America's first religious freedom law described compelled financial support of churches. The Virginia Statute for Religious Freedom, written by Thomas Jefferson and shepherded through the legislature by James Madison, explains that "to compel a man to furnish contributions of money for the propagation of opinions which he disbelieves and abhors, is sinful and tyrannical" and "that even . . . forcing him to support this or that teacher of his own religious persuasion, is depriving him of the comfortable liberty" of making voluntary financial contributions.[17] Compelled support of religion is tyranny.

This compelled-support principle has been implemented in most state constitutions, often multiple times. There are differences in language, operation, strength, exceptions, etc., and scholars differentiate between the clauses accordingly. There are "no-funding clauses," "no-aid clauses," "compelled-support clauses," and others. Those finer points need not concern us, and I'll refer to these collectively as "compelled-support clauses" because that is primarily what they prevent—the government wielding its taxing power to compel support of religion.

The compelled-support principle is vital to ensure true religious freedom and is woven into Line #3. No citizen can have religious freedom when the government can force them to donate to a sect that promises them eternal torture if they happen to exercise that freedom. "Religion then of every man must be left to the conviction and conscience of every man," wrote James Madison, certainly not left to the taxing power of the state.[18] That power cannot be wielded to oblige Muslims to bankroll temples, or to compel Jews to subsidize Christian churches, or to force Christians to fund mosques. The compulsory support of a religion or god that is not your own is anathema to American principles.

This is the principle the crusading justices demolished—inverted, really—in the children's ministry case.

Missouri's constitution has three religious freedom clauses, including two compelled-support clauses, all of which enhance religious freedom with different specific guarantees that set the clear boundaries in

Line #3.[19] To comply with these clauses, applicants for the scrap-tire grants had to certify that they were "not owned or controlled by a church . . . and the grant would not directly aid any church,"[20] language that mirrored the constitutional language.

This church confessed that the learning center "is a ministry" in its application.[21] It was clear about this when it filed the lawsuit, too. "The Learning Center is a ministry of the Church and incorporates daily religion. . . . Through the Learning Center, the Church teaches a Christian worldview to children of members of the Church, as well as children of non-member[s]. . . . The Church has a sincere religious belief to be associated with the Learning Center and to use it to teach the Gospel to children of its members, as well to bring the Gospel message to non-members."[22] The church didn't hide the fact that this was a ministry, but the Supreme Court later would.

Since the church wanted that state to violate Line #3, Missouri's DNR rejected the church's grant.

The Crusaders must have rejoiced. This was the perfect case for Crusaders and the court to break Line #3 and its compelled-support principle. They could tell the world that this was about playgrounds, skinned knees, and keeping children safe, not overturning a founding American principle. The Alliance Defending Freedom took this case for its public relations value and baptized it "The Playground Case."[23] NPR, PBS, and reputable media adopted the name.[24] The Crusade was now camouflaged with kids' skinned knees.

On the day of oral argument, just three days after Easter, the Crusaders put on a show in front of the Supreme Court.[25] In the plaza, they set up a red Little Tikes playground slide. Mylar balloons spelled out "Fair Play."[26] The lectern had a bright, safety-yellow sign that read, "Every Child's Safety Matters." #FairPlay hashtags were everywhere. Children in yellow "#FairPlay" hats held "#FairPlay" signs featuring kids on playgrounds. Other children held signs that said, "Keep Me Safe Too! #FairPlay," "Make Playtime Safe Again," and "Every Kid Loves Playtime. Let Us Play Safe. #FairPlay."[27] Women and children, including an occupied double stroller, flanked the lectern, everyone pushed close together to provide a photogenic background for the cameras. This was the perfect distraction for robbing American taxpayers of the greatest protection for their financial freedom and cracking open the public treasury.

Concerned Women for America—a Christian nationalist outfit whose goal is to "bring biblical principles into all levels of public policy"—hosted the rally but was otherwise not involved in the case.[28] (CWA is tied to Leo's network, and you may remember the group from its gaudy pink bus tour supporting Amy Coney Barrett's nomination.[29]) ADF President Mike Farris and Faith & Freedom Coalition chairman Ralph Reed spoke, as did others from ADF, the Heritage Foundation, Focus on the Family, the Family Research Council, and the US Conference of Catholic Bishops.[30] Several members of Congress, all Christian nationalists, sent over statements to be read, including Senator Ted Cruz and Representatives Bob Goodlatte, Vicky Hartzler (who wrote a book called *Running God's Way* to lay out "the proven campaign techniques in God's Word"), and Trent Franks. Franks resigned in disgrace a few months later to avert a sexual harassment investigation.[31]

In a few short years, these same Crusaders would eviscerate public health during a pandemic to pursue their privilege, but for now, they claimed to care about children's safety.[32] Fairness and children's safety are more popular than taxing citizens to fund evangelizing children. Tolerance, not taxes, and fairness instead of forced tithing. Look at this, not that.

It worked. ADF won the public messaging battle. People shrugged, not realizing that their religious freedom was threatened.

The Supreme Court was so eager to take the perfect case that it ignored crucial procedural safeguards. Our legal system is adversarial. Two opposing sides argue a dispute before an impartial judge. If the parties agree, there's no dispute, no adversity, and courts dismiss such cases because there's a danger that rights will get trampled in unforeseen and unexpected ways. That's what happened here.

By the time the case reached the Supreme Court, Missouri had agreed to fund the children's ministry. Governor Eric Greitens ordered the DNR to ignore Line #3 and stop denying funds to churches. "We're fighting for religious liberty here in Missouri," said Greitens, announcing the new order.[33] The DNR eliminated the constitutional requirements for the grants.

The new Missouri attorney general took office four months before oral argument at the Supreme Court. Prior to that, Josh Hawley had actually worked this case *on the church's side*, arguing that the grant program "unfairly discriminate[d] against religious organizations," citing the Santeria case three times to open the brief and again to close it out.[34] He wrote the brief with his wife—both are former clerks of Chief Justice Roberts. Before this, Hawley worked for a Crusader, the Becket Fund, even helping on the Hobby Lobby case.[35] Hawley became Missouri's US senator in 2019, and is still dedicated to the Crusade. He infamously supported Trump's insurrection and voted to disenfranchise millions of Americans on January 6, 2021. "Hawley's idea of freedom is the freedom to conform to what he and his preferred religious authorities know to be right," observed Katherine Stewart in op-ed about January 6 that featured the infamous photo of Hawley with his fist raised in solidarity with the Capitol mob that attempted to overthrow our election.[36]

So by the time the Supreme Court was ready to hear oral argument, Crusaders controlled both sides of the case. Everyone involved sided with the Christian ministry and against Line #3. The Supreme Court should have dropped the case. It refused, ostensibly because the parties, which agreed on the outcome, also agreed that the case could continue.[37] Hawley selected an attorney who would argue the "old position" at the Supreme Court. It begins to look like collusion.

The parties, of course, also agreed that Line #3 was not implicated or violated in the case. It was violated, as every lower court had found, but that was back when one side actually argued the dispute. The Supreme Court said that there was no constitutional problem with taxing citizens and then giving the money to a church because the parties said it was OK.[38] Justices Sotomayor and Ginsberg were appropriately incensed at this, writing in their dissent: "Constitutional questions are decided by this Court, not the parties' concessions." Nevertheless, the court ignored a central pillar of true religious freedom.

The court also ignored reality, adopting the public relations message from the plastic playground press conference in front of the building. "To hear the court tell it, this is a simple case about recycling tires to resurface a playground," wrote Sotomayor and Ginsburg. "The stakes are higher. The case is about nothing less than the relationship between religious institutions and the civil government—that is, between church and state. The court today profoundly changes that relationship by holding, for the first time, that the Constitution requires the government to provide public funds directly to a church." Roberts and the other six justices completely elided the fact that the state grant was supporting a children's ministry. The church repeatedly and unabashedly admitted that this playground is a ministry. Roberts, just as unabashedly, ignored that fact.

Sotomayor didn't: "The Church's playground surface—like a Sunday School room's walls or the sanctuary's pews—are integrated with and integral to its religious mission. The conclusion that the funding the Church seeks would impermissibly advance religion is inescapable."[39]

Given these numerous flaws, it's almost pointless to ask what Roberts actually decided, as it had little bearing on reality.

Roberts cited the Santeria case at least ten times; it was one of the cases that he relied on the most, to show that the compelled-support principle is hostile to and discriminates against Christianity. Do you see the fatal catch-22 here? By arguing that the grant program discriminates against religion, Roberts admits that the grants would fund religion. His discrimination argument admits to the constitutional violation of Line #3. He claims that this is both religious freedom and somehow also not funding religion. Roberts invoked religion to benefit the church—the church has a right to religious freedom—but then pretended religion was not relevant to Line #3 state/church separation. To get the benefit, yes, recognize religion; if there's a burden, no, ignore the religion. We saw these nauseating acrobatics earlier in the Bladensburg Cross case, and we'll see them again.

Roberts tried to get around this fatal flaw by claiming that the state was discriminating against the *character* of the church, *rather* than the use of the funds. Doing so required a rewrite of precedent and reality.

Roberts relied on a 2004 case for use/character distinction. Washington State awarded scholarships to college students, but not for devotional religious degrees. Crusader Jay Sekulow and his American Center for Law & Justice argued that excluding "pastoral ministries" degrees from the program targeted religion, just like the Santeria case. The court upheld the exclusion partly because of the compelled-support principle and Line #3.[40] Enforcing these principles ensure equality, so such denials are not discrimination. Chief Justice Rehnquist noted, "Since the founding of our country, there have been popular uprisings against procuring tax-payer funds to support church leaders." (Scalia and Thomas began their dissent with the Santeria case, one of the only times it was cited prior to Alito resurrecting it in the 2016 pharmacy opinion (see pages 106–7).

Roberts also rewrote reality—rather easily, given the parties' agreement. First, the church admitted it was seeking the grant for a ministry meant to convert people, especially children, into church members. That's a religious use. Second, it's often impossible to sepa-rate a church's religious identity from its activities. A childcare center standing alone might not be religious. There are many. But this is not one. Churches use what might be secular activities to further religious missions. This was Sotomayor's point about walls and pews. The use versus character fallacy shouldn't have mattered; Line #3 should have.

Once upon a time, the Supreme Court explained that the gov-ernment "cannot hamper its citizens in the free exercise of *their own* religion. Consequently, it cannot exclude individual Catholics, Lutherans, Mohammedans, Baptists, Jews, Methodists, nonbelievers, Presbyterians, or the members of any other faith, because of their faith, or lack of it, from receiving the benefits of public welfare legislation."[41] But protecting citizens' religious freedom also means not forcing them to support religions that are not "their own"—that all contributions to religion are strictly voluntary. This is a universal right that lies with all citizens; defending it is not hostility or discrimination. That was the true flaw in Roberts's opinion. He should have defended religious free-dom as a universal right but instead focused on the religious freedom of the church alone. The Supreme Court ignored everyone else. The court privileged Christians and moved *their* religious freedom to the top of the hierarchy of rights.

Roberts came painfully close to grasping the court's error: "It is true the Department has not criminalized the way Trinity Lutheran worships or told the Church that it cannot subscribe to a certain view of the Gospel."[42] The church wasn't being coerced into not being a church—but because of the court's decision, citizens are coerced into supporting that church. The government is forcing citizens to financially support a ministry that targets children. This is, as Thomas Jefferson told us two and a half centuries ago, "sinful and tyrannical."

What would have happened if Line #3 had been upheld? What calamitous outcome would have befallen the church? Nothing. It'd be in the same position. In fact, the same position American churches have been in for centuries. Some might be tempted to point to the dire demographic and financial state that American churches find themselves in as they face plummeting attendance and dwindling donations. But that is to prove again the central point—the government cannot prop up failing religions by taking money from its citizens. It does not possess this power.

The Missouri ministry decision weaponized religious freedom. Roberts ignored procedure to decide a collusive case; ignored the facts to pretend that a religious ministry was not a religious ministry, while still claiming religious freedom as the central rationale; and focused only on the rights of these churchgoing Christians to the exclusion of every other American. That ignorance is now enshrined in precedent.

The Supreme Court has cited this "playground case" ten times in recent years, and three times in major Line #3 disputes, including a case I litigated for the Freedom From Religion Foundation and won, with a unanimous 7–0 opinion from the New Jersey Supreme Court.[43]

IN FOUR SHORT YEARS, MORRIS COUNTY, NEW JERSEY, took $5 million from citizens and gave it to churches. If those numbers held statewide, that's a transfer of wealth from taxpayers to New Jersey churches of about $250 million over a decade.[44] We challenged this violation.

The question of whether history is important, and should be preserved, is different from the question of whether the government can support active religious congregations. As a society, we should preserve historic church buildings, especially, for instance, if they played a role in the Revolutionary War or the Underground Railroad. But taxpayers cannot be forced to financially support active congregations, preaching hellfire for nonbelievers on Sundays, and hosting bible study on Wednesdays. This holds even, and perhaps especially, if their congregations are dwindling and unable to maintain historic structures.

This was the struggle in New Jersey. Morris County taxed citizens. Some taxes funded a trust to preserve "the county's exceptional abundance of historic resources." The fund gave $5,530,322 to churches over four years, more than half the money it doled out, all of it to active congregations with regular worship. One church took in more than a million dollars to "historically preserve the building allowing its *continued use by our congregation for worship services . . . ,*" according to the grant application. The church's mission, also stated in the grant application, is to "proclaim faithfully the Good News of the Gospel in fresh and compelling ways" and "nurture relevant thoughtful, committed disciples." Another church was given $616,000 to "ensure continued safe public access to the church *for worship*."[45]

The churches are preserving their ability to worship first and foremost; the history is secondary (at best).

Like New York's public health measures, the historic preservation grants actually favored churches. Only three types of entities were eligible for grants: the government, charities dedicated to historic preservation, and churches. Individuals, businesses, and most secular nonprofits were excluded from the program, even if they owned and maintained historic buildings, unless they were also dedicated to historic preservation. So most were excluded, while *all* churches owning a historical building were eligible.

With a local plaintiff, the Freedom From Religion Foundation sued under the compelled-support clause written into the New Jersey constitution of 1776. The language is clear and on point: "No person shall . . . under any pretense whatever . . . be obliged to pay tithes, taxes, or other rates for building or repairing any church or churches, place or places of worship, or for the maintenance of any minister or ministry, contrary to what he believes to be right or has deliberately and voluntarily engaged to perform."[46]

The case was that simple. The New Jersey constitution says that the government cannot tax citizens to build or repair churches, and the county taxed citizens to repair churches. "Without doubt, a religious liberty right is threatened in this case," we explained to the New Jersey Supreme Court. "But the imperiled right does not lie with the churches; it lies with David Steketee, the local resident who was forced to pay taxes to repair houses of worship. Morris County used its taxing power, which is inherently coercive, to repair churches and thereby fund religious worship. It is this tyranny that Jefferson and Madison sought to abate with their religious freedom statue, which then influenced the First Amendment. That is the religious freedom issue here: the right of all citizens not to be taxed to support religion."[47]

The churches and county had two relevant counterarguments. First, historical preservation is important and a legitimate government interest. It is. But, as we explained, the compelled-support principle in Line #3 "dates back to the American founding and is among our most sacred and hallowed rights. Over that long history, there has never been any indication that this fundamental protection does not apply if the government has a noble purpose. A stated purpose of historic preservation would not excuse Morris County from violating other fundamental rights—Free Speech or the right to bear arms, for example."[48]

Their second argument relied on the Missouri ministry decision just discussed. The county and churches wanted the court to ignore the clear language of the state constitution, just like the Supreme Court did in Missouri. They even argued that fixating on the churches' rights and ignoring everyone else somehow advanced equality. This is, of course, backward. Equality is enshrined in every compelled-support clause—*every* citizen is protected from forced tithing. Removing that protection to repair old, neglected churches is favoritism, not just of religious entities over every other citizen, but also of older, more established sects over newer sects.

Unlike the US Supreme Court in the Missouri ministry case, the New Jersey Supreme Court got it right.[49] It rejected the Missouri ministry case because, even under Roberts's untenable use/character distinction, the New Jersey churches had admitted they needed the grants to continue worshipping—the state was funding active congregations.

We had won. Over the next decade, New Jersey taxpayers would save about a quarter billion dollars that would have been taken from them by their government and given to churches that they did not attend.[50] I love my job.

After the New Jersey Supreme Court handed down its opinion, the Crusaders jumped in. The Becket Fund asked the US Supreme Court to take up the Morris County case in mid-September 2018.

Four justices must agree for the Supreme Court to accept a case. Kennedy had announced his retirement on June 27, 2018. Leo and Trump were bound to nominate a more rabidly conservative replacement, and Trump began interviewing potential picks days later, on July 2. Later that month, Becket requested a one-month extension on the deadline to ask the Supreme Court to review the New Jersey case, which Justice Alito granted. This extension ensured that Trump's more conservative replacement would weigh in on Becket's request to review the case. That replacement was Brett Kavanaugh.[51] And, because of Leonard Leo, Becket almost certainly knew that Kavanaugh was the choice before the public did. Leo was on Becket's board when all this was happening and, as we've seen, ran the Federalist Society, which selected Trump's judges.[52] Becket was biding time until the Crusader network could ensure a more favorable judiciary was in place.

The Morris County case was so strong and the New Jersey Supreme Court opinion so clear that only three justices considered taking the case: Alito, Gorsuch, and, the new appointment, Brett Kavanaugh.

Kavanaugh wrote a statement accompanying the court's refusal to take the case.[53] That itself is odd. But he'd done quite a bit of that lately, including joining a statement in a case seeking to ban abortion[54] and another arguing that the court should review the case of a public school football coach who wanted to use his public position to pray on the field at games (we met this coach in the Kim Davis chapter).[55] Kavanaugh's statement on the New Jersey case was perhaps his fourth substantive Supreme Court writing, and two of the three previous also sought to weaponize religious freedom.[56] He leapt into the Crusade.

Kavanaugh, Alito, and Gorsuch didn't say the court should review Morris County, they actually agreed with the refusal. Instead, they told their fellow Crusaders what they wanted to see in the next case so that they could accept it. These justices *want* to take these cases—they're eager to aid the Crusade to overturn the compelled-support principle.

AFTER THE NEW JERSEY SUPREME COURT handed down its unanimous opinion, a statewide historic trust body approved thirty-three historic grants totaling over $1 million, including $43,186 to the Moravian Church in Gloucester County and $5,000 to the Middle Valley

Chapel in Morris County.[57] Both buildings are historic churches, but at the time of the grants, neither had active congregations or were used for religious worship. The church is now county-owned, and the chapel had been repurposed as a community center. Taxes funded historic preservation and not religion. This honored the spirit of the law and the rights of every citizen, and protected the state's history. And it wasn't that hard. History and Line #3 can be balanced.

14

No, Really, Religious Freedom
Is Taxing Us

*(Espinoza v. the Montana
Department of Revenue)*

"Yes, Jesus would destroy the public education temple."

—Kyle Olson, cofounder and cochair of
National School Choice Week[1]

In June 2020, almost three years to the day after it decided the Missouri ministry case, the court violated the rights of every American taxpayer again.[2]

Before walking over to the Senate to preside over President Trump's first impeachment trial, Chief Justice John Roberts heard oral argument in a neo-voucher case out of Montana.[3] (I won't get into the many varieties of vouchers and neo-vouchers in this book: traditional vouchers, education savings accounts, tuition tax-credits, or any of the other deviously creative neo-vouchers. Vouchers are an ever-evolving hydra, but always rely on the government's taxing power to fund private education that is overwhelmingly religious and Christian, often well over 90 percent and sometimes 100 percent.[4] Using the taxing power is both the hallmark and the problem.)

Rather like the Missouri ministry case, the central issue in the Montana case was whether religious liberty is an exclusive weapon belonging to Christians or a universal right belonging to every citizen. The court said it was the former.

The Montana constitution protects the religious freedom of every taxpayer; the state "shall not make *any direct or indirect* appropriation or payment from *any* public fund or monies, or any grant of lands or other property for *any* sectarian purpose or to aid any church, school, academy, seminary, college, university, or other literary or scientific institution, controlled in whole or in part by any church, sect, or denomination."

And yet. The Montana legislature in 2015 adopted a scheme to funnel public money to Christian schools.[5] Governor Bullock vetoed a nearly identical bill in 2013, explaining that "we shouldn't undermine our public education system that serves students well in order to fund these private institutions."[6] That's precisely what the 2015 law did.

This neo-voucher scheme was a bizarre shell game that depended entirely on the state's taxing power. Here's how it worked: Taxpayers owe Montana money. Instead of paying the state, Montana allowed taxpayers to divert tax payments to a private scholarship fund that paid for private, mostly religious education. The state then forgave the debt. One dollar sent to a scholarship fund was one dollar off your taxes.[7]

Early versions of the bill called the donations "directed tax payments," an honest circumlocution—Montana was directing tax payments to religious schools. The state appropriated $3 million to cover the anticipated shortfall from forgiving those debts. Taxpayers were funding Christian education.

The scholarships could only be used for private schools, not homeschooling or costs associated with sending children to another public school. Only one scholarship fund was created, Big Sky Scholarships. Of the schools eligible to receive the Big Sky Scholarships, all but one was Christian. And in the year before litigation, all but three of the scholarships went to Christian schools (94 percent).

Big Sky Scholarships was a financial waypoint, an empty husk of an organization run by a failed Republican statehouse candidate who posts Christian nationalist propaganda on her social media and who ran Big Sky as a volunteer along with her full-time day job because it required so little effort. It was a shell created to circumvent the state constitution. This is money laundering by another name.

The Montana Department of Revenue was tasked with certifying scholarship organizations and wrote the rules for administering the program. The new law said that the neo-voucher program "must be administered in compliance" with the compelled-support clauses of the Montana Constitution.[8] Taking its duty to uphold the constitution more seriously than state legislators, the Department of Revenue crafted a rule that incorporated all the relevant constitutional language preventing public money flowing to churches or schools "controlled in whole or in part by any church."[9]

Three Christian parents sued over the rule. The Institute for Justice, which took the case, sold the media stories of people struggling financially, eager to get their children an education.[10] But behind the IJ's carefully crafted tale are parents seeking a *Christian* education for their children, not a *better* education.

All three Christian parents—Kendra Espinoza, Jeri Anderson, and Jaime Schaefer—sent their children[11] to Stillwater Christian School in Kalispell.[12] There are good, free public schools in the area that rank and rate competitively with Stillwater Christian on the many websites that grade schools. But quality was less essential than Christianity to these parents. Espinoza wanted to *avoid* public school in favor of Stillwater because "the school teaches the same Christian values that I teach at home."[13] There was another private school near Espinoza, but she did "not wish to send her daughters to this school because it does not teach Christian values."[14] Anderson explained, "I am a Christian and appreciate that Stillwater [Christian School] teaches religious values."[15] The parents wanted Christianity inculcated, and they wanted us to pay for it.

Stillwater Christian preaches a "biblical worldview," the tenets of which include "authority" and "memorization" and, more specifically, that "the Bible is our sole authority for belief and behavior" and "we study the Bible to train students to be obedient to God's revealed will."[16] The school's statement of faith is typical of a deeply conservative Christian sect. It includes classics, like biblical inerrancy and creationism, and modern hits, like abortion ("pre-born babies"), biblical marriage ("God created marriage to be exclusively the union of one man and one woman"), and, especially, dehumanizing LGBTQ folks ("God . . . immutably creates each person as male or female, and . . . these two distinct, complementary sexes reflect the image and nature of God").[17] In a promotional video, the school portrays itself as a culture warrior. "The culture," we're told, is "working against" Christian families, and Stillwater Christian "work[s] very hard to counter these cultural forces by teaching the truth of God's Word."[18] In February 2021, a Stillwater employee was arrested and charged with repeatedly raping a young girl, beginning when she was thirteen years old.[19]

In fall 2012 the school raked in $20,000 raffling off an "AR-15 rifle."[20] Despite this windfall, Stillwater was struggling financially; all the local Christian schools seemed to be.[21] Before the promise of public money, Stillwater Christian had been hemorrhaging students. Enrollment dropped by nearly a quarter in one year, according to local reports about plummeting private school enrollment.[22] One of the Christian schools receiving Big Sky scholarships has since permanently closed.[23]

Espinoza initially homeschooled her children, but circumstances sent her back to work full-time and her kids to public school.[24] Espinoza was "not happy with my daughters' public school," because when the eldest—who was nine or ten at the time—"started a daily Bible study for her friends that took place during recess, she was repeatedly bullied by other students and called a 'goody two shoes.'"[25] In my work, I encounter many administrators and parents who regard public schools as a mission field, as a way to access other people's children in the 4/14 window. Some Christian parents encourage their children to proselytize their peers; there are Christian groups that provide training for "peer-to-peer" proselytizing.[26] It's rare for nine-year-old children voluntarily and without prompting to start "daily Bible study" groups instead of playing at recess. They're *told* to start bible study groups. And having your children proselytize other people's children in public school is, yes, likely to cause some friction. The simple solution is to stop using your child to smuggle your religion into public schools. Let them go play at recess.

Espinoza "never worr[ied] about my daughters being bullied at Stillwater," but that's less because of the welcoming nature of the school and more because of its bigoted theology. It's doubtful that LGBTQ families or non-Christians would feel welcome. One freshman unknowingly explained this: "There is a sad lack of diversity but people get along pretty well."[27] Others agree. The lack of diversity is why one student who wanted to start a Gay-Straight Alliance club didn't think it would go anywhere; "most people have the same religious and political views. Sadly, our school is very unaccepting of various sexual orientations. Teachers lecture against it, and because of that there are many students who have very negative, even violent opinions about gay people."[28] Even the wrong kind of Christians are ostracized: "If you are a Christian family that embraces all people regardless of status, wealth, looks or history, your child and your family may be uncomfortable here."[29] Said one alum, "In terms of what is considered diversity today, it's a stretch to find kids that aren't white. Homosexuality is so wrong that just being gay is hell-worthy. Acceptance is not for everyone there."[30] This is the school taxpayers were meant to fund.

Christian parents wanted their children to go to a Christian school and demanded everyone else pay for it. However much we empathize with struggling people trying to give their children a better life (not what we have here), the solution is not to use the state's taxing power to indoctrinate children into a particular religion. The solution is better public schools.

We have a public school system that admits and benefits everyone. Not just people with kids, but everybody, because an educated workforce and electorate are necessary in a democracy. Montana already funded public education for all; funding a parallel system was counterproductive and wasteful. The people of Montana added this preference to their constitution, which says that "it is the goal of the people to establish a system of education which will develop the full educational potential of each person," guarantees "educational opportunity" to every person in the state, and says that the state shall provide "free quality public elementary and secondary schools."[31] The delegates at the 1972 Constitutional Convention explained that this meant to provide "unequivocal support . . . for a strong public school system.'"[32] And that "any diversion of public funds or effort from the public school system would tend to weaken that system in favor of schools established for private or religious purposes."[33] The state constitution is designed to protect and fund public education, as well as protect Line #3.

"School choice" is as much about destroying this quality public education as it is about funding religious education. "School choice" activists blame the erosion of traditional Protestantism on public schools. "For many supporters, of course, the underlying motive for voucher programs is not to improve education but to eliminate non-sectarian education," according to Katherine Stewart.[34] Public schools, with their focus on math, reading, science, and every other subject that is not religious education or indoctrination, are driving children away from the church. Christian parents feared that one bible class on a Wednesday evening, even if partnered with church and Sunday School, wasn't enough to keep kids in the faith. Without daily rein-forcement, children would stop believing (this says rather a lot about the content of religious claims).

Rarely are proponents of neo-vouchers open about this goal, but occasionally the mask slips. Jerry Falwell "hope[d] to see the day when . . . we don't have public schools. The churches will have taken them over and Christians will be running them."[35] Kyle Olson cocre-ated and chaired National School Choice Week.[36] As its executive direc-tor, Olson wrote, "I would like to think that, yes, Jesus would destroy the public education temple and save the children from despair and a hopeless future."[37] Olson also wrote the book *Indoctrination: How "Useful Idiots" Are Using Our Schools to Subvert American Exceptional-ism*, and he ran the Education Action Group Foundation in Michigan, partially funded by former US secretary of education Betsy DeVos.[38] DeVos and her family promoted vouchers "to help advance God's Kingdom," she told The Gathering, the annual meeting of the coun-try's richest Christians.[39] And because "The church—which ought to be in our view far more central to the life of the community—has been displaced by the public school as the center for activity."[40] Recentering the church is more important to these activists than most people real-ize. That means ending reliance on the government, and even ending government programs, like public education (see chapter 16).

The Montana Supreme Court struck down the entire neo-voucher program. No neo-vouchers for private religious or private secular schools, because the scheme funded a parallel education system and drained resources from public education. Religious parents were, of course, still free to opt out of this fully funded public education system and put their kids in religious schools. They were free to exercise that choice. But it is not then the taxpayers' responsibility to fund a second parallel system that erodes the first. Nor is it discrimination to refuse to do so, said the state court.[41]

The Montana Supreme Court also struck down the entire program because the department's rule essentially corrected the law: "An agency cannot transform an unconstitutional statute into a constitutional statute with an administrative rule."[42]

The decision protected public education and reined in an overreaching agency. If ever there were a case for states' rights and the judicial restraint that conservative judges love to preach about, this would be it. Instead, six months after Brett Kavanaugh was confirmed, the Institute for Justice asked the Supreme Court to take the case, and the justices leapt at the chance to attack Line #3.

The Koch brothers funded IJ with bags of seed money.[43] In *Dark Money: The Hidden History of the Billionaires Behind the Rise of the Radical Right*, journalist Jane Mayer uses the Koch-funded founding of IJ as the prototypical example of how the billionaires established countless conservative nonprofits, ventures even the activists themselves thought nobody would fund. Charles Koch gave $1.5 million and retained some control over IJ's work and mission.[44] Other IJ funders included the National Christian Charitable Foundation (recall that its biggest donor was tied to Hobby Lobby) and the foundation Betsy DeVos uses to funnel money to anti–public education groups.[45] IJ has ties to many right-wing power brokers (such as the American Legislative Exchange Council) and activists, (such as Kyle Olsen's National School Choice Week).[46]

Clint Bolick and William "Chip" Mellor cofounded the Institute for Justice. Bolick and Mellor were lawyers in the Reagan White House and known for dedicating their careers to opposing affirmative action.[47] Bolick was an aide to Clarence Thomas back then. The *New York Times* called Bolick the "prime architect behind school voucher plans in Milwaukee and Cleveland," the oldest in the country, and noted that Clarence Thomas is godfather to one of Bolick's children.[48] Bolick is now a justice on the Arizona Supreme Court.

The Cato Institute published Bolick's 2003 book, *Voucher Wars: Waging the Legal Battle over School Choice*, and from the first poorly crafted sentence, the dishonest nature of the school choice fight is laid bare: "It is almost surrealistic that my colleagues and I have had to spend the past dozen years litigating to establish the basic legal premise that parents may exercise school choice." Twaddle. Parents are free to send their children to private school. The issue is whether taxpayers must fund that private choice, when they already fund a public school system that does the same job. No—from the standpoints of both sound fiscal policy and religious freedom, taxpayers should not be funding private schools.

Some of IJ's first cases included suing in Chicago and Los Angeles, and arguing that these public school systems *must* create private school vouchers because the public schools were bad.[49] In another, it sued to challenge a school district's desegregation plan. We'll explore the intimate relationship between vouchers and segregation in the next chapter.[50]

IJ asked the US Supreme Court to resurrect the neo-voucher program for the three Christian parents. The case was similar to the first cases IJ took in Chicago and Los Angeles; it was arguing for a right to a publicly funded private education. But this time, it had religious freedom as a weapon and a packed court.

Chief Justice Roberts wrote the 5–4 majority opinion. Thomas, Alito, Gorsuch, and Kavanaugh joined him. They destroyed the compelled-support principle, that critical part of Line #3 that protects us from forced tithing.

Montana and a phalanx of other groups argued, as I have in these chapters, that the compelled-support principle embodied in the Montana constitution protects religious freedom, that any use of the taxing power to fund religion violates religious freedom.

Roberts ignored these huge swaths of American law and history, and one of our founders' truly original contributions to the world, disposing of it all in one sentence. "We do not see how," wrote Roberts, the compelled-support principle in Line #3 and in the Montana constitution "promotes religious freedom." That's it. Two hundred years of legal principle swatted aside in one willfully blind sentence.

Essentially, Roberts inverted Line #3 and redefined state/church separation as discrimination. Roberts bastardized a principle that protects equality into a tool for Christian privilege. He pulled off that magic trick by focusing only on Christians and ignoring everyone else, writing, "The Department's argument is especially unconvincing because the infringement of religious liberty here broadly affects both religious schools and adherents." Roberts "doesn't see" how compelled-support clauses protect religious freedom because he willfully blinds himself to everyone except the Christian parents and Christian schools. Roberts decided the case by ignoring and excluding the rights of minorities. There's a word for that: discrimination. This isn't hyperbole; it's bigotry—in print, in a Supreme Court decision. And it went entirely unremarked.

Bigotry played another role in this decision. Roberts revived the hostility argument to bolster his claims of discrimination. He cited the Santeria case and the Missouri ministry case (which relied on the Santeria case) to argue that the Montana constitution discriminated against—was hostile to—Christians. Except that, this time, the attempt was to paint every compelled-support clause in every state constitution as the product of anti-Catholic bigotry. Specifically, Roberts and other justices claimed that compelled-support clauses were born of anti-Catholic bigotry in the nineteenth century and therefore must be struck down.

State constitutions differ significantly from local ordinances passed by a town whipped into a fervor (as in the Santeria case) or from the offhand comment of a civil servant that can be overwrought by a judge removed in time and place (as in the cake case). They're written in conventions and approved by voters of that state. There are records of the debates and discussions. We know the why and how. To claim that an entire provision of a state constitution is deliberately and intentionally anti-Catholic is extraordinary and requires serious evidence. To claim that every provision that prevents the flow of taxpayer funds to religious entities must therefore also die the death of a bigot requires a great deal more.

The evidence supports neither claim. Anti-Catholic bigotry existed in America and was an issue during the fight over public schools, but that bigotry did not taint the compelled-support principle, the clauses that implement it, or the universal nature of that religious freedom protection. These provisions are pro-religious freedom, pro-Constitution, and pro-equality. Often the clauses were first instituted at the founding, long before the wave of Catholic immigration and anti-Catholic bigotry, and readopted long after the bigotry had died.[51] Florida voters refused to overturn that state's compelled-support clause in 2012 by more than twenty-five points. There was "no hint of anti-Catholic animus" when the clause was first adopted or in this 2012 vote.[52] Congress even required new states to adopt these provisions.[53] But, also, the only clause that mattered in this case was Montana's, and the history there was clear: there was no anti-Catholic bigotry at the state's first constitutional conventions or from any official participating in those conventions. Similarly, there's simply no plausible argument that bigotry motivated that clause in Montana's new 1972 constitution.[54]

The anti-Catholic bigotry strain of the "hostility" argument is new, sort of a forerunner to the Crusade. Justice Thomas first advanced it in a 2000 case that challenged government loans of equipment, books, transportation, and even teachers to Catholic schools in Louisiana.[55] Thomas wrote the controlling opinion, but only Kennedy, Scalia, and Chief Justice Rehnquist joined him. Justices Sandra Day O'Connor and Breyer agreed in the result, but not Thomas's reasoning, including his novel anti-Catholic bigotry claim. Since Thomas convinced only a plurality of four justices, his bigotry claims weren't binding precedent.

Thomas's anti-Catholic argument ran to two paragraphs. Seven sentences. Two hundred words to lay out a new history and new argument, before he sweepingly declared, "This doctrine, born of bigotry, should be buried now."[56] He didn't argue that a specific state constitutional clause was passed amid a hail of anti-Catholic slurs and enforced against only Catholics. Instead, he's arguing that *the principle* of refusing to tax citizens and give that money to religious schools is unconstitutional— the entire "doctrine" amounts to anti-Catholic bigotry.

Thomas touches on history only in the first four of his seven sentences.[57] He cites a single historical source, a law review article by Professor Steven Green.[58] Green is a leading expert on the history of compelled-support clauses and is often cited, especially his two law reviews articles on these constitutional provisions.[59] The first was published eighteen months before the Santeria decision. This is the one Thomas cites. But, in it, Green examines the debate over a failed federal compelled-support clause (known as "the Blaine Amendment") and how that disproves an originalist stance (that Thomas holds) on an esoteric legal doctrine called incorporation.[60] There's something vindictive about Thomas citing this article, and for a completely different purpose or, at the very least, something unscholarly. "My article was taken out of context," Green tells me. "Anti-Catholicism existed at the time, but that's not the only thing that was going on. Thomas' opinion and Becket Fund's brief misconstrued my work."[61] Green adds, "I cringed before I even saw the opinion. It was very galling to have Thomas quote my work for that claim."

Green's second article was "a rebuttal to Thomas['s]" abuse of his work.[62] "Contrary to Justice Thomas' assertions," Green concludes, "opposition to public funding of sectarian schools rests on longstanding constitutional principles of religious liberty, non-coercion, and non-favoritism. 'No-funding' is a principle with a pedigree that we should not hesitate to reaffirm." (The no-funding principle is what I am calling compelled support). So the sole, factual support of Thomas's anti-Catholic argument is wrong, according to the very expert Thomas cited or, rather, miscited.

Before Thomas in 2000, the last case in which the court mentioned the "Blaine Amendment" actually discusses anti-Catholic bigotry, but in Spain.[63] The 1968 opinion doesn't even suggest the compelled-support principle is anti-Catholic. It even includes an appendix with a 1967 letter from influential Cardinal Francis Spellman, which was to be read at every Catholic mass under his jurisdiction. Spellman asked people to support a new state constitution without a compelled-support clause, but this Catholic cleric, calling on Catholics to undo the clause, somehow forgot to mention its anti-Catholic pedigree.[64]

Where did Thomas get his potent, fallacious argument? The party arguing for government loans to religious schools barely raised the argument, mentioning it only in a few paragraphs.[65] That was the same lawyer who thought up the religious liberty law clinic that the Becket Fund established at Stanford a decade later.[66] Though they are connected, it was actually the Becket Fund's friend-of-the-court brief that focused on the anti-Catholic bigotry argument. Becket showed that anti-Catholic bigotry was prevalent in America, but could only tie it to one constitutional provision, when anti-Catholic Know Nothings briefly controlled the Massachusetts government.[67] But even that history is dubious, partly because the compelled-support principle was first adopted by Massachusetts during the American founding at the behest of believers like Isaac Backus, a Baptist preacher, who proposed a resolution in 1775 arguing that complete "freedom from being taxed by civil rulers to religious worship, is not a mere favor, from any man or men in the world, but a right and property granted us by God."[68] And also because later constitutional conventions readopted the principle with overwhelming Catholic support. According to Boston College historian James O'Toole, at the 1917 constitutional convention, eighty-five of the ninety-four Catholic delegates voted in favor of the supposedly anti-Catholic amendment.[69] Historically, American Catholics have supported the principle in theory for these same reasons, even suing under compelled-support clauses to win crucial state/church cases in the late 1800s.[70] The government did not have the power to tax citizens for the benefit of religion in Massachusetts long before the bigoted Know Nothings won power, and American Catholics supported the principle long after.

The anti-Catholic argument against the compelled-support principle was invented by a Crusader founded by a Catholic and named after a Catholic prelate who wanted special privileges for his church. The court adopted it in a fractured plurality opinion written by Justice Thomas, perhaps the most devout Catholic to sit on the bench. Thomas attended St. Pius X Catholic High School in Savannah and then transferred to a Catholic boarding school that trained students for the priesthood. He then began college at Conception Seminary College before transferring to a fourth Catholic school, College of the Holy Cross. He goes to mass every day before work because, "It gives you, a sinner—it starts you in a way of doing this job—secular job—the right way for the right reasons."[71] (We know from studies that people vote more conservatively if their polling location is in a church. What does daily church before adjudicating cases do to a justice's decisions?) Thomas humbly claimed that his life was governed by "miraculous . . . divine providence."[72] He summed up his beliefs in a speech at Christendom College, a Catholic school: "I am decidedly and unapologetically Catholic."[73]

With a deft pen, the three dissenters buried Thomas's poor argument for twenty years.[74] But then the Crusade was launched, and Leo, Trump, and McConnell packed the courts. Chief Justice Roberts resurrected this bigotry claim in the Montana case, hedging in a way that muddied the clear absence of anti-Catholic bigotry in Montana's constitution, the only state constitution at issue.[75] The only court opinion Roberts cited was Thomas's shoddy twenty-year-old singularity.[76] Kavanaugh (like Thomas, a Catholic and product of Catholic schools) joined in during oral argument, claiming that compelled-support clauses are "certainly rooted in grotesque religious bigotry against Catholics."[77] Alito, also a Catholic, joined in at oral argument too, but really hammered the anti-Catholic bigotry claim in a rambling, bitter concurring opinion.[78] Alito pointed to twenty-one amicus briefs that mention the anti-Catholic history claim, as if many mouths regurgitating the same bad history from the same sources somehow makes it true. Nearly all cite Thomas's 2000 opinion. Some, such as the Cato Institute's brief, cite no authority at all.[79] Others like the Koch-funded Pioneer Institute, cite the history as written and published by the Crusader itself.[80] None showed an anti-Catholic influence in the Montana constitution, again the only relevant question.

But the history doesn't really matter to Crusaders. The goal is to transform a case about taxing all citizens *to fund* Christianity into a case about hostility *toward* Christianity. Hostility shifts focus from everyone to the Christians. The protection shifts with it. Roberts understands that if he can fit these cases into the mold of the Santeria case, he'll win overwhelming support on the court and in the media. Roberts declared that the compelled-support principle and Line #3 are hostile to and discriminate against religion. Roberts wrote that the Montana Supreme Court itself discriminated against Christian parents by applying a principle that guarantees religious equality.[81] And then Roberts ordered the Montana Supreme Court to resurrect the neo-voucher scheme.

The five justices in the majority—all of them products of Catholic schools and/or churches[82]—ignored the fact that nondiscriminatory education already exists and is supported by tax dollars. The religious liberty at issue here didn't lie with the Christian parents or religious schools, but with every Montana taxpayer. Because that taxing power is inherently coercive, when used directly, or even indirectly, to benefit religious education, it violates the conscience of each citizen. So in the end, religious liberty *was* violated in this case—by the US Supreme Court.

AS ALWAYS, WE MUST ASK THE QUESTION: What would have happened if the court had decided this differently? What terrible calamity would have befallen the Christians of Montana without state funding for their religious schools? Nothing. The children would have received a free public education that wouldn't have strained the budgets of struggling families. They would have learned to read, write, multiply and divide, and play music. Everyone would have received the same baseline benefit, free from discrimination. Parents would still be free to augment that baseline with whatever religion they wish or substitute religious instruction completely.

At its most basic level, these cases—the children's ministry in Missouri, the New Jersey churches, and the Christian schools in Montana—share a similar goal. Christians want to use the machinery and power of the state to collect money from everyone for churches. Everything else is window dressing. The funding schemes have grown more creative and circuitous, but they are based on the power the state has to tax citizens. The state is passing, with the force of law, the churches' collection plates. It's forced tithing.

The ban on government-enforced tithing exists because humanity suffered through centuries of that terrible curse before America created Line #3. By gutting this principle and these protections, the Supreme Court is not protecting citizens' freedom; rather, the court is stripping us of our basic human rights. The court is robbing us of a shield and leaving every citizen exposed to the sword of God.

15

Religious Freedom and Segregation Academies

(School Vouchers Cases)

> "If you are against segregation and against racial separation,
> then you are against God."
>
> —**Bob Jones**, evangelist and founder of
> Bob Jones University[1]

Religious freedom saved the Montana voucher scheme, but the modern push for vouchers and school choice was not born of religious freedom; it was born of racism and later cloaked in religious freedom. And now, religious freedom is destroying public schools.

When public pools were first integrated, white people spilled the blood of any Black American attempting to swim. Or they drained the pools. Or filled them with dirt. Or cement.[2] Or, like local officials in Jackson, Mississippi, closed most pools and then leased the remaining to private organizations that discriminated and segregated, like the Young Men's Christian Association (at the time, still very much Christian). The result was the same: no Blacks allowed.[3]

Segregationists tried the same thing with public education after the Supreme Court ordered public schools desegregated "with all deliberate speed" in 1954. We revere *Brown v. Board of Education* as a unanimous decision in which the Supreme Court finally did the right thing after decades of upholding a gross moral wrong, but the court wasn't in a hurry.[4] "All deliberate speed" left room for delay. Lots. Continuing segregated education in the face of *Brown*'s order was more complicated than destroying public pools or leasing them to racists, but not much.

The authors of "The Racist Origins of Private School Vouchers" use Prince Edward County, Virginia, as the lens to tell this history.[5] When desegregation became inevitable and separate schools unconstitutional, the county closed the entire public school system. First, it slashed budgets and refused to levy taxes for public schools. Then, the state passed a voucher program to send kids to private schools. The authors explain that when the county "locked and chained its schools' doors . . . white children continued their education at the private Prince Edward Academy, a 'segregation academy' that would serve as a model for other communities in the South. The county's Black students, however, were not permitted to attend Prince Edward Academy nor granted tuition grants to attend other private schools." The Supreme Court eventually ordered the county to reopen and integrate its schools.[6]

Voucher programs were created to perpetuate segregation. The purpose was to circumvent the Constitution. To create a parallel, white public school system, that was ostensibly private and therefore outside of the constitutional commands of equality. Inequality was the intent. (This is effectively what Crusaders accomplished in Montana.)

Similar situations were repeated across the nation. White Americans and local governments across the country destroyed and defunded public schools. Then they created publicly funded vouchers for white students to attend segregated private schools, often private religious schools, leaving the dismantled and broken public system to Black Americans. Like the Jackson pools, White America essentially leased out education to segregationists and destroyed what was left over for minorities.

In this chapter, we'll look at that clear and well-documented history. Standing alone, this history should end the Crusaders' voucher offensive. In the last chapter, we saw Crusaders and the Supreme Court manipulate history to declare that constitutional provisions separating state and church are anti-Catholic, discriminatory, and therefore invalid. If the Supreme Court were consistent, if it were guided by legal principle and not the Crusade, it would end vouchers because of their undeniably racist history. But this court is not consistent or motivated by principle. This history shows not just that vouchers were born of bigotry and should die an ignominious death, but that the entire Crusade was. The story of vouchers is the story of the birth of the Crusade.

The evolution of vouchers follows the infamously explicit course Lee Atwater laid for the Southern Strategy,[7] an electoral plan to exploit the racial fears and prejudice of white voters. Atwater explained:

> You start out in 1954 by saying, "Nigger, nigger, nigger." By 1968 you can't say "nigger"—that hurts you, backfires. So you say stuff like, "forced busing," "states' rights," and all that stuff, and you're getting so abstract. Now, you're talking about cutting taxes, and all these things you're talking about are totally economic things and a byproduct of them is, blacks get hurt worse than whites. . . . "We want to cut this," is much more abstract than even the busing thing and a hell of a lot more abstract than "Nigger, nigger."[8]

Atwater "start[ed] out in 1954" deliberately. That was the year the Supreme Court decided *Brown v. Board.* Vouchers followed a similar progression, starting in 1954. N-word, to segregation academics, to vouchers, to school choice, to free market competition, to something even more potent: religious freedom.

"School choice" began as one of these economic dog whistles. Segregationists and racists framed publicly funded private education to maintain the color barrier as an issue of choice. "Mississippi segregationists' main weapon of resistance," writes Mississippian and political historian Joseph Crespino, "became 'freedom-of-choice' desegregation plans, which ostensibly gave every student in the district the right to choose which school he or she attended."[9] Betsy DeVos loves to focus on free market "competition." But even the oracle of free market competition, Milton Friedman, adopted religious freedom, too. In his hugely influential book *Free to Choose* (a favorite of Ronald Reagan's, who plays a role in this story), Milton Friedman wrote that paying for public schools "abridge[s] the religious freedom of parents who do not accept the religion taught by the public schools."[10] Notice that

Friedman makes this both an "economic thing" and about religious freedom. But "freedom of choice" really meant segregation. "We can kill" school desegregation, explained one Mississippi county Republican Party chairman by "growing a freedom of choice system."[11]

Mississippi provides several striking case studies for white vouchers.

Senator Cindy Hyde-Smith (R-MS) is dedicated to the Crusade.[12] She's also a vocal supporter of vouchers and school choice, and has joked about going to "a public hanging" (also known as a lynching).[13] In 2021, she introduced a resolution for National School Choice Week.[14] Hyde-Smith attended Lawrence County Academy, a segregation academy that was "started because people didn't want their kids going to school with minorities," in the words of a local NAACP affiliate and local public school board member.[15] Hyde-Smith is not the only product of Mississippi voucher academies who's bent on redefining religious freedom. Former Mississippi governor Phil Bryant graduated from McCluer Academy, a segregation academy run by the Citizens' Council, which began after *Brown* to maintain segregation.[16] Bryant signed several religious freedom laws, including the one discussed in Chapter 1. Hyde-Smith's academy opened just as the Supreme Court, fed up with interminable delays on *Brown*'s "all deliberate speed," ordered states to "immediately terminate dual school systems based on race and operate only unitary school systems."[17] Her school was one of thirty-nine segregation academies that opened in the months following that mandate. That same year, white enrollment in one public school system dropped from 771 students to 28. By the next year, it was 0.[18]

In *The Atlantic*, education journalist Sarah Carr wrote of "how segregation academies are still going strong" well into the modern voucher and school choice movement. Indianola, Mississippi, has "two school systems—one public and black, one private and white."[19] Whites defunded the public schools, leaving them rotting, with sinkholes, no heat, no air conditioning, and worse. "They didn't want black kids to get an education," one student told Carr. To this day, the whites "would prefer not to pay a dime to the public schools," said one of the first students to integrate. This, in turn, drives the narrative that vouchers are needed to save kids from failing public schools.

Starting a new school system overnight raised several practical and logistical problems. It required significant money and resources. Money was the big problem for these segregation academies, but also for the white families who couldn't afford the added expense of suddenly sending all their kids to private school.

Robbery was one possible solution. White students and staff pillaged the public schools on their way out the door, stealing athletic gear, textbooks, supplies, and anything else they could use in their new segregation academies. They even took school "school colors, symbols, and mascots."[20] Local governments developed devious methods for paying teachers from the public treasury to work at the private white schools. For instance, they paid the public school teachers a full lump-sum salary at the beginning of the year; then the teachers would quit and teach at the white school for free that year instead.[21]

Churches were part of the solution, too. Logistically, church infrastructure was necessary. Overnight the bigots needed large spaces to accommodate students and personnel, and a racist ideology that would support a parallel school system. Churches provided rent-free space, volunteers, and a divine, moral justification to continue segregation.

Vouchers were an integral part of the solution for the segregationist parents. After the Supreme Court's immediate desegregation order, the governor of Mississippi pledged on television to establish a private school system as a "workable alternative" for white children and told the legislature to "seek ways and means of rendering assistance" to private schools. "Ways and means" is government-speak for funding.[22] Governments everywhere used vouchers to pay tuition costs at these segregation academies. In Mississippi alone, up to 96 percent of private school tuition was paid by taxpayers through vouchers.[23]

The system is an insidious feedback loop. Pillage public schools to establish segregation academies (with the help of churches). At the same time, defund the public school system that's now entirely Black. Shift those funds into the private segregation academies using vouchers. Then point to the failing, crumbling public schools that were deliberately destroyed as evidence of the need to fund more vouchers. Privatizing education becomes the solution to the problem created by privatizing education. The feedback loop ties nicely into the mission of destroying the "temple" of public schools—burning them all down, as the troll from the cake case said.

Churches were part of the "solution" to maintain segregation, too, and not just in terms of merely material support. If the impetus to flee and destroy public schools was deep-seated racism, it quickly blended and became indistinguishable from Christianity. As Dr. Anthea Butler explains in *White Evangelical Racism*, you can't really divorce the two. American Christianity and especially evangelicalism have deep racist roots; it's "a movement that could and should have moved on from its roots in nineteenth-century racism and slavery . . . yet it has not," writes Butler.[24]

Graduates of segregation academies have begun telling their stories, which show that the Christian churches were willing partners with segregationists.[25] "White churches were involved with segregation academies at every step," explained one alum.[26] They tell of parents declaring that maintaining segregation in spite of a constitutional mandate and a Supreme Court order is "the Christian thing to do," and of how "Protestant churches gave essential support to segregation academies in community after community. Typically, churches helped new academies by volunteering use of their Sunday school rooms until an actual academy's construction." One class of 1973 alum wrote that these schools "cloaked themselves in the American flag, the Bible and fervent, evangelical patriotism"—what we know as Christian nationalism today.[27]

By 1973, "Christian schools and segregation academics are almost synonymous," writes Crespino.[28] And often they were from the start. The Briarcrest Baptist School System was conceived in a dozen local churches the same year a new busing order took effect. Briarcrest insisted that it would allow Black students to enroll, but the local NAACP director called it "a racist place . . . no matter what its admission policy. No black family would want its children educated in such an atmosphere."[29] Crespino writes, "Few church school defenders actually denied that racism played some part in the remarkable growth of private schools from the mid-1960s to the mid-1970s."[30]

The bigots found their solution to continuing segregation in American churches, but the federal government found a counter-solution: tax the segregation academies.

Black families in Mississippi successfully challenged both the voucher schemes and the IRS's initial policy of allowing tax exemptions for segregation academies. That success forced a shift in IRS policy.[31] In 1970, the IRS declared that "it would no longer allow tax exemptions for private schools unless they announced a racially non-discriminatory policy as to students."[32] Taxation would kill the parallel school system and help realize equality in education.

This push to tax segregation academies forever altered the American political landscape. That looming threat created a new alliance. The story has been told many times.[33] Paul Weyrich, a Catholic who founded the Heritage Foundation with money from the Coors brewing empire, Jerry Falwell, a Southern Baptist mega-preacher and founder of Liberty University, and others deliberately sought to unite segregationists, racists, conservative politicians, white politicians, Southern politicians, and conservative Christians in a political mission. Bringing together their mailing lists, media streams, and access, they forged a new alliance in the fires of racism, aiming to maintain segregation. Later, they would *choose* abortion as their wedge issue, not for its moral dimension, but for its power to motivate and unite followers under a religious banner that couldn't be questioned. The Religious Right and the Moral Majority, Weyrich's term that Falwell latched on to, were born.

The talk of taxing segregation academies spawned the talk of religious freedom. The pull of churches to house segregated schools grew beyond mere infrastructure and logistics once the government started talking taxes because churches can claim religious freedom.

But this put the segregationists on the horns of a dilemma. They needed tax exemptions *and* public money to survive. To maintain their tax exemption, they had to claim religious freedom. One segregated Christian school in Hattiesburg, Mississippi, objected to the IRS investigation into its tax exemption because the inquiry violated its "constitutionally protected right of religious freedom and liberty which extends to raising and teaching children in the nurture and admonition of the Lord."[34] But claiming religious freedom put their publicly funded vouchers at risk because taxing citizens to support religion has always been unconstitutional. The initial voucher programs for segregation academies often excluded religious schools when they were first instituted to avoid this legal vulnerability.[35] When they claimed religious freedom to avoid taxes, the publicly funded vouchers could be challenged as a violation of Line #3.

The Supreme Court took up one such challenge in 1971, *Lemon v. Kurtzman*, issuing a seminal state/church separation opinion.[36] You'll remember the *Lemon* test as an unavoidable piece of jargon I used earlier, in the Bladensburg cross chapter. The court synthesized a Line #3 test by pulling the legal principles from every previous case where religion and the law collided. The case underlying the test was about money flowing to private religious schools, most of which were segregated.

Alton Lemon served in the army, graduated from Morehouse College with a mathematics degree, played basketball with Martin Luther King Jr., served in several government jobs, was a Black humanist, and vindicated the Constitution at the Supreme Court.[37] Pennsylvania passed a law that propped up religious schools with taxpayer money. It was rather like the unscrupulous Mississippi program that paid teachers a lump salary, only to have them quit and work at the private white school for the year. Essentially, the state would pay for teachers to work at religious schools, if they were not teaching religion classes. The program was rather like vouchers for teachers' salaries instead of student tuition. The Supreme Court combined the Pennsylvania case with a nearly identical Rhode Island case in which all 250 of the teachers paid under that plan were working at Catholic schools.[38]

Pennsylvania had paid out about $5 million by the time Alton Lemon challenged the program. Lemon argued "that the nonpublic schools are segregated in Pennsylvania by race and religion" and that this new program "perpetrates and promotes the segregation of races." The end result was that the state was "promoting two school systems in Pennsylvania—a public school system predominantly black, poor and inferior and a private, subsidized school system predominantly white, affluent and superior."[39] The lower courts winnowed out the racial issues, and the Supreme Court didn't revive them.

The Supreme Court correctly struck down this program as a violation of the separation of state and church. The court actively enforced

Line #3, rather than treating it as hostile to religious freedom, as the court does now.[40] The concurring justices explained that striking down the program *enhanced* religious freedom: "When taxpayers of many faiths are required to contribute money for the propagation of one faith, the Free Exercise Clause is infringed."[41]

The court got this right, overwhelmingly, in an 8–1 decision that forced a choice on Christian segregation academies: lose your tax exemption or lose your vouchers. The newly formed political bloc created by Weyrich and Falwell counterattacked on both fronts. They set out to protect their tax exemption while discriminating and, at the same time, to smuggle vouchers through Line #3.

BOB JONES WAS A RACIST. "If you are against segregation and against racial separation, then you are against God," declared the evangelist in his 1960 Easter sermon. For Jones, segregation was a divine mandate. Desegregationists, were "infidels" and "Satanic propagandists" creating "Satanic agitation striking back at God's established order." He added, "Religious liberals are the worst infidels." Slavery was actually a good thing, hinted Jones, because "God almighty . . . turned the colored people in the south into wonderful Christian people."[42]

The racist was a successful evangelist, a forerunner to today's megapreachers and televangelists. His racism wasn't idle. Jones founded an eponymous school, which put these tenets into practice.[43] Bob Jones University was formed to educate (a word used loosely here) students while also:

> combatting all atheistic, agnostic, pagan, and so-called scientific adulterations of the Gospel; unqualifiedly affirming and teaching the inspiration of the Bible (both the Old and the New Testaments); the creation of man by the direct act of God; the incarnation and virgin birth of our Lord and Savior, Jesus Christ; His identification as the Son of God; His vicarious atonement for the sins of mankind by the shedding of His blood on the cross; the resurrection of His body from the tomb; His power to save men from sin; the new birth through the regeneration by the Holy Spirit; and the gift of eternal life by the grace of God.[44]

Every school activity and class started and ended with prayer. Daily church was mandatory, as were religion courses.[45] BJU believed that implementing biblical Christianity literally also meant admitting only whites.[46]

After the IRS announced in 1970 that it would not grant tax exemptions to segregated schools, the agency asked every private school in the country, including BJU, about its admission policy. BJU exploited the IRS request to fundraise. "The whole cause of Christ is at stake in this matter," read its fearmongering letter. BJU would "stall" the IRS so that people could "give as generously as possible" in the few tax-exempt weeks remaining: that "may mean somebody is going to have to sacrifice, but Bob Jones University is sacrificing for this cause, too."[47]

At the end of 1970, BJU told the IRS that it "has no Blacks in its student body, and it is the unanimous conviction of [the Board of Trustees] that the University shall not enroll Blacks. These convictions . . . in no way change the status of Bob Jones as a non-profit religious and educational institution."[48] BJU "does not feel it is wise to have black students in its student body. It is not felt that this policy is discriminatory in the legal sense." BJU's president issued a statement that harkened back to its founder's "segregation is scriptural" message, bemoaning that "the whole emphasis today is on a breaking down of racial barriers which God has set up; and where God sets up barriers, He does it for human good."[49]

So the IRS revoked BJU's tax exemption. Or tried to. BJU sued the IRS to prevent that from happening.

BJU sued before the seismic shift in American politics, before the Moral Majority, and decades before the Crusaders' legal arm—that host of organizations born in the 1990s—could coordinate the assault in the courts.[50]

The case bounced up and down the courts for more than a decade before the Supreme Court issued the final decision (a consolidated case that included another segregation academy[51]). Throughout, BJU fiddled with its racist admissions policies, relenting slightly.[52] In 1971, BJU allowed "married Negroes" to apply, but prohibited unmarried

Black people, Black people who married outside their race, and expelled any "students who date outside their own race."[53] "Race mixing" rules like these manifested "a fear that dated back to the Reconstruction and Redemption periods after the Civil War," explains Dr. Butler. "White women . . . were put on a pedestal to promote moral and social 'purity.' Black men were vilified and often lynched over myths about their sexual prowess and their desire for white women."[54] By the time litigation was rolling, BJU had admitted one, unmarried, part-time Black student[55]—not enough to reclaim the tax-exemption. The minor policy shifts were not the major issue in the case; religious freedom was.

"Observers often depict the case as a clash of two competing rights: racial equality versus religious free exercise," wrote Columbia law professor Olatunde Johnson.[56] Racial equality or religious freedom became the focus of the tax exemption fight at the Supreme Court. Or, rather, religious freedom became the justification for segregation *and* tax-exemption.

The Supreme Court had already held in 1976 that segregated private schools without an element of religion could not be tax exempt.[57] So the question in this case was whether religious freedom changed that calculus. In the BJU case, the Supreme Court said no, it didn't: "The Government has a fundamental, overriding interest in eradicating racial discrimination in education—discrimination that prevailed, with official approval, for the first 165 years of this Nation's history. That governmental interest substantially outweighs whatever burden denial of tax benefits places on petitioners' exercise of their religious beliefs."[58] This balancing of burden and government interest is a typical legal test we've replaced and simplified with our three lines. The court also explained, again, that belief and action are treated differently under the law (Line #1) and reiterated the many instances where it is appropriate for the government to regulate action, even when religiously motivated (Line #2), including to collect taxes and enforce child labor laws.[59] The court defended Line #3.

What's the worst that would have happened if BJU were not tax exempt? Would it be forced to violate its religion if it actually had to render unto Caesar, as Jesus said it ought? Would its free exercise of religion have been prohibited? No.

The question was not whether BJU could discriminate, but whether it could discriminate *and* avail itself of a federal tax privilege established by Congress. BJU could still separate the races as its god required. It just wouldn't get a tax exemption to do so. The court agreed: "Denial of tax benefits will inevitably have a substantial impact on the operation of private religious schools, but will not prevent those schools from observing their religious tenets," said the court.[60] Tax exemption is a privilege, not a right, and the government can attach strings to that privilege. The case wasn't a clash between religious freedom and equality, but between a tax exemption created by Congress and equality.

Like the *Lemon* case a decade earlier, the BJU decision was 8–1. The sole dissent in the case, Rehnquist, still agreed that the government had the power to "[deny] § 501(c)(3) status to organizations that practice racial discrimination" and that doing so "would not infringe on petitioners' First Amendment rights."[61] So on the question of whether religious freedom includes a right to a tax exemption, the court unanimously said no.

Unfortunately, the decision didn't have the impact it should have. The entire case depended on IRS policy, and in the decade BJU's case ping-ponged around the courts, Weyrich and Falwell's Religious Right grew powerful enough to influence that policy. Reagan even spoke at Bob Jones University in January 1980, during the presidential campaign. He told a cheering crowd that BJU was a "great institution" and denounced the IRS rules as "evil."[62] The Moral Majority and this new Religious Right helped Reagan win the presidency. One of the founders of that movement, Bob Billings, even worked for Reagan's campaign and in Reagan's Department of Education alongside Clarence Thomas.[63] In return, Reagan undid the IRS policy and permitted segregated Christian schools to remain tax exempt.[64]

So Weyrich and Falwell lost the legal battle on the first front, tax-exemption, at the Supreme Court, but won the political battle, securing their tax exemption. The legal loss was galvanizing and convinced some in the new Christian political movement that they needed committed lawyers on their side. This realization contributed to the explosion of Crusader groups over the next decade.

The BJU case also upheld and reiterated Lines #2 or #3. Religious freedom was insufficiently weaponized in the late 1990s, so Christians needed another way to smuggle vouchers through state/church separation. Explained one scholar, "For vouchers to survive, the Court needed to see them as advancing academic achievement, not religious freedom. This was especially true as long as Justice O'Connor remained the swing vote on Establishment Clause cases."[65] Pursuing this strategy, the Crusaders began peddling disinformation to sell vouchers to the public and the Supreme Court.

We know all this because they told us. Clint Bolick, then the founder of the Crusader group Institute for Justice—which we met in the last chapter—now an Arizona Supreme Court justice, explained this choice in his book *Voucher Wars*. In 1997, Bolick pulled together the "top legal luminaries" on his side (all white men), including former O'Connor clerks. They met in a hotel across the street from the National Education Association and so dubbed this their "Shadow of the Beast conference."[66] They targeted Justice O'Connor as the swing vote in any voucher case involving Line #3 and agreed that O'Connor "would be especially sensitive" to economic and sociological arguments packaged as a good story. Or, as one scholar put it, O'Connor would allow a voucher program "if she believed it was an effective way to help poor, minority children trapped in terrible schools."[67]

Out of this need came the voucher myths that have been ripping apart public education as part of that destructive feedback loop mentioned earlier. This disinformation also advanced "school choice" farther along Atwater's progression of appropriate ways to impose racism on America. This is why, when reading this chapter, some of you have wondered, "How can vouchers be racist when they're rescuing kids from failing inner city schools?" Because the Crusaders sold this fiction when nothing else worked.

Vouchers don't rescue kids in struggling schools. Back in the late '90s, the NAACP passed a resolution against vouchers because they "destroy public education and black people will suffer more and more."[68] Vouchers benefit the most advantaged students, not the least. Georgia created its neo-voucher program in 2007, and "most of the students receiving the scholarships had not come from public schools," explained the *New York Times.*[69] The lawmakers' admitted on tape to crafting neo-vouchers that "would support students already in private schools."[70] The same was true in Wisconsin, where three-quarters of the eligible voucher students *already* attended private schools.[71] For the 2017–18 school year, 100 percent of the schools registered for the Wisconsin Parental Choice Program were religious, and all but three were Christian.[72]

To this day and despite the rescue rhetoric, vouchers often exacerbate segregation. Studies repeatedly show that race-neutral voucher programs intensify racial segregation.[73] The Department of Justice sued Louisiana in 2013 because the vouchers made segregation in the schools *worse* in a state still trying to desegregate after *Brown v. Board.*[74] "Vouchers impeded the desegregation process" by sending state money to private religious schools that discriminate, explained the DOJ.[75]

The voucher dream was not for better education or competition to spur public school performance; the dream was for white Christian education. And that's the voucher reality across the country: enrollment in most private schools is disproportionately white.[76] In fact, "the strongest predictor of white private enrollment is the proportion of black students in the area," according to the Civil Rights Project at Harvard University.[77]

Rescuing students is but one myth. Disinformation about vouchers is rampant. Vouchers don't improve educational or academic outcomes for most kids. Voucher schools are rarely better environments or facilities because private religious schools can ignore rules and regulations, a loophole that has led to some disgusting abuses of the system. Voucher schools also discriminate on virtually any basis, including race, disability, gender, sexual orientation, or religion. Today, this means excluding students with disabilities, LGBTQ students, or anyone else who doesn't fit their ideal—historically, that meant Black Americans, too.[78]

They claim religious freedom to repulse government regulation, but also claim religious freedom to access government money. Even the schools' religious freedom claims are a myth. When minority religions want a slice of taxpayer pie, voucher-loving politicians suddenly remember Line #3. "I actually support funding for teaching the fundamentals of America's Founding Fathers' religion, which is Christianity, in public schools, or private schools," said one Louisiana legislator after discovering that the word "religion" in the voucher bill she helped pass meant "religion," not just "Christianity." While she "liked the idea of giving parents the option of sending their children to a public school or a Christian school," she felt differently about "Muslim schools . . . I do not support using public funds for teaching Islam anywhere."[79]

Before religious freedom was weaponized, Crusaders tailored this disinformation to Justice O'Connor in a case challenging an Ohio voucher program under Line #3 because "96.6 percent of all voucher recipients go to religious schools."[80] Before this Ohio voucher case, there were a few incorrectly decided instances of transportation and textbooks benefiting religious schools, but no direct funding. That changed when O'Connor bit on the myths. The court voted 5–4 to uphold vouchers in the 2002 case, even though it had previously struck down similar programs, including in the *Lemon* case.[81]

The court contended that there was no direct government funding of religion, even though the government's taxing power was the engine for the entire scheme, because of private choice. (Recall that we touched on this briefly with the Hobby Lobby decision's hypocrisy in chapter 10.) Five justices claimed that there was no state/church problem with using the government's taxing power because it was a program of "true private choice."[82] This brings us full circle to the public rationale for starting the segregation academies and the modern private school push in the first place: freedom of choice. "We can kill" school desegregation by "growing a freedom of choice system," said that Mississippi Republican leader.[83]

Freedom of choice opened the door for religious freedom in 2002. The court pushed the needle further in religion's favor in the recent cases we've explored in this book, relying more on religious freedom than ever before. And this court is still not done. *Enough* is not a concept that exists for weaponized religious freedom and the Crusaders.

16

Religious Freedom and
"Promoting the General Welfare"

(*Fulton v. Philadelphia,* Same-Sex Foster Parents Case)

"This [case] could signal a dangerous, broader movement on
the court to give license to discrimination, based on religious beliefs,
especially against gays, lesbians and transgender people."

—**Erwin Chemerinsky**, Dean and Jesse H. Choper Distinguished
Professor of Law, University of California, Berkeley, School of Law[1]

There's a more sinister aspect to the Crusade. Weaponizing religious freedom enshrines Christian privilege into the Constitution, but it also cripples our government's ability to "promote the general welfare," one of the central purposes for which it is ordained, according to the Preamble to the Constitution. This is an unspoken goal of the Crusade. Making civil government impossible ushers us closer to replacing the rule of law with God's Law.

When the Supreme Court asked 150 years ago of our laws, "Can a man excuse his practices to the contrary because of his religious belief?" it answered "no," because to answer otherwise was to invite anarchy. "To permit this would be to make the professed doctrines of religious belief superior to the law of the land, and, in effect, to permit every citizen to become a law unto himself. Government could exist only in name under such circumstances."[2] With a weaponized religious freedom, every law that doesn't agree with conservative Christian dogma

229

will be riddled with exceptions. Every government at every level will be overwhelmed with cases involving religious claims of exemption from the law. Courts will be overwhelmed. Laws will become either a joke or Christian. Chaos and anarchy. But if you're eager for the end times, or want Christian dominion and a Christian nation, crippling the civil government is not counterproductive.

Hell, that chaos will drive people to Christianity. For centuries, Christianity has used social safety nets to win converts. There are, of course, many individuals who help the needy and vulnerable simply because people need help. They take Jesus's words about helping the poor and sick to heart. They try to live that laudable message. But Christianity has also provided relief in order to reach vulnerable souls. Need is a way into people's lives, especially those who are most vulnerable. Justice Scalia said as much in "The Common Christian Good," a speech at the Pontifical Gregorian University in Rome: "I know of no country in which the Churches have grown fuller as the governments have moved leftward. The churches of Europe are empty. . . . Far from doing Christ's work, state provision of welfare positively impedes it."[3] He's upset not that the general welfare is promoted and that people are receiving assistance, but that churches weren't "full" as a result. It's charity to stave off demographic decline—transactional charity.

When the Becket Fund and the Little Sisters of the Poor concocted their religious freedom attacks on the largest expansion of American health care in history, nobody questioned the sincerity of the religious beliefs of the women who took vows of poverty and chastity. There has never been a proper discussion of the fact that expanded and universal health care might make the order obsolete. If the government actually cares for the sick, elderly, poor, and vulnerable, the nuns lose the carrots that bring vulnerable people into their orbit. A history of their order described how it used charity to proselytize. Three nuns left to open a new branch; they "went happy . . . to run after fresh sacrifices and humiliations, but also after fresh victims of misfortune and other souls redeemed at the price of the Blood of the Lord Jesus Christ."[4] The nuns were hamstringing a competitor.

Plenty of churches use charity to prey on the vulnerable. They open schools to avoid kids leaving the faith, and seek to destroy public schools with vouchers. They feed and clothe the homeless, but might first require church attendance. Or even tithing when the people get a job; "that's God's money," said one church-run homeless shelter director.[5] They help place kids in loving homes, but only homes that their god and holy book sanction.

If this seems like harsh criticism, consider that many religious charities choose to shut down when they cannot use their charitable work to impose their religion on the vulnerable.

When Illinois recognized civil unions in 2011, Catholic Charities could no longer legally discriminate against gay couples when placing foster children in homes. Instead of helping those children find loving homes with two parents of the same or opposite sex, Catholic Charities opted to shut down altogether, shuttering services across the state when more than 1,000 children needed homes. The same thing happened in Boston and Washington, DC, when gay marriage was legalized there.[6] Sunrise, a Baptist organization in Kentucky that served 1,000 children, chose the same path for the same reasons in 2021.[7] If they were primarily motivated by a desire to help orphans, they would be helping orphans. At best, helping people is secondary. Charity is secondary.

The Illinois foster care shutdown happened just as the Crusade was getting started, and it was framed as a "religious liberty battle" and an issue of "freedom of religion."[8] After a decade, this particular battle came to a head before this Supreme Court.

Philadelphia wanted to treat its citizens equally. It didn't want to discriminate or pay contractors to provide city services to only some citizens. It didn't want to fund discrimination. Philadelphia also had a duty to care for children in dangerous circumstances and hopefully to place these 6,000 foster children in safe homes. These two duties came together in the Philadelphia Fair Practices Ordinance, which ensured the widest possible pool of foster caregivers by prohibiting discrimination based on color, race, religion, and gender identity or sexual orientation. This is especially important because disproportionately high numbers of LGBTQ youth are homeless and need help. The city was actively trying to recruit more foster families who were sensitive to at-risk LGBTQ youth.[9]

Catholic Social Services had no such scruples regarding discrimination, believing instead that discrimination was required by its god. That disagreement led to a collision at the Supreme Court, with the Becket Fund arguing in favor of discrimination.

Philadelphia contracted out many of the administrative duties of the foster care system, including vetting—interviewing, screening, training, and certifying—families that might foster children. From 2017 to 2018, the city contracted with thirty different groups to provide such vetting, all with identical contracts. CSS vetted caregivers, but didn't actually place children with families.

In March 2018, CSS told Philadelphia it wouldn't vet caregivers who did not meet their god's ideal of what a family should look like.[10] Put another way, CSS refused to do the job it was contracted and paid to do.

James Amato, who ran CSS, testified, "I am following the teachings of the Catholic Church."[11] Catholic Social Service's full name is "Catholic Social Services of the Archdiocese of Philadelphia." It's an extension of the Catholic Church. But it's also "a ministry of the Church, we serve in communion with Jesus of Nazareth who came to bring good news to the poor."[12] It does good work, hard work; but it works to bring the most vulnerable into the church.[13]

The archbishop, Charles Chaput, was widely known for his anti-LGBTQ bigotry.[14] He blamed the rampant child rape, abuse, and coverups in the Catholic Church on "homosexuality."[15] Chaput was supposedly installed to clean up that disaster in this diocese, the subject of multiple grand jury investigations and two major reports.[16] But Chaput was more focused on attacking Obamacare. One local observer hypothesized that Chaput's "anti-Obama crusade is a distraction" from that chronic moral abomination.[17] The Becket Fund gave Chaput a medal in 2009 for his anti-Obama campaign (the same medal it awarded to Leonard Leo in 2017, see page 141), so he was uniquely placed to pull the Becket Fund into the case.[18]

After CSS refused to vet LGBTQ caregivers, the city terminated its contract for foster care. The city still contracted with CSS to provide other services for which it paid CSS $18.5 million, so the contract termination had nothing to do with religion or anti-Catholic bigotry.[19] CSS refused to do a job it contracted for and was paid to do. But CSS believed that it had a right to contract with the city, to take taxpayer money, and discriminate in the name of its god. So it sued.

By now, you should be able to predict the outcome.

The Supreme Court held that terminating this contract violated CSS's religious freedom. Roberts wrote the unanimous opinion and cited the gay wedding cake case early. And, as in the gay wedding cake case, the outcome is awful. Rebecca Markert, a constitutional attorney and cohost of the *We Dissent* legal podcast, put it well. She was "glad the decision wasn't worse, but the LGBTQ community deserves better."[20] Indeed. Forget about legal tests and precedent and how the case will be used in the future, and try to appreciate what *every* justice on the court did in this case. They sanctioned discrimination against a minority in the name of god. That should shock us all.

The general take in the legal profession and academy was that the court punted on the bigger legal questions.[21] There's a lot of disagreement, but most seem to think the court reached some kind of political compromise to minimize the case and its impact. That Roberts based his decision on a technicality and the opinion reads like the court looking for a loophole and the technical formality was enough to bring in all nine justices. Many view it as a limited opinion. But that may have been premature. I fear that it effectively overturned the final roadblock to a weaponized religious freedom, the drug counselor decision we explored in chapter 8 and in which the court defended our lines so vigorously. And Roberts undermined this final barrier by clever, esoteric means that will seem clear in retrospect but are veiled now.

Essentially, Roberts held that unless a law applies to everyone all the time, anyone claiming religious freedom is exempted from the law. The drug counselor case said that there are no religious freedom exceptions from broad, generally applicable laws. This opinion effectively redefines what a broad, generally applicable law is so that no such law exists. That's because every law has exemptions, so the drug counselor roadblock will never be applied again. The unemployment rules in the drug counselor cases were riddled with exceptions themselves, meaning that, under this opinion, the drug counselor precedent wouldn't even apply to itself.[22] It's overturning the precedent without saying so. But Roberts's framing this in the way he did—as an exception to the road-block case, rather than undermining it—is why some people read the case as narrow. Recall that this is essentially what the court did in the shadow docket decision out of California, the challenge to public health orders that impeded in-person bible studies.

Does one exemption in the law based on nonreligious criteria mean that Christianity should get an exemption, too? This case says, "yes." Think about precisely what this means for our society. Go back to the example from the beginning of the book with the religious group in your backyard or the Mormons knocking on your door to under-stand how outlandish this is. You stand in your backyard, nonplussed, as a preacher spews hellfire near your firepit. Trespass is illegal, and the law is on your side. Unfortunately, there are many nonreligious excep-tions to the law of trespass, including emergencies (necessity), to stop or abate a nuisance or prevent harm, to fulfill law enforcement duties, or simply to return something.[23] Some exceptions date back centuries. These exemptions to trespass have nothing to do with religion and in no way impugn religion. But under the court's new regime, the exemp-tions exist, and exemptions for religion do not. That means that the law is hostile to and discriminatory against religion. Therefore, religion—Christians—must be exempt from the law of trespass. The court is unlikely to go that far, but that's the principle it's adopted in this case. It rejected the lines we've used in favor of this unworkable absurdity.

The Crusaders immediately seized on this interpretation. They began arguing that any law that is *capable* of exemptions *must* exempt Christians. Steven Hotze is a right-wing radio host, QAnon adher-ent, and wealthy Republican activist in Texas who spends most of his time and money opposing LGBTQ equality. He believes that "to solve our nation's social and moral problem, our government must enforce biblical law." He's so extreme that he thought Texas governor Greg Abbott's pandemic response was too liberal and sued over Abbott's "draconian" mask order, and again over the stay-at-home order, and again over the state's contact-tracing program. Hotze also left a voice mail for Abbott about Black Lives Matter protesters: "I want to make sure that he has National Guard down here and they have the order to shoot to kill if any of these son-of-a-bitch people start rioting . . . shoot to kill the son of a bitches. That's the only way you restore order. Kill 'em."[24] Hotze runs the Liberty Center for God and Country and several "wellness centers" that sell "supplements."[25] On behalf of those businesses, and with a church added for good measure, Hotze sued so that the businesses could discriminate against LGBTQ employees. He claimed, "I am a Christian and I operate each of my businesses according to my Christian beliefs found in the Bible . . . in accordance with Christian biblical principles."[26] He chose to sue in a venue that virtually guaranteed a win, in front of one of the most conservative and activist judges in the country (the judge that gutted Obamacare, among many other decisions).[27]

Judge Reed O'Connor, a George W. Bush appointee, held that Hotze's businesses "may hire and fire in accordance with sincerely held religious beliefs and employment policies," even though the anti-discrimination provisions of Title VII of the Civil Rights Act of 1964 prohibit precisely this.[28] O'Connor cited the Covid shadow docket cases, the Hobby Lobby case, and the Santeria case. When he described the drug counselor case, the last remaining barrier to this Crusade, he immediately and extensively pivoted to this Philadelphia case to show that it effectively rewrote and reworked that final barrier.[29] The appeal will go to the Fifth Circuit, packed with activist Leo/Trump judges who will almost certainly agree with this rewriting of the final barrier. And then on to the Supreme Court.

Another problem with Roberts's decision in the Philadelphia foster care case is Line #3. The court held that the Catholic Church's religious freedom includes a right to contract with the government *and* that it can impose its religion through that contract. Once again, the Supreme Court trampled Line #3. The Catholic Church is allowed to use the power and imprimatur of the state to impose its religion on other people. The state has delegated the power to vet families to the church, and the church is using that power to impose its religious will on citizens, using tax dollars. We also see again the fatal catch-22 from the Bladensburg cross and Montana neo-voucher cases. The court claims religious freedom to demand the right to contract with the government, but disclaims the religious nature of Catholic Social Services when it comes to taking taxpayer funds to exercise that religious freedom. Claiming religion to get benefits, disclaiming religion to avoid burdens.

The opinion also reads like a defense of the court itself, an impression intensified by the opinion's unanimity. The Crusade, the abuse of the shadow docket, the anti-abortion lawlessness, and other conservative activism had generated lots of court reform talk, and Congress proposed important bills to reform and expand the courts. Historically, when that happens, the court changes course or checks the reins. This decision checked some of the momentum for court reform. I had meetings with congressional offices on court reform bills that were canceled after this case. But the message we should glean from the opinion is precisely the opposite—that court reform is needed now more than ever because the court is playing politics with our constitutional rights.

The Philadelphia foster care opinion moved us toward Christian supremacy. It furthered the Crusade, which is already using it to argue that religious freedom means Christianity is exempt from every law and that equality is an insufficient justification to deny such exemptions. Time will tell, but I'm not as sanguine about the limited nature of this decision. It's also possible that Roberts simply blew up the final barrier to the Crusade in a way that we'll only realize later, perhaps after the 2022 midterms.

CLASHES WITH CHRISTIANITY ARE INEVITABLE the more the government "promotes the general welfare," as our Constitution demands. "Why does the United States seem to rely on religious charities, service providers, and disaster relief more than any other developed nations? Why are these core functions not part of our expectations for government action?" asked Nick Fish, president of American Atheists.[30]

It's tempting to think that the Crusaders and, more broadly, conservatives operate on the assumption that only charity (and therefore religion) can provide the social safety net, not government. Plenty claim as much, pointing to some mythical past.[31] Mitt Romney deviated from this orthodoxy when he declared in 2012, "I'm not concerned about the very poor. We have a safety net." Liberty Counsel, the Crusader who defended Kim Davis and undermined public health measures, attacked: "Romney wrongly assumes that it is the role of government to provide more entitlements to help the poor. In fact, that is not the role of government. The historical biblical view of helping the poor is that they are best helped by individuals and the faith community." The Crusader goes on to talk of "enslav[ing] the poor" in poverty before concluding, "it is the duty of the church, the faith community, to look after the poor, the orphans, and the widows."[32] They see government services as competition for doing what the church does to grow its ranks. Scalia said as much in his transactional charity speech. For them, small government means big church. That also means that American Christianity is invested in the government not working well, in failing to provide a social safety net. Small Government/Big Church conservatives want to neuter the government's ability to care for the most vulnerable among us. Better yet, outsource that care to churches, along with taxpayer funding. For American Christians, that's the best of both worlds. It's Jerry Falwell's dream—not just schools but all social services: "Churches will have taken them over and Christians will be running them."[33]

It's no coincidence that education and health care are two contested areas that repeatedly come up in this book—the young and the sick are among the most vulnerable. Nor that equality is another contested area. The equality clash often centers around the provision of services: marriage licenses, wedding vendors, foster care, and adoption. The government provides services that churches want to provide too, or instead. For instance, "Foster care is a governmental function, not a liturgical function," wrote Connecticut's solicitor general; "the state has a grave responsibility to play its part as *parens patriae* and provide for the well-being of a child when 'parental control falters.'"[34] Religion is free to have its understanding of the family and parenting. To some extent, religion can demand that adherents obey that understanding. But under the three lines we've explored in this book, lines dictated by genuine freedom and constitutional principles, Christianity isn't free to impose that understanding on government services.

Enforcing the three lines in this book protects basic human rights. These lines enshrine equality. One person's religious rights are not a license to violate someone else's rights. If the opposite were true, the believer's rights are held by the law to be supreme—this is the reality the Crusade is fighting for. If one person can use the power and machinery of the state to impose their religion on others, to showcase their religion for the world, to collect money for their religion, it's a violation of every citizen's rights.

"There is no such thing as a single-issue struggle because we do not live single-issue lives," wrote Audre Lorde. The fight to weaponize religious freedom is another front of the fight against equality. So while secularism, which is the fight to uphold these three lines, may seem like a fight for the few, the lucky, the privileged, it's a fight for all of us. These lines have been dying since John Roberts took over the Supreme Court. Or, rather, Roberts, Alito, Thomas, Gorsuch, Kavanaugh, and Barrett are killing them.

17

What's Next?

"The phrases 'religious liberty' and 'religious freedom'
will stand for nothing except hypocrisy so long as they remain
code words for discrimination, intolerance, racism, sexism,
homophobia, Islamophobia, Christian supremacy,
or any form of intolerance."
—**Chairman Martin R. Castro**, US Commission
on Civil Rights, September 2016[1]

This book isn't comprehensive. It's meant to reacquaint readers with true religious freedom, expose this Crusade, and show that there are simple solutions to the religious freedom cases we're told are intractable—solutions that put the onus of religious belief on the believer. The clear lines between belief and action, action that harms others and action that doesn't, and between state and church have served us well. "Those who would renegotiate the boundaries between church and state must therefore answer a difficult question: Why would we trade a system that has served us so well for one that has served others so poorly?" asked Justice Sandra Day O'Connor in one of the twin Ten Commandments cases decided in 2005, the case the court got right.[2]

I also wanted to show how far this court has marched across the lines toward Christian supremacy. Because that is what the Crusade offers as a replacement for our lines: inequality.

I left out many cases. There are simply too many to cover, and because the court is eager to consummate the Crusade, more are coming. Said one veteran law professor in late 2020, "I have never seen such a spurt of religious-liberty cases in such a short time, especially where over and over again there is a victory for religious-liberty claims."[3] The religious freedom docket exploded after Amy Coney Barrett joined the court and had not slowed as this book went to press. The court is taking more Crusader cases than ever before. Things will be worse by the time you read this.

Here's a short rundown of some of the important kinds of cases that didn't get full treatment.

Children

Consider the following cases about children:

- The crowd looks on passively as the man cuts off the foreskin, places his mouth over the infant's penis, and sucks the blood and skin into his mouth, exchanging bodily fluids with the infant. The ritual infects some infants with herpes. Some die. Others spend weeks in the hospital. This is happening in America right now. And the government refuses to stop it because of religious freedom.[4]

- An Idaho graveyard is full of children born to parents in the Followers of Christ, a sect with an infant-mortality rate ten times higher than the rest of the state. Beyond prayer, their parents won't interfere with "God's plan." They refuse even the most basic medical aid—antibiotics or insulin—that would save children's lives (see *The Founding Myth*, chapter 22).

- A law allows minors eleven years old and up to receive CDC-recommended vaccines without parental consent if a doctor approves. Robert F. Kennedy Jr.'s anti-vaxxer organization sued, arguing that the law violates parents' religious freedom.[5]

- In another lawsuit, parents and a Catholic school argue that masking measures violated their religious freedom because: "A mask shields our humanity. And because God created us in His image, we are masking that image. . . . As the Catholic faith teaches, we are relational beings. And our existence as relational beings points to the Holy Trinity. A mask is disruptive to this essential element of the Catholic faith."[6] (The pope disagreed.[7])

- The Amish prefer to pull children out of school after they turn fourteen because the more educated and knowledgeable they are, the more likely they are to choose to leave the religious order. And so the Amish circumvent compulsory education laws to preserve their religion at the expense of children.

Adults should not be able to suck an infant's penis in the name of god—that this sentence needs to be written is a condemnation of today's religious freedom. Exemptions from criminal law that protect parents who pray their children to death in lieu of seeking medical care are inhumane and should be abolished (roughly thirty states have such exemptions.[8]) Nor should religious freedom claims protect parents or stop children from getting life-saving vaccines or wearing masks during a pandemic.

In these cases, *granting* religious freedom claims causes harm; denying the claims causes none. There's no harm in saving a child's life and health with medical interventions that fend off some god's plan until the child is old enough to understand the inevitable result of refusing life-saving medicine. The same goes for ritual circumcision. Wait until the child can consent to having their foreskin removed, including by another man's mouth, if they so wish. There's no legitimate medical reason to do this on children incapable of consent, unless one thinks that thoughtful, grown adults are unlikely to agree to having part of their genitalia sliced away. But if the justification for imposing the procedure on children is that they won't voluntarily consent as adults, be it to an unnecessary surgery or to stay with a particular sect, then it rather proves the harm in granting the religious freedom claim in the first place.

Courts get these cases wrong when judges focus on the religious freedom of the parents and ignore the harm to the child—when they fail to examine Line #2. Take the Amish example, the fact pattern people find most sympathetic to a religious freedom argument. At worst, the child will learn more. How is this a harm? The child may not then choose the religious path, but they are free to do so; *that* is religious freedom. Forcing them to remain unlearned as a way to keep them in a religious sect is religious bondage. In 1972, the Supreme Court decided Amish parents could stop their children's education early, despite a law requiring schooling. Viewing the sect through condescending, rose-colored glasses, the court saw "rural" communities "aloof from the world," devoted to "a life in harmony with nature and the soil," and romanticized an "Amish society [that] emphasizes informal 'learning through doing;' a life of 'goodness,' rather than a life of intellect; wisdom, rather than technical knowledge" (as if these things are mutually exclusive). The court even claimed that this sect has "never been known to commit crimes, that none had been known to receive public assistance, and that none were unemployed." Professor Marci Hamilton, the leading expert on the misuse of religious freedom to abuse children, has described the decision as "a love letter to the Amish."[9] The court focused on the religious freedom of the community and parents, and utterly subordinated the rights of the children. The court condemned Amish children to that rural, aloof life, without once asking about their "preferred course," as the dissent suggested. The court chose for the children, robbing them of their freedom in the name of religious freedom.

When it comes to religious freedom, we'd do better to think of parents as having duties and responsibilities *to* children, not rights *over* children. These cases can be humanely resolved by treating the children like people with their own rights, including self-autonomy and health. Government telling parents how to raise their children is a fearsome boogieman in the American mind, and justified in some communities (think of Al Smith, chapter 8). The Supreme Court touched on this fear in 1925 when it allowed children to receive private school education under compulsory education laws: "The child is not the mere creature of the State; those who nurture him and direct his destiny have the right, coupled with the high duty, to recognize and prepare him for additional obligations."[10] That is why these cases are harder. But that doesn't make them impossible. And it doesn't mean that while a young life is incapable of caring fully for itself, religion can impose on it things that the adult wouldn't consent to. Responsibility for others does not imply impunity.

We learned at the beginning of this book that parents do not have unlimited rights over their children. The principle is greater than the

Abraham and Isaac hypothetical. Parents don't have a right to risk the life or safety of their children because they believe a god commands it. A parent who viciously beats a child should be punished without regard to biblical edict. Parents who neglect the health of their diabetic child, leading to the child's death, should not be exempt from homicide and neglect laws.

The law cannot allow children to be sacrificed on the altar of religious freedom. The law must be the arresting hand that stops Abraham from plunging the knife into his son, not the legal sanction for the murder.

Employment Discrimination

I also didn't cover a series of increasingly frequent cases involving religious freedom as a defense to employment discrimination lawsuits. Churches have a constitutional dispensation to hire and fire clergy as they see fit. Carte blanche. This actually makes sense *for clergy* under nearly any conception of religious freedom. Catholic churches should be allowed to hire only Catholic priests—Line #3 cuts both ways. But, of course, the Crusaders wanted more. This is now being applied to any nominally religious position, and some clearly nonreligious positions, at any religious organization. The Becket Fund sued, and in 2012, the Supreme Court stated this basic rule, known as the "ministerial exception," but applied it to non-ministers. A Lutheran school fired a teacher for having a disability. She sued under the Americans with Disabilities Act, and the court refused to examine her case because "the constitutional guarantee of religious freedom protects the group's right to remove the employee."[11]

Congress explained how religion and the ADA interact with a helpful hypothetical:

> Assume that a Mormon organization wishes to hire only Mormons to perform certain jobs. If a person with a disability applies for the job, but is not a Mormon, the organization can refuse to hire him or her. However, if two Mormons apply for a job, one with a disability and one without a disability, the organization cannot discriminate against the applicant with the disability because of that person's disability.[12]

Under the ADA, churches can account for religion, but not for disability. They may impose religious requirements on positions but must not discriminate against a person with disabilities who meets those requirements.

But the court has done something different with the ministerial exception. It asks whether an employee is a minister or not. If she is, then the court cannot even hear the case. The appellate court didn't think that the teacher at the Lutheran school was a minister because her "primary duties were secular . . . she spent the overwhelming majority of her day teaching secular subjects using secular textbooks," and the school didn't rely on her for indoctrination.[13] The Supreme Court upheld the termination anyway.

One of Roberts's favorite incrementalist tactics is to pry open the law in a way that privileges Christians, while claiming the same decision is limited (one reason to fear the Philadelphia foster care case). Roberts knows when he cracks the door, the Crusaders will kick it in.[14] Before this case, a host of cases held that "lay teachers" couldn't be fired with impunity. A school firing a teacher is not the same as a church firing a clergyman. Roberts changed that, and it got worse immediately. Religious schools and organizations rewrote their employment contracts to label employees as ministers and give them a few nominal religious duties.[15]

And, of course, the Crusaders came back to the court. In 2020, the Supreme Court decided a pair of Becket Fund cases in favor of Catholic schools and against employees. One employee was fired while getting breast cancer treatment; she died, and her estate sued for wrongful termination. The other brought an age-discrimination lawsuit against her employer.[16] Neither school claimed it fired either teacher for religious reasons, but both schools sought refuge from civil rights laws in religious freedom. The Supreme Court said that, because of the ministerial exception, Catholic schools can declare that teachers are ministers and fire them, despite clear anti-discrimination laws. The Catholic court allowed Catholic schools to successfully argue that women, *who cannot be ordained in the Catholic Church*, are ministers and so can be fired on a whim.

These cases cannot be made to agree with the decisions in the Montana case and Missouri ministry case. Christian schools want to be considered religious and special when it comes to firing their gay employees or their employees with disabilities or their employees undergoing chemotherapy, but they want equal treatment when it comes to public funding. Catholic schools now demand a right to access public funds; by one estimate, religious schools took in between $4 and $8 billion in Paycheck Protection Program funds during the pandemic,[17] many while flouting public health orders, also in the name of religion. This weaponized religious freedom means taxpayer funds must flow to churches and that regulation cannot accompany the checks.

State and church used to be two wary animals pacing on either side of a wall, out of one another's territory. Now, one is a host and the other a parasite. Churches have argued and won: "If you treat us differently in a way we don't like, it's discrimination. If you treat us differently in a way that benefits us, it's because religious freedom requires it." That, my friends, is religious privilege. Churches want to have their cake—which they think American taxpayers must buy—and eat it too.

Tangentially Religious

I also left out cases where religion wasn't the central question but will become so in the future. For instance, sometimes this court will get something right but leave the door cracked for religious freedom. Not as part of the incrementalist approach, but as a back door to advance the Crusade, sometimes in an opinion the other side will love. In 2020, the court finally agreed that sexual orientation and gender identity are necessarily protected under federal civil rights laws that protect against gender discrimination. Gorsuch and Roberts defected in the 6–3 decision. This was a huge win for LGBTQ people and is legally and logically sound. "It is impossible to discriminate against a person for being homosexual or transgender without discriminating against that individual based on sex," wrote Gorsuch.[18] He's right, "An employer who fires an individual for being homosexual or transgender fires that person for traits or actions it would not have questioned in members of a different sex."[19] Perfectly correct.

But Gorsuch left the gate open for the Crusaders. He even drew their attention to it: "employers in other cases may raise free exercise [of religion] arguments that merit careful consideration," though the employers in this case didn't argue that "Title VII will infringe their own religious liberties in any way."[20] Gorsuch even noted that the Religious Freedom Restoration Act (see chapter 9) is a "super statute" that "displaces" other federal statutes, such as civil rights laws like Title VII.

The Crusaders are already storming through the Gorsuch gate. Recall, from chapter 16, the lawsuit brought by Steven Hotze, the right-wing radio host, QAnon Texan, and GOP powerbroker who thinks Texas governor Greg Abbott is too liberal. The activist conservative judge in that case explained that Gorsuch "expressly left open the implications for religious liberties and other matters arising from its decision."[21] The judge then decided the religious freedom question in favor of the bigot, giving Hotze a license to discriminate.

Given how the Philadelphia decision circumvented the final barrier to religious exemptions from any and every law, we should expect to see this weaponized religious freedom argued everywhere. Every liberal, progressive, democratic, and Democratic win before this court will have an asterisk that reads, "until a religious freedom case on this point is litigated."

AS THIS BOOK GOES TO PRESS, THE FLOW OF RELIGIOUS FREEDOM CASES to the court is increasing. The court once decided these cases every few years. Then, in the decade following the *Deus vult*, they increased to deciding one a term. Now, they're deciding three, four, or perhaps as many as seven or eight religious freedom cases a term if we include the shadow docket (as we must). In 2020 and 2021 alone, the court forced taxpayers to fund religious schools (chapter 13), struck down public health using religious freedom in several cases on the shadow docket (chapter 11),[22] gave the Catholic Church a license to discriminate while performing government contracts (chapter 16)[23] and forced Boston to fly the Christian flag over its City Hall at the request of a group that is dedicated to indoctrinating "the next generation . . . with the knowledge of how America was founded as a Christian nation."[24] (On Jan. 6, 2021, Christian Nationalists and insurrectionists paraded the flag on the floor of the US Senate after they breached the Capitol. It marked their territory on January 6 and will do the same flying over the seat of government in one of our oldest cities.) The court also accepted

Crusader-brought cases involving another voucher program to benefit religious schools, the football coach who imposes prayer on students (see page 55), and, in early 2022, it also agreed to hear a rerun of the gay wedding cake case brought by the same Crusader and involving a graphic designer who had never been approached by a gay couple or denied anyone service or been found to have violated a civil rights law.[25]

The outcomes are predictable. If the facts don't fit the Crusade, the court will alter reality, like the Town of Greece prayers, gay wedding cake, and Missouri ministry cases. Recall that in religion cases at the Roberts Court, Christianity won 85 percent of the time, up from 44 percent before every other Supreme Court. These justices' overriding principle won't be reality or the law or the Constitution or the three lines or even any of the legal tests unnamed in this book, but simply this: Christians win. With some due consideration given to the legitimacy of the court to preserve the opinions and, therefore, the wins for White Christian America.[26]

There is also a coming attack on the last citadel of Line #3: American public schools. Courts have been unwilling to allow the machinery of the state that educates our children to be hijacked to impose religion on children. This has forced Crusaders into the strategy of eroding public schools and establishing a parallel religious education system. They've secured funding for their parallel system and done all they can to destroy and lower the quality of public schools. They're pushing for a reckoning that will either force Christianity into the public schools or force public school students into the Christian schools. I suspect that the court's opinion in the Maine voucher case, brought by the Institute for Justice and First Liberty Institute, might open this door. In the Missouri ministry case, the court pretended that the grant recipient wasn't a children's ministry and neglected Line #3 because the parties agreed. In the Montana neo-voucher case, the court simply ignored Line #3 and everyone other than the Christian families. But in the Maine case, the court might say straight out that public money can fund religious education and indoctrination. The Christian schools in that case had even indicated that they wouldn't accept public funds.[27] Again, the captured court wants to take these cases.

I also expect to see the culmination of the "hostility toward Christianity" argument. The court has essentially declared that the separation of state and church is hostile to religious freedom even though that separation is the solution to hostility, not the source. The court might deliver the *coup de grace* to Line #3 and possibly the school citadel in the case of the praying football coach. It could declare that public school teachers, employees, and administrators have a religious freedom right to abuse government power and position to impose their religion on the children under their care. This is the "deceitful narrative" case in which the coach moved out of state a year and a half before the Crusader asked the Supreme Court to take the case. If the court decides yet another moot case, and in favor of the Institute's "deceitful narrative," it will say little about the law and much about the justices' desire to rewrite religious freedom law. Again.

Demographics, Dominance, and the Flip Side of the Coin

I also omitted a whole genre of fascinating new cases that are the flip side of this religious liberty coin.

The changing demographics that instill such fear in White Christian America, that seem to threaten its dominance, have also been pushing the boundaries of religious freedom law. Professor Jay Wexler has explored some of these cases in *Our Non-Christian Nation: How Atheists, Satanists, Pagans, and Others Are Demanding Their Rightful Place in Public Life.*[28] The same demographic desertion that is driving the fear and Crusade—there are now more atheists and agnostics than Mormons, Jews, Hindus, Muslims, Jehovah's Witnesses, and Buddhists combined, and the "nones" are now the biggest religious self-identification denomination in the country—is challenging our understanding of religious freedom.[29] It raises truly interesting questions that get at the heart of our Constitution's guarantees of equality and religious freedom.

Ask yourself, why is religion protected by the law? What makes it special? Ignore, for a moment, the historical drivers: the "torrents of blood . . . spilt in the old world."[30] (Equal protection in the Constitution and civil rights laws have that covered for now.) Why do we carve out special protection for religious beliefs from a philosophical standpoint?

Religion is special in two ways: the *degree* of belief and the *basis* of the belief. Degree? They really, really believe it. Why? Faith.[31] Religious freedom is a specially protected right because people really, really believe certain things without evidence.

On reflection, that seems a tad unreasonable. It also seems backward. This rationale incorporates a judgment about the relative value of ideas, and it's reversed. Unreasoned beliefs deeply held are given greater legal protection than reasoned beliefs deeply held. One who is told, "This is a moral rule because that god said so," has more legal protections for that belief and ability to act on the belief than another who arrives at the moral rule through careful thought and study. Obedience is valued over rationality. Tradition over reason. "Because he said so" over "because it is right."

We saw this inverted valuation earlier. Think back to the unemployment cases in chapter 8, the runaway freedom-of-religion train the court tried to derail in the drug counselor case. Those decisions in favor of Seventh-day Adventists had created a system whereby people who believed their god commanded them not to work on certain days and who were out of work as a result would be given unemployment benefits. This same thing happened in similar cases. Church leaders told Eddie Thomas what his god desired, and Eddie believed it, so he received unemployment benefits after quitting a job manufacturing military armaments.[32] Someone with the same pacifist position, reached after much personal edification and soul-searching, who quits the same job would be denied those benefits.[33]

A Hindu or Buddhist prisoner might demand and receive vegetarian meals on religious grounds. (Jacob Chansley, the self-proclaimed "QAnon Shaman" and the horned, painted face of the January 6 insurrection, was given organic food in jail because his religious beliefs required that he only eat "traditional food that has been made by God."[34]) The thoughtful vegetarian who has studied the impact of consuming animals on the climate crisis and learned of their capacity to suffer might demand the same and get nothing.

Courts have struggled with this inverted valuation. In the military draft cases, they even attempted to correct it. Some pacifist sects oppose war because their god said so. That belief gets special protection and exemptions from military service and the draft. Some thoughtful citizens drafted to fight in Vietnam held conscientious objections to killing another human, arriving at the conclusion after ethical and moral musing. Surely that latter refusal is more principled than a person who's simply following what they're told is a divine command? The court struggled with this and said, though not quite in these words, that religious freedom really protects matters of deepest conscience, including these deeply held nonreligious convictions.[35]

Under this conception, religion is not so special. Matters of conscience are worth protecting, and religion is such a matter. Indeed, the founders often spoke of "rights of conscience." During the debate about what would become the First Amendment, this broader understanding of religious freedom was crucial. One of the only Catholic founders, Daniel Carroll, argued in favor of the First Amendment because, "The rights of conscience are a peculiar delicacy and will little bear the gentlest touch of government's hand."[36] When James Madison first introduced the provisions, conscience was the language he used. He proposed that "no State shall violate the equal right of conscience," spoke of "the great rights," including "liberty of conscience," and called "freedom of the press and rights of conscience, those choicest privileges of the people."[37] This understanding conceives of religion as one facet of the freedom of thought that we protect, but not as the only one and not as special.

Epistemologically, religious belief is inferior to conscience. After all, if the divinity of the command is the issue, then the content of the command is irrelevant. And if the worth of the belief is derived from the morality of the belief or act, and not the divinity of the underlying command, why give religion protection instead of conscience? Protecting conscience, as opposed to just religion, protects the thoughtful vegan and rational pacifist. As it stands now, it's inequitable and backward that individuals with identical positions are treated so differently under our law. Given the demographic shift away from religion, the inequity is only going to grow more stark. This disparity will, of course, be further exacerbated by the Crusade, which seeks inequality through religious freedom.

It is this exacerbated inequality that is creating this genre of cases and opening these fascinating legal horizons. At their most basic levels, people are seeking the same privileges the law extends to Christians who claim the privilege with the ease of one word, "god." Let's look at just a few.

For more than a decade, nonreligious members of our military—the second largest religious demographic in the military, you'll recall—have been asking for nonreligious or humanist chaplains. They want and deserve the same kind of support that Christian soldiers receive (only about 70 percent of the military identifies as Christian, but more than 97 percent of all chaplains are Christian).[38] Nonreligious chaplains may sound like a contradiction. Tony Perkins, who runs the Crusader group Family Research Council and who Trump tapped for a position on the United States Commission on International Religious Freedom, mocked the idea: "Atheist chaplains are like vegetarian carnivores. They don't exist!"[39] They exist; and, in the military, chaplains have serious advantages over, for instance, mental health counselors. When chaplains are told things in confidence, "No commander, court, or anyone else can compel a chaplain or chaplain assistant to reveal such privileged information" without consent.[40] This nearly absolute confidentiality is unequaled in the military for personal health and counseling. Military courts have even overturned criminal convictions if key information was disclosed by the chaplain.[41] By contrast, while there is a presumption against reporting psychological issues to soldiers' commanding officers, they *must* be reported up the chain of command in nine broad instances, including a catchall, "harm to mission."[42] This perverse incentive means that some secular counselors and advisors even turn soldiers away, instructing them to go and visit chaplains, to whom they can speak safely and freely.[43] The Department of Defense has refused to treat these freethinkers equally and fought multiple lawsuits to prevent humanist chaplains from serving this growing demographic in the ranks.

Secular Americans have given hundreds of invocations at local government meetings nationwide.[44] They prefer to uphold Line #3, but if the government insists on prayers, they want their chance to solemnize public meetings, to be included rather than excluded. Those giving secular invocations meet with genuine hostility and discrimination occasionally, and have won and lost lawsuits on their inclusion. I argued and lost a case about an atheist, Dan Barker, delivering a prayer to open the US House of Representatives. The House chaplain discriminated against him, and the second-highest court in the land sanctioned that discrimination. Anyone who compares previous prayers to Barker's proposed invocation—"Let us rejoice in the inalienable liberty of conscience our forefathers and foremothers risked their lives to establish and our country continues to defend against those enemies who despise freedom of religion, freedom of speech, and freedom of thought"—cannot find fault or inferiority.[45] The court found fault in that he didn't include certain magic words that it permitted the chaplain to impose.

The Satanic Temple, a group of nontheists, is raising some of these cutting-edge legal questions. TST's activism is causing some judges to rethink their blind acceptance of the sincerity of religious beliefs. TST also created a "religious abortion ritual, a ceremony rooted in our deeply held beliefs," that will collide with virtually every abortion restriction in the country—and in the name of religious freedom. The ceremony is based on members' deeply held belief in bodily autonomy, and supported by evidence, thought, and philosophy. TST has also sought to put up monuments to fallen soldiers, just like the Christian cross in Bladensburg, around which the group also hosted a ritual to honor Satanic veterans and "celebrated th[e] government-sanctioned monument in the name of Satan."[46]

We should expect to see a few challenges to the coming abortion bans that are rooted in religious freedom, both because some religions mandate abortions for adherents if, for instance, the life of the mother is in danger, and because the loss of reproductive freedom is, at its heart, the imposition of one particular branch of conservative Christianity on us all.

More challenges to our traditional understanding of religious freedom will inevitably arise as more Americans leave Christianity behind.

Instead of expanding the concept of religious freedom to encompass our rich and growing diversity, religious freedom is contracting. Crusaders are circling the wagons around the dwindling dominant caste, and while religious freedom is contracting overall, religious freedom is actually expanding within that smaller circle to encompass other characteristics of White Christian America that aren't religious, but which are given the "religion" label so as to receive the protection. The Crusade is robbing Americans of their religious freedom, while extending the protections of religious freedom to, for instance, the political beliefs of White Christian America. A wave of new scholarship shows that, rather than religion driving people's political ideology, it's the other way around; politics is driving religious belief.[47] This has monumental implications for religious freedom law.

If the "politics drives religion" argument is not wholly convincing, at the very least there is a feedback loop, where the politics pressures religion and religion pressures the politics. One such toxic mix of religion and politics we've come to know is Christian nationalism. It becomes hard to disentangle the political from the religious, but they believe each fervently, so they slap the religion label on it and go to court.

This happened with vaccines and masks as the pandemic wore on. No major religion objected to Covid vaccines. The sharp increase in people claiming religious exemptions from required vaccines—exemptions that shouldn't exist—shows the after-the-fact nature of religious justifications for behavior. No new biblical scroll about vaccines was discovered, no new divine revelation handed down from heaven. People opposed life-saving medical science for political reasons, but there was no political exemption for vaccines, so instead they used the magic word, "god." This happened with masks too. Louisiana attorney general Jeff Landry distributed form letters that read: "I do not consent to forcing a face covering on my child, who is created in the image of God. Masks . . . interfere with religious commands to share God's love with others, and interfere with relationships in contravention with the Bible."[48] One father refused to let his kids wear masks in school because "the Bible says we're made in the image of God and Satan tries to cover that up."[49] An Ohio lawmaker said, "This is the greatest nation on earth founded on Judeo-Christian Principles . . ."—this is not true, please go read *The Founding Myth*. "One of those principles is that we are all created in the image and likeness of God. That image is seen the most by our face. I will not wear a mask. That's the image of God right there."[50] Pastor Greg Locke, who burned *The Founding Myth* with a blowtorch, banned masks at his church. There's no theology[51] or reality to back up those statements, but it doesn't matter in the legal context of religious freedom because they'll claim it's religious. Right now, our collective deference to religious beliefs sharpens religious freedom as a weapon. That is, you will recall, the point of this potent weapon. It can and will be applied in virtually every context.

Unless, of course, we can stop the court and reverse the Crusaders' damage.

Conclusion

The End of
Religious Freedom?

I t's traditional to end books like this with a solution to the problem
presented. The solution here is simple: expand and rebalance the
Supreme Court. The six-member conservative bloc on the court is
the problem. We need immediate and massive court reform.

The solution is as clear as it is unlikely. It requires shattering the
myth of an impartial, non-partisan institution guided by legal principles. Whatever the court was, that is not what this court is. It is a
broken body. Destroy that myth, fix that court, then we can look at
reversing the Crusade's damage.

Court reform is a good idea no matter what issue you care about:
voting, LGBTQ, women's, consumer, disability, housing, or immi-
grant rights; fighting for racial, criminal, environmental, or reproductive justice; ending the climate crisis. We need serious democratic
reform—with a small *d*. We need to empower people and voters, not
corporations and churches. White Christian Americans are choosing
that identity over our democracy. They are willingly walking into the
arms of fascists and authoritarians because equality feels like a threat.

Unfortunately, every policy solution and litigation strategy we can
employ to cure America's ills leads to the Supreme Court. All remedial
roads lead to 1 First Street, NE. To solve these problems, we first need
a solution to this Supreme Court. After much study and agonizing,
I'm convinced that the only effective solution is adding seats to the
Supreme Court to rebalance its extreme shift to the right. Anything else
is a half measure or temporary fix. The court was stolen by monied special interests intent on fomenting this Crusade. We have to take back
the court. My great fear is that we'll look back on the two-year window
from 2021 to 2022 as the last chance America had to save itself.

It's tempting to point to the shifting demographics as a bright spot, and they are, but they're not a solution. Demographics are shifting against the court and the Christian supremacy asserted in these religious freedom "victories." Professor Leslie Griffin observed that the victories are really losses, including for many members of the religious institutions bringing the challenges.[1] Christians attack life-saving vaccines, masks, public health orders, and shun them for the "blood of Jesus." Christians discriminate against LGBTQ couples and foster parents and children. They discriminate in their schools against LGTBQ people, people with disabilities, and non-Christian students, and demand that taxpayers foot the bill. No wonder record numbers of young Americans are claiming that they have no religious affiliation.

Stacked against this demographic shift are the lifetime appointments of about 230 Trump judges who comprise more than a quarter of the federal judiciary.[2] They were chosen *because* they are young, conservative ideologues. *Now*, with lifetime appointments and the only check the impossibly high bar of impeachment. The Crusaders went after the judiciary as a tool of minority rule. Without court reform and expansion, the Crusaders will continue to enshrine Christian privilege for another half century. Longer, once they successfully extend their Crusade into voting rights and democratic reforms.

Everything comes back to court reform and expansion.

WHAT'S THE WORST THAT WOULD HAVE HAPPENED if the religious freedom claims were rejected in the cases we explored in this book? It's not a question ever asked by the court, but one we explored. What is the worst that would've happened in these cases? A corporation that's never been to church would have had to provide comprehensive health insurance to its employees; a business wouldn't have been able to discriminate against customers because of their sexual orientation or, for that matter, race; public health measures would save people's lives; drug counselors fired for doing drugs wouldn't receive unemployment because they were fired for cause; clerks would have to issue lawful licenses; Christian parents who want to opt out of the public school system that our taxes already fund would have to do so on their own dime; the government would have to put up inclusive memorials;

nuns might have to fill out a brief, five-part form to notify the government that they're taking a religious exemption. In every case, the people claiming religious freedom were still allowed to pray, to go to church when it didn't risk killing others, to hate gay people, to not use contraception, to not get an abortion, to put a cross on their grave, or to send their kids to a private Christian school.

Even if the court gets a case wrong, heaven won't fall. No god would be dethroned. We should not fear offending religion, but fear failing justice. *Fiat justitia ruat cælum.* This Latin legal maxim means something like, "Let justice be done though the skies may fall."[3] When it comes to religion and the law, we might amend the maxim slightly: "Let justice be done, though heaven fall." If you believe in an all-powerful god, there's no danger that judicial decisions will trouble him in his heaven.

If, however, we ask *what's the worst that can happen with a weaponized religious freedom?*, the answer is alarming. What's the worst that could happen if we allow any religiously motivated action an exemption from a law? The rule of law disappears. When the Supreme Court asked the same question 150 years ago, anarchy was the answer. Every citizen would "become a law unto himself. Government could exist only in name under such circumstances."[4] In systems that value an individual's right to act on any religious belief, there is no law; there is only what that individual believes their god commands. And, often, that will devolve into a matter of political convenience that's simply assigned religious significance after it's been politicized, as with masks and vaccines. We'll have traded the rule of law for the rule of each conservative Christian's personal god.

When Pope Urban II launched the first crusade to cheers of *Deus vult!*, he emphasized in his sermon that the "Turks" had attacked Christians, destroyed churches, and "devastated the Kingdom of God."[5] Another possible translation is that they "laid waste to God's kingdom."[6] He pitched the crusade as us versus them, a zero-sum game. The medieval crusaders had to drop their plowshares, strap on their swords, and march to the Holy Land to retake and rebuild the Kingdom of God. Conquest. The message that Amy Coney Barrett had for the new lawyers she roused was not dissimilar. Being a lawyer "is but a means to an end . . . and that end is building the Kingdom of God."[7]

Crusaders sit on our Supreme Court. They are working to prove the swords-to-plowshares prophecy true. That lovely turn of phrase signified a new era of peace. But in the biblical story, that peace comes only after conquest and forcible conversion. "And it shall come to pass in the last days, that the mountain of the Lord's house shall be established in the top of the mountains, and shall be exalted above the hills; and all nations shall flow unto it," says the Book of Isaiah. "And he shall judge among the nations, and shall rebuke many people: and they shall beat their swords into plowshares."[8]

Only after the Kingdom of God has been established and imposed on "all nations" will there be peace. War is peace.

Once their crusade is successful, once conservative white Christians sit atop the hierarchy, the mountain, in the privileged position gained with their weaponized religious freedom, they'll sue for peace.

Acknowledgments

Books are rarely the product of one person, and this one is no exception. Books are a team effort for which we authors take the credit. There are many people who deserve my thanks for making this book possible. Here are a few:

My family, for their unwavering support. In particular, EC, OU, SA, and TL, who bore the heaviest burdens.

Callahan Miller for her amazing research and willingness to help out when I desperately needed it. Ryan Jayne for his thoughtful comments and editing.

Sam Grover for his nuance, creativity, and erudition when arguing finer points with me on our morning runs.

My colleagues and co-counsel at the Freedom From Religion Foundation, Americans United for the Separation of Church and State, American Civil Liberties Union, American Atheists, Center for Inquiry, American Humanist Association, and Secular Coalition for America, and the hundreds of local groups and activists working to defend true religious freedom and the wall of separation.

Sukhvir Singh for tracking down a difficult piece of legal history for me. Ayesha Khan for all her generous time. Monica Miller for her time and insight.

Andrew Torrez and Thomas Smith of the *Opening Arguments* podcast for making this book inevitable by having me on so many times (here's to lowering the Lukumi bar).

Charlie Craig and Dave Mullins for giving me their time and trust.

Professors Leslie Griffin, Marci Hamilton, Dan Canon, Andrew Lewis, Mark Satta, and the other experts and professionals who weighed in on particular aspects of these arguments. The Supreme Court clerks and admissions team for helping me with a few thorny questions. The City of Hialeah library staff for trying.

Hemant Mehta at the *Friendly Atheist* for accurately cataloging religion news in America, from whimsical shenanigans to lethal immorality; his site nearly always came up when I was researching a specific event. The other was Right Wing Watch, brilliant, tireless folks—Kyle Mantela, in particular.

Professor Erwin Chemerinsky for graciously taking time to write the foreword. Jane Dystel for guiding me through and encouraging me to do a second book, even when the timeline seemed impossible. Barbara Berger for her superb editing skills and her unerring ability to rein me in or let me rage as necessary.

And, most of all, to my many supporters, in particular my original coffee crew. This fight is impossibly hard. Sisyphean. It'd be impossible without your support, encouragement, and caffeine.

Notes

EPIGRAPH

1 Will Durant and Ariel Durant, *The Story of Civilization: The Life of Greece* (New York: Simon & Schuster, 1939), 520. The Durants are paraphrasing Plato, who was quoting Socrates.

FOREWORD

1 410 U.S. 113 (1973).

2 *Everson v. Board of Education*, 330 U.S. 1, 18 (1947).

3 I develop these reasons more fully in Howard Gillman and Erwin Chemerinsky, *The Religion Clauses: The Case for Separating Church and State* (New York: Oxford University Press, 2020), 62–66.

4 139 S.C. 2067 (2019). | 5 572 U.S. 565 (2013).

6 137 S.Ct. 2012 (2017) | 7 140 S.Ct. 2246 (2020).

8 494 U.S. 872 (1990). | 9 141 S.Ct. 1868 (2021).

10 Id. at 1882 (Barrett, J., concurring).

11 *McCreary County, Ky. v. American Civil Liberties Union of Ky.*, 545 U.S. 844, 882 (2005) (O'Connor, J., concurring).

INTRODUCTION

1 *McCreary County, Ky. v. American Civil Liberties Union of Ky.*, 545 U.S. 844, 882 (2005) (concurring).

2 Michael Nicks, "Parma Driver Said She 'Let God Take the Wheel' After Slamming into Another Car and a House," WOIO News Cleveland, July 12, 2021, https://bit.ly/317LvDG; Talia Naquin, "Woman Lets 'God Take the Wheel' as a Test of Faith in Beachwood High-speed Crash," Fox 8 Cleveland WJW, July 13, 2021, https://bit.ly/3xUoxyd, July 13, 2021.

3 Special thanks to Hemant Mehta, who tracks these better than anyone. Hemant Mehta, "Driver Who Let Jesus Take the Wheel Before Crashing Wanted to 'Test Her Faith,'" *Friendly Atheist*, July 17, 2021, https://bit.ly/3N5CSNj.

4 Taylor Romine, "Police: Pennsylvania Woman Drives into Path of Oncoming Vehicle While Waiting for Calling from God," CBS Philly, Jan. 17, 2020, https://cbsloc.al/3DU4ccp; "Pennsylvania Woman Drove into Oncoming Traffic to 'Test Her Faith,' Police Say," CNN, Jan. 20, 2020, https://cnn.it/3ERxUQE.

5 Police found quite a bit of alcohol and drugs in the car. "THP: Maryville Man Flips Truck 5 Times After 'Jesus Advised Him to Let Go of the Wheel,'" WVLT-CBS affiliate, Knoxville, TN, Jan. 23, 2018, https://bit.ly/3wmtfnB.

6 "Lebanon Woman Charged with Crashing into Multiple Cars Says 'God Told Her to Do It,'" WLWT Cincinnati, Sept. 26, 2019, https://bit.ly/3NiYQwy; Chris Mayhew, "Lebanon Woman Accused of Driving into Cars Indicted on 12 Attempted Murder Charges," *Cincinnati Enquirer*, Nov. 26, 2019, https://bit.ly/3ugqRff (she was found incompetent to stand trial); Lawrence Budd, "Driver Charged in Multi-car Crash in Lebanon Makes Insanity Defense," *Dayton Daily News*, Jan. 21, 2020, https://bit.ly/3ikWjUi.

7 Ian Cohen, "Police: Man Said Jesus Told Him to Drive Ferrari off Dock," *Palm Beach Daily News*, Jan. 14, 2019, https://bit.ly/3Dd7pV7; Ian Cohen, "Police: Man Drove Ferrari off Dock on Purpose," *Palm Beach Daily News*, Jan. 3, 2019, https://bit.ly/3iqNd8m.

8 Sara Wagner, "Motorcyclist: I Said to Myself Today Is the Day I Die," WANE.com, July 18, 2014, https://bit.ly/3Mz5PjM; Hemant Mehta, "Woman Who Ran Over Pedestrian Because She Was 'Distracted' by God Gets 32 Years," *Friendly Atheist*, Nov. 7, 2018, https://bit.ly/3tqD3Lg.

9 "Supreme Court Backs Beards," BBC News, Oct. 4, 1999, https://news.bbc.co.uk/2/hi/americas/465220.stm; *Fraternal Order of Police v. City of Newark*, 170 F.3d 359 (3d Cir. 1999).

10 Isaiah 2:4.

11–12 "From George Washington to the Hebrew Congregation in Newport, Rhode Island, 18 Aug. 1790," Founders Online, National Archives, https://founders.archives.gov/documents/Washington/05-06-02-0135.

13 Thomas Paine, *Rights of Man: Being an Answer to Mr. Burke's Attack on the French Revolution* (London: J. S. Jordan, 1791), 78 (emphasis in original), https://bit.ly/3aqsOiY.

14 Isabel Wilkerson, *Caste: The Origins of Our Discontents* (New York: Random House, 2020), 387.

15 "Washington to the Hebrew Congregation in Newport," Aug. 18, 1790.

16 Literally. *See* chapter 17, note 24, and accompanying text.

17 Audrey Clare Farley, "The Eugenics Roots of Evangelical Family Values," *Religion and Politics*, May 12, 2021, https://bit.ly/3tgKzrB.

18 Matt Gertz and Zachary Pleat, "The Familial Ties That Bind the Anti-Garland Judicial Crisis Network to Its Dark Money Funder," Media Matters for America, Apr. 4 , 2016, https://bit.ly/3ETgYsO; Jay Michaelson, "Billionaires Try to Buy the Supreme Court," *Daily Beast*, Apr. 13, 2017, https://www.thedailybeast.com/billionaires-try-to-buy-the-supreme-court; Jon Skolnik, "Behind the Dark-Money Web That Put Barrett (and Kavanaugh and Gorsuch) on the Supreme Court," *Salon*, Mar. 30, 2021, https://bit.ly/3trGcKU.

19 Carol Brzozowski, "Love of God Is Shrouded in Secrecy Opus Dei Wants Others to Understand Devotion," *Sun Sentinel*, May 25, 1990, https://www.sun-sentinel.com/news/fl-xpm-1990-05-25-9001100227-story.html.

20 Michaelson, "Billionaires Try to Buy the Supreme Court." | 21 Ibid.

22 Anna Massoglia and Andrew Perez, "Secretive Conservative Legal Group Funded by $17 Million Mystery Donor Before Kavanaugh Fight," OpenSecrets, May 17, 2019, https://bit.ly/3ESjGPr; "Judge Amy Coney Barrett Confirmed," Judicial Crisis Network, Oct. 27, 2020, https://judicialnetwork.com/in-the-news/judge-amy-coney-barrett-confirmed/; Mica Soellner, "Judicial Crisis Network Launches $2.2M Ad Buy Backing Trump Supreme Court Pick," *Washington Examiner*, Sept. 21, 2020, https://washex.am/3L5VjQh.

23 JCN about page, at https://bit.ly/onlySev (archived Dec. 19, 2019).

24 Jay Michaelson, "The Secrets of Leonard Leo, the Man Behind Trump's Supreme Court Pick," *Daily Beast*, July 24, 2018, https://bit.ly/3anycn6.

25 See, e.g., "HHS Budget Would Fund Discrimination at Expense of Civil Rights Enforcement," Center for American Progress, Apr. 25, 2019, https://ampr.gs/3CuMFHK. For the division announcement of Jan. 18, 2018, see https://bit.ly/SeverinoHHS-WRF. For denial of care, see "San Francisco Successfully Blocks Discriminatory Health Care Rule," City Attorney of San Francisco, Nov. 19, 2019, https://bit.ly/3voV4uI.

26 Elizabeth Williamson, "With Barrett Nomination, a D.C. Conservative Power Couple Nears Its Dream," *New York Times*, Oct. 15, 2020, https://nyti.ms/3zcUsu9.

27 Lee Fang and Nick Surgey, "Ginni Thomas Plans New Conservative Supergroup to 'Protect President Trump,'" *The Intercept*, June 4, 2019, https://theintercept.com/2019/06/04/ginni-thomas-trump-conservative-group/. Jane Mayer explored some of these ties in the *New Yorker*. In Apr. 2020, when Ginni Thomas was serving as one of eight members on the Council for National Policy Action board—described by Mayer as "a dark-money wing of the conservative pressure group the Council for National Policy"—it was chaired by Kelly Shackelford, the president and CEO of First Liberty Institute, a Crusader involved in several major cases before the court, including the Bladensburg cross, the football coach pressuring students to pray, and the Maine neo-voucher cases. "In addition to these cases, First Liberty has filed lawsuits that challenge Covid-19 restrictions on religious grounds—an issue that has come before the Court—and Ginni Thomas and Shackelford have served together on the steering committee of the Save Our Country Coalition, which has called Covid-19 health mandates 'unconstitutional power grabs.'" Jane Mayer, "Is Ginni Thomas a Threat to the Supreme Court?," *New Yorker*, Jan 21, 2022, https://bit.ly/3PWIJpB.

28 Robert Barnes, "Ginni Thomas Apologizes to Husband's Supreme Court Clerks after Capitol Riot Fallout," *Washington Post*, Feb. 2, 2021, https://wapo.st/3v0Bxhp.

29 Ibid.; see also Mayer, "Is Ginni Thomas a Threat to the Supreme Court?"

30 Gertz and Pleat, "The Familial Ties That Bind."

31 John Kruzel, "It's True: Millions in Dark Money Has Been Spent to Tilt Courts Right," *PolitiFact*, Sept. 11, 2019, https://bit.ly/3MrqE0q.

32 All told, Trump released four lists of potential nominees. Eleven names on May 18, 2016, to which ten more were added on Sept. 23, 2016. Gorsuch was chosen from that augmented list. Trump released a third list on Nov. 17, 2017; both Kavanaugh and Barrett were on it. The final list came on Sept. 9, 2020. See, e.g., Robert O'Harrow Jr. and Shawn Boburg, "A Conservative Activist's Behind-the-Scenes Campaign to Remake the Nation's Courts," *Washington Post*, May 21, 2019, https://wapo.st/3cTyUX9; Shane Goldmacher, Eliana Johnson, and Josh Gerstein, "How Trump Got to Yes on Gorsuch," *Politico*, Jan. 31, 2017, https://bit.ly/3xZRtEW.

33 O'Harrow and Boburg, "A Conservative Activist's Behind-the-Scenes Campaign."

34 Alex Shepherd, "Oligarch of the Month: Leonard Leo," *New Republic*, Oct. 12, 2020, https://newrepublic.com/article/159683/oligarch-month-leonard-leo.

35 Jay Michaelson, "The Secrets of Leonard Leo, the Man Behind Trump's Supreme Court Pick," *Daily Beast*, July 24, 2018, https://bit.ly/3vQFZAO.

36 Michelle Boorstein, "Agency that Monitors Religious Freedom Abroad Accused of Bias," *Washington Post*, Feb. 17, 2010, https://wapo.st/38ugCwW.

37 David Corn and Nick Baumann, "'Ground Zero Mosque' Foes Bankrolled by Feds," *Mother Jones*, Aug. 23, 2010, https://bit.ly/3kmWkYR.

38 Chrissy Stroop, "About Those Trump Voters for God? Stop Calling Them 'Fake Christians,'" *Not Your Mission Field*, May 3, 2017, https://bit.ly/3rSB01h.

39 Elizabeth R. Platt, Katherine Franke, Kira Shepherd, and Lilia Hadjiivanova, "Whose Faith Matters? The Fight for Religious Liberty Beyond the Christian Right," The Law, Rights, and Religion Project, Columbia Law School, Nov. 2019, https://bit.ly/3reycML.

40 Elizabeth R. Platt, "'Religious Liberty' Is Coming for Voting Rights," *The Hill*, Mar. 10, 2021, https://bit.ly/3x9kZ93. Even the least expected arenas could see the claims. "Infrastructure and religious freedom are two things not often heard in the same sentence," wrote a group that seeks to help persecuted Christians, adding, "The current infrastructure bill represents much-needed funding for America's crumbling infrastructure, while others see possible threats to one of America's most cherished freedoms." "Some Fear the Infrastructure Bill Threatens Religious Liberty," *Persecution*, Aug. 11, 2021, https://bit.ly/3N5N1tn.

41 MS House Bill 132 (2015).

42 Mississippi also passed the Student Religious Liberties Act in 2013 (SB2633) and a Religious Freedom Restoration Act in 2014 (SB2681).

43 MS House Bill 1523 (2016).

44 *Barber v. Bryant*, 193 F. Supp. 3d 677, 688 (S.D. Miss. 2016), rev'd, 860 F.3d 345 (5th Cir. 2017).

45 Ibid., 716.

46 *Barber v. Bryant*, 860 F.3d 345 (5th Cir. 2017). The judges employed a once-common tactic in cases where religion and the law collide, claiming that the people challenging the law "do not have standing" because none of them were injured by the law. Since the Trump judges have been packed into the federal judiciary and now constitute majorities in many courts, I expect standing recede. Now that they have the votes to decide cases on the merits, they'll dispense with the jurisdictional issues.

47 Miss. Code Ann. § 11-62-3.

48 Claire Provost and Nadine Archer, "Revealed: $280m 'Dark Money' Spent by US Christian Right Groups Globally," Open-Democracy, Oct. 27, 2020, https://www.opendemocracy.net/en/5050/trump-us-christian-spending-global-revealed/.

49 In *Barber v. Bryant*, 193 F. Supp. 3d 677, 688 (S.D. Miss. 2016), more than 60 pages of emails were submitted showing Alliance Defending Freedom's coordination with various Mississippi officials. For the affidavit laying the founding for these exhibits, see https://bit.ly/ADF-aff. For the affidavit, with the emails attached as exhibits, see: https://bit.ly/3vkDGXU. Docket entry for Barber v. Bryant Case 3:16-cv-00442-CWR-LRA Document 49. One email to Gov. Bryant's staff reads, "I've sending [*sic*] two different drafts. We looked through a number of Gov. Bryant's signing statements and tried to use his voice. . . . Let me know how else we can be helpful, and if you need anything else today. We're here to serve." ADF was not serving the people of Mississippi; it was using them and their government to further its Crusade.

50 Michelle Goldberg, "Trump's CIA Pick Wants a Holy War," *Slate*, Jan. 12, 2017, https://bit.ly/3m5mP5J.

51 Report of the Commission on Unalienable Rights, https://bit.ly/37KdixI; Pompeo's ad hoc rights line is in Michael R. Pompeo, "Unalienable Rights and U.S. Foreign Policy," *Wall Street Journal*, July 7, 2019, https://on.wsj.com/3rVDX14.

52 Letter to Michael Pompeo, July 23, 2019, signed by 178 NGOs and 251 individuals, https://bit.ly/3yev5If.

53 Diana C. Mutz, "Status Threat, Not Economic Hardship, Explains the 2016 Presidential Vote," *Proceedings of the National Academy of Sciences*, Apr. 23, 2018, 115 (19) E4330-E4339, DOI: 10.1073/pnas.1718155115; Ashton Yount, "Fear of Losing Status, Not Economic Hardship, Drove Voters in 2016 Presidential Election," Annenberg School for Communication News, Apr. 23, 2018, https://bit.ly/3y3FkyZ; Chauncey Devega, "White Fear Elected Trump: Political Scientist Diana Mutz on the "Status Threat" Hypothesis," *Salon*, May 7, 2018, https://bit.ly/3MBUobM. | 54 Wilkerson, *Caste*, 181.

55 "US Nationalists: 'You Will Not Replace Us,'" BBC News, Aug. 12, 2017, https://bbc.in/3PUHAyW; Nellie Bowles, "'Replacement Theory,' a Racist, Sexist Doctrine, Spreads in Far-Right Circles," *New York Times*, Mar. 18, 2019, https://nyti.ms/3GWIhUt.

56 Bill O'Reilly ranted about this to John McCain in 2007: "They want to break down the white, Christian, male power structure . . . and they want to bring in millions of foreign nationals to basically break down the structure that we have." "Preserving the 'White, Christian, Male Power Structure,'" *ThinkProgress*, May 13, 2007, https://bit.ly/3EWD2CR. Video: https://youtu.be/ysoOB9w0tF4.

57 Rosemary L. Al-Kire, Michael H. Pasek, Jo-Ann Tsang, and Wade C. Rowatt, "Christian No More: Christian Americans Are Threatened by Their Impending Minority Status," PsyArXiv, Aug. 27, 2021, doi:10.31234/osf.io/mfyj5.

58 Samuel L. Perry, Landon Schnabel, and Joshua B. Grubbs, "Christian Nationalism, Perceived Anti-Christian Discrimination, and Prioritising 'Religious Freedom' in the 2020 Presidential Election," *Nations and Nationalism*, Aug 31., 2021, 1–12, https://doi.org/10.1111/nana.12764.

59 Samuel Perry, Twitter post, Dec. 16, 2020, https://twitter.com/socofthesacred/status/1339185844951928832.

60 Ronald Brownstein, "The Supreme Court Is Colliding with a Less-Religious America," *The Atlantic*, Dec. 3, 2020, https://bit.ly/3vS5qlP.

AUTHOR'S NOTE

1 Confirmation Hearing on the Nomination of John G. Roberts Jr. to Be Chief Justice of the United States: Hearing Before the S. Comm. on the Judiciary, 109th Cong. 56 (2005).

2 Specifically from 1999 through 2007.

3 *Town of Greece v. Galloway*, 572 U.S. 565 (2014)

4 Brief Amicus Curiae of the Freedom from Religion Foundation in Support of Respondents, *Town of Greece v. Galloway*, 2013 WL 5348583 (U.S.) (U.S., 2013), at 30, https://bit.ly/3xsvVhX. This brief was filed under Rich Bolton's name but was primarily authored by me with extensive help from Patrick Elliott, Rebecca Markert, and Elizabeth Cavell. | 5 *Town of Greece v. Galloway*, 572 U.S., 565, 587 (2014).

6 Sept. 2021 conversation with author.

7 Kagan does set the record straight in her dissent.

1: CHRISTIAN LEGAL SUPREMACY

1 Ralph Waldo Emerson, *Emerson in His Journals*, diary entry Nov. 8, 1838 (Cambridge, MA: Belknap/Harvard Univ. Press, 1982), 206.

2 Alabama Code Title 15. Criminal Procedure § 15-18-83.

3 President Clinton appointed Charles R. Wilson and Stanley Marcus, and President Obama appointed Beverly B. Martin.

4 *Ray v. Commissioner, Alabama Department of Corrections*, 915 F.3d 689, 697, 700 (11th Cir. 2019).

5 *Dunn v. Ray*, 139 S. Ct. 661 (2019).

6 The meeting with the warden was on Jan. 23, 2019. He filed the lawsuit on Jan. 28, 2019. *Ray v. Commissioner, Alabama Department of Corrections,* 915 F.3d 689, 693.

7 Ivana Hrynkiw, "AL Executes Domineque Ray for 1995 Killing of Teen," AL.com, Feb. 8, 2019, https://bit.ly/3JtP1Jz.

8 Address by Justice Samuel Alito to the Federalist Society 2020 National Lawyers Convention, Nov. 12, 2020, https://youtu.be/tYLZL4GZVbA.

9 Julia Jacobs, "Muslim Inmate's Execution Is Blocked Over Denial of Request for Imam," *New York Times,* Feb. 6, 2019, https://nyti.ms/3Lt4w5G.

10 *Masterpiece Cakeshop, Ltd. v. Colorado Civil Rights Commission*, 138 S. Ct. 1719, 1722–23 (2018).

11 I read about the case as I was boarding a plane to DC. I was so incensed that I wrote an op-ed for *Religion Dispatches* on the plane on my phone. Andrew L. Seidel, "Supreme Court Conservatives Allow Execution of Muslim Prisoner Despite Religious Freedom Violation," *Religion Dispatches,* Feb. 8, 2019, https://bit.ly/3LARzGQ.

12 Cameron Langford, "On Eve of Execution, Inmate Fights for Buddhist Priest," Mar. 27, 2019, https://www.courthousenews.com/on-eve-of-execution-inmate-fights-for-buddhist-priest/.

13 Howard Friedman, "Another Death Row Inmate Denied Chaplain of His Choice During Execution," *Religion Clause,* Mar. 27, 2019, https://religionclause.blogspot.com/2019/03/another-death-row-inmate-denied.html.

14 *Murphy v. Collier*, 919 F.3d 913, 915 (5th Cir. 2019). | 15 *Murphy v. Collier*, 139 S. Ct. 1475, 1476 (2019).

16 Jolie McCullough and Elizabeth Byrne, "Texas Bans Chaplains from Its Execution Chamber," *Texas Tribune,* Apr. 3, 2019, https://bit.ly/3w0zLQC.

17 Amy Howe, "Court Won't Allow Alabama Execution without a Pastor," SCOTUSblog, Feb. 12, 2021, https://www.scotusblog.com/2021/02/court-wont-allow-alabama-execution-without-a-pastor/.

18 "*Ramirez v. Collier*," SCOTUSblog, Sept. 7, 2021, https://bit.ly/3OaxurZ.

19 It's a microcosm of the broader Crusade: The Court tramples rights of minorities (Black Muslim in Alabama). There's an outcry and litigation that vindicates the same minority right (for the Texas Buddhist). Now Christians are bringing cases. Except that, in this context, the state is not just oppressing prisoners but trying to kill them.

2: THE COURT AND THE CRUSADE

1 Jonathan Phillips, *Holy Warriors: A Modern History of the Crusade* (New York: Random House, 2009), 3. For a more detailed discussion on the sermon, see Georg Strack, "The Sermon of Urban II in Clermont and the Tradition of Papal Oratory," *Medieval Sermon Studies* 56 (2012), 30–45, https://www.mag.geschichte.uni-muenchen.de/downloads/strack_urban.pdf.

2 Wade Payson-Denney, "So, Who Really Won? What the Bush v. Gore Studies Showed," CNN, Oct. 31, 2015, https://cnn.it/3NQCqC2. Full review, "Florida Ballots Project," National Opinion Research Center, Dec. 17, 2001.

3 See, e.g., Geoffrey R. Stone, "Equal Protection? The Supreme Court's Decision in *Bush v. Gore*," Fathom Archive, 2001, https://bit.ly/3rYzif1. "No one familiar with the jurisprudence of Justices Rehnquist, Scalia and Thomas could possibly have imagined that they would vote to invalidate the Florida recount process on the basis of their own well-developed and oft-invoked approach to the Equal Protection Clause."

4 Jeffrey Toobin, *The Nine: Inside the Secret World of the Supreme Court* (New York: Knopf, 2008), 208.

5 Garrett Epps, "Requiem for the Supreme Court," *The Atlantic,* Oct. 7, 2018, https://bit.ly/3vOdp33. Anita Hill was interviewed by the FBI, signed an affidavit, and produced a corroborating witness. See, e.g., Nina Totenberg, "A Timeline of Clarence Thomas–Anita Hill Controversy as Kavanaugh to Face Accuser," NPR, Sept. 23, 2018, https://n.pr/365omnK.

6 *McCreary County, Ky. v. American Civil Liberties Union of Ky.*, 545 U.S. 844 (2005); *Van Orden v. Perry*, 545 U.S. 677 (2005).

7 *Locke v. Davey*, 540 U.S. 712 (2004).

8 *Santa Fe Independent School District v. Doe*, 530 U.S. 290 (2000).

9 *Locke v. Davey* in 2004 can be considered a win too, but it is also framed as what the free exercise of religion *does not require*, as opposed to what the separation of state and church *does require*. The court rejected the idea that state/church separation is hostile toward religion, which it adopted later in the Crusade.

10 *Mitchell v. Helms*, 530 U.S. 793 (2000).

11 *Zelman v. Simmons-Harris*, 536 U.S. 639 (2002).

12 Linda Greenhouse, "The Court and the Cross," *New York Times,* Mar. 14, 2019, https://nyti.ms/3lgKY9H.

13 *Arizona Christian School Tuition Organization v. Winn*, 563 U.S. 125 (2011).

14 *Hosanna-Tabor Evangelical Lutheran Church and School v. Equal Employment Opportunity Commission*, 565 U.S. 171 (2012); *Our Lady of Guadalupe School v. Morrissey-Berru*, 140 S. Ct. 2049 (2020).

15 Override: *Burwell v. Hobby Lobby Stores, Inc.*, 573 U.S. 682 (2014). Prayers: *Town of Greece, N.Y. v. Galloway*, 572 U.S. 565 (2014).

16 *Trinity Lutheran Church of Columbia, Inc. v. Comer*, 137 S. Ct. 2012 (2017).

17 *Masterpiece Cakeshop, Ltd. v. Colorado Civil Rights Commission*, 138 S. Ct. 1719.

18 *Trump v. Hawaii*, 138 S. Ct. 2392, 2420–21 (2018).

19 *American Legion v. American Humanist Association,* 139 S. Ct. 2067 (2019).

20 *Espinoza v. Montana Department of Revenue*, 140 S. Ct. 2246 (2020).

21 *Roman Catholic Diocese of Brooklyn v. Cuomo*, 592 U.S. ___ (2020) (per curiam); *High Plains Harvest Church v. Polis*, 592 U.S ___ (2020); *Tandon v. Newsom*, 141 S. Ct. 1294 (2021).

22 *Fulton v. City of Philadelphia*, No. 19-123 (U.S. June 17, 2021).

23 "Supreme Court Success Rate on a Writ of Certiorari," *Supreme Court Press*, Nov. 27, 2021, https://supreme-courtpress.com/chance_of_success.html.

24 I first wrote about this back in 2017, with Sam Grover, in the wake of the deadly Las Vegas shooting: Andrew Seidel and Sam Grover, "Gun Control and Religious Freedom: How Thinking in Constitutional Absolutes Is Killing People," *Freethought Now*, Oct. 2, 2017, https://bit.ly/3zA1lGd.

25 Michael Waldman, "How the NRA Rewrote the Second Amendment," *Politico Magazine*, May 19, 2014, https://politi.co/3kkMpD6.

26 *District of Columbia et al. v. Heller*, 554 U.S. 570, 582 (2008).

27 Warren Burger, *The MacNeil/Lehrer NewsHour*, Dec. 16, 1991, https://youtu.be/Eya_k4P-iEo .

28 Linda Greenhouse, "The Supreme Court Nears the Moment of Truth on Religion," *New York Times*, Feb. 27, 2020, https://nyti.ms/3z7Dqhc.

29 The Warren Court is the exception and an odd contradiction, given that Warren was one of the court's most political additions; he was the 1948 Republican vice-presidential nominee.

30 Ted Cruz, "The Right Stuff," *National Review*, July 20, 2005, https://bit.ly/3PTNfoX.

31 Rehnquist became the most conservative member of the court and undid much of the Warren and Burger court's progress.

32 McKay Coppins, "Is Brett Kavanaugh Out for Revenge?," *The Atlantic*, May 13, 2021, https://bit.ly/3tbaIZ7

33 Toobin, *The Nine*, 276.

34 Michael A. Fletcher, "What the Federalist Society Stands For," *Washington Post*, July 29, 2005, https://wapo.st/3nZphwG; Samuel Alito, Attachment to PPO Non-Career Appointment Form of Samuel Alito, Nov. 15, 1985, https://bit.ly/AlitoGOP4eva. See also Robin Cook, "Confirmation of High Court Justices Akin to Political Campaign, Leo Says," Univ. of Virginia School of Law, Fall 2006, https://bit.ly/3CuTZDs.

35 Kenneth P. Vogel, "Ginni Thomas Reportedly Quits Group," *Politico*, Nov. 16, 2010, https://www.politico.com/story/2010/11/ginni-thomas-reportedly-quits-group-045142.

36 Daniel Schulman, "Bush's Shadow Justice Department: Did the Federalist Society Have a Hand in Attorney Firings?," *Mother Jones*, June 7, 2007, https://bit.ly/3N9yKfj; Dylan Matthews and Byrd Pinkerton, "The Incredible Influence of the Federalist Society, Explained," *Vox*, June 3, 2019, https://bit.ly/3sjghnV.

37 The briefs can be found at https://bit.ly/CJRobBrief1 and https://bit.ly/CJRobBrief2.

38 For a comprehensive report on Roberts's awful state/church record at the time of his nomination, see Americans United for the Separation of Church and State, "Religious Minorities at Risk: A Report in Opposition to the Nomination of John G. Roberts Jr. to the United States Supreme Court," 713–31; Confirmation Hearing on the Nomination of John Roberts, Committee on the Judiciary, United States Senate, 109th Congress, 1st session, S. HRG. 109–158, (Sept. 12–15, 2005) Serial No. J–109–37, https://bit.ly/AUrepCJRob; see also "Final Pre-Hearing Report in Opposition to the Confirmation of John Roberts to the United States Supreme Court," special report, People for the American Way, Sept. 2005, http://media.pfaw.org/stc/PH-report.pdf#page=91.

39 See, e.g., transcript of Hugh Hewitt interview with Jay Sekulow, *The Hugh Hewitt Show*, Aug. 16, 2005, https://bit.ly/37m5DVF. Sekulow said of Roberts, "For instance, the Ten Commandments case . . . while we carried the day in Texas with a 5–4 vote, our side lost the Kentucky case. I definitely think that a John Roberts on the Court, with his view of the establishment clause, would have come out the other way on that. We would have carried the day."

40 Brief for Appellant, *Renzi v. Connelly School of the Holy Child, Inc.*, No. 99-2352, 2000 WL 33982797 (4th Cir.) (Jan. 20, 2000), 9 (emphasis added). "Efforts to accommodate religion are invariably constitutional when the State simply chooses to relieve religious institutions of burdens placed on secular elements of society or society at large."

41 David E. Rosenbaum, "An Advocate for the Right," *New York Times*, July 28, 2005, https://nyti.ms/3PTNosv.

42 "Final Pre-Hearing Report in Opposition to the Confirmation of John Roberts," 86–87. Memorandum from John G. Roberts to Fred F. Fielding re: Address by Secretary Bennett to Supreme Council Meeting of Knights of Columbus, Aug. 6, 1985, https://bit.ly/3MX2wn3.

43 For instance, "The Blaine Amendment was 'born of bigotry' and 'arose at a time of pervasive hostility to the Catholic Church and to Catholics in general'; many of its state counterparts have a similarly 'shameful pedigree.'" *Espinoza v. Montana Dept. of Revenue*, 140 S. Ct. 2246, 2259 (2020). However, Roberts began shifting "hostility" to "discrimination" in this opinion and concluded, "That supreme law of the land condemns discrimination against religious schools and the families whose children attend them."

44 He wrote of one line in a Reagan draft speech, "The President refers to the role of religion in shaping the American character, noting that most Americans derive their religious belief from the Holy Bible. This formulation strikes me as broad enough to be generally unoffensive (except perhaps to the ACLU)," Memorandum from John G. Roberts to Fred F. Fielding re Proposed Presidential Address, Fudan Univ., Apr. 13, 1984, "Final Pre-Hearing Report in Opposition to the Confirmation of John Roberts."

45 Americans United for the Separation of Church and State, "Religious Minorities at Risk," 11, citing Memorandum from Roberts to Fielding (June 11, 1985) written in support of SJ Res. 3, 99th Cong. (1985) and HRJ Res. 279, 99th Cong. (1985).

46 *Wallace v. Jaffree*, 472 U.S. 38 (1985).

47 Americans United for the Separation of Church and State, "Religious Minorities at Risk," 12, citing Memorandum from Roberts to Fielding (June 4, 1985).

48 Samuel Alito, Attachment to PPO Non-Career Appointment Form of Samuel Alito, Nov. 15, 1985, https://bit.ly/AlitoGOP4eva. "In college, I developed a deep interest in constitutional law, motivated in large part by disagreement with Warren Court decisions, particularly in the areas of criminal procedure, the Establishment Clause, and reapportionment." Arguing against reapportionment is just as bad; he's questioning the principle of one person, one vote.

49 People for the American Way, "The Record and Legal Philosophy of Samuel Alito," Jan. 2006, 122–34, http://media.pfaw.org/stc/alito-final.pdf.

50 David Kirkpatrick, "Nominee Is Said to Question Church-State Rulings," *New York Times*, Nov. 4, 2005, https://www.nytimes.com/2005/11/04/us/nominee-is-said-to-question-churchstate-rulings.html.

51 David Porter, "Justice Alito Says Country Increasingly 'Hostile' to 'Traditional Moral Beliefs,'" *Chicago Tribune*, Mar. 15, 2017, https://bit.ly/3amVABc. The group, the "'Advocates of Christ' are Catholic lawyers and judges who have entered into an elite fellowship of those who are committed to both the legal profession and the profession of their faith," said the 2016 brochure, "Advocati Christi: The Fellowship of Catholic Lawyers," https://bit.ly/3rcP7iH.

52 Joan Biskupic, *American Original: The Life and Constitution of Supreme Court Justice Antonin Scalia* (New York: Farrar, Straus and Giroux, 2009), 186, 259.

53 Jennifer Senior, "In Conversation with Antonin Scalia," *New York Magazine*, Oct. 4, 2013, https://nymag.com/news/features/antonin-scalia-2013-10/; "Constitution a 'Dead, Dead, Dead' Document, Scalia Tells SMU Audience," *Dallas Morning News*, Jan. 13, 2013, https://bit.ly/3vQxOGu.

54 His flip from the drug counselor case to Hobby Lobby (chapters 8–10) shows a shift after the *Deus vult* call to crusade and a healthy dose of bigotry. He'd probably not have decided that peyote case if it were against Catholic drug counselors taking communion. But that is also the point of the Crusade: Christian supremacy.

55 Kruzel, "It's True: Millions in Dark Money Has Been Spent to Tilt Courts Right."

56 Neil Gorsuch, "Liberals 'n' Lawsuits," *National Review Online*, Feb. 7, 2005, https://bit.ly/3OHhyPa.

57 *American Atheists, Inc. v. Davenport*, 637 F.3d 1095 (10th Cir. 2010) (Gorsuch dissenting).

58 See *Green v. Haskell County Board of Commissioners*, 574 F.3d 1235 (10th Cir. 2009) denying en banc. He made a similar decision in another decalogue case; see *Pleasant Grove City v. Summum*, 555 U.S. 460 (2009).

59 Eliana Johnson, "Kavanaugh's Friends Promoted Him. Now They Have to Rescue Him," *Politico*, Sept. 25, 2018, https://politi.co/3kjRPOQ.

60 Ruth Marcus, *Supreme Ambition: Brett Kavanaugh and the Conservative Takeover* (New York: Simon & Schuster, 2019), 159.

61 *Bush v. Holmes*, 919 So. 2d 392 (Fla. 2006).

62 The New Jersey Legal Resource Council was the legal arm of the New Jersey Family Policy Council and is now the New Jersey Family Policy Alliance: "Join us for a New Jersey where God is honored, religious freedom flourishes," etc. See https://familypolicyalliance.com/?fpastate=NJ and https://bit.ly/NJFPC-BK.

63 Andrew L. Seidel, "How Kavanaugh Will Use Religion to Turn Back the Clock," *ThinkProgress*, July 10, 2018, https://bit.ly/3vloOIx.

64 *Santa Fe Independent School Dist. v. Doe*, 1999 WL 1272963 (1999), https://bit.ly/34xy6Xr. The American Center for Law & Justice filed the case, but Liberty Counsel, First Liberty Institute (then Liberty Legal Institute), all waded in.

65 *Santa Fe Independent School District v. Doe*, 530 U.S. 290, 309–10 (2000). "School sponsorship of a religious message is impermissible because it sends the ancillary message to members of the audience who are nonadherants 'that they are outsiders, not full members of the political community, and an accompanying message to adherants that they are insiders, favored members of the political community.' The delivery of such a message—over the school's public address system, by a speaker representing the student body, under the supervision of school faculty, and pursuant to a school policy that explicitly and implicitly encourages public prayer—is not properly characterized as 'private' speech."

66 Gail R. Chaddock, "A Judicial Think Tank—or a Plot?," *Christian Science Monitor*, Aug. 4, 2005, https://www.csmonitor.com/2005/0804/p01s01-uspo.html.

67 Zalman Rothschild, "Free Exercise Partisanship," *Cornell Law Review* 107, no. 4 (2022), https://ssrn.com/abstract=3707248 or http://dx.doi.org/10.2139/ssrn.3707248. He agrees that the partisan divide on religious freedom cases predates the pandemic but notes that "the trend toward increased free exercise partisanship is starkly manifested by free exercise cases related to the pandemic."

68 Jacob Gershman, "Challenges to Covid-19 Lockdowns Have Been Mostly Losing in Court," *Wall Street Journal*, Feb. 13, 2021.

69 Ibid. See also Michael Heise and Gregory C. Sisk, "Free Exercise of Religion Before the Bench: Empirical Evidence from the Federal Courts," *Notre Dame Law Review* 88, 1371, 1374 (2013); Sepehr Shahshahani and Lawrence J. Liu, "Religion and Judging on the Federal Courts of Appeals," *Journal of Empirical Legal Studies* (2017), 716, 734.

70 Lewis Michael Wasserman, "U.S. Supreme Court Justices' Religious and Party Affiliation, Case-Level Factors, Decisional Era and Voting in Establishment Clause Disputes Involving Public Education: 1947–2012" (Sept. 7, 2012), *British Journal of American Legal Studies* 2 (2013), https://ssrn.com/abstract=2143406 or http://dx.doi.org/10.2139/ssrn.2143406; Lee Epstein and Eric A. Posner, "The Roberts Court and the Transformation of

Constitutional Protections for Religion: A Statistical Portrait," *Supreme Court Review* (Apr/ 3, 2021), https://ssrn.com/abstract=3825759. Posner and Epstein added to Wasserman's data, bringing it up through the 2019 term.
71 Epstein and Posner, "The Roberts Court." "The court ruled in favor of religion 58% of the time. Win rates do not differ significantly for Free Exercise clause cases (59%) and Establishment clause cases (57%). Across the Warren, Burger, and Rehnquist courts the religious side prevailed about half the time, with gradually increasing success."
72 Ibid. | 73 Ibid. | 74 Ibid.

3: DRAWING LINES

1 *Cantwell v. Connecticut*, 310 U.S. 296, 303–4 (1940).
2 *Employment Division, Department of Human Resources of Oregon v. Smith*, 494 U.S. 872, 877 (1990) ("The free exercise of religion means, first and foremost, the right to believe and profess whatever religious doctrine one desires"); *Sherbert v. Verner*, 374 U.S. 398, 402, (1963) ("The door of the Free Exercise Clause stands tightly closed against any governmental regulation of religious *beliefs as such*" (emphasis added), citing *Cantwell v. Connecticut*, 310 U.S. 296, 303 (1940)); *Wisconsin v. Yoder*, 406 U.S. 205, 219–20 (1972) (recognizing the belief-action dichotomy and that "it is true that activities of individuals, even when religiously based, are often subject to regulation by the States in the exercise of their undoubted power to promote the health, safety, and general welfare."); *Torcaso v. Watkins*, 367 U.S. 488, 495 (1961) ("We repeat and again reaffirm that neither a State nor the Federal Government can constitutionally force a person 'to profess a belief or disbelief in any religion'").
3 Micah Schwartzman, Twitter post, Nov. 2, 2021, https://bit.ly/3reHisT.
4 Andrew Koppelman, "Has the Supreme Court Been Infected with Long Trump Syndrome?," *Balkinization*, Nov. 2, 2021, https://balkin.blogspot.com/2021/11/has-supreme-court-been-infected-with.html?m=1.
5 Mike Essen, moderator, Andrew L. Seidel and Tom Trento debate, "Does the God of the Bible Exist?," Feb. 2021, https://youtu.be/PubtwJIqKZ0 (exchange at 20:05).
6 Sheila Stogsdill, "Mother Found Insane in Toddler's Death to Be Released to Halfway House," *Tulsa World*, Feb. 24, 2019, https://bit.ly/37eBWWp; Associated Press, "Mom Accused in Son's Drowning Ruled Insane," *Tulsa World*, Sept. 21, 2013, https://bit.ly/3NpVPKM.
7 Susan Ayres, "'[N]ot a Story to Pass On': Constructing Mothers Who Kill," *UC Hastings Women's Law Journal* 15, no. 39 (2004), https://repository.uchastings.edu/hwlj/vol15/iss1/2, citing Anne Belli Gesalman, Andrea Yates Redux, *Newsweek* web exclusive, May 17, 2003. See also "Attorney: Woman Thought God Told Her to Kill Sons," CNN.com, Mar. 30, 2004, https://www.cnn.com/2004/LAW/03/29/children.slain/index.html.
8 Julia Glick, "Husband of Woman Accused of Cutting off Baby's Arms Testifies," *Midland Reporter-Telegram*, Feb. 13, 2006, https://bit.ly/3DdGto4.
9 "Mike Pence Disappointed God Has Never Asked Him to Kill One of Own Children," *The Onion*, Feb. 6, 2017, https://bit.ly/3kkQt6o.
10 "Did Vice President Mike Pence Lament God Never Asked Him to Sacrifice His Children?," Snopes.com, Feb. 7, 2017, https://www.snopes.com/fact-check/mike-pence-laments-no-sacrifice/.
11 "VI. Notes on Locke and Shaftesbury, 11 Oct.–9 Dec. 1776," Founders Online, National Archives, https://bit.ly/3Oi23fz. Punctuation and capitalization modernized slightly, spelling corrected; emphasis added.
12 *Reynolds v. U.S.*, 98 U.S. 145, 166–67 (1878). Some authorities list the year as 1879.
13 Richard H. Greene and Hada Messia, "Book: Pope John Paul II Self-flagellated to Get Closer to Jesus," CNN, Jan. 29, 2010, https://cnn.it/3ObT6o3.
14 Vic Ryckaert, "Son Had 36 Bruises. Mom Quoted the Bible as Defense," *Indianapolis Star*, Aug. 31, 2016, https://bit.ly/3uC4WzD; Vic Ryckaert, "Mom Who Cited Religious Freedom Pleads Guilty," *Indianapolis Star*, Oct. 28, 2016, https://bit.ly/3I82Gow; Senate Enrolled Act No. 101, Indiana General Assembly, 2015 Session, https://iga.in.gov/legislative/2015/bills/senate/101#document-92bab197.
15 Again, not as far-fetched as you'd think. See, e.g., "Florida Couple's 'Dream' Wedding at Mansion Hits Snag When Actual Mansion Owner Calls 911," *Palm Beach Post*, Apr. 22, 2021, https://bit.ly/3Nmx2HH. Trespassers "said it was God's plan that the couple marry there."
16 "Is Religious Liberty a Shield or a Sword?," PRRI, Feb. 10, 2021, https://bit.ly/39p7wlG.
17 *Lee v. Weisman*, 505 U.S. 577, 606–7 (1992) (Blackmun concurring). "The mixing of government and religion can be a threat to free government, even if no one is forced to participate. When the government puts its imprimatur on a particular religion, it conveys a message of exclusion to all those who do not adhere to the favored beliefs. A government cannot be premised on the belief that all persons are created equal when it asserts that God prefers some." Jay Sekulow, a Crusader who runs the American Center for Law & Justice, "served as co-counsel representing school officials who wished to invite clergy to deliver invocations at school ceremonies," according to his website (jaysekulow.com), and his name appears on the briefs.
18 Andrew L. Whitehead and Samuel L. Perry, *Taking America Back for God: Christian Nationalism in the United States* (New York: Oxford Univ. Press, 2020), 161.
19 Associated Press, "Hindu Prayer in Senate Disrupted," July 12, 2007, nbcnews.com/id/wbna19729245.
20 Haley Davies, "Hindu Chaplain Rajan Zed Leads State Senate in Opening Prayer," *San Francisco Chronicle*, Aug. 27, 2007, https://bit.ly/3JMoFTu.
21 The Family Research Council was quick to erase all traces of this bigoted response, which also said, "As for our Hindu priest friend, the United States is a nation that has historically honored the One True God. Woe be to us on that day when we relegate Him to being merely one among countless other deities in the pantheon

of theologies." Several sources piece it together: Jim Abrams, Associated Press, "Hindu Prayer in Congress Criticized," *Beliefnet*, Sept. 21, 2000, https://bit.ly/3iDPVYr; "Congress' Hindu Blessing," *Hinduism Today*, https://bit.ly/311bOMu. Religious Tolerance has a fuller explanation of Family Research Council's walkback: "Hinduism: Hindu Invocation in Congress, Religious Tolerance.org, Nov. 4, 2005, https://bit.ly/3iCu83n.

22 Frederick Douglass and William Lloyd Garrison, *Narrative of the Life of Frederick Douglass, an American Slave* (Boston: Anti-Slavery Office, 1849), 78, https://www.loc.gov/item/82225385/.

23 W. E. B. Du Bois, *The Souls of Black Folk* (Chicago: A. C. McClurg, 1903), chapter 10.

24 See, e.g., Brigit Katz, "Heavily Abridged 'Slave Bible' Removed Passages That Might Encourage Uprisings," *Smithsonian*, Jan. 4, 2019, https://bit.ly/3804F1z.

25 Library of Congress writeup for "Draft of Elizabeth Cady Stanton's *The Woman's Bible*, ca. 1895," in Elizabeth Cady Stanton Papers, https://bit.ly/3KtyVje (citing Elizabeth Cady Stanton and Mary Ann McClintock, "Letter to the Editor," *Semi-Weekly Courier*, Seneca Falls, NY, 1848, *The Papers of Elizabeth Cady Stanton and Susan B. Anthony*, microfilm edition, reel 6:779–81). See also Elizabeth Cady Stanton, "The Degraded Status of Woman in the Bible," *Free Thought Magazine* 14, no. 541, Sept. 1896, https://bit.ly/3GTcbZK. In "Degraded Status," Stanton also explained that the "Bible and the church . . . have been the greatest block in the way of her [woman's] development. . . . It is not to Bibles, prayer books, catechisms, liturgies, the canon law and church creeds and organizations, that woman owes one step in her progress, for all these alike have been hostile, and still are, to her freedom and development."

26. *Fulton v. City of Philadelphia*, Oyez, www.oyez.org/cases/2020/19-123, 1:44:25. Barrett is unfit for the Supreme Court, unrelated to her record and ideology. Before her name was announced, I explained why in "Trump's Nominee to Fill RBG's Seat Is Unfit," *Religion Dispatches*, Sept. 21, 2020, https://religiondispatches.org/trumps-nominee-to-fill-rbgs-seat-is-unfit-by-definition/. No principled jurist could have accepted that nomination for the ethical reasons I laid out in the piece. By accepting the nomination, she confessed herself to be unfit for the office.

27 "Thomas Jefferson: Autobiography, 6 Jan.–29 July 1821, 6 Jan. 1821," Founders Online, National Archives, https://founders.archives.gov/documents/Jefferson/98-01-02-1756. He was writing about the Virginia Statute for Religious Freedom.

28 The "Year of our Lord" mentioned in the date near the signatures—it's not appended to the other dates that appear in the text—is not legally or historically significant, as I've detailed elsewhere. It was added at the last moment by the scribe while the founders were debating whether to keep or destroy the records of the secret convention, and it's almost certain that none of the signers approved or even noticed this language, which was also never fully ratified by the states. See "Dating God: What Is 'Year of Our Lord' Doing in the U.S. Constitution?," *Constitutional Studies*, vol. 3 (2018), 129–51, https://bit.ly/3zGbn8Z.

29 The preamble of the version produced by the Committee of Detail on Aug. 6, 1787, read: "We the People of the States of New-Hampshire, Massachusetts, . . ." Gouverneur Morris changed it and added the Preamble's goals. See Max Farrand, ed., *The Records of the Federal Convention of 1787*, vol. 2, (New Haven: Yale Univ. Press, 1911), 177, https://bit.ly/3uy1G8d.

30 See U.S. Constitution, Article 1, Section 18; *McCulloch v. Maryland*, 17 U.S. 316 (1819).

31 As Madison would later explain about his and Jefferson's religious freedom statute: "Here the separation between the authority of human laws, and the natural rights of Man excepted from the grant on which all political authority is founded, is traced as distinctly as words can admit, and the limits to this authority established with as much solemnity as the forms of legislation can express." "Detached Memoranda, ca. 31 Jan. 1820," Founders Online, National Archives, https://founders.archives.gov/documents/Madison/04-01-02-0549.

32 Hamilton may not have used the exclamation mark all that readily, but in 1986, the town of Hamilton, Ohio, officially changed its name to Hamilton! UPI, "Hamilton, Ohio, Acts to Become Hamilton!," *New York Times*, May 16, 1986, https://nyti.ms/36WJZo1.

33 They weren't alone. "To give up the independence of conscience, upon merely human authority, to any government, is making a sacrifice to it, which they have no right to make," explained one English minister in 1772. Joseph Fownes, *An Enquiry into the Principles of Toleration* (London: J. Buckland, 1772), 23, https://books.google.com/books?id=rVsVAAAAQAAJ&pg=PA23.

34 The First Amendment applies beyond "Congress" through other provisions of the Constitution, such as the 14th Amendment. There are some judges—including Clarence Thomas on the Supreme Court and keyboard warriors—who dispute this rather clear extension. They are fringe but have a growing presence.

35 "From James Madison to Edward Livingston, 10 July 1822," Founders Online, National Archives (emphasis added), https://founders.archives.gov/documents/Madison/04-02-02-0471.

36 Definition of "demean," *Merriam-Webster*, accessed Nov. 27, 2021, https://www.merriam-webster.com/dictionary/demean.

37 *Reynolds v. United States*, 98 U.S. 145, 167 (1878).

38 Sessions learned this theology in the White House Bible Study led by Christian Nationalist preacher and organizer of Capitol Ministries Ralph Drollinger. Andrew L. Seidel, "The White House Bible Study Group That Influenced Trump's Family Separation Policy," *ThinkProgress*, June 19, 2018, https://bit.ly/3OJvKHp.

39 "Attorney General Sessions Addresses Recent Criticisms of Zero Tolerance by Church Leaders," U.S. Department of Justice, Justice News, June 14, 2018, https://bit.ly/3NpJqGO.

40 Tucker Higgins, "White House on Separating Migrant Children from Parents: 'It's Very Biblical to Enforce the Law,'" CNBC, last modified June 15, 2018, https://cnb.cx/3hXcrep.

41 "Attorney General Sessions Issues Guidance . . . ," U.S. Department of Justice, Justice News, Oct. 6, 2017, https://bit.ly/3NrjUB6; for the 25-page memo, see "Federal Law Protections for Religious Liberty," Office of the Attorney General, Oct. 6, 2017, https://www.justice.gov/opa/press-release/file/1001891/download; Pete Madden, "Jeff Sessions Consulted Christian Right Legal Group on Religious Freedom Memo, ABC News, Oct. 6, 2017, https://abcn.ws/3Nvgj54.

42 For a nice introduction, see Alan Noble, "The Evangelical Persecution Complex," *The Atlantic*, Aug. 4, 2012, https://bit.ly/3Mya4Mm.

43 Betsy Cooper, Daniel Cox, E. J. Dionne Jr., Rachel Lienesch, Robert P. Jones, and William A. Galston, "How Immigration and Concerns about Cultural Change Are Shaping the 2016 Election," Public Religion Research Institute(PRRI)/Brookings Immigration Survey, June 23, 2016, 6–17, https://bit.ly/3km3pbW.

44 Daniel Cox and Robert P. Jones, "Majority of Americans Oppose Transgender Bathroom Restrictions," PRRI, Mar. 10, 2017, https://bit.ly/36TwMPX.

45 Jonathan Swan, "Christian Group Honors Kim Davis with Award," *The Hill*, Sept. 25, 2015, https://bit.ly/3OCDRpb.

4: DRAWING LINES: BIGOTRY IN KENTUCKY

1 Richard Socarides, "Is There Hope for Francis on Gay Rights?," *New Yorker*, Mar. 13, 2013, https://bit.ly/38eDpN9; see also "Nuevo Papa Francisco I Se Pronunció en 2010 Contra el Matrimonio Gay," Globovision, Mar. 13, 2013, https://bit.ly/3IW7wpX.

2 This allusion has been made by many; see, e.g., Jennifer Rubin, "Trashing the Rule of Law," *Washington Post* (Sept. 4, 2015), https://wapo.st/3D2PluW. The Rowan County Clerk's office is in the Rowan County Court Building.

3 *Obergefell v. Hodges*, 576 U.S. 644 (2015) was decided on Friday, June 26, 2015. Davis's announcement ran in the local paper on Monday, June 29, 2015. See "Clerk Not Issuing Marriage Licenses," *Daily Independent Online*, June 29, 2015, https://bit.ly/3CZmLdK. "Rowan County Clerk Kim Davis says her office will not be issuing any marriage licenses at this time. She said she made this decision based on her Christian beliefs and because she does not want to discriminate against anyone. This issue arose after Friday's U.S. Supreme Court ruling invalidating a ban in all 50 states on same sex marriage."

4 Davis was held for contempt of court, remained in custody for five days, and was released because her clerks began issuing marriage licenses to the couples and promised to continue to do so. In her release order, the judge wrote, "Davis *shall not interfere* in any way, directly or indirectly, with the efforts of her deputy clerks to issue marriage licenses to all legally eligible couples" (emphasis in original), *Miller v. Davis*, case 0:15-cv-00044, dckt #89 (E.D. KY Sept. 8, 2015), https://bit.ly/3v8j5Ge.

5 Alan Blinder and Richard Fausset, "Kim Davis, a Local Fixture, and Now a National Symbol," *New York Times* (Sept. 1, 2015), https://nyti.ms/3i6PIgB; see also Keith Kappes, "Davis Wins Squeaker in County Clerk's Race," *Daily Independent Online*, Oct. 26, 2020, https://bit.ly/363QsQi.

6 Sarah Kaplan and James Higdon, "The Defiant Kim Davis, the Ky. Clerk Who Refuses to Issue Gay Marriage Licenses," *Washington Post*, Sept. 2, 2015, https://wapo.st/3ub68sU.

7 Blinder and Fausset, "Kim Davis."

8 Emily McFarlan Miller, "What's an Apostolic Christian and Why Is Kim Davis's Hair So long?," *Washington Post*, Sept. 30, 2015, https://wapo.st/3kF4rRq.

9 Blinder and Fausset, "Kim Davis." "But others said Ms. Davis put her faith into action. Donald K. Hall Sr., the former county jailer, said Ms. Davis had approached him and asked if she could operate a Bible study for detainees at the county jail. He gave her permission, and she held classes for female detainees on Monday evenings."

10 Fox News, "Exclusive: Kim Davis Opens Up About Faith, Threat to Freedom," Sept. 24, 2015, https://video.foxnews.com/v/4504743812001#sp=show-clips.

11 There was a legislative solution in the end; clerks' names no longer appeared on marriage licenses.

12 German Lopez, "Meet the Little-known Christian Law Firm Behind the New Wave of Anti-LGBTQ Bills," *Vox*, Apr. 14, 2016, https://bit.ly/3EB4pCB.

13 Liberty Counsel, "About Liberty Counsel," accessed Nov. 27, 2021, https://lc.org/about-liberty-counsel.

14 Ibid.

15 Southern Poverty Law Center, "Liberty Counsel," accessed Nov. 27, 2021, https://bit.ly/3k4Nm25.

16 These unethical promises allow groups to pass costs of the Crusade on to taxpayers. Andrew L. Seidel, "How 'Pro Bono' Offers to Defend Religious Monuments Are Stressing Local Governments," Religion News Service, Mar. 7, 2018, https://bit.ly/36Ioomk.

17 Brian Tashman, "Kim Davis' Lawyer Says She's Just Like a Jew Living in Nazi Germany," Right Wing Watch, Sept. 3, 2015, https://bit.ly/3ESgJi1.

18 Fox News, "Exclusive: Kim Davis Opens Up About Faith, Threat to Freedom."

19 ABC News, "Kentucky Clerk Kim Davis Denies Same-Sex Marriage License," Sept. 1, 2015, https://youtu.be/_Xg1Dh2xhXg?t=53.

20 Blinder and Fausset, "Kim Davis." "Davis understood (and understands) this oath to mean that, in upholding the federal and state constitutions and laws, she would not act in contradiction to the moral law of God, natural law, or her sincerely held religious beliefs and convictions."

21 *Kennedy v. Bremerton School District*, Dckt 21-418.
22 Matthew 6:5–6 NLT.
23 Salman Rushdie, *Real Time with Bill Maher*, HBO, Sept. 11, 2015, https://youtu.be/EmMyrt_Vbew?t=183.
24 Steve Bittenbender, "Apostolic Christianity Fuels Kentucky Clerk's Gay Marriage Fight," Reuters, Sept. 4, 2015, https://reut.rs/3x4cXwW.
25 Mike Huckabee, "Kim Davis's Right to Religious Liberty Has Been Grossly Violated," Fox News, Sept. 14, 2015, https://fxn.ws/38e5nsm.
26 Blinder and Fausset, "Kim Davis."
27 "Statement from Rowan County Clerk Kim Davis," *Richmond Register*, Sept. 1, 2015, https://bit.ly/3I22ZAQ.
28 Joel Martinez, "Standoff Continues in Kentucky over Gay Marriage," WWLP., July 1, 2015, https://bit.ly/3xQEsgO.
29 "David Ermold and David Moore Wedding," *MSU Trail Blazer*, Oct. 31, 2015, https://youtu.be/7ZJAqOvlaLY?t=121.
30 Matthew 19:26. | 31 Judges 1:19. | 32 Compare Exodus 21:23–25 and Matthew 5:39.
33 Luke 14:26; see also Matthew 10:34–36. | 34 1 Samuel 13:14; Acts 13:22. | 35 1 Kings 11.
36 Genesis 38; Judges 21:20–24; Exodus 21; Deuteronomy 22.
37 Numbers 31. | 38 Deuteronomy 21:10–14. | 39 See, e.g., 1 Corinthians 7.
40 Paul Oestreicher, "Was Jesus Gay? Probably," *The Guardian*, Apr. 20, 2012, https://bit.ly/3vAUecY; "Brazil: Netflix 'Gay Jesus' Parody Film Ban Overturned," BBC News, Jan. 10, 2020, https://bbc.in/3vzYpWx.
41 The most popular verse to support this claim seems to be the Genesis account of a man leaving his family, finding a woman, and the two becoming "one flesh," a passage the Books of Matthew and Mark claim Jesus repeated and which Paul quotes in his letter to the Ephesians, Genesis 2:24; Matthew 19:5–6; Mark 10:7–9; Ephesians 5:31–32. The Genesis lines come immediately after the biblical god fashions woman out of man's rib—except that, in the previous chapter, the same god had already made woman and man, both "male and female he created them," Genesis 1:27. See, e.g., 1 Corinthians 7:2; Ephesians 5:22–33.
42 *Davis v. Ermold*, 141 S. Ct. 3 (2020) (Thomas and Alito respecting the denial of certiorari).
43 Andrew L. Seidel, "Could This Supreme Court Undo Marriage Equality?," *Religion Dispatches*, Sept. 23, 2021, https://bit.ly/39b245D.

5: IT WAS NEVER ABOUT A CAKE

1 Robert Barnes, "The Spurned Couple, the Baker and the Long Wait for the Supreme Court," *Washington Post* (Aug. 13, 2017), https://wapo.st/3lecPXX.
2 Charlies Craig and David Mullins, interview with author, Feb 4, 2021, recording and transcript on file with author, edited for clarity. The discrimination occurred on July 19, 2012.
3 Interview with author.
4 Debbie Munn, "How It Feels When Someone Refuses to Make Your Son a Wedding Cake," Yahoo! News, Oct. 24, 2017, https://yhoo.it/3xZW22c.
5 Interview with author.
6 "Baker in Supreme Court Gay Wedding Cake Jack Phillips Shares His Story | The View," YouTube, June 30, 2017, https://youtu.be/coBIZle18kM.
7 Ken McIntyre, "24 Questions for Jack Phillips, the Baker Who Gave Up Wedding Cakes for God," *Daily Signal*, Aug. 19, 2015, https://dailysign.al/3Lk36KG.
8 Interview with author.
9 Combined Appendix for Cert Petition, 2015 SC 738 (Oct. 23, 2015), 69, https://bit.ly/3kjTMLa.
10 Interview with author.
11 Interview with author. See also Joint Appendix, No. 16-111, 50, https://bit.ly/3y2s7WW.
12 Colorado Civil Rights Division determination in Charge No. P20130008X (Mar. 5, 2013) in Combined Appendix for Cert. Petition, 93, https://bit.ly/3ESmRGK.
13 Colorado Civil Rights Division final agency order (May 30, 2014) in Combined Appendix for Cert Petition, 82. An administrative law judge later adopted the commission's remedies verbatim.
14 Editorial Board, "Wedding Cakes and Conscience," *Chicago Tribune*, Dec. 6, 2017, https://bit.ly/3NPDjeb.
15 Interview with author.
16 Alan Sears and Craig Osten, *The Homosexual Agenda: Exposing the Principal Threat to Religious Freedom Today* (Nashville, TN: Broadman and Holman, 2003), 147.
17 Erik Eckholm, "Legal Alliance Gains Host of Court Victories for Conservative Christian Movement," *New York Times* (May 11, 2014), https://nyti.ms/1l0vm1Z.
18 Sarah Jones, "Who's Afraid of Higher Education?," *New York Magazine*, Nov. 8, 2021, https://nymag.com/intelligencer/article/bari-weiss-university-of-austin-nothing-new.html.
19 Alliance Defending Freedom, Form 990 for period ending June 2019, https://bit.ly/3hYew9S.
20 Chip Somodevilla, "Why Is Alliance Defending Freedom a Hate Group?," Southern Poverty Law Center, Apr. 10, 2020, https://bit.ly/3azTaPH.
21 And plenty more. It's easy when your budget is that big and you've packed the courts.
22 "About Us," Alliance Defending Freedom, accessed Nov. 26, 2021, https://www.adflegal.org/about-us.
23 "Exclusive Interview with Pure Flix Entertainment for *God's Not Dead* Movie," Alliance Defending Freedom, Feb. 14, 2014, https://archive.is/CT6xU; Hemant Mehta, "Let's Debunk the 'Christian Persecution' Court

Cases That Inspired the *God's Not Dead* Films," Patheos, *The Friendly Atheist*, Apr. 8, 2016, https://bit.ly/34x-OZRP. On persecution, see, e.g., *God's Not Dead* website, "Is Religious Persecution in America Spinning Out of Control?"Aug. 24, 2014, https://bit.ly/3x4eS6b

24 "Legal Training: Overview," Alliance Defending Freedom, accessed Nov. 26, 2021, https://www.adflegal.org/training/overview.

25 "Blackstone Legal Fellowship," Alliance Defending Freedom, accessed Nov. 26, 2021, https://www.adflegal.org/training/blackstone.

26 Archive of the site shows this quote from the first time the site was archived in Feb. 2010 until July 2014, Resources, Blackstone Legal Fellowship, https://bit.ly/3KnR1mn.

27 Rob Boston, "Don't Want to Be Called a Hate Group? Then Stop Hating," Protect Thy Neighbor: A Project of Americans United for Separation of Church and State, Aug. 13, 2018, https://bit.ly/3lRoBHJ.

28 Amy Coney Barrett, Financial Disclosure Report, nomination filing (2017), https://bit.ly/3NVAI2k; Alex Amend, "Anti-LGBT Hate Group Alliance Defending Freedom Defended State-Enforced Sterilization for Transgender Europeans," Southern Poverty Law Center, July 27, 2017, https://bit.ly/37HvJmJ.

29 Jessica Glenza, "The Multimillion-dollar Christian Group Attacking LGBTQ+ Rights," *The Guardian*, Feb. 21, 2020, https://bit.ly/3OETY5r.

30 See, e.g., Max Burns, "Will Amy Coney Barrett Finally Explain Her Ties to Anti-Gay Hate Group?," *Daily Beast*, Oct. 13, 2020, https://bit.ly/3pXcPy2.

31 Sarah Kramer, "The Newly Confirmed Justice Amy Coney Barrett Will Hear an ADF Case Later This Term," ADF Blog, Oct. 27, 2020, https://bit.ly/3OJ8vgo.

32 Sarah Posner, "Inside the Christian Legal Army Weakening the Church-State Divide," Type Investigations, Oct. 4, 2019, https://bit.ly/3OHk0Fm.

33 Sarah Posner, "The Christian Legal Army Behind 'Masterpiece Cakeshop,'" *The Nation, Nov. 28, 2017, https://bit.ly/3Nmy8mi.

34 Posner, "Inside the Christian Legal Army Weakening the Church-State Divide."

35 Interview with author.

36 Brief of Amici Curiae Corporate Law Professors in Support of Respondents, *Masterpiece Cakeshop, Ltd. v. Colorado Civil Rights Commission (hereafter "Masterpiece Cakeshop")* 2017 WL 5127303 (U.S.) (U.S.,2017) https://bit.ly/3y5NczE. In rare instances, the separation between the legal corporation and the person, sometimes called the corporate veil, can be "pierced"; that is, the courts can treat the owners and corporation as not separate. Typically, this happens in instances of fraud or abuse, or where the owner himself has not treated the entities as separate. But this is rare.

37 *United States v. Bestfoods*, 524 U.S. 51, 61 (1998) (citations and internal quotations omitted).

38 See Brief of Amici Curiae Corporate Law Professors, supra note 38.

39 "Certificate and Articles of Incorporation of Masterpiece Cakeshop Incorporated," Dec. 12, 1992, https://bit.ly/3PSUXzL.

40 "Articles of Organization" [for Masterpiece Cakeshop, Ltd.], July 5, 2017, https://bit.ly/3aEajYE.

41 Andrew L. Seidel, "God's Not Fixing Climate Change, He's Making It worse," *Freethought Now*, June 1, 2017, https://freethoughtnow.org/gods-not-fixing-climate-change/.

42 Cornwall Alliance, "An Evangelical Declaration on Global Warming," May 1, 2009, https://bit.ly/37JsScX.

43 *Dole v. Shenandoah Baptist Church*, 899 F.2d 1389 (4th Cir. 1990).

44 See, e.g., *Mitchell v. Pilgrim Holiness Church Corp.*, 210 F.2d 879 (7th Cir. 1954).

45 *Tony and Susan Alamo Foundation v. Secretary of Labor*, 471 U.S. 290, 292 (1985). | 46 Ibid.

47 Combined Appendix for Cert Petition, 74.

48 Oral argument, *Masterpiece Cakeshop*, Oyez, Dec. 5, 2017, 00:09:55, www.oyez.org/cases/2017/16-111.

49 Ibid., 00:08:50.

50 Three paragraphs in the cert petition, three paragraphs in the bakery's merits brief, and the last five paragraphs in the bakery's merits reply. The argument was raised in a few amicus briefs. These can, of course, be quibbled with. For instance, some might wish to include the bias discussion of analogous contexts.

51 Generously, from 40:48 to 42:33, and again briefly at 50:10. There was some additional brief discussion of "bias."

52 Walter Olson, "The Oral Argument in the Supreme Court's Masterpiece Cakeshop Same-Sex Marriage Case Is Heartening," Dec. 6, 2017, Cato Institute, https://bit.ly/3kh1xBl. Amy Howe, an unbiased journalist for SCOTUSblog, noted the exchange in her coverage. Amy Howe, "Argument Analysis: Conservative Majority Leaning Toward Ruling for Colorado Baker (UPDATED), SCOTUSblog, Dec. 5, 2017, https://bit.ly/3kk8ykQ. Others didn't mention this line of argument as important. *See* Mark Walsh, "A 'View' from the Courtroom: Setting the Table for a Major Ruling," SCOTUSblog, Dec. 5, 2017, https://bit.ly/3aTYopE.

53 See letter of "Notice Regarding Clarification of the Record" filed by Counsel of Record for Respondent Colorado Civil Rights Commission," Jan, 8, 2018, https://bit.ly/3qhFdLx.

Because Kennedy misattributed the quote, we know precisely where he pulled it from. Only one other submission to the court made the same error, and it was not from the parties: Brief of Amici Curiae Ethics and Religious Liberty Commission of the Southern Baptist Convention et al. *Masterpiece Cakeshop*, 2017 WL 4005657 (U.S.) (U.S.,2017), https://bit.ly/36aHeBW. That brief was written by Matthew Whitehead, an attorney with close ties to the ADF and other Crusaders, according to his firm website, https://thewhiteheadfirm.com.

54 *Masterpiece Cakeshop*, 138 S. Ct. 1719, 1728).

55 In re: *Charlie Craig and David Mullins v. Masterpiece Cakeshop, Inc.* hearing before the Colorado Civil Rights Commission Meeting, July 25, 2014, Colorado State Capitol, transcribed from an audio recording, https://bit.ly/3ldDJiG.

56 Interview with author.

57 Address by Justice Samuel Alito to the Federalist Society 2020 National Lawyers Convention, Nov. 12, 2020, https://youtu.be/tYLZL4GZVbA: "Consider what a member of the Colorado Human Rights Commission said to Jack Phillips, the owner of the now notorious Masterpiece Cakeshop, when he refused to create a cake celebrating a same-sex wedding. She said that freedom of religion had been used 'to justify all kinds of discrimination throughout history, whether it be slavery, whether it be the Holocaust, we can list hundreds of situations where freedom of religion has been used to justify discrimination.' You can easily see the point. For many today, religious liberty is not a cherished freedom. It's often just an excuse for bigotry, and it can't be tolerated, even when there is no evidence that anybody has been harmed."

58 All quotes from Diann Rice are from an interview with author, on file with author. Quotes confirmed with Rice on Nov. 26, 2021, via email.

59 Frank Newport, "Religion a Big Factor for Americans Against Same-Sex Marriage," Gallup, Dec. 5, 2012, http://bit.ly/2Nf6qxv.

60 Chief Justice Roberts said discrimination *against* religion was "odious" in 2017. *Trinity Lutheran Church of Columbia, Inc. v. Comer*, 137 S. Ct. 2012, 2025 (2017). Justice Thomas referred, correctly, to segregation as "despicable" in *Missouri v. Jenkins*, 515 U.S. 70, 118 (1995). Justices Blackmun, Brennan, Marshall, and Stevens said that racial discrimination is "abhorrent" in *McCleskey v. Kemp*, 481 U.S. 279, 346 (1987).

61 *Pena-Rodriguez v. Colorado*, 137 S. Ct. 855, 868 (2017) quoting *Rose v. Mitchell*, 443 U.S. 545, 555 (1979).

62 *Masterpiece Cakeshop*, 138 S. Ct. 1719, 1729 (citations omitted). This was the May 30, 2014, commission meeting at which they discussed the administrative law judge's findings.

63 Joint appendix, No. 16-111, 205.

64 *Burwell v. Hobby Lobby Stores, Inc.*, 573 U.S. 682, 769 (2014).

65 Joint Appendix, No. 16-111, 207.

66 *Elane Photography, LLC v. Willock*, 309 P.3d 53, 79-80 (N.M. 2013) ¶¶ 91–92.

67 All quotes from Raju Jairam are from an interview with author, on file with author. Quotes confirmed with Jairam on Nov. 26, 2021, via email.

68 Sarah Huckabee Sanders, press briefing, June 5, 2018, https://bit.ly/3DXDvUn.

69 *Masterpiece Cakeshop*, 138 S. Ct., 1729.

70 Ian Millhiser, "The Christian Right's Bizarre Plan to Destroy Civil Rights Laws by Trolling," ThinkProgress, June 6, 2018, https://bit.ly/3y2vcX0.

71 The facts in this case are from the Colorado Anti-Discrimination Act's three "determinations" in the cases, which appear as exhibits in the Joint Appendix, No. 16-111, 226–159.

72 "About Us," Worldview Academy, accessed Nov. 21, 2021, https://worldview.org/about/.

73 Stephanie Mencimer, "Did the Supreme Court Fall for a Stunt?," *Mother Jones*, June 7, 2018, https://bit.ly/3Md0Jcg; Kyle Mantyla, "Kevin Swanson and Co-Host Say Schools That Violate God's Law Should Be Burned Down," Right Wing Watch, Aug. 11, 2017, https://bit.ly/39fM02l; Catherine Tsai, "Bible Museum Tours Cast Doubt on Science," *Washington Post*, Feb. 16, 2006, https://wapo.st/3p31Bqf.

74 Ken McIntyre, "24 Questions for Baker Who Gave Up Wedding Cakes for God," *Daily Signal,* Aug. 21, 2015, https://dailysign.al/3Lk36KG.

75 See, Administrative Law Judge Robert Spence's initial opinion, undisputed fact #6, Dec. 6, 2013, in Combined Appendix for Cert Petition, 2015 SC 738 (Oct. 23, 2015).

76 *Masterpiece Cakeshop*, 138 S. Ct., 1730. | 77 Ibid., 1727.

78 Each year on Martin Luther King Day, I reread his "Letter from the Birmingham Jail." King was arrested for asking and organizing for equal rights. He was unjustly jailed for violating an unconstitutional court injunction that, the Tuscaloosa News wrote, "bans every imaginable form of demonstration." "Negroes to Defy Ban," *Tuscaloosa News*, Apr. 11, 1963, 21, https://bit.ly/3vH5Ta4. The injunction was directed at King and more than 100 other civil rights activists and meant to stop their 1963 campaign for civil rights in Birmingham. On Good Friday, King and about 50 others walked down the street, arms linked, obeying traffic laws and singing. After four blocks, they were arrested and thrown in the Birmingham jail. King was put in solitary confinement. He wrote on scraps of paper, toilet paper, newspaper, and a greasy paper bag, anything that could hold a few of the letter's almost 7,000 words. Lawyers slipped the scraps out of the jail, and Willie Pearl Mackey King pieced it together and typed up the full letter. "Woman Who Helped MLK Change the Nation Talks about Famous Letter," CBS News DFW, Jan. 19, 2015, https://dfw.cbslocal.com/2015/01/19/woman-who-helped-mlk-change-the-nation-talks-about-famous-letter/. There are numerous, slightly different texts of the letter. The Martin Luther King Jr. Research and Education Institute at Stanford has an early draft. https://kinginstitute.stanford.edu/king-papers/documents/letter-birmingham-jail. This text was taken from "Letter from Birmingham Jail," Estate of Martin Luther King, Jr., Apr. 16, 1963, https://bit.ly/3CLEDux.

79 The original reads "cross county," but the "night after night" suggests that this is a typo.

80 Georgia House Bill 757, 2015–16 Regular Session.

81 Gary Tuchman, "Why One Georgia Florist Won't Serve Gay Couples," CNN, *Anderson Cooper 360*, Apr. 1, 2015, https://cnn.it/3cQRoaP.

82 Such things happened regularly during Jim Crow. For a modern example, see Mark Joseph Stern, "Anti-Gay Doctor Refuses to Treat Lesbian Parents' 6-Day-Old Baby," *Slate*, Feb. 19, 2015, https://bit.ly/3OJzZmj.

83 Netta Barak Corren, "Religious Exemptions Increase Discrimination toward Same-Sex Couples: Evidence from *Masterpiece Cakeshop*," *Journal of Legal Studies* 50, no. 1 (2021), https://www.journals.uchicago.edu/doi/10.1086/713289; see also Netta Barak Corren, "How One Supreme Court Decision Increased Discrimination Against LGBTQ Couples," *The Atlantic*, updated Feb. 8, 2021, https://bit.ly/3OI5I77.

84 In "Religious Exemptions Increase Discrimination," Corren estimated "the odds that same-sex couples would experience discrimination post-Masterpiece [are] between 61% and 85%. The effect is significantly more pronounced in religiously dense environments."

85 See, e.g., Amanda Holpuch, "Chick-fil-A Appreciation Day Brings Huge Crowds to Fast-food Chain," *The Guardian*, Aug. 1, 2012, https://bit.ly/38pjBXj.

86 Jim Campbell, "I Represent Christian Baker Jack Phillips. Believe Me, He's a Good Man." *Daily Signal*, June 19, 2018, https://dailysign.al/39alasr.

87 "Support Jack Phillips," Continue to Give, fundraiser archived at https://bit.ly/3tdPoBZ

88 "Masterpiece Cakeshop," Go Fund Me, fundraiser archived at https://bit.ly/3ais7Z5.

89 Rachel Kramer Bussel, "June 2020 Memoir 'The Baker' by Jack Phillips Will Discuss Supreme Court Case about His Refusal to Bake Cake for Same-Sex Couple," *Forbes*, Jan. 31, 2020, https://bit.ly/367QG9c.

90 Market regulation corrects for our irrational ways. Adam Smith didn't like government regulations that constrained competition, but he was fine with regulation of the market in general. He wrote, referring to a specific regulatory system involving London's tailors, that regulation was great: "Regulation, therefore, in favour of the workmen, it is always just and equitable; but it is sometimes otherwise when in favour of the masters." Adam Smith, *Wealth of Nations* (New York: Cosimo Classics, 2007), 151.

91 John F. Kennedy, "Excerpt from a Report to the American People on Civil Rights, 11 June 1963," https://bit.ly/3MwK8AI.

92 *Heart of Atlanta Motel, Inc. v. United States*, Oyez, oral argument at 9:32, Jan. 14, 2021, www.oyez.org/cases/1964/515. (The transcription fails to correctly render the southern accent of Moreton Rolleston, the attorney and hotel owner. I have corrected the quote.)

93 *Atlanta Motel v. United States*, 379 U.S. 241, 278 (1964).

94 Elise Hu, "A History of Human Fingers Found in Fast Food," NPR, May 17, 2012, https://n.pr/3HZHIsP.

95 *Atlanta Motel v. United States*, 379 U.S. 241, 278 (1964).

96 *Masterpiece Cakeshop*, 2017 WL 4023118 (U.S.), 25 (U.S.,2017). See also Deroy Murdock, "Why Christians Are Losing the War over Gay-wedding Cakes," *New York Post*, Apr. 29, 2016, https://bit.ly/3teo0nm.

97 *Newman v. Piggie Park Enterprises, Inc.*, 256 F. Supp. 941, 947 (D.S.C. 1966), rev'd, 377 F.2d 433 (4th Cir. 1967), aff'd, 390 U.S. 400 (1968).

98 Christian Farias, "We've Already Litigated This," *Slate*, Dec. 4, 2017, https://bit.ly/39bDvFy.

99 Letter from L. Maurice Bessinger of the Columbia Chapter of the National Association for the Preservation of White People, Feb. 10, 1963, https://bit.ly/3md0HGM. The footer of NAPWP's letterhead told the reader, "You are white because your ancestors believed in segregation."

100 Michelle Fine and Lois Weis, eds., *Beyond Silenced Voices: Class, Race, and Gender in United States Schools*, rev. ed., (Albany: State Univ. of New York Press, 2005), 223.

101 John Monk, "Barbecue Eatery Owner, Segregationist Maurice Bessinger Dies at 83," *The State*, Feb. 24, 2014, https://bit.ly/3koO8qM.

102 David Firestone, "Sauce Is Boycotted, and Slavery Is the Issue," *New York Times*, Sept. 29, 2000. "I am not pro-slavery," he said, "but no man on earth can make me deny what the Bible says about slavery. The stores are just yielding to outside pressure from people who want to destroy the Constitution and remake America to fit their globalism strategy."

103 The sign can be seen on Google Maps through 2014 images, http://bit.ly/2XQ2c1r, but is gone in 2019 images. See also Rien Fertel, *The One True Barbecue: Fire, Smoke, and the Pitmasters Who Cook the Whole Hog* (New York: Atria Books, 2017), 161. | 104 Fertel, *The One True Barbecue*, 162.

105 *Newman v. Piggie Park Enterprises, Inc.*, 390 U.S. 400, 403n.5 (1968).

106 Maurice Bessinger, *Defending My Heritage: The Maurice Bessinger Story* (West Columbia, SC: Lmbone-Lehone, 2001), 134. I believe this is truly one of the most heinous books I've ever read.

107 Even recorded interviews with Anne Newman focus on her husband's work. See, e.g., Marvin Ira Lare, ed., *Champions of Civil and Human Rights in South Carolina*, Vol. 1: *Dawn of the Movement Era, 1955–1967* (Columbia: Univ. of South Carolina Press, 2016). See book for transcript of Lare interview with Newman, https://bit.ly/3PQOUeL.

108 For the oral argument, see *Masterpiece Cakeshop*, Oyez, Dec. 5, 2017, https://www.oyez.org/cases/2017/16-111.

109 *Loving v. Virginia*, 388 U.S. 1 (1967). | 110 Oral argument, *Masterpiece Cakeshop*.

111 *Masterpiece Cakeshop*. Sotomayor on Piggie Park, at 16:00; Kagan on interracial marriage, 17:05; "Race is different," 17:52; Francisco, 26:03.

112 *Masterpiece Cakeshop*, 1:25:50. | 113 Oral argument in *Masterpiece Cakeshop*, at 1:00:01.

114 Opinion announcement, *Obergefell v. Hodges*, Oyez, www.oyez.org/cases/2014/14-556. For instance, polygyny and polygamy have been common throughout human history. And same-sex marriage between individuals was not unheard of. Roman men—including Emperor Nero, apparently—married other men. See

Elizabeth Abbott, *A History of Marriage* (New York: Seven Stories Press, 2011). It was also common among many native people prior to Christian influence, in part because gender was fluid and multifaceted, rather than rigid and dichotomous.

115 Court watchers noted the anger where an average observer might not. See, e.g., Erwin Chemerinsky, "Justice at Risk," *American Prospect*, Winter 2017, https://prospect.org/power/justice-risk/.

116 Ashton Pittman, "No 'Mixed' or 'Gay' Couples, Mississippi Wedding Venue Owner Says on Vide," Deep South Voice, Sept. 1, 2019, https://bit.ly/39mIJhX.

117 Interview with author.

6: HOSTILITY IN HIALEAH

1 James Baldwin, *No Name in the Street* (New York: Dial Press, 1972).

2–4 Facts and quotes for these three footnotes are taken from the district (*Church of the Lukumi Babalu Aye, Inc. v. City of Hialeah,* 723 F. Supp. 1467, 1476, (S.D. Fla. 1989) and Supreme Court opinions (*Church of the Lukumi Babalu Aye, Inc. v. City of Hialeah,* 508 U.S. 520 (1993)), the petitioners brief (*Church of the Lukumi Babalu Aye, Inc. v. City of Hialeah,* 1992 WL 541280 (U.S.), 34), and two scholarly works: Stephan Palmié, "Which Centre? Whose Margin? Notes Towards an Archaeology of U.S. Supreme Court Case 91-948, 1993," in *Inside and Outside the Law: Anthropological Studies of Authority and Ambiguity,* ed. Olivia Harris (New York: Routledge, 1996), http://bit.ly/2Yb0hF2; and Fred M. Frohock, "The Free Exercise of Religion: Lukumi and Animal Sacrifice," a paper delivered at the Institute for Cuban and Cuban-American Studies Occasional Paper Series, Nov. 2001, https://bit.ly/3kjSpff. This paper eventually became part of Fred M. Frohock, *Bounded Divinities: Sacred Discourses in Pluralist Democracies* (London: Palgrave Macmillan, 2016).

5 *Church of the Lukumi Babalu Aye, Inc. v. City of Hialeah,* 723 F. Supp., 1477.

6 Katherine Hagedorn, *Divine Utterances: The Performance of Afro-Cuban Santería* (Washington, DC: Smithsonian Books, 2001). Some Santeria practitioners sacrifice cats and dogs, though this particular church refused to do so, perhaps because it was trying to become more mainstream.

7 Genesis 6:19 and 7:2–3. Or perhaps seven additional animals, not seven pairs; the translations are contradictory. Compare, e.g., the King James Version and New Revised Standard Version translations.

8 Genesis 8:16–22. | 9 Hebrews 10:4. | 10 1 John 2:2.

11 A. J. Dickerson, "Lawyers Jeered for Their Advice on Closing Church," Associated Press, June 10, 1987. See also Ana Maria Guadayol "Hialeah Vote on Santeria Meaningless, Lawyer Says," *Miami News*, June 10, 1987, 10.

12 The basic 1987 timeline is this: *June 9:* Mob meeting, Resolution 87-66 and Ordinance 87-40 adopted. City asks Florida Attorney General for an opinion. *July 13:* Florida Attorney General issues opinion: Prohibiting ritual animal sacrifice is OK. *Aug. 11:* Resolution No. 87-90 adopted. *Sept. 8:* Ordinance 87-52 adopted. *Sept. 11:* Pope visits Miami, where church was trying to root out Santeria from its ranks. *Sept. 22:* Ordinance 87-71 and 87-72 were passed.

13 The full text of Resolution 87-66 and the four ordinances appears in an appendix to the Supreme Court opinion, *Church of the Lukumi Babalu Aye, Inc. v. City of Hialeah,* 508 U.S. 520, 548.

14 Florida Attorney General Advisory Legal Opinion—AGO 87-56, July 13, 1987, https://bit.ly/38rfiL8.

15 See, e.g., *Church of the Lukumi Babalu Aye, Inc. v. City of Hialeah,* oral argument at 43:46, https://www.oyez.org/cases/1992/91-948. The church couldn't even sacrifice in a slaughterhouse. | 16 Ibid., 12:35.

17 There are very important questions about the animal rights side of this issue, and there is interesting, cutting-edge legal work being done by groups like the Nonhuman Rights Project, but resolving those fascinating questions is outside the scope of this book.

18 *Church of the Lukumi Babalu Aye v. City of Hialeah,* 508 U.S. 520 (1993).

19 "VI. Notes on Locke and Shaftesbury, 11 Oct.–9 Dec. 1776," Founders Online, National Archives, https://bit.ly/3Oi23fz. [Original source: *The Papers of Thomas Jefferson,* vol. 1, *1760–1776,* ed. Julian P. Boyd (Princeton, NJ: Princeton Univ. Press, 1950), 544–50.] Punctuation and capitalization modernized slightly; spelling corrected; emphasis added.

20 Palmié, "Which Centre? Whose Margin?," 147.

21 A. J. Dickerson, "Florida City Opposes Santeria Church Plans," Associated Press, June 7, 1987, *Albuquerque Journal,* June 8, 1987, A14.

22 Mike Clary, "Florida's Caribbean Immigrants Are Putting Their Faith in Santeria: The Religion Has Flourished Since a Favorable 1993 Supreme Court Ruling. But Growth Has Bred Controversy in Ranks of Believers" *Los Angeles Times,* Aug. 9, 1995, https://lat.ms/3PZAhpJ.

23 Frohock, "The Free Exercise of Religion," 30. | 24 Ibid., 28. | 25 Palmié, "Which Centre? Whose Margin?," 147.

26 *Church of the Lukumi Babalu Aye, Inc. v. City of Hialeah,* 508 U.S., 541–42.

27 Palmié, "Which Centre? Whose Margin?," 147.

28 "Crowd Protests Santeria Church," *Miami News,* June 10, 1987, 1.

29 Bill Reinke, Interview with Miami Archbishop Edward McCarthy, "Pope Not Coming to Scold Us" *Miami News,* July 11, 1987, 1A, 6A.

30 "Miami Archbishop Edward McCarthy, 87," obituary, *Washington Post,* June 9, 2005, http://wapo.st/3oqxvL9.

31 George Volsky, "Religion from Cuba Stirs Row in Miami," *New York Times,* June 29, 1987, https://nyti.ms/29zHVa9.

32 Including mine. Leslie C. Griffith and Andrew L. Seidel, *Law and Religion: Cases and Materials, 5th ed.* (St. Paul, MN: Foundation Press, 2022).

33 One student observed as much at the time. Gabrielle G. Davison, "The 'Extreme and Hypothetical' Come to Life: *Church of the Lukumi Babalu Aye, Inc. v. City of Hialeah*," *Catholic Univ. Law Review* 43, no. 2 (1994), 641, https://scholarship.law.edu/lawreview/vol43/iss2/9.

34 *Church of the Lukumi Babalu Aye, Inc. v. City of Hialeah*, 508 U.S., 563.

35 On Nov. 16, 1993.

36 See, e.g., Sean Clerget, "Timing Is of the Essence: Reviving the Neutral Law of General Applicability Standard and Applying It to Restrictions Against Religious Face Coverings Worn While Testifying in Court," *George Mason Law Review* 18, no. 4 (2011), 1013, 1019: ("One must understand the Court's application of *Smith* in *Church of Lukumi* and Congress's response to *Smith* via the 1993 Religious Freedom Restoration Act."); Lino A. Graglia, "Church of the Lukumi Babalu Aye: Of Animal Sacrifice and Religious Persecution," *Georgetown Law Journal* 85, no. 1, 3 (1996), "To the extent that the Justices hoped to avoid adverse congressional action by demonstrating the Court's continuing commitment to the cause of religious freedom, the attempt failed."

37 Kenneth L. Karst, "The Stories in Lukumi: Of Sacrifice and Rebirth," in Andrew Koppelman and Richard W. Garnett, eds., *First Amendment Stories* (St. Paul, MN: Foundation Press/Thomson Reuters, 2012), 474.

38 Most of the facts in this section—facts omitted by the courts—come from the two scholars, Fred M. Frohock and Stephane Palmié, both of whom interviewed the parties many times. Palmié was a scholar and friend of the Pichardo family.

39 Tom Lassiter, "Hialeah Official Convicted in Extortion," *South Florida Sun-Sentinel*, Feb. 28, 1987, https://bit.ly/3kkbcHi.

40 Tom Lassiter, "Mayor Testifies in Bribe Case," *South Florida Sun-Sentinel*, Feb. 26, 1987, https://bit.ly/38xzeMw.

41 Laura Parker, "Florida Corruption Probes Proliferate," *Washington Post*, Aug. 13, 1990, https://wapo.st/3681vYG.

42 Sandra Marquez Garcia and Joseph Tanfani, "Hialeah Mayor, Protester Mix It Up at Traffic Blockade," *Miami Herald*, July 1, 1999, 12, https://bit.ly/3MFUgHD.

43 Dan Sewell, "Raul Martinez Leads Hialeah Again—But Prison Looms," Associated Press, Dec. 26, 1993, https://bit.ly/3y3MNOx; Associated Press, "Hialeah Mayor Guilty of Selling His Influence," *New York Times*, Mar. 27, 1991, A16, https://nyti.ms/29nb1GV. | 44 Sewell, "Raul Martinez Leads Hialeah Again."

45 David M. O'Brien, *Animal Sacrifice and Religious Freedom: "Church of the Lukumi Babalu Aye v. City of Hialeah"* (Lawrence: Univ. Press of Kansas, 2004), 37.

46 Just FYI, Julio Navarro was the property owner, according to Palmié.

47 Frohock, "The Free Exercise of Religion," 27; Palmié, "Which Centre? Whose Margin?," 150.

48 Frohock, "The Free Exercise of Religion," 26; Palmié, "Which Centre? Whose Margin?," 150. Sebastian Dorrego was the councilman. For more, read Carlos Harrison, "Federal Corruption Probe Has Long, Tangled History," *Miami Herald*, Apr. 4, 1990, 1.

49 Frohock, "The Free Exercise of Religion," 27; Palmié, "Which Centre? Whose Margin?," 150.

50 Frohock, "The Free Exercise of Religion," 27.

51 "Santeria: Ancient Afro-Cuban Religion, Animal Sacrifices Surface in Miami," *Florida Today*, July 26, 1987, 1D, 2D, https://www.newspapers.com/clip/13098011/santeria-1987/.

52 Frohock, "The Free Exercise of Religion," 27–28. | 53 Palmié, "Which Centre? Whose Margin?," 149–50.

54 *Miami News*, Oct. 30, 1987, page 8A, Donna Gehrke story, interview with Salvatore D'Angelo.

55 Frohock, "The Free Exercise of Religion," 30. | 56 Ibid.

57 O'Brien, *Animal Sacrifice and Religious Freedom*, 37. | 58 Ibid.

59 The original address was 173 W. 5th Street, almost exactly 1,500 feet from the storefront at 345 Palm Avenue.

60 O'Brien, *Animal Sacrifice and Religious Freedom*, 220.

61 The property search folio number is 04-3118-001-2131, https://www.miamidade.gov/Apps/PA/propertysearch/#/. The property got a new address on 6th Street along the way. An interesting note in the sales records states that two sales were "disqualified" in 1993, the year the decision came down, "as a result of examination of the deed."

7: THE MUSLIM BAN

1 Brian Tashman, "Trump: Under Obama, Only Muslim Immigrants Allowed into America," Right Wing Watch, May 16, 2015, https://bit.ly/3NWuVJQ; Linh Ta, "National Security in Focus for GOP Field in Iowa," *Des Moines Register*, May 16, 2015, https://bit.ly/34wfPty.

2 In *School District of Abington Township v. Schempp*, 374 U.S. 203, 205 (1963), the court said, "The State may not . . . show hostility to religion," but that it wasn't doing so in that case. Rehnquist: "We neither abdicate our responsibility to maintain a division between church and state nor evince a hostility to religion by disabling the government from in some ways recognizing our religious heritage." *Van Orden v. Perry*, 545 U.S. 677, 683–84 (2005). Breyer mentions it too, in *Rosenberger v. Rector and Visitors of University of Virginia*, 515 U.S. 819, 845–846 (1995), warning against the "risk [of] fostering a pervasive bias or hostility to religion, which could undermine the very neutrality the Establishment Clause requires." They didn't cite *Lukumi*, though, and the cases weren't decided based on hostility per se.

3 *Vidal v. Girard's Executors*, 43 U.S. 127, 197 (1844). Then not again for 99 years. For a full history of the hostility concept, see Mark Satta, "Unclear Hostility: Supreme Court Discussions of 'Hostility to Religion' from

Barnette to *American Legion*," *Buffalo Law Review* 68, no. 2 (2020), 641, https://digitalcommons.law.buffalo.edu/buffalolawreview/vol68/iss2/5. | 4 Satta, "Unclear Hostility," 641.

5 Using "depth of treatment" on Westlaw as a marker for support. *City of Boerne v. Flores*, 521 U.S. 507, 529 (1997); *Locke v. Davey*, 540 U.S. 712, 720 (2004), brought by a Crusader, the American Center for Law and Justice.

6 *Stormans, Inc. v. Wiesman*, 136 S. Ct. 2433 (2016).

7 Wash. Admin. Code § 246–863–095 and § 246–869–010. The Ninth Circuit explained well. *Stormans, Inc. v. Wiesman*, 794 F.3d 1064, 1073 (9th Cir. 2015). | 8 *Stormans*, 136 S. Ct., 2440.

9–11 *Trinity Lutheran Church of Columbia, Inc. v. Comer*, 137 S. Ct. 2012 (2017). | *Masterpiece Cakeshop, Ltd. v. Colorado Civil Rights Commission*, 138 S. Ct. 1719 (2018). | *Trump v. Hawaii*, 138 S. Ct. 923 (2018). | *American Legion v. American Humanist Association*, 139 S. Ct. 2067, 2085 (2019). Alito did not cite *Lukumi*, but upheld the massive concrete Christian cross on government land in part because moving it would "be aggressively hostile to religion." | *Espinoza v. Montana Department of Revenue*, 140 S. Ct. 2246 (2020). Not having a scholarship program for children to attend private religious schools was hostile to religion, and "so long as this hostility remains, fostered by our distorted understanding of the Establishment Clause, free exercise rights will continue to suffer." | *Roman Catholic Diocese of Brooklyn v. Cuomo*, 141 S. Ct. 63 (2020). | *South Bay United Pentecostal Church v. Newsom*, 141 S. Ct. 716 (2021). | *Tandon v. Newsom*, 141 S. Ct. 1294 (2021) cites *Cuomo* and *South Bay* and *Lukumi* in the last paragraph, though not for hostility. But that simply shows that it lowered the bar. Now the crusading justices can cite *their* cases for hostility, not the original high bar set in *Lukumi*. | *Fulton v. City of Philadelphia, Penn.* 141 S. Ct. 1868, 1882 (2021), citing *Lukumi*, 508 U.S. at 546–547. Less for the hostility per se, but rather to say that any exceptions in a law that also did not include religious exception was necessarily discriminatory or hostile, as in the Santeria case: "The creation of a system of exceptions under the contract undermines the City's contention that its non-discrimination policies can brook no departures."

12 See Miriam Valverde, "Trump's Travel Restrictions Survive Supreme Court, Fall Short of Promised Muslim ban," *PolitiFact*, Nov. 14, 2018, https://bit.ly/3vWUfcY.

13 Donald Trump, Twitter post, June 5, 2017, archived at https://bit.ly/312qoCK.

14 "People were so upset when I used the word Muslim," he said, "'Oh, you can't use the word Muslim. Remember this.' And I'm okay with that, because I'm talking territory instead of Muslim." See Miriam Valverde, "Trump's Travel Restrictions Survive Supreme Court."

15 The American Presidency Project, Presidential Debates: Presidential Debate at Washington Univ. in St. Louis, Missouri, Oct. 9, 2016, https://bit.ly/3OE0NEm.

16 Jenna Johnson and Abigail Hauslohner, "'I Think Islam Hates Us': A Timeline of Trump's Comments about Islam and Muslims," *Washington Post*, May 20, 2017, http://wapo.st/3p2sOZ7.

17 Adam Liptak, "'There's No Reason to Apologize' for Muslim Ban Remarks, Trump Says," *New York Times*, Apr. 30, 2018, https://nyti.ms/2FwUY6K.

18 Michael Keller, "Tracking Trump's Web of Conflicts," Bloomberg Politics, May 18, 2017, https://www.bloomberg.com/graphics/tracking-trumps-web-of-conflicts/.

19 See Alana Abramson, "What Trump Has Said About a Muslim Registry," ABC News, Nov. 18, 2016, https://abcnews.go.com/Politics/trump-muslim-registry/story?id=43639946; Michael Scherer, "Donald Trump Says He Might Have Supported Japanese Internment," *Time*, Dec. 8, 2015, https://bit.ly/3MVstTi.

20 Sunnivie Brydum, "The Deafening Silence of 'Religious Freedom' Defenders on Trump's Muslim Ban," *Religion Dispatches*, Jan. 31, 2017, https://bit.ly/3sX35Wm. The Alliance Defending Freedom has almost no history of representing non-Christians, according to an exhaustive investigative report. See Sarah Posner "The Christian Legal Army Behind 'Masterpiece Cakeshop,'" *The Nation*, Nov. 28, 2017, https://bit.ly/3Nmy8mi.

21 The list appears at "Trump v. Hawaii," SCOTUSblog, https://www.scotusblog.com/case-files/cases/trump-v-hawaii-3/. Among those Christian champions were Roy Moore's Foundation for Moral Law, Phyllis Schlafly's Eagle Forum Education and Legal Defense, and 17 states led by Texas Attorney General and Christian nationalist Ken Paxton.

22 Brydum, "The Deafening Silence of 'Religious Freedom' Defenders on Trump's Muslim Ban."

23 Brief Amicus Curiae of the Becket Fund for Religious Liberty in Support of Neither Party, *Trump v. State of Hawaii*, 2018 WL 1314147 (U.S.) (U.S., 2018), iv, https://bit.ly/39RjJMj.

24 Brief for Alliance Defending Freedom as Amicus Curiae Supporting Neither Party, *Trump v. Hawaii*, 2018 WL 1156655 (U.S.) (U.S., 2018), https://bit.ly/35YqkmW.

25 *Trump v. Hawaii*, 138 S. Ct. 2392, 2420–21 (2018). | 26 Ibid., 2421. | 27 Ibid. | 28 Ibid., 2433.

8: IT WAS NEVER ABOUT THE DRUGS

1 Oral argument, *Employment Division, Department of Human Resources of Oregon v. Smith*, Oyez, exchange begins at 21:11, accessed Feb. 25, 2022, www.oyez.org/cases/1989/88-1213.

2 Garrett Epps, *Peyote vs. the State: Religious Freedom on Trial* (Norman: Univ. of Oklahoma Press, 2012), 89.

3 A 501c3 incorporated in 1971. The IRS Employment Identification Number is 93-0611783.

4 Brief for Petitioners, Employment Division, Department of Human Resources, of the State of Oregon, *Ray Thorne, Administrator and ADAPT, Petitioners v. Alfred Smith (No. 86-946) and Galen W. Black (No. 86-947), Respondents*, 1987 WL 880306 (U.S.), 2–3.

5 *Black v. Employment Division*, 75 Or. App. 735, 737 (1985).

6 Smith said later, "When I went to work for them, did I consider ADAPT would consider peyote a drug? Yes." Epps, *Peyote vs. the State,* 86.
7 "Oregon Peyote Law Leaves 1983 Defendant Unvindicated," *New York Times,* July 9, 1991, https://nyti.ms/3nZzMQt.
8 Epps, *Peyote vs. the State,* 88. | 9 Ibid., 90–91. | 10 Ibid., 96.
11 *Black v. Employment Division,* 75 Or. App. 735, 739. | 12 Epps, *Peyote vs. the State,* 58.
13 Ibid., 96. | 14 Ibid., 97. | 15 Ibid., 95–99. | 16 Ibid.
17 *Smith v. Employment Division, Department of Human Resources,,* 301 Or. 209, 212 (1986).
18 Epps, *Peyote vs. the State,* 8.
19 The stories of unmarked mass graves have, so far, centered on Canada, which has done more to reckon with its past than the United States. That's changing. See, e.g., Peter Smith, "US Churches Reckon with Traumatic Legacy of Native schools," Associated Press, July 22, 2021, https://bit.ly/3leyIXa; and Susan Montoya Bryan, "US to Review Native American Boarding Schools' Dark History," Associated Press, June 22, 2021, https://bit.ly/37MRFN7.
20 Epps, *Peyote vs. the State,* 13.
21 Patricia Nelson Limerick, "The Repression of Indian Religious Freedom," Native American Rights Fund 18, no. 2 (Summer 1993), 11, https://bit.ly/3EWg2Uw.
22 Garrett Epps, "To an Unknown God: The Hidden History of *Employment Division v. Smith*," *Arizona State Law Journal* 30, no. 4 (Winter 1998), 1019.
23 *Sherbert v. Verner,* 374 U.S. 398 (1963).
24 The fears of such fraud were racist. If one person has "80 names, 30 addresses, 12 Social Security cards and is collecting veterans' benefits on four non-existing deceased husbands" and Social Security, Medicaid, food stamps, and welfare, as Ronald Reagan claimed, a line in the unemployment statute limiting distribution of benefits to those who lost jobs "for cause" is not going to stop that person or that kind of fraud. "'Welfare Queen' Becomes Issue in Reagan Campaign," *New York Times,* Feb. 15, 1976, https://nyti.ms/3p8s7Pe.
25 Oral argument, *Employment Division, Department of Human Resources of Oregon v. Smith (1987),* Oyez, 32:49 www.oyez.org/cases/1987/86-946.
26 *Smith v. Employment Division,* 301 Or. 209, 215 (Or. 1986).
27 *Black v. Employment Division,* 301 Or. 221, 223 (Or. 1986).
28 Oral argument, *Employment Division, Department of Human Resources of Oregon v. Smith* (1989), exchange begins at 21:11, Oyez, www.oyez.org/cases/1989/88-1213.
29 Oregon Revised Statutes 475.992 (1993).
30 *Employment Division, Department of Human Resources of Oregon v. Smith,* 494 U.S., 872, 877 (1990).
31 Ibid., 878. | 32 Ibid., 888.
33 Oral argument, *Employment Division, Department of Human Resources of Oregon v. Smith (1987),* Oyez, 32:49, accessed Oct. 19, 2020, www.oyez.org/cases/1987/86-946.
34 Paul E. McGreal, "The Making of the Supreme Court's Free Exercise Clause Jurisprudence: Lessons from the Blackmun and Powell Papers in Bowen v. Roy," *Southern Illinois Univ. School of Law Journal* 34 (2010), 469, 471, https://law.siu.edu/academics/law-journal/issues/spring-2010.html.
35 "Justice Antonin Scalia: The US Constitution Is 'Dead,'" FORA.tv clip, YouTube.com, Mar. 25, 2009, https://youtu.be/DTRe5xDLfXw.
36 "Constitution a 'Dead, Dead, Dead' Document, Scalia Tells SMU Audience," *Dallas Morning News,* Jan. 13, 2013, https://bit.ly/3OAUYHT.
37 Jeffrey Rosen, *The Supreme Court: The Personalities and Rivalries That Defined America* (New York: Henry Holt, 2007) 219, quoting Ralph A. Rossum, *Antonin Scalia's Jurisprudence: Text and Tradition* (Lawrence: Univ. Press of Kansas, 2006), 205–6. Rossum and Rosen suggest that this worked for Scalia, but Rossum's methodology was not intended to be exhaustive. For a thorough examination of Scalia's influence, see Brian T. Fitzpatrick and Paulson K. Varghese, "Scalia in the Casebooks," *Univ. of Chicago Law Review* 84 (2017), 2231–42, http://www.jstor.org/stable/45063674.
38 See, e.g., Richard L. Hasen, "The Most Sarcastic Justice," *18 GREEN BAG 2D* (2015), 215, 216 (noting that Scalia's sarcasm was partly to gain attention for his ideas.), https://bit.ly/3EWgeTK; Yury Kapgan, "Of Golf and Ghouls: The Prose Style of Justice Scalia," *Legal Writing: The Journal of the Legal Writing Institute* 71 (2003), 96, https://bit.ly/3KLSFP8; for popular media, see J. Lyn Entrikin, "Disrespectful Dissent: Justice Scalia's Regrettable Legacy of Incivility," *Journal of Appellate Practice and Process* 18 (2017), 275, https://lawrepository.ualr.edu/appellatepracticeprocess/vol18/iss2/5.
39 Tina Nguyen, "Scalia's Comment on Black Students Draws Gasps in Supreme Court," *Vanity Fair,* Dec. 10, 2015, https://bit.ly/3kq3zit; Barney Frank, "Justice Scalia Is a Homophobe," *Politico,* June 26, 2015, https://politi.co/3vjTYjJ; Sam Fulwood III, "The Racially Insensitive Legacy of Justice Antonin Scalia," Center for American Progress, Feb. 24, 2016, https://ampr.gs/3tLMGDo; Rachel Anspach, "Scalia Was Not a Hero. He Was a Bigot," *HuffPost,* Feb. 17, 2017, https://www.huffpost.com/entry/scalia-was-not-a-hero-he-_b_9245850.
40 *Lyng v. Northwest Indian Cemetery Protective Association,* 485 U.S., 439 (1988).
41 *Northwest Indian Cemetery Protective Association v. Peterson,* 565 F. Supp. 586, 590 (N.D. Cal. 1983).
42 Ibid. at 592. | 43 *Lyng v. Northwest Indian Cemetery Protective Association,* 485 U.S., at 442.
44 *Northwest Indian Cemetery Protective Association v. Peterson,* 565 F. Supp., at 590, 595.
45 "The building of a road or the harvesting of timber on publicly owned land cannot meaningfully be distinguished from the use of a Social Security number." *Lyng v. Northwest Indian Cemetery Protective Association,* 485 U.S., at 449.

46 The environmental impact report on the road found the religious use depended on "certain qualities of the physical environment, the most important of which are privacy, silence, and an undisturbed natural setting." Ibid.

47 See, e.g., Laura Underkuffler, "The Separation of the Religious and the Secular: A Foundational Challenge to First Amendment Theory," *William and Mary Law Review* 36 (1995), 837, 854, https://scholarship.law.wm.edu/wmlr/vol36/iss3/2 (arguing that "the collapse of the compelling interest test into a generalized concern for the protection of the secular state reached its culmination in [*Lyng*] and [*Smith*].").

48 Oral argument, *Employment Division, Department of Human Resources of Oregon v. Smith (1989)*, Oyez, 29:55 www.oyez.org/cases/1989/88-1213. | 49 *Employment Division*, 494 U.S., 890 (emphasis added).

50 Linda Greenhouse, "Use of Drugs in Religious Rituals Can Be Prosecuted, Justices Rule," *New York Times*, Apr. 18, 1990, A22, https://nyti.ms/3I2Jsl5; Stephen Chapman, "Should Religious Freedom Include Peyote Users?," *Chicago Tribune*, Feb. 3, 1991, https://bit.ly/3ESyT2Z; "The Necessity of Religion: High Court Says Religious Freedom Is a Luxury—Wrong," *Los Angeles Times*, Apr. 19, 1990, https://lat.ms/3vH8hxy; see, e.g., Michael W. McConnell, "Free Exercise Revisionism and the Smith Decision," *Univ. of Chicago Law Review* 57, no. 4 (1990), 1109–53, accessed July 11, 2021, doi:10.2307/1599887.

51 Religious Freedom Restoration Act of 1991 Hearings (HR 2797), Subcommittee on Civil and Constitutional Rights, Committee on the Judiciary, House of Representatives, 102nd Cong., 2nd Sess. May 13–14, 1992, https://bit.ly/3Lnrpat.

9: RESTORING CHRISTIAN SUPREMACY

1 Sandhya Somashekhar, "Georgia Governor Vetoes Religious Freedom Bill Criticized as Anti-Gay," *Washington Post*, Mar. 28, 2016, https://wapo.st/34YgCnn.

2 The bill was not passed unanimously, as is suggested nowadays, but by a justly maligned consent procedure that doesn't record votes. Prof. Marci A. Hamilton explains in *God vs. the Gavel: The Perils of Extreme Religious Liberty*, rev. ed. (New York: Cambridge Univ. Press,) 2014: "The House didn't even do a roll call vote, which would have recorded each member's vote. It was passed by "unanimous consent," the reprehensible procedure by which leadership puts up a bill for a vote with no one there and no record of where each member stands. Today, supporters of the Religious Freedom Restoration Act routinely claim it was passed 'unanimously,' but that is just not true."

3 Rep. Shepherd of Utah, Congressional Record H2353, May 11, 1993, https://bit.ly/3KlOdGA.

4 Rep. Jack Brooks (Tex.), Congressional Record H2356, May 11, 1993, https://bit.ly/37MRNw4.

5 By Mr. Biden S. 3254, Congressional Record S17331, Oct. 26, 1990, https://bit.ly/38pn7AZ.

6 See, e.g., https://bit.ly/3wWsqBW, PDF pp 3 ("will we begin to change the standard by which we judge whether a religious practice can be impacted upon by a governmental body?,") 33, 166–68.

7 I am indebted to Prof. Marci Hamilton for all her work on the unconstitutionality of the Religious Freedom Restoration Act. See, e.g., http://rfraperils.com/wp-content/uploads/2014/03/brief.pdf.

8 *Sherbert v. Verner*, 374 US, 409–10; *Thomas v. Review Board of Indiana Employment Security Division*, 450 US 707 (1981); *Hobbie v. Unemployment Appeals Commission of Florida*, 480 US 136 (1987).

9 She began on Aug. 8, 1938. Joined the Seventh Day Adventist church on Aug. 6, 1957. On June 5, 1959, Spartan Mills made Saturdays mandatory. She was fired on July 27, 1959. The Supreme Court's recitation of the facts is very short and conclusory. See, instead, the lower court's facts. *Sherbert v. Verner*, 240 S.C. 286, 288, 125 S.E.2d 737, 737 (1962), *rev'd*, 374 US, 398 (1963).

10 Jeffrey Leiter, Rhonda Zingraff, and Michael Schulman, *Hanging by a Thread: Social Change in Southern Textiles* (Ithaca, NY: Cornell Univ. Press, 1991), 208.

11 *Sherbert v. Verner*, 374 US, at 402, n.2.

12 Ibid., 399–401. | 13 Ibid., 404.

14 John Hart Ely, "Legislative and Administrative Motivation in Constitutional Law," *Yale Law Journal* 79, no. 7 (1970), 1207.

15 There's good evidence that Constantine made the shift to Sunday; his reasons are less clear. Robert K. McIver, "When, Where, and Why Did the Change from Sabbath to Sunday Worship Take Place in the Early Church?," *Andrews Univ. Seminary Studies* 53, no. 1, (2015), 15–35, https://bit.ly/3y01ulw. "There is, in fact, evidence that can be put forward to support the claim that Constantine was a crucial player in the shift of the day of worship from Sabbath to Sunday. There is even evidence to support the claim that Constantine had a long association with sun worship."

16 *Sherbert v. Verner*, 240 S.C. 286, 303 (1962).

17 Section 64 of the South Carolina Code of 1952 banned sporting and working on Sundays. By then, the state's textile business was so lucrative that the legislature passed a special provision directed solely at banning any work in a textile mill on Sunday. Section 64-4: "It shall be unlawful for any person owning, controlling or operating any textile manufacturing, finishing, dyeing, printing or processing plant to request, require or permit any regular employee to do, exercise or perform any of the usual or ordinary worldly labor or work in, of, about or connected with such employee's regular occupation or calling or any part thereof in or about such textile manufacturing, finishing, dyeing, printing or processing plant on Sunday." *Code of Laws of South Carolina, 1952*, https://bit.ly/3MD8k5p.

18 *Xepapas v. Richardson*, 149 S.C. 52, 146 S.E. 686, 687 (1929).

19 "Art. VIII. § 1. The free exercise and enjoyment of religious profession and worship, without discrimination or preference, shall forever, hereafter, be allowed within this State to all mankind; provided, that the liberty

of conscience hereby declared shall not be so construed as to excuse acts of licentiousness, or justify practices inconsistent with the peace or safety of this State." *City Council of Charleston v. Benjamin*, 33 S.C.L. 508, 509 (S.C. App. L. 1848).

20 David Barton, *The Myth of Separation: What Is the Correct Relationship Between Church and State?* (Aledo, TX: WallBuilder Press, 1992); cites the case seven times; see, e.g., pp 73–75.

21 John Belton O'Neall, *The Negro Law of South Carolina* (Columbia, SC: J. G. Bowman, 1848), 23, sect. 42, https://bit.ly/39okOyD.

22 Ulysses Robert Brooks, *South Carolina Bench and Bar*, 22, 30. (Columbia, SC: State Company, 1908), This is a simplified portrait of O'Neall, who was the child of Quakers and who was reviled by his fellow whites for not being hard enough on slaves in *The Negro Law*. Then again, his first book was Bunyan's *Pilgrim's Progress*, a founding book of Protestantism.

23 *City Council of Charleston v. Benjamin*, 33 S.C.L. 508, 521 (S.C. App. L. 1848). | 24 Ibid., 524. | 25 Ibid., 527.

26 *Estate of Thornton v. Caldor, Inc.*, 472 U.S. 703, 709–10 (1985). | 27 *Sherbert v. Verner*, 374 U.S., 406.

28 The court noted that "all of the textile plants, including the Spartan Mills, operate six days per week." *Sherbert v. Verner*, 240 S.C. 286, 294 (1962). And it seems clear, given the economic strain the industry was under, that it would have welcomed the chance for a 17% increase in output.

29 Leslie Griffin and Marci Hamilton. "Why We Like Smith: We Want Neutral and General Laws to Prevent Harm," *Verdict*, Apr. 19, 2021, https://bit.ly/3KopcKX.

30 *Sherbert v. Verner*, 374 U.S., 406.

31 *Hobbie v. Unemployment Appeals Commission of Florida*, 480 US 136 (1987). Paula Hobbie worked for a chain of Florida jewelers. After two and a half years of work, some promotion, and having to work Fridays and Saturdays, Hobbie converted to and was "baptized into the Seventh-day Adventist Church." She explained to her bosses that, for religious reasons, she would "no longer be able to work on her Sabbath, from sundown on Friday to sundown on Saturday." At 138.

32 It's a real thing. See "The 'Zeal of the Convert': Is It the Real Deal?," Pew Research Center, Oct. 28, 2009, https://www.pewforum.org/2009/10/28/the-zeal-of-the-convert-is-it-the-real-deal.

33 There's remarkably little information on these individuals. I scoured the papers, as did my talented researcher.

34 *Sherbert v. Verner*, 374 US, at 422.

35. *Thomas v. Review Board of Indiana Employment Security Division*, 450 US 707, 720 (1981) J. (Rehnquist dissenting).

36 Paul Baumgardner and Brian K. Miller, "Moving from the Statehouses to the State Courts? The Post-RFRA Future of State Religious Freedom Protections," *Albany Law Review* 82, no. 4 (2019), 1385, 1392–93, https://bit.ly/37JyuUz. "State RFRAs [Religious Freedom Restoration Acts] have progressed through three distinct stages since their origin. The first stage—the bipartisan stage—began with the passage of the first state RFRAs in the mid-1990s and continued through the enactment of Louisiana's RFRA in 2010. During this initial stage, state RFRAs were depicted as simple, constructive, and non-ideological safeguards that promised to better protect religious adherents and institutions." Many of these RFRAs were a response to the Supreme Court reclaiming a bit of sovereignty in 1997 and holding that the federal RFRA could not apply to state governments in *City of Boerne v. Flores*.

10: THE WAR ON WOMEN

1 Jessica Valenti, "The Hobby Lobby Ruling Proves Men of the Law Still Can't Get over 'Immoral' Women Having Sex," *The Guardian*, June 30, 2014, https://bit.ly/3Mzhb7o.

2 National Women's Law Center, "Status of the Lawsuits Challenging the Affordable Care Act's Birth Control Coverage Benefit," Oct. 27, 2015, https://bit.ly/3vUtSEH. There have been nearly 2,000 lawsuits filed against the ACA and its regulations. For a full survey of the litigation, see Abbe R. Gluck and Erica Turret, "The Affordable Care Act's Litigation Decade," *Georgetown Law Journal* 108, no. 6 (2020), https://ssrn.com/abstract=3671670.

3 See, e.g., Lori Windham, Counsel for Becket Fund, testimony at the House Judiciary Committee, Sept. 12, 2012, Serial No. 112–45, https://bit.ly/3KmBqDQ.

4 Organizations were eligible if they were a (1) nonprofit (2) whose purpose was to inculcate religion (3) that employed and (4) served people who share those religious beliefs. See Group Health Plans and Health Insurance Issuers Relating to Coverage of Preventive Services Under the Patient Protection and Affordable Care Act, 77 Fed. Reg., Number 31, 8725, 8728, Feb. 15, 2012 (codified at 45 CFR Part 147), https://bit.ly/3voQ7lz.

5 Marty Lederman, "*Hobby Lobby* Part III: There Is No "Employer Mandate," *Balkinization*, Dec. 16, 2013, https://bit.ly/3rXbc49.

6 26 U.S. Code § 4980H(c) (1). See, e.g., Kaiser Family Foundation and Health Research and Educational Trust, "Employer Health Benefits: (2013 Summary of Findings)," https://bit.ly/3tJWyxy.

7 $100 per day for each "individual to whom such failure relates." 26 U.S. Code § 4980D(b) (1).

8 Aaron Blake, "Huckabee: Dems Think Women Can't Control Their Libido," *Washington Post*, Jan. 23, 2014, https://wapo.st/3lhxx9g.

9 My favorite example also happens to be my favorite bible story: the story of the woman taken in adultery in the Book of John. The priests catch the couple mid-coitus, but only the woman stands before the stone-bearing zealots—the man is nowhere to be found. Interestingly, this story is not original to the bible and appears in none of the older manuscripts. Nor does the style or vocabulary match the surrounding text. It was clearly added much later by scribes.

10 Ian Haney López, a Univ. of California, Berkeley, law professor, wrote specifically about this, in "Today's Dominant Racial Dog Whistle? Obamacare," *HuffPost*, Mar. 3, 2014, https://www.huffpost.com/entry/obamacare-dog-whistle-politics_b_4759499, citing Michael Tesler, "The Spillover of Racialization into Health Care: How President Obama Polarized Public Opinion by Racial Attitudes and Race," *American Journal of Political Science* 56 (2012), 690–704, and Eric D. Knowles, Brian Lowery, and Rebecca L. Schaumberg, "Racial Prejudice Predicts Opposition to Obama and His Health Care Reform Plan," *Journal of Experimental Social Psychology* 46 (2010), 420–23.

11 Republicans who controlled the committee blocked Fluke from testifying, preferring to keep the panel mostly men and mostly clergy. Fluke testified instead to a Democratic steering committee.

12 Molly Moorhead, "In Context: Sandra Fluke on Contraceptives and Women's Health," *PolitiFact*, Mar. 7, 2012, https://bit.ly/38AwIoQ.

13 Guttmacher Institute, "Many American Women Use Birth Control Pills for Noncontraceptive Reasons," Nov. 15, 2011, https://bit.ly/3vV3sCy.

14 Archived transcript for Limbaugh show of Feb. 29, 2012, https://bit.ly/RushLimSlut.

15 Jeremy Holden, "Limbaugh's Misogynistic Attack on Georgetown Law Student Continues with Increased Vitriol," *Media Matters for America*, Mar. 1, 2012, https://bit.ly/RushLimSlut2.

16 Sarah B. Boxer, "Romney: Limbaugh Remarks 'not Language I Would Have Used,'" CBS News, Mar. 3, 2012, https://cbsn.ws/3mivEcx.

17 Maureen Dowd, "Have You No Shame, Rush?," *New York Times*, Mar. 4, 2012, https://nyti.ms/3xxrhiU.

18 Mimi Swartz, "Mothers, Sisters, Daughters, Wives," *Texas Monthly*, Aug. 2012, https://www.texasmonthly.com/news-politics/mothers-sisters-daughters-wives/.

19 Valenti, "The Hobby Lobby Ruling Proves Men of the Law Still Can't Get over 'Immoral' Women Having Sex."

20 Dahlia Lithwick, "For Men, This Supreme Court Term Was Uncontroversial. For Women, It Was a Disaster," *Slate*, July 9, 2014, https://bit.ly/37Jz04X.

21 David Green, "Christian Companies Can't Bow to Sinful Mandate," *USA Today*, Sept. 12, 2012, https://bit.ly/2Zv9Cf3.

22 His father and his five siblings are preachers or preachers' wives. Brian Solomon, "Meet David Green: Hobby Lobby's Biblical Billionaire," *Forbes*, Sept. 18, 2012, https://bit.ly/37MTbig. | 23 Ibid.

24 Andrew L. Seidel, "An Atheist Visits the Museum of the Bible," *Freethought Now*, Mar. 29, 2018, https://freethoughtnow.org/atheist-visits-bible-museum-of-the-bible/.

25 Andrew L. Seidel, "Hobby Lobby's 'In God We Trust' Ad Is Still Untrustworthy," *Freethought Now*, July 19, 2016, https://freethoughtnow.org/hobby-lobbys-igwt-ad-is-still-untrustworthy/. See also Freedom from Religion Foundation, "In Hobby Lobby We Don't Trust," https://ffrf.org/hlr/HobbyLobby.html.

26 Alison Frankel, "Duped Again on Biblical Artifacts, Hobby Lobby Sues Once-renowned Oxford Prof.," Reuters, June 3, 2021, https://reut.rs/3nWL0VW.

27 Grace Wyler, "Hobby Lobby Is Trying to Bring the Bible to America One Court Battle at a Time," *Vice*, July 3, 2014, https://bit.ly/3Kr2DFc.

28 Associated Press, "Obamacare Foe Met Privately with Okla. School Officials on Bible Class," CBS News, May 22, 2014, https://cbsn.ws/3lc8Uuz.

29 Michele Chabin, "Hobby Lobby's Steve Green's Bible Curriculum Is a Hit in Israeli Schools," Religion News Service, June 15, 2015, https://bit.ly/39bHjGQ; Adelle M. Banks, "Hobby Lobby President's Bible Curriculum Shelved by Oklahoma School District," Religion News Service, Nov. 26, 2014, https://bit.ly/3vR73QD/.

30 Complaint, p. 19, heading IV. 2012 WL 4009450 in *Hobby Lobby Stores, Inc. v. Sebelius*, 870 F. Supp. 2d 1278 (W.D. Okla. 2012), http://s3.amazonaws.com/becketpdf/Hobby-Lobby-Complaint-stamped.pdf.

31 These funds are notoriously opaque, so this holds for 2009. See Eli Clifton, "Hobby Lobby's Secret Agenda: How It's Quietly Funding a Vast Right-wing Movement," *Salon*, Mar. 27, 2014, https://bit.ly/3KpfM1D.

32 Becket Fund, "History," https://www.becketlaw.org/about-us/history/.

33 Sean Coughlan, "Saint or Sinner?," BBC News, Jan. 31, 2006, https://news.bbc.co.uk/2/hi/uk_news/4663032.stm.

34 *The Lives of Thomas Becket.*, Michael Staunton, ed. and translator (Manchester, UK: Manchester Univ. Press, 2001), 30, note 18.

35 Becket Fund, *Ahlquist V. City of Cranston, Rhode Island* (2011–present), Nov. 28, 2021, https://bit.ly/3EVxd8X.

36 Paul Gabrielsen, "Stanford Law School Opens Religious Liberty Clinic," Stanford News, July 13, 2013, https://news.stanford.edu/pr/2013/pr-religious-liberty-clinic-011613.html.

37 "When I was there the halls at the Becket Fund were lined with anti-Catholic cartoons from the 1880s and 1890s. . . . I was told that the philosophy is 'we protect everybody, because if we don't stop liberals, they'll be at our door next." Jay Michaelson, "The Secrets of Leonard Leo, the Man Behind Trump's Supreme Court Pick," *Daily Beast*, July 9, 2018, https://bit.ly/3vQFZAO.

38 Becket Fund, "2017 Canterbury Medalist," https://www.becketlaw.org/2017-canterbury-medalist/; Becket Fund, "Stalwart defender" quote in the promotional video, "Announcing the 2017 Canterbury Medalist," Mar. 14, 2017, https://youtu.be/3QpOaqTNns0.

39 See, e.g., Robert Barnes, "High Court with Vocally Devout Justices Set to Hear Religious Objections to Healthcare Law," *Washington Post*, Mar. 23, 2014, https://wapo.st/3xDRRa4.

40 Roberts and Thomas both worked for the Reagan administration, Roberts in the White House. Alito served in the Department of Justice Office of Legal Counsel from 1985 to 1987 under Reagan. Scalia served in the

same office under Nixon and Ford, and sought to serve as Solicitor General under Reagan. Kennedy was from California and had a cozy relationship with Reagan, but did not serve in any administration.

41 Michelle Boorstein, "Founder of Hobby Lobby's Law Firm Pioneered Debate over Religious Freedom," *Washington Post*, June 30, 2014, http://wapo.st/1qr5cvZ.

42 Complaint . . . in *Hobby Lobby Stores, Inc. v. Sebelius*, paragraph 57.

43 Physicians for Reproductive Health, the American College of Obstetricians and Gynecologists, the Assoc. of Reproductive Health Professionals, the American Society for Reproductive Medicine, the Society for Adolescent Health and Medicine, the American Medical Women's Assoc., the National Assoc. of Nurse Practitioners in Women's Health, the Assoc. of Forensic Nurses and others, to name but a few. Amicus Curiae Brief of Physicians for Reproductive Health, American College of Obstetricians and Gynecologists, et. al. in the Hobby Lobby consolidated case, *Conestoga Wood Specialties v. Sebelius*, 2013 WL 1792349, https://bit.ly/3I0HZvF

44 *Burwell v. Hobby Lobby Stores, Inc.*, 573 US 682, 691 (2014) (emphasis added).

45 *United States v. Seeger*, 380 US 163, 185 (1965).

46 Andrew L. Seidel, *Religion Dispatches*, "First Roe, then Contraception," May 20, 2021, https://bit.ly/FirstRoe.

47 *Conestoga Wood Specialties Corp. v. Sebelius*, 2014 WL 316722 (US), 23 (US,2014).

48 Daniel Okrent, "Prohibition Life: Politics, Loopholes and Bathtub Gin," NPR, *Fresh Air* interview with Terry Gross, May 10, 2010, https://www.npr.org/transcripts/126613316.

49 Sam Hananel, "Hobby Lobby 401(k) Invests in Birth Control Makers," Associated Press, Apr. 2, 2014, https://bit.ly/3w87KFt; Molly Redden, "Hobby Lobby's Hypocrisy: The Company's Retirement Plan Invests in Contraception Manufacturers," *Mother Jones*, Apr. 1, 2014, https://bit.ly/3MrDagq.

50 Using ImportGenius.com, U.S. Customs Records for Hobby Lobby Inc. Warehouse, which show, under the "suppliers" section, that 85 to 90 percent of the company's containers originate in China, with "China Taiwan" making up another sizable chunk. Performed in summer 2021, https://bit.ly/3J63ETw.

51 Matthew 19:21.

52 See *Zelman v. Simmons-Harris*, 536 US 639, 653 (2002). | 53 Ibid., 652.

54 Complaint . . . in *Hobby Lobby Stores, Inc. v. Sebelius*, paragraphs 2–3, 18–24, 38.

55 "The plaintiffs have failed, for example, to provide the district court with complete information about the financial strain they would bear if they did not provide health care insurance coverage to their employees. They allege that they would face a penalty of $26 million but do not allege or prove the offsetting expenses they would save. See Maj. Op. at 1141. These facts are relevant to substantial burden and other preliminary injunction factors." *Hobby Lobby Stores, Inc. v. Sebelius*, 723 F.3d 1114, 1181 at n.4 (10th Cir. 2013) (Matheson dissenting).

56 At oral argument, Hobby Lobby's attorney said, "We believe it's important to provide our employees with qualified health care." *Burwell v. Hobby Lobby Stores*, Oyez, www.oyez.org/cases/2013/13-354. Paul Clement arguing for Hobby Lobby at 26:55.

57 Ibid., 28:15. This seemed like a new argument to the justices, and the lawyer fumbled and failed to make his position clear, but it was clear from the beginning. The first filing in the case explained, "As part of their religious obligations, the Green family also provides excellent health insurance coverage to Hobby Lobby" employees.

58 The Greens forced stores to stay open and then fired thousands of employees, leaving them without health insurance in Apr. 2020. Dahlia Lithwick, "Of Course Hobby Lobby Thinks It's Above the Law," *Slate*, Apr. 3, 2020, https://slate.com/news-and-politics/2020/04/hobby-lobby-scotus-coronavirus.html; Liz Dye "Hobby Lobby Orders Stores to Stay Open, Citing HR Memo from Jesus Christ," *Above the Law*, Mar. 23, 2020, https://bit.ly/3MCcBVK; Bethany Biron, "In Leaked Letter, Hobby Lobby Prepares to Lay off Employees and Slash Salaries to Cut Costs in States with Mandated Store Closures Due to the Coronavirus," *Business Insider*, Mar. 26, 2020, https://bit.ly/3sjqxMX.

59 Complaint . . . in *Hobby Lobby Stores, Inc. v. Sebelius*, paragraph 2.

60 *Burwell v. Hobby Lobby Stores, Inc.*, 573 US at 724.

61 Had the Greens wanted to run the company as a religious outfit according to their religion, they could have organized the corporation without this separation. For instance, a sole proprietorship gives individuals the ability to get a trade name, such as "Hobby Lobby," but there is no separation between the person and the corporation; the finances and liabilities are mixed. It's not clear that a religious freedom claim would succeed in such an instance; such a claim has failed against Social Security taxes in the past, particularly when hiring employees who have their own rights, but at least such an organization wouldn't have the deliberate legal separation as here.

62 Five or less. Internal Revenue Service, "FAQ: Can you give me plain English definitions for the following: (1) a closely held corporation, (2) a personal holding company, and (3) a personal service corporation?," accessed Nov. 4, 2021, https://bit.ly/3MjzFIn.

63 *Burwell v. Hobby Lobby Stores, Inc.*, 573 US at 739 (Ginsburg dissenting). | 64 Ibid., 740.

65 *Newman v. Piggie Park Enterprises, Inc.*, 390 US 400 (1968).

66 *State by McClure v. Sports Health Club*, 370 N.W.2d 844, 848 (Minn. 1985).

67 *Elane Photography, LLC v. Willock*, 309 P.3d 53 (N.M. 2013).

68 Alito took what's perceived as a dig at RFRA, but can also be seen as a call to the Crusaders to bring these cases under the First Amendment next time: "The wisdom of Congress's judgment on this matter is not our concern. Our responsibility is to enforce RFRA as written." 134 S. Ct. at 2785.

69 *Burwell v. Hobby Lobby Stores, Inc.*, 573 US at 769 (Ginsburg dissenting) citing *United States v. Lee*, 455 US 252, 261 (1982).

70 See, e.g., Lauren Markoe, "Should Congress Repeal the Law Behind the Hobby Lobby Case?," *Washington Post*, July 3, 2014, https://wapo.st/3E1wlhM.

71 HR 1378 in the 117th Congress and HR 1450 in the 116th Congress.

72 Patrick Deneen, "Even If Hobby Lobby Wins, We Lose," *American Conservative*, Mar. 25, 2014, https://www.theamericanconservative.com/hobbylobby/.

73 Studies regularly show that two-thirds of American Catholic women use medical contraception of some kind. See, e.g., Glenn Kessler, "The Claim That 98 percent of Catholic Women Use Contraception: A Media Foul," *Washington Post*, Feb. 17, 2012, https://wapo.st/3li7hvs. Other similar measures show that "more than 99 percent of people in the United States who identify as religious have ever used contraceptive methods such as the birth control pill, IUDs and condoms; only 1 percent have solely used natural family planning," according to the Guttmacher Institute. Rachel K. Jones, "People of All Religions Use Birth Control and Have Abortions," *Ms.* Magazine, Oct. 21, 2020, https://bit.ly/3PYHOoG.

74 For the archived form, see "EBSA Form 700—Certification," Aug. 2014, https://bit.ly/309lKSK.

75 Almost 30 at one point. Lyle Denniston, "Analysis: The Little Sisters Case and EBSA Form 700," SCOTUSblog, Jan. 4, 2014, https://bit.ly/3th0Z3v.

76 *University of Notre Dame v. Sebelius*, 743 F3d 547, 557 (7th Cir 2014).

77 Emphasis in original. *Priests for Life v. Burwell*, No 14-1453, SCOTUSblog, brief of respondents, Department of Health and Human Services et al. in opposition, (Aug. 12, 2015) 2015 WL 4883185, 23, https://www.scotusblog.com/wp-content/uploads/2015/10/priests.archdiocese.bio_.pdf.

78 "President Trump Signs Religious Liberty Executive Order," C-SPAN.org, May 4, 2017, https://bit.ly/3xbExKb, 29:30.

79 Address by Justice Samuel Alito to the Federalist Society 2020 National Lawyers Convention, Nov. 12, 2020, https://youtu.be/tYLZL4GZVbA.

80 Amy Howe, "Opinion Analysis: Court Rejects Challenge to Exemptions from Birth-control Mandate, SCOTUSblog, July 8, 2020, https://bit.ly/3kk5gOM.

81 *Little Sisters of the Poor Saints Peter and Paul Home v. Pennsylvania*, 140 S. Ct. 2367 (2020); Adam Liptak, "Supreme Court Upholds Trump Administration Regulation Letting Employers Opt Out of Birth Control Coverage," *New York Times*, July 8, 2020, https://nyti.ms/3PZKYsh.

82 *Little Sisters of the Poor Saints Peter and Paul Home v. Pennsylvania*, 140 S. Ct. 2367, 2400.

83 See, e.g., Emily Bazelon, "Alito v. O'Connor: How the Nominee Tried to Restrict Roe," *Slate*, Oct. 31, 2005, https://slate.com/news-and-politics/2005/10/how-alito-tried-to-restrict-roe.html.

84 For updated numbers, see Guttmacher Institute, "Requirements for Ultrasound," https://www.guttmacher.org/state-policy/explore/requirements-ultrasound.

85 Eleanor Clift, "There's No Separation of Church and State on the Supreme Court," *Daily Beast*, updated May 13, 2022, https://bit.ly/39bIt5F; Sarah Posner, "Overturning *Roe* Is the Crowning Achievement of Christian Nationalism," *The Nation*, May 9, 2022, https://www.thenation.com/article/society/dobbs-christian-right; Jennifer Rubin, "Opinion: The Supreme Court's Religion-Driven Mission Sets Off a Firestorm, *Washington Post*, May 3, 2022, https://wapo.st/3xma1hM.

86 To see the delays, look at how many times the case was distributed for judicial conference and rescheduled before it was finally accepted. "Dobbs V. Jackson Women's Health Organization," SCOTUSblog, July 27, 2020, https://bit.ly/3PZLgiR.

87 Senate Bill 8, 87th Leg., Reg. Sess. (Tex. 2021).

88 This bait and switch based on the court's personnel appeared to bother Roberts, who asked Mississippi about it during oral argument: "*In your petition for cert, your first question and the only one on which we granted review was whether all pre-viability prohibitions on elective abortions are unconstitutional.* And then I think it is fair to say that when you got to the brief on the merits, you kind of shifted gears and talked a lot more about whether or not *Roe* and *Casey* should be overruled." Oral argument in *Dobbs v. Jackson Women's Health Organization*, Oyez, www.oyez.org/cases/2021/19-1392 at 34:50.

89 Peter Montgomery, "Pastor Robert Jeffress Hopes Trump's Supreme Court Picks Will 'Uphold Their Part of the Deal' and Overturn *Roe v. Wade*," Right Wing Watch, May 18, 2021, https://bit.ly/3hTOe8V.

90 Oral argument in *Dobbs v. Jackson Women's Health Organization* at 26:35.

91 *Conestoga Wood Specialties Corp. v. Sebelius*, 2014 WL 316722 (US), 23 (US,2014).

11: RELIGIOUS FREEDOM IS KILLING US

1 Gary Tuchman, "Despite Warnings, Churchgoers Explain Why They're Still Going to Services," CNN, Apr. 4, 2020., https://cnn.it/3riC2V0. | 2 Ibid.

3 The sermon is here: https://subsplash.com/srcarchives/media/mi/+w8zkyv4,Apr. 2, 2020. The CNN report, at 1:35, shows the same pastor, Pastor Lawrence Bishop II, who also identifies himself as such. A copy of the sermon is on file with the author should it be deleted. | 4 Emphasis in original.

5 "We are going to remain open . . . we are not going to give in to the chaos. We are not gonna fold to the fear." Pastor Greg Locke, "Our Response to Church Closures," Facebook, Mar. 17, 2020, https://fb.watch/9zfexrga2_/.

6 A note for Greg. People who wear work boots typically call them boots. Posers trying to be a man of the people might call them "work boots." Hemant Mehta, "MAGA Cultist Pastor Unleashes Tirade Against Mask Mandates at Dunkin' Donuts," *Friendly Atheist*, July 30, 2020, https://bit.ly/3ks9QKw.

7 Hemant Mehta, "MAGA Cultist Pastor: At My Church, We Refuse to Social Distance or Wear Masks," *Friendly Atheist*, July 5, 2020, https://bit.ly/3KpUqkS.

8 Andrew L. Seidel, "Events, People, and Networks Leading up to January 6," in *Christian Nationalism at the January 6, 2021, Insurrection*, 23–24, jointly published by the Baptist Joint Committee for Religious Liberty, the Freedom from Religion Foundation, and Christians Against Christian Nationalism, Feb. 9, 2022, https://bjconline.org/jan6report/. See also Rob Kuznia and Majlie de Puy Kamp, "The Pastors," in *Paths to Insurrection*, CNN, June 2021, https://cnn.it/3Nl9v9q.

9 Michael J. Mooney, "Trump's Apostle," *Texas Monthly*, July 8, 2021, https://bit.ly/3PZNWNn/; Adelle M. Banks, "The Key Evangelical Players on Trump's Advisory Board," *National Catholic Reporter*, Sept. 5, 2017, https://bit.ly/3td0W8E.

10 First Baptist Dallas, "Celebrate Freedom Sunday," Youtube.com, June 28, 2020, https://youtu.be/XYQlAunB_xl?t=4746, 1:19:30.

11 Rosalind Adams, Dan Vergano, and Ellie Hall, "A Dallas Megachurch Had a Coronavirus Cluster. Then It Hosted Mike Pence," BuzzFeed News, July 1, 2020, https://bit.ly/38yvnyP; Jamie Ehrlich, "Choir of More Than 100 People Perform Without Masks at Pence Event," CNN, June 29, 2020, https://cnn.it/3OCXHjU.

12 Adams, Vergano, and Hall, "A Dallas Megachurch."

13 Hemant Mehta, "Street Preacher: 'You Need Jesus More Than You Need Toilet Paper!,'" *Friendly Atheist*, Mar. 19, 2020, https://bit.ly/39iz7oh.

14 Sacramento County, "COVID-19 Update, April 1," *SacCounty News*, accessed Nov. 28, 2021, https://bit.ly/3HXHqTt; Hilda Flores, "One-third of COVID-19 Cases in Sac County Tied to Church Gatherings," KCRA 3, Apr. 1, 2020, https://bit.ly/3kkQyab. Churches in the area later defied health orders. Mike Luery, "Sacramento Church Holds Indoor Services Despite County's 'Widespread' COVID Tier," KCRA, Nov. 16, 2020, https://bit.ly/3vndsE7.

15 Anita Chabira, Sean Greene, and Rong-Gong Lin II, "Pentecostal Church in Sacramento Linked to Dozens of Coronavirus Cases," *Los Angeles Times*, Apr. 2, 2020, https://lat.ms/3lrA91u. (One of the church's pastors, Victor Miroshnichenko, was also convicted on ten counts of child sexual assault. Ibid.) See also "Defendant Convicted of 10 Counts of Child Sexual Assault," press release, Sacramento County District Attorney's Office, Feb. 16, 2018, https://bit.ly/3xfqfZ8; Rone Tempest, "For Gays, a Loud New Foe," *Los Angeles Times*, Oct. 13, 2006, https://lat.ms/3t14HgH.

16 Steve Almasy, "Almost 100 People in Ohio Were Infected with Coronavirus after Man Attended Church Service," CNN, Aug. 6, 2020, https://cnn.it/3fO0x4w.

17 Ohio Department of Health, "Aug. 4, 2020, COVID-19 SPREAD: Case Study," https://bit.ly/3roKfqy; Ohio Department of Health, "COVID-19 Update: Masks in Schools, Rapid Testing, Community Spread and Spread from Faith-Based Settings, Dr. Amy Acton," Aug. 4, 2020, https://bit.ly/37K14VT.

18 Mecklenburg County, NC, "COVID-19 Update on United House of Prayer for All People Convocation Events," Nov. 19, 2020, https://bit.ly/3rhyVfR; Alison Kuznitz, "More COVID-19 Deaths Linked to Super-Spreader Event at Charlotte Church," *Charlotte Observer*, Nov. 4, 2020, https://bit.ly/3knru2f. The updated numbers for Ms. Kuznitz's story can be found here: "COVID-19 Update on United House of Prayer for All People Convocation Events," Mecklenburg County, NC, Nov. 19, 2020, https://bit.ly/3rgc3NP. For "daddy," see, e.g., "We Are Holding On to Our Faith," United House of Prayer for All People, Jan. 4, 2020, https://bit.ly/317spNK; "The United House of Prayer for All People Celebrates Convocation and Centennial Anniversary," *Savannah Tribune*, Sept. 4, 2019, https://bit.ly/3t0amEG.

19 North Carolina Department of Health and Human Services, "COVID-19 Clusters in North Carolina, Updated Dec. 6, 2021," https://bit.ly/3DxUqNG . The Dec. 6, 2021, update was the last issued by the department.

20 Tracy Loew, "More COVID-19 Cases Linked to Peoples Church as Pastor Vows to Keep In-person Services," *Salem Statesman Journal*, May 13, 2021, https://bit.ly/3y1aPcE.

21 See, e.g., Andrew L. Seidel, "Senators Can and Must Ask About Nominees' Religious Beliefs," *Rewire News*, Feb. 7, 2019, https://bit.ly/3ziTvR3; Andrew L. Seidel, "Yes, Questions of Religion Can Be Fair Game for Senate Confirmation Hearings," *Freethought Now*, Sept. 20, 2017, https://freethoughtnow.org/questions-religion-fair-game/.

22 Michael S. Winters, "Raising Questions About Amy Barrett's Beliefs is Not an Anti-popery Riot," *National Catholic Reporter*, July 6, 2018, https://bit.ly/3LsSSb3; Massimo Faggioli, "Why Amy Coney Barrett's Religious Beliefs Aren't Off Limits," *Politico*, Sept. 24, 2020, https://politi.co/3aq5XEj.

23 As Senator Sheldon Whitehouse explained it during her hearing, "You're entitled to your own beliefs, you're entitled to your own faith, and it's nobody's business but your own unless you can't leave it in the robing room, and you're going to start making judicial decisions not on the law, but based on your personal views."

24 John H. Garvey and Amy Coney Barrett, "Catholic Judges in Capital Cases," *Marquette Law Review* 81 (2005), 303–50, https://lawdigitalcommons.bc.edu/cgi/viewcontent.cgi?article=1105&context=lsfp. Since becoming a judge, Barrett has ruled on abortion and capital cases.

25 Stephanie Kirchgaessner, "Revealed: Amy Coney Barrett Supported Group That Said Life Begins at Fertilization," *The Guardian*, Oct. 1, 2020, https://bit.ly/3F1quui.

26 "Letter to Synod Fathers from Catholic Women," Ethics and Public Policy Center, Oct. 1, 2015, https://eppc.org/synodletter/.

27 Amy Coney Barrett, "Associate Professor Amy Coney Barrett, Diploma Ceremony Address," 2006), Notre Dame Law School, Commencement Programs 13, https://scholarship.law.nd.edu/commencement_programs/13. Some have argued that this language was metaphorical, but it seems clear that it was not. "FFRF's Full Report on Amy Coney Barrett," Freedom from Religion Foundation, Sept. 30, 2020, https://bit.ly/3tJZGti.

28 People of Praise says it is literal. Andrew L. Seidel, Twitter post, Sept. 26, 2020, https://twitter.com/AndrewLSeidel/status/1309896974477545473.

29 "People of Praise: Former Member of Group Tied to SCOTUS Front-Runner Amy Barrett Calls It a 'Cult,'" *Democracy Now*, Sept. 23, 2020, https://www.democracynow.org/2020/9/23/coral_anika_theill_people_of_praise.

30 Lucien Bruggeman, "Supreme Court Favorite Judge Amy Coney Barrett Faces Renewed Attention for Religious Affiliation," ABC News, Sept. 24, 2020, https://abcn.ws/3ri6UoM; Michael Biesecker and Michelle R. Smith, "Barrett Tied to Faith Group Ex-members Say Subjugates Women," Associated Press, Sept. 28, 2020, https://bit.ly/3CZIHps.

31 Ibid. (both).

32 Jeffrey Toobin, *The Nine: Inside the Secret World of the Supreme Court* (New York: Knopf, 2008), 276.

33 The media actually crowdsourced it. "Here's Everyone at the White House Rose Garden SCOTUS Event Now Called a Likely 'Superspreader.' Help Us ID Them All," *USA Today*, Oct. 7, 2020, https://bit.ly/32zjZPX.

34 Ibid. There were representatives from the Alliance Defending Freedom, Becket Fund, and First Liberty, and Christian nationalists such as Pence, Paula White, Franklin Graham, Tony Perkins, Senator Josh Hawley, Ralph Reed of the Faith and Freedom Coalition, Trump's incompetent Christian nationalist attorney Jenna Ellis (who wrote a book for Christians to understand their Constitution and dedicated it to Jesus), Gary Bauer, the Scalia family, and Fox News personalities Laura Ingraham and Pete Hegseth; representatives from other conservative organizations attended as well, including the Heritage Foundation, American Conservative Union, Judicial Watch, Citizens United, and the Judicial Crisis Network.

35 T. Bedford, J. Logue, P. Han, C. Wolf, et al. (2020), "Viral Genome Sequencing Places White House COVID-19 Outbreak into Phylogenetic Context," medRxiv, Nov. 2020, https://www.medrxiv.org/content/10.1101/2020.10.31.20223925v1. See also Lena H. Sun, Yasmeen Abutaleb, and Josh Dawsey, "A Week into a White House Outbreak, CDC Still Playing Only a Limited Role," *Washington Post*, Oct. 8, 2020, https://wapo.st/3p-4JD6V; Amy Schoenfeld Walker and Michael Conlen. "Tracking Coronavirus Infections in the White House and Trump's Inner Circle," *New York Times*, Dec. 8, 2020, https://nyti.ms/3E1NWWS.

36 Jack Jenkins and Emily Macfarlan Miller, "Trump Evangelical Advisers Exposed to COVID-19 Flout CDC Guidelines, Preach in Public," Religion News Service, Oct. 7, 2020, https://bit.ly/38AWhpK.

37 "White House Hosted Covid 'Superspreader' Event, Says Dr Fauci," BBC News, Oct. 10, 2020, https://www.bbc.com/news/election-us-2020-54487154.

38 See, e.g., Aaron Blake, "The Reckless Timeline of Trump's Positive Coronavirus Test," *Washington Post*, Dec. 1, 2021, https://wapo.st/33Jebo0; Ashley Parker and Josh Dawsey, "Seven Days: Following Trump's Coronavirus Trail," *Washington Post*, Dec. 5, 2021, https://wapo.st/3vxuwar.

39 *Jacobson v. Massachusetts*, 197 US 11, 26 (1905).

40 *Prince v. Massachusetts*, 321 US 158, 16–67 (1944).

41 *Harvest Rock Church, Inc. v. Newsom*, No. EDCV206414JGBKKX, 2020 WL 7639584, at *11 (C.D. Cal. Dec. 21, 2020), *appeal dismissed*, No. 20-56357, 2021 WL 2555491 (9th Cir. May 19, 2021) *citing Terminiello v. Chicago*, 337 US 1, 37 (1949) (dissenting opinion).

42 *South Bay United Pentecostal Church v. Newsom*, 590 U. S. ___ (2020), and *Calvary Chapel Dayton Valley v. Sisolak*, 591 U. S. ___ (2020).

43 Using these two trackers: "Coronavirus in the US: Latest Map and Case Count," *New York Times*, https://www.nytimes.com/interactive/2021/us/covid-cases.html; "COVID Live Update," Worldometer—Real Time World Statistics, https://www.worldometers.info/coronavirus/.

44 *Roman Catholic Diocese of Brooklyn v. Cuomo*, No. 20A87, 2020 WL 6948354 (US Nov. 25, 2020); *Agudath Israel v. Cuomo*, No. 20A90, 2020 WL 6954120 (US Nov. 25, 2020). Cases and opinion consolidated under *Roman Catholic Diocese of Brooklyn v. Cuomo*, 141 S. Ct. 63 (2020).

45 Obviously, these can be dispensed with. However, in watching many of these services in the course of writing this book, I saw that the customs were still practiced and still directed from the pulpit: "Turn to your neighbor . . . ," etc.

46 Kate Conger, Jack Healy, and Lucy Tompkins, "Churches Were Eager to Reopen. Now They Are Confronting Coronavirus Cases," *New York Times*, July 10, 2020, https://nyti.ms/3iG8GJw.

47 This comparison holds even when it's not just attending worship, but also other religious events. New York City's first Covid cluster exploded because a 50-year-old man attended a bat mitzvah and a funeral at his synagogue. Opposition to Application for Writ of Injunction, *Roman Catholic Diocese of Brooklyn v. Cuomo*, No. 20A87, page 5, https://bit.ly/3hZAVna.

48 Executive Order 202.68, New York, Oct. 6, 2020, https://on.ny.gov/3NUdEkK.

49 New York Department of Health, Interim Guidance on COVID-19 Test-Out for Public and Non-Public Schools Located in Areas Designated as "Red or Orange Micro-Cluster Zones" under the New York State Micro-Cluster Action Initiative, Nov. 3, 2020, https://bit.ly/3wUbSsT.

50 *Roman Catholic Diocese of Brooklyn v. Cuomo*, 141 S. Ct. 63, 68 (2020).

51 "Press Briefing by Press Secretary Kayleigh McEnany," White House, May 22, 2020, https://bit.ly/38yxDpN.

52 Jill Colvin and Zeke Miller, "Trump Declares Churches 'Essential,' Calls on Them to Reopen," Associated Press, May 22, 2020, https://bit.ly/3MjDnSb.

53 Peter Baker, "Firing a Salvo in Culture Wars, Trump Pushes for Churches to Reopen," *New York Times*, May 23, 2020, https://nyti.ms/3I13e0f: "We hope that local officials across the country will heed the president's words and respect houses of worship, including our clients," said Mark Rienzi, the president of Becket, a religious liberty law firm representing the Minnesota churches. "Religion is an essential service for the well-being of society that cannot be subordinated to the economic interests of the states"; Marisa Schultz, "Trump Announces That Houses of Worship Are 'Essential,' Calls on Governors to Open Them Up," Fox News, May 22, 2020, https://fxn.ws/3FLBIll: "The discrimination that has been occurring against churches and houses of worship has been shocking," said Kelly Shackelford, president of First Liberty Institute, a legal organization dedicated to defending religious freedom. "We applaud the President's strong stance today demanding that these attacks must stop and that churches and houses of worship be freed to safely open. Americans are going to malls and restaurants. They need to be able to go to their houses of worship"; Tony Perkins, "Trump Insists It's Open Season for Churches," Family Research Council, May 26, 2020, https://www.frc.org/updatearticle/20200526/open-season.

54 *Roman Catholic Diocese of Brooklyn v. Cuomo*, 141 S. Ct. 63, 69 (2020).

55 Conger, Healy, and Tompkins, "Churches Were Eager to Reopen."

56 "The Sickness and The Cure" sermon, supra note 3, at 33:15.

57 *Roman Catholic Diocese of Brooklyn v. Cuomo*, 141 S. Ct., 68.

58 Both cases had been up and down the courts for some time. Justices Thomas, Alito, and Gorsuch would have struck down the public health measures entirely, while Justices Kagan, Breyer, and Sotomayor would have upheld them all. Justices Roberts, Kavanaugh, and Barrett split on the various measures. See, e.g., Stephen I. Vladeck, "The Most-Favored Right: COVID, the Supreme Court, and the (New) Free Exercise Clause," *New York Univ. Journal of Law and Liberty* 15 (2022), 25–26, forthcoming, https://papers.ssrn.com/sol3/papers.cfm?abstract_id=3987461.

59 "California Coronavirus Map and Case Count," *New York Times*, https://nyti.ms/3tI24S4.

60 Amy Howe, "Divided Court Blocks California's COVID-related Restrictions on In-home Religious Gatherings," SCOTUSblog, Apr. 10, 2021, https://bit.ly/3MAmcwn. The opinion was unsigned (per curiam), but we know that Roberts did not agree and that Kagan, Breyer, and Sotomayor dissented. *Tandon v. Newsom*, 141 S. Ct. 1294, 209 L. Ed. 2d 355 (2021). | 61 *Tandon v. Newsom*, 992 F. 3d 916 (9th Cir. 2021).

62 Christopher C. Lund, "A Matter of Constitutional Luck: The General Applicability Requirement in Free Exercise Jurisprudence," *Harvard Journal of Law and Public Policy* 26 (2003), 627, 664, https://digitalcommons.wayne.edu/lawfrp/213/; Caroline Mala Corbin, "Religious Liberty in a Pandemic," *Duke Law Journal Online* 72 (2020), https://scholarship.law.duke.edu/dlj_online/72/; Richard Schragger and Micah Schwartzman, "Religious Antiliberalism and the First Amendment," *Minnesota Law Review* 104 (2020), 1341, 1396, https://bit.ly/3MFAbRo; Alan Brownstein, "Protecting Religious Liberty: The False Messiahs of Free Speech Doctrine and Formal Neutrality," *Journal of Law and Politics* 18 (2002), 119, 199, https://bit.ly/3Hw8UQd.

63 Jim Oleske, "Tandon Steals Fulton's Thunder: The Most Important Free Exercise Decision Since 1990," SCOTUSblog, Apr. 15, 2021, https://bit.ly/3rYlKjy.

64 Stephen Vladeck, "The Supreme Court Is Making New Law in the Shadows," *New York Times*, Apr. 15, 2021, https://nyti.ms/3FSdrdl. After this manuscript was drafted, Prof. Vladeck pre-published a law review article on this subject. See Stephen I. Vladeck, "The Most-Favored Right: COVID, the Supreme Court, and the (New) Free Exercise Clause."

65 Steven I. Vladeck, "The Supreme Court's "Shadow Docket" Helped Trump 28 Times. Biden Is 0 for 1," *Washington Post*, Aug. 26, 2021, https://wapo.st/3EWk2Ek; Stephen I. Vladeck, "The Solicitor General and the Shadow Docket," *Harvard Law Review* 133 (2019), 123; Lawrence Hurley, Andrew Chung, and Jonathan Allen, "The 'Shadow Docket': How the US Supreme Court Quietly Dispatches Key Rulings," Reuters, Mar. 23, 2021, https://reut.rs/3ievtxl.

66 Hurley, Chung, and Allen, "The 'Shadow Docket.'"

67 Ibid.

68 As the omicron variant surged in January 2022, Justice Gorsuch would not wear a mask into the courtroom for oral argument, though every other justice did, and this forced Justice Sotomayor, who has diabetes and so is at higher risk for complications with Covid, to participate in the oral arguments telephonically. His recklessness and the reporting on it caused quite a stir. See, e.g., Nina Totenburg, "Gorsuch Didn't Mask Despite Sotomayor's Covid Worries, Leading Her to Telework," NPR, updated Jan. 21, 2022, https://n.pr/3BRD1yH; Kelly McBrie, "NPR Reporting on Supreme Court Mask Controversy Merits Clarification," NPR, Jan. 20, 2022, https://n.pr/350CApG.

12: *DEUS VULT* REVISITED

1 "New Highway Will Be Yank Memorial," *Washington Times*, May 25, 1919, in Joint Appendix for *American Legion v. American Humanist Association*, 2018 WL 6706093 (vol. II of IV), 428, https://bit.ly/35pwjns.

2 The top of the cross was regularly covered with a protective tarp. In May 2015, architects completed a "crack survey," catalogued massive cracks, rust, discoloration, deterioration, efflorescence, missing panels, biological growth, and exposed rebar. Davis Buckley Architects and Planners, "Crack Survey of the Memorial Peace Cross in Blandensburg, Maryland," May 7, 2015, in Joint Appendix for *American Legion v. American Humanist Association*, 2018 WL 6704186 (vol. IV of IV), 1342, https://bit.ly/AHAJointAppIV. The other three volumes

are vol. I, 2018 WL 6706093, 43 https://bit.ly/AHAJointAppI; vol. II, 2018 WL 6715176, https://bit.ly/AHAJointAppII; vol. III 2018 WL 6715177, https://bit.ly/AHAJointAppIII; and vol. IV 2018 WL 6704186, https://bit.ly/AHAJointAppIV.

3 The bushes were ripped out during the case in an effort to strengthen it for the government. *American Humanist Association v. Maryland-National Capital Park and Planning Commission (hereafter Am. Humanist Assoc. v. Maryland-Nat. Cap. Park)*, 874 F.3d 195, 201 (4th Cir. 2017), *rev'd and remanded sub nom. American Legion v. American Humanist Association* 139 S. Ct. 2067 (2019).

4 It seems rather like something from colonialism or the Doctrine of Discovery (which originated in the Catholic Church), when European nations would sail the world planting flags and crosses to claim lands for their monarch and, often, the Catholic Church, as if the native people did not exist.

5 Joint Appendix for *American Legion v. American Humanist Association*, 2018 WL 6706093 (vol. I). Capitalization altered here for legibility (original in all capitals).

6 *Am. Humanist Assoc. v. Maryland-Nat. Cap. Park*, 874 F.3d, 200.

7 The American Legion assumed control in 1922, three years before the cross's dedication. The town transferred the land to the American Legion at the same time: "The Town Commissioners of Bladensburg, Maryland do hereby assign and grant to the [local American Legion post], that parcel of ground upon which the cross now stands. . . ." *Am. Humanist Assoc. v. Maryland-Nat. Cap. Park*, 147 F. Supp. 3d 373, 377 (D. Md. 2015) (subsequent history omitted).

8 *Am. Humanist Assoc. v. Maryland-Nat. Cap. Park*, 874 F.3d, 200–201; United Daughters of the Confederacy, Joint Appendix for *American Legion v. American Humanist Association*, vol. I, 212.

9 While the claims about the transfer were disputed, it was clear that the American Legion tended, maintained, and claimed the cross and island. However, in 1956, a court ruled that the land belonged to Maryland. Even then, there was still some doubt because six years later, in 1961, the American Legion assigned any interest it may have had back to the state. So, for about four decades, ownership of the land was at best unclear, but it seems to have been in private hands.

10 Joint Appendix for *American Legion v. American Humanist Association*, vol. I, 191.

11 No records show the 1985 ceremony rededicating the cross to all veterans. Justice Ginsburg was careful with this in her dissent, writing that it "was rededicated in 1985 and is now *said to honor* "the sacrifices made [in] all wars" (at 2104), but is from Jeffrey Lyles, "Peace Cross Used to Celebrate Veterans, Town," *Gazette Community News*, July 5, 2001. "Peace Cross was built in memory of the World War I veterans, but now we believe it stands for the hope of peace and the sacrifices made from all wars," Bladensburg Councilwoman Marion Hoffman (Ward 1) said. "In this area, [the Cross] has always denoted Bladensburg and today it stands as the connection between the Ports Towns of Bladensburg, Colmar Manor and Cottage City." Joint Appendix for *American Legion v. American Humanist Association*, vol. III, 868.

12 That rededication ceremony included opening and closing prayers by Father Karl A. Chimiak of St. Matthias Catholic Church, about six miles away. The church would become mired in an abuse scandal in 1995 after victims came forward, and four priests admitted to sharing the victims around in the 1970s. Chimiak was not accused of anything. Debbi Wilgoren, "Priests Face New Charges of Abusing Boys in P.G.: More Men Claim They Were Molested by 3," *Washington Post*, Mar. 15, 1995, https://www.bishop-accountability.org/news/1995_03_15_Wilgoren_PriestsFace.htm.

13 "Humanists Challenge Cross War Memorial in Maryland," press release, American Humanist Assoc. Aug. 23, 2012, https://bit.ly/3d1kFQ0.

14 *Trunk v. City of San Diego*, 629 F.3d 1099 (9th Cir. 2011).

15 *American Atheists, Inc. v. Davenport*, 637 F.3d 1095 (10th Cir. 2010).

16 Lawrence Hurley, "Maryland 'Peace Cross' Can Stand on Public Land, US High Court Rules," Reuters, June 20, 2019, https://reut.rs/3reJmkz. Trump's Justice Department called it "a win for protecting religious freedom"; "Historic Victory at the Supreme Court," First Liberty Institute, June 21, 2019, https://bit.ly/3CUY8iF. First Liberty Institute also said: "This is a historic victory and a landmark decision for religious freedom . . . [It] is just the beginning of a new era for religious liberty in America." The Institute's CEO wrote the same thing in a Fox News op-ed: "A major victory for religious freedom" and "a landmark victory for religious freedom." Kelly Shackelford, "Supreme Court Peace Cross Decision Is a Major Victory for Religious Freedom," Fox News, June 20, 2019, https://fxn.ws/3D0mZS9.

17 Stella Morabito, "Thanks to Anti-Religion Lawsuit, This WWI Anniversary Could Be the Last for the Bladensburg Cross," *The Federalist*, Nov. 10, 2018, https://bit.ly/3rZmeWO.

18 *Am. Humanist Assoc. v. Maryland-Nat. Cap. Park*, 874 F.3d, 212.

19 Nina Totenberg, "Cross Clash Could Change Rules for Separation of Church and State," NPR.org, Feb. 25, 2019, https://n.pr/31aJDd2.

20 Brief for the Jewish War Veterans of the United States of America, Inc. as Amicus Curiae in Support of Respondents, *The American Legion v. American Humanist Association*, 2019 WL 410763 (US), 12–13 (US,2019).

21 An old slander, which attempts to wrap its exclusion of atheists in a deep, if erroneous, observation about human nature. The origin of the modern turn of phrase is not certain, but it appears to have begun in World War I with chaplains and a YMCA representative—both of whose livelihoods depended on the claim—saying that there were no atheists in trenches. "There Are No Atheists in Foxholes," Quote Investigator, Nov. 2, 2016, https://quoteinvestigator.com/2016/11/02/foxhole/. There's an old rejoinder I've heard many nonreligious

veterans and servicemembers retell in response, "Yeah, well, I've never seen a chaplain in a foxhole." Some prefer a variation of "If there were more atheists, there would be fewer foxholes."

22 These numbers are not reliable, and the military rarely publishes data about the religious makeup of its force. They lump the "nones" as "Other/Unclassified/Unknown." Kristy N. Kamarck, *Diversity, Inclusion, and Equal Opportunity in the Armed Services: Background and Issues for Congress* (Washington, D.C,: Congressional Research Service, 2019), https://fas.org/sgp/crs/natsec/R44321.pdf. The Military Association of Atheists and Free-Thinkers has been using FOIA to compile data for a decade. http://militaryatheists.org/demographics/.

23 Brief Amici Curiae for the Military Religious Freedom Foundation and Sixteen High-Ranking Military Officials and Veterans in Support of Respondents, *American Legion v. American Humanist Association*, 2019 WL 446514 (US), 4 (US,2019) (internal quotations omitted).

24 See the archive of the Free Market Foundation website, https://web.archive.org/web/20010204120300/http://www.freemarket.org:80/. Settling on "First Liberty" is something of a mistake; the group wrongly claims that "religious liberty is the first phrase of the first amendment to our US Constitution." Andrew L. Seidel, "Undeniably Awful: Lobbyists for Christian Privilege Issue Fallacious 'Report,'" *Freethought Now*, Mar. 1, 2016, https://bit.ly/3OO1oUe.

25 Form 990 (2001), https://bit.ly/3voWxAR. In 1997, Texas Freedom Network pegged its income at $314,004, Texas Freedom Network, Religious Right Watch: Far-Right Organizations in Texas, https://tfn.org/religious-right-watch-far-right-organizations-in-texas/#LI.

26 It helps to look at older versions of these various groups' websites, before they started inventing their own creation myths. E.g., see "History," Liberty Institute, Sep. 9, 2011, https://bit.ly/3xXpvJR.

27 Form 990 (2017), https://bit.ly/3pUsRss.

28 See, for example, Kelly Shackelford, "Religious Liberty on Trial," streamed live, July 4, 2021, https://youtu.be/1N3zJZ7vtdM.

29 "About Liberty Institute," accessed 2010, https://bit.ly/3MxnKHo.

30 "About Liberty Institute," accessed 2015 (emphasis in original), https://bit.ly/3zjCFl2.

31 On evolution: "'God Unleashed His People,'" Texas Freedom Network, Oct. 8, 2009, https://tfn.org/god-unleashed-his-people/. On Bible classes: Seema Mehta, "Bible Finds a Place in Schools," *Los Angeles Times*, Aug. 5, 2007, https://lat.ms/3rhLqrN. On Jesus portrait: Associated Press, "Ohio School: Jesus Portrait Has Been Taken Down," *USA Today*, Apr. 3, 2013, https://bit.ly/3Fc7hpT. On prayer: see the case involving a football coach in Bremerton, WA, in which the coach wants to use his power and position to pray on the field with students and model prayer for students; discussed infra. See also Claudia Kolker, "Girl Gets Special 'Blessing' for Football Game Prayer: Religion: Federal Judge Intervenes for Texas Senior. Louisiana, Arkansas Had Also Been Affected by a Court Ban," *Los Angeles Times*, Sept. 4, 1999, https://lat.ms/3E4r9cV.

32 See, e.g., Patrick Elliott, "Nothing to Cheer about in the Texas Cheerleader Case," *Freethought Now*, Oct. 6, 2017, https://freethoughtnow.org/3559-2/.

33 *Kennedy v. Bremerton School District*, 4 F.4th 910, 912 (9th Cir. 2021) (Smith concurring).

34 Petition for a writ of certiorari in *Kennedy v. Bremerton School District*, No. 21-418 (Sept. 14, 2021). "The questions presented are: 1. Whether a public-school employee who says a brief, quiet prayer by himself while at school . . ."

35 See Suggestion of Mootness of Bremerton School District, filed (Feb. 18, 2022), https://www.scotusblog.com/case-files/cases/kennedy-v-bremerton-school-district-2/.

36 "It is the duty of counsel to bring to the federal tribunal's attention, 'without delay,' facts that may raise a question of mootness," *Arizonans for Official English v. Arizona*, 520 U.S. 43 (1997).

37 Of course, government attorneys don't necessarily agree with every argument they make. But it ought not to have been a surprise. *Salazar v. Buono*, Oyez, www.oyez.org/cases/2009/08-472.

38 *American Legion v. American Humanist Association*, 139 S. Ct., 2091 (Breyer concurring) (internal quotations omitted).

39 Brief of Amicus Curiae Forge Youth Mentoring in Support of Petitioners, in *Espinoza v. Montana Department of Revenue*, 2019 WL 4640665 (US) (US,2019). Four Institute lawyers are listed on the brief, including Shackleford.

40 Oral argument. *The American Legion v. American Humanist Association*. Oyez, May 4, 2021, 18:48, www.oyez.org/cases/2018/17-1717.

41 Nina Totenberg, "Cross Clash Could Change Rules for Separation of Church and State," NPR.org, https://n.pr/31aJDd2.

42 "First Liberty in the National Spotlight: Will the Bladensburg Memorial Case Transform American History?," First Liberty, Feb. 26, 2019, https://firstliberty.org/news/will-the-bladensburg-memorial-case-transform-american-history/.

43 Brief of Baptist Joint Committee for Religious Liberty et al., *American Legion v. American Humanist Association*, 2019 WL 495118, https://bit.ly/3E3Hwq3.

44 *Elk Grove Unified School District v. Newdow*, 542 US 1 (2004); "'In God We Trust' has nothing whatsoever to do with the establishment of religion. Its use is of a patriotic or ceremonial character and bears no true resemblance to a governmental sponsorship of a religious exercise." See also *Aronow v. United States*, 432 F.2d 242, 243 (9th Cir. 1970).

45 *Lynch v. Donnelly*, 465 US 668 (1984).

46 139 S. Ct. at 2084–85. | 47 Ibid.

48 It's not dead, partly because of how terribly fractured the court's opinions were in this case. They couldn't agree on a replacement. Even Thomas and Gorsuch, who clearly loathe the test and want it gone, wrote shortly after

this decision, "This Court has not overruled *Lemon v. Kurtzman.*" *Georgia v. Public Resource.Org, Inc.*, 140 S. Ct. 1498, 1521 n.6 (2020).

13: TARGETING CHILDREN, TAXING EVERYONE

1 "From Benjamin Franklin to Richard Price, 9 Oct. 1780," Founders Online, National Archives, https://founders.archives.gov/documents/Franklin/01-33-02-0330.

2 "Christian Number Cruncher: Profile George Barna," Religion News Service, Jan. 1, 1997, https://bit.ly/3OCZQfs.

3 George Barna, *Transforming Children into Spiritual Champions* (Grand Rapids, MI: Baker Books, 2003), 35.

4 Katherine Stewart, *The Good News Club: The Christian Right's Stealth Assault on America's Children* (New York: PublicAffairs, 2012), 130. | 5 Ibid., 127.

6 Child Ministries, Trinity Lutheran Church, Columbia MO, archived website., https://bit.ly/3LvXIo2.

7 Trinity Lutheran Child Learning Center, archived website, https://web.archive.org/web/20130702202411/ https://tlclckids.com/. This is the website as it appeared in 2013, the first available on Archive.org and the year that the district court decided the case,

8 Author conversation with Geoffrey Blackwell, May 19, 2022.

9 Trinity Lutheran Child Learning Center, archived website. | 10 Ibid.

11 "US Supreme Court Sets Oral Argument Date for Highly Important Religious Freedom Case," Alliance Defending Freedom, press release, Feb. 17, 2017, https://bit.ly/3OIkCdM.

12 Mission, Trinity Lutheran Church Columbia, MO, archived website, https://bit.ly/3kkHFxc.

13 Missouri Dept. of Natural Resources, "Scrap Tire and Illegal Dumping Unit—General Information," archived version, https://bit.ly/3koxwzv. Tires are particularly attractive breeding grounds for mosquitos and in populated areas can be the preferred breeding grounds for mosquitos that carry disease. G. Ferede, M. Tiruneh, E. Abate, et al, "Distribution and Larval Breeding Habitats of *Aedes* Mosquito Species in Residential Areas of Northwest Ethiopia," *Epidemiological Health*, Apr. 23, 2018, doi:10.4178/epih.e2018015.

14 Missouri Dept. of Natural Resources, "Scrap Tire Uses at the Missouri State Fair," archived https://bit.ly/39iBrvv.

15 Missouri Dept. of Natural Resources, Waste Management Program, Playground Scrap Tire Surface Material Grant Application Form (Jan. 30, 2003), https://dnr.mo.gov/forms/780-2143-f.pdf.

16 Trinity Lutheran grant application, https://bit.ly/TrinLuthGrantAppWRF.

17 "82. A Bill for Establishing Religious Freedom, 18 June 1779," Founders Online, National Archives, https://founders.archives.gov/documents/Jefferson/01-02-02-0132-0004-0082.

18 "Memorial and Remonstrance against Religious Assessments, [ca. 20 June] 1785," paragraph 1, Founders Online, National Archives, https://founders.archives.gov/documents/Madison/01-08-02-0163.

19 Missouri Constitution, Article I, sections 5, 6, and 7.

20 See Missouri Department of Natural Resources Playground Scrap Tire Surface Material Grant Application, Form 780-2143, original version, https://bit.ly/3KrpsIT. For instructions, see "Playground Scrap Tire Surface Material Grant Application Instructions for Form 780-2143," Nov. 2012, https://bit.ly/3rZDMC8.

21 Letter of Ownership and Approval, attachment A to application, p. 6, https://bit.ly/3kEEp0K.

22 *Trinity Lutheran Church of Columbia, Inc. v. Pauley*, 976 F. Supp. 2d 1137, 1150 (W.D. Mo. 2013), aff'd, 788 F.3d 779 (8th Cir. 2015), *rev'd and remanded sub nom. Trinity Lutheran Church of Columbia, Inc. v. Comer*, 137 S. Ct. 2012, 198 L. Ed. 2d 551 (2017).

23 The Alliance Defense Fund filed the lawsuit, *Trinity Lutheran Church of Columbia, Inc. v. Sara Parker Pauley*, https://bit.ly/3NlpS67; they made a website, too: "Trinity Lutheran Wins! Supreme Court Rules Missouri Engaged in Religious Discrimination," https://www.adflegal.org/the-playground-case. They made a website, too ThePlaygroundCase.com.

24 Nina Totenberg, "Playground Case Could Breach Barrier Between Tax Coffers, Religious Schools," Apr. 19, 2017, NPR, https://n.pr/3rYrVnR; Mark Sherman and Sam Hananel, "Supreme Court Rules in Favor of Missouri Church in Playground Case," PBS, June 26, 2017, https://to.pbs.org/3MlpKC4; Lauren Markoe, "Supreme Court Rules for Missouri Church in 'Playground' Case," Religion News Service, June 26, 2017, https://bit.ly/3thM9JW. *USA Today* reported on the "playground dispute": Richard Wolf, "Supreme Court Justices Side with Church in Playground Dispute," *USA Today*, Apr. 19, 2017, https://bit.ly/37K3Z0N.

25 Oral argument was Wednesday Apr. 19, 2017, Easter on Apr. 16.

26 "DC: Religious Freedom Rallies Take Place Outside Supreme Court as Court Case Involving Trinity Lutheran Church [*sic*]," Getty Images, https://bit.ly/3MHpwWF.

27 Michael Gryboski, "States Can't Discriminate Against Churches in Secular Aid Programs, Supreme Court Rules," *Christian Post*, June 26, 2017, https://bit.ly/3LnA10W; see also MRCTV, "Children Rally for Religious Freedom in SCOTUS Playground Case," YouTube, Apr. 19, 2017. https://youtu.be/Bp3j-GN2Pvk.

28 Concerned Women for America website, "About Us," "What We Do," https://concernedwomen.org/about/ who-we-are/, archived https://bit.ly/3EYCUTJ; Jeff Malet Photography, "Supreme Court Hears Trinity Lutheran Church V. Comer/ State Aid to Church Programs (Apr. 19, 2017)," YouTube, Apr. 20, 2017, https:// youtu.be/Ltp_f-XC7H8.

29 Greta Moran, "The Dark Money-Funded Women's Group Rallying Behind Amy Coney Barrett," The Intercept, Oct. 24, 2020, https://bit.ly/3MIXUFN.

30 Faith and Freedom Coalition, "Ralph Reed to Appear at Washington, DC, Rally Tomorrow in Support of Religious Freedom," press release, Apr. 18, 2017, https://bit.ly/3lfguEO; Peter Montgomery, "Religious Right

Rallying for Supreme Court to Weaken Church-State Separation with Gorsuch's Help," Right Wing Watch, Apr. 18, 2017, https://bit.ly/3vRfn2H.

31 Katie Rogers, "Trent Franks, Accused of Offering $5 Million to Aide for Surrogacy, Resigns," *New York Times*, Dec. 8, 2017, http://nyti.ms/3jNQkXP.
32 Photo accompanying Tara I. Burton, "What a SCOTUS Decision over a Church Playground Means for Religious Freedom in America," Vox, June 26, 2017, https://bit.ly/3OJO57e.
33 He concluded, "God bless you all," https://www.facebook.com/watch/?v=10155199351954747; see also https://bit.ly/3NSxSLs.
34 Benjamin Peters, "Attorney General's Office Recuses Self from Trinity Lutheran Case, Citing Greitens' Executive Order," *Missouri Times*, Apr. 18, 2017, https://bit.ly/37K4p7n. In Apr. 2016, Hawley submitted an amicus brief to the U.S. Supreme Court. Brief for the General Council of the Assemblies of God as Amicus Curiae in Support of Petitioner, *Trinity Lutheran Church of Columbia, Inc. v. Pauley*, 2016 WL 1639717 (US) (US,2016), https://bit.ly/3ktn61v. Hawley filed the brief with his wife, Erin Morrow Hawley, a former clerk for Chief Justice Roberts, law professor, and author of a book that supposedly "offers young mothers a chance to grow in their identity as children of God simply by observing their own little ones," entitled *Living Beloved: Lessons from My Little Ones About the Heart of God* (Colorado Springs, CO: Focus on the Family, 2018).
35 Michael Kranish, "Grievance, Rebellion and Burnt Bridges: Tracing Josh Hawley's Path to the Insurrection," *Washington Post*, May 11, 2021, https://wapo.st/3avwbVO.
36 Katherine Stewart, "The Roots of Josh Hawley's Rage," *New York Times*, Jan. 11, 2021, https://nyti.ms/3zfNFA9.
37 137 S. Ct. at 2019 n.1.
38 "The parties agree that the Establishment Clause of that Amendment does not prevent Missouri from including Trinity Lutheran in the Scrap Tire Program." 137 S. Ct. at 2019.
39 137 S. Ct. at 2029. "The Church seeks state funds to improve the Learning Center's facilities, which, by the Church's own avowed description, are used to assist the spiritual growth of the children of its members and to spread the Church's faith to the children of nonmembers. The Church's playground surface—like a Sunday School room's walls or the sanctuary's pews—are integrated with and integral to its religious mission. The conclusion that the funding the Church seeks would impermissibly advance religion is inescapable."
40 *Locke v. Davey*, 540 US 712, 720 (2004).
41 *Everson v. Board of Education of Ewing*, 330 US 1, 16 (1947) (emphasis added).
42 *Trinity Lutheran Church of Columbia, Inc. v. Comer*, 137 S. Ct. 2012, 2022 (2017) quoting *Lyng v. Northwest Indian Cemetery Protective Association*, 485 US 439, 450 (1988).
43 With one of the Freedom from Religion Foundation's very talented attorneys, Ryan Jayne, and our dogged local counsel, Paul Groswald. After the FFRF's legal team spent years investigating and trying to resolve the case without a lawsuit, FFRF and local taxpayer David Steketee sued, with myself and Jayne and Paul Groswald. Jayne and Groswald primarily litigated the case. Constitutional scholar and UC Berkeley law professor Erwin Chemerinsky joined the team when the county and churches tried to take it to the U.S. Supreme Court.
44 Andrew L. Seidel, "How Important Is FFRF's Morris County Victory?," *Freethought Now*, Apr. 20, 2018, https://freethoughtnow.org/morris-county-victory-impact/.
45 *Freedom from Religion Foundation v. Morris County Board of Chosen Freeholders*, 232 N.J. 543, 573, 181 A.3d 992, 1009 (2018). The county and churches later stipulated that the churches taking taxpayer money all "have active congregations that regularly worship, or participate in other religious activities," and all hold "regular worship services in one or more of the structures that they have used, or will use" taxpayer-funded grants to repair.
46 Yale Law School, Lillian Goldman Law Library, Constitution of New Jersey, 1776, https://avalon.law.yale.edu/18th_century/nj15.asp.
47 Plaintiffs' Reply Memorandum, NJ Sup Ct, https://ffrf.org/images/04FFRFMorrisCountyreplybrief.pdf. Again, Jayne, one of the finest attorneys I know, and Groswald did the bulk of the work. I wrote the introduction and closing of the brief quoted here.
48 Plaintiffs' Reply Memorandum, NJ Sup Ct, https://ffrf.org/images/04FFRFMorrisCountyreplybrief.pdf.
49 It held "that the plain language of the Religious Aid Clause bars the use of taxpayer funds to repair and restore churches, and that Morris County's program ran afoul of that longstanding provision." *Freedom from Religion Foundation v. Morris County Board of Chosen Freeholders*, 232 N.J. 543, 548, 181 A.3d 992, 994 (2018).
50 Seidel, "How Important Is FFRF's Morris County Victory?"
51 Morris County asked for an extension on July 27, 2018. Alito granted it on July 31, 2018. Morris County filed its cert petition on Sept. 18, 2018. Kavanaugh took his oath on Oct. 6, 2018.
52 About Us, Board, Becket Fund website, archived at https://bit.ly/3vqqwsr.
53 *Morris County Board of Chosen Freeholders v. Freedom from Religion Foundation*, 139 S. Ct. 909 (2019).
54 *June Medical Services, L.L.C. v. Gee*, 139 S. Ct. 663 (2019). Kavanaugh also wrote the dissent when the court temporarily halted the enforcement of a state rule that targeted reproductive rights in his short time on the bench. In other words, Kavanaugh would have effectively let an abortion ban go into effect (which he was able to do when Amy Coney Barrett was added to the bench two years later).
55 *Kennedy v. Bremerton School District*, 139 S. Ct. 634 (2019). For more on why this is wrong, see Andrew L. Seidel, "Legal Ministry to File Suit against School District So Coach Can Illegally Pray with Students," *Freethought Now*, Oct. 27, 2015, https://bit.ly/38AaGCj.

56 The first opinion he authored was *Henry Schein, Inc. v. Archer and White Sales, Inc.*, 139 S. Ct. 524, (Jan. 8, 2019). He then joined four other substantive decisions: 139 S. Ct. 544, 682, 738, 893 (2019). He joined another statement on a denial of cert and a dissent from a ruling staying the enforcement of a law.

57 See "Sept. 19, 2018—New Jersey Historic Trust Announces Preserve New Jersey Preservation Grant Award Recommendations," press release, Sept. 19, 2018, https://nj.gov/dca/news/news/2018/approved/20180919a. html.

14: NO, REALLY, RELIGIOUS FREEDOM IS TAXING US

1 Kyle Olson, "Jesus Isn't in Michigan," Town Hall, Mar. 18, 2011, https://bit.ly/2ZNBYRv.

2 *Espinoza v. Montana Department of Revenue*, 140 S. Ct. 2246 (2020).

3 Oral argument was on Jan. 22, 2020, *Espinoza v. Montana Department of Revenue*, Oyez, www.oyez.org/cases/2019/18-1195.

4 To take one example at random, 97% of Ohio voucher money went to religious schools for the 2015–16 school year. Patrick O'Donnell, "Almost All of Ohio's Voucher Cash Goes to Religious Schools," Cleveland.com., Mar. 12, 2017, https://bit.ly/3NnJvKJ. $143 million went to Christian schools, and just over $3 million to schools with other religious affiliations (Jewish and Muslim). For the 2017–18 school year, 100% of the schools registered in the Wisconsin Parental Choice Program were religious: 163 of 163 schools were religious, 160 were Christian. Wisconsin Department of Public Instruction, "163 Private Schools Register for Wisconsin Parental Choice Program," press release, Jan. 31, 2017, https://bit.ly/3xtZQ9x.

5 MT SB 410 (2015), https://legiscan.com/MT/text/SB410/id/1209179.

6 MT SB 81 (2013), https://legiscan.com/MT/bill/SB81/2013; for Bullock's statement, see Mike Dennison, "School Choice Bills Still Alive at Legislature," *Billings Gazette*, Oct. 13, 2015, https://bit.ly/3a0ZVXU. It's unclear why Bullock didn't veto the bill again in 2015. He didn't sign the bill either, but it then became law. Associated Press, "School's Choice Bill Becomes Law without Governor's Signature," May 11, 2015, https://bit.ly/3scJzBw. | 7 MT SB 410 Sect 8(7).

7 Only one scholarship organization, Big Sky Scholarships, formed under the neo-voucher program. It supported 13 schools, 12 of which were religious. Big Sky Scholarships, archived website, https://perma.cc/L8RB-AD69. Cottonwood Day School was the only nonsectarian private school.

9 The Big Sky website and personnel made this clear. Ann Morren, a Montana House candidate who lost her Republican primary, runs the organization; for her affidavit, see Affidavit of Ann Morren in Support of Plaintiffs' Motion for Stay of Judgment, paragraph 4, https://bit.ly/3pQwQ9p. For the electoral loss, see Ballotpedia, https://ballotpedia.org/Ann_Morren.

10 MT SB 410 (2015), section 7.

11 *Espinoza v. Montana Department of Revenue*, 2018 MT 306, ¶ 10, 393 Mont. 446, 457 (2018). More specifically, the Department of Revenue defined eligible schools to be secular schools: (1) A "qualified education provider" has the meaning given in Mont. Code Ann. § 15-30-3102, and pursuant to Mont. Code Ann. § 15-30-3101, may not be: (a) a church, school, academy, seminary, college, university, literary or scientific institution, or any other sectarian institution owned or controlled in whole or in part by any church, religious sect, or denomination; or (b) an individual who is employed by a church, school, academy, seminary, college, university, literary or scientific institution, or any other sectarian institution owned or controlled in whole or in part by any church, religious sect, or denomination when providing those services. (2) For the purposes of (1), "controlled in whole or in part by a church, religious sect, or denomination" includes accreditation by a faith-based organization.

12 Kendra Espinoza signed two affidavits telling her story, in 2018 and in 2016. Both appear in the Joint Appendix to the Cert Petition, 150 and 156, https://bit.ly/3tLrFso.

13 The parents testified that the children—seven, eight, nine, ten, and twelve years old at the time—were also all Christian.

14 Formerly Sunnybrook Christian School and formerly Covenant Community School.

15 Kendra Espinoza 2018 affidavit paragraph 12, https://bit.ly/3Mz5hdC.

16 *Kendra Espinoza v. Montana Department of Revenue*, Complaint, paragraph 78, Dec. 15, 2015 at https://bit.ly/3EVcvpK .

17 Jeri Ellen Anderson affidavit, paragraph 8, https://bit.ly/37SkvM7.

18 "Biblical Worldview," Stillwater Christian School, accessed Nov. 26, 2021, https://www.stillwaterchristian-school.org/academics/biblical-worldview/.

19 The Statement of Faith appears in the Pastor's Reference letter, https://bit.ly/3NUiAGi. See also "Who We Are," Stillwater Christian School, accessed Nov. 26, 2021, https://www.stillwaterchristianschool.org/about-us/who-we-are/.

20 "Partnering with Parents," Stillwater Christian School, YouTube, Oct. 23, 2019, https://youtu.be/2SlLJn5Turg.

21 He had resigned when authorities began investigating. Andy Viano, "Kalispell Man Charged with Sexually Assaulting Teen," Feb. 24, 2021, *Flathead Beacon*, https://bit.ly/3MfkgsE; Scott Shindledecker, "Former School Employee Accused of Rape," Daily Inter Lake, Feb. 25, 2021, https://bit.ly/3O0uKxr.

22 Felicity Barringer, "In Montana Town's Hands, Guns Mean Cultural Security," *New York Times*, Feb. 20, 2013, https://nyti.ms/3NqQDpC.

23 David Bitton, "A Christian Focused Education," *Stillwater News Press*, Aug. 8, 2016, https://bit.ly/3kokEtk.

24 "Private School Enrollment Falls with Economy," *Flathead Beacon*, Dec. 9, 2010, https://bit.ly/3mfHAfl. "At Stillwater Christian School, enrollment dropped by 47 elementary students from last year to this year's total of 151. The school saw its numbers peak in 2005, when it reached 216 students."

25 The archived website for the scholarships, https://perma.cc/L8RB-AD69, lists Fortis Leadership Academy as a school and Google now lists it as permanently closed. It too had been struggling financially. See Matt Hoffman, "West End Private School Becoming Nonprofit Amid Financial Struggles," *Billings Gazette*, Dec. 9, 2016, https://bit.ly/37lszo1.

26 Espinoza's second affidavit was signed at the end of 2018, and she said her children were thirteen and ten. The husband left the family in 2011, when her kids were around six and three, respectively.

27 Espinoza 2018 affidavit paragraphs 2–4. Complaint paragraph 63, https://bit.ly/3MGAA6Z.

28 See, e.g., Katherine Stewart, *The Good News Club*, chapter 10.

29–32 Niche.com 3-star reviews—by freshman, Jan. 29, 2017; by student, June 24, 2014; by parent, Nov. 27, 2018; by alum, Mar. 9, 2020: see all at https://bit.ly/3aJ5zkv.

33 Montana Constitution, Article X, Section 1.

34 Montana Constitutional Convention, Verbatim Transcript, Mar. 11, 1972, 2008–11, https://courts.mt.gov/portals/189/library/mt_cons_convention/vol6.pdf#page=188. | 35 Ibid.

36 Katherine Stewart, *The Power Worshippers: Inside the Dangerous Rise of Religious Nationalism* (London: Bloomsbury, 2020), 191. See also Katherine Stewart, *The Good News Club*, 5.

37 Jerry Falwell, *America Can Be Saved!* (Murfreesboro, TN: Sword of the Lord, 1979), 52–53.

38 Peter Montgomery, "National School Choice Week: PR for Privatizers?," Right Wing Watch, Jan. 29, 2015, https://www.rightwingwatch.org/post/national-school-choice-week-pr-for-privatizers/.

39 Kyle Olson, "Jesus Isn't in Michigan."

40 The Dick and Betsy DeVos Family Foundation contributed $5,000/year from 2011 to 2013, according to Conservative Transparency, http://conservativetransparency.org/org/education-action-group-foundation.

41 Benjamin Wermund, "Trump's Education Pick Says Reform Can 'Advance God's Kingdom,'" *Politico*, Dec. 2, 2016, https://politi.co/3zkbFCe. | 42 Ibid.

43 The Supreme Court even upheld funding private nonreligious schools and not private religious schools in 1973. "The Religion Clauses of the First Amendment strictly confine state aid to sectarian education. Even assuming, therefore, that the Equal Protection Clause might require state aid to be granted to private nonsectarian schools in some circumstances—health care or textbooks, for example—a State could rationally conclude as a matter of legislative policy that constitutional neutrality as to sectarian schools might best be achieved by withholding all state assistance." *Norwood v. Harrison*, 413 US 455, 462 (1973).

44 *Espinoza v. Montana Department of Revenue*, 2018 MT 306, ¶ 44. "It is the Legislature's responsibility to craft statutes in compliance with Montana's Constitution, which it failed to do here."

45 Before Koch funding became an albatross, the Institute for Justice awarded the brothers its Cornerstone Award. "Charles Koch provided the initial seed funding that made it possible to launch the Institute in 1991. David Koch has been a generous benefactor each year of IJ's first decade. We are deeply grateful." "IJ Thanks Its Cornerstone Supporters: Charles and David Koch," *Liberty and Law 10, no. 6* (Nov. 2001), 10, https://ij.org/wp-content/uploads/1426/05/LL_11_01.pdf.

46 Mayer wrote: "Typical was the experience in 1991 of two former Reagan administrations lawyers, Clint Bolick, a former aide to Clarence Thomas, and William 'Chip' Mellor III, in search of seed money for a new kind of aggressive, right-wing public interest law firm that would litigate against government regulations in favor of 'economic liberty'; Mellor recalled thinking, 'Who else would give us enough money to be serious?'" Jane Mayer, *Dark Money* (New York: Penguin Random House, 2017), 178.

47 Lateshia Beachum, "Kochs Key among Small Group Quietly Funding Legal Assault on Campaign Finance Regulation," Center for Public Integrity, Nov. 15, 2017, https://bit.ly/3OIXmME; Erica L. Green, "The DeVos 'Nice List,'" *New York Times*, Dec. 23, 2017, https://nyti.ms/3E9Ndmk.

48 Green, "The DeVos 'Nice List.'"

49 Steven A. Holmes, "Political Right's Point Man on Race," *New York Times*, Nov. 16, 1997, https://nyti.ms/3FRmfk5. Bolick began law school at the Univ. of California, Davis, while it was at the center of the 1978 Supreme Court case that upheld affirmative action. Bolick started at the school the year after the case was decided.

50 Ibid.

51 See Greg D. Andres, "Private School Voucher Remedies in Education Cases," *Univ. of Chicago Law Review 62* (1995), 795, 802. See also *Jenkins v. Leininger*, No. 92 CH 05578, slip op ((Ill) Cir Ct, Cook County, Mar 30, 1993); *Arviso v. Dawson*, No B 077772, slip op ((Cal) Ct App, 2d App Dist, 3d Div, Mar. 23, 1995), aff'g grant of demurrer, No BC 057321, slip op ((Cal) Super Ct, Los Angeles County, June 4, 1993).

52 *Stone v. Prince George's County Board of Education*, 977 F.2d 574 (4th Cir. 1992), unpublished opinion.

53 Montana threw out its 1889 constitution and adopted an entirely new one in 1972 that included a compelled support clause. Jill Goldenziel, "Blaine's Name in Vain?: State Constitutions, School Choice, and Charitable Choice," *Denver Univ. Law Review 83* (2005), 57, 65–66, see text in notes 69–73. Even Roberts admits that this new Constitution was adopted without anti-Catholic animus. "Montana even re-adopted its own [compelled support clause] in the 1970s, for reasons unrelated to anti-Catholic bigotry." 140 S. Ct. at 2259.

54 "Ban on Aid to Religious Groups Could Be Removed," WUSF Public Media, Nov. 30, 2017, https://bit.ly/3miAkPG.

55 The Senate essentially required potential states to have the provision in their state constitutions as a condition of admission to the Union, and that language could not be modified without congressional consent. Frank J. Conklin and James M. Vaché, "The Establishment Clause and the Free Exercise Clause of the Washington Constitution—A Proposal to the Supreme Court," *Seattle Univ. Law Review* 8 (1985), 411, 433, https://digitalcommons.law.seattleu.edu/sulr/vol8/iss2/7/. For instance, in 1889 Congress passed the enabling act that allowed the Dakotas, Montana, and Washington to become states and said that each "shall provide, by ordinances irrevocable without the consent of the United States and the people of said States . . . for the establishment and maintenance of systems of public schools, which shall be open to all the children of said States, and free from sectarian control." 50 Stat. 676–684 (1889).

56 See Brief for Respondents 16–27, in *Espinoza v. Montana Department of Revenue*, 140 S. Ct. 2246 (2020); 2019 WL 5887033, https://bit.ly/3Iez4pz. Montana recounts the history in the anti-Catholic bigotry argument context on pp. 16–27.

57 *Mitchell v. Helms*, 530 US 793 (2000). The court agreed to hear this on June 14, 1999, six years, almost to the day, after it decided the Santeria case, 527 US 1002 (1999).

58 *Mitchell v. Helms*, 530 US 793, 828–29 (2000).

59 Ibid.; that fifth sentence begins, "Notwithstanding its history . . ."

60 Steven K. Green, "The Blaine Amendment Reconsidered," *Journal of American Legal History* 36 (Jan. 1992), 42.

61 Ibid.; and Steven K. Green, "Blaming Blaine: Understanding the Blaine Amendment and the No-Funding Principle," *First Amendment Law Review* 2 (2003), 107, https://unc.live/3F625nj.

62 Incorporation is the process by which the courts apply rights and restrictions in the U.S. Constitution to the states through the language of the Fourteenth Amendment. For instance, the plain text of the First Amendment applies only to the federal government, but the Fourteenth Amendment's text applies the First Amendment to state action as well. Green's first article discusses how the history of the Blaine Amendment fails to support the originalist position Thomas has repeatedly advanced suggesting that the First Amendment does not and should not apply to the states.

63 Interview with author. | 64 Interview with author. Quote confirmed by Green.

65 Justice Douglas does not mention this in his dissent directly, but he includes a letter written by Cardinal Spellman as Appendix B to his dissent in *Board of Education of Central School District No. 1 v. Allen*, 392 US 236, 265 (1968). See also *McCollum v. Board of Education of School District No. 71, Champaign County, Illinois*, 333 US 203, 218 and n.6 (1948); *School District of Abington Township, Pennsylvania v. Schempp*, 374 US 203, 255–57 (1963).

66 *Board of Education of Central School District No. 1 v. Allen*, 392 US 236, 268. None of these mention the principle as anti-Catholic.

67 Brief for Petitioners, *Mitchell v. Helms*, 1999 WL 639126 (US), 37–38. Michael McConnell never raised the issue in oral argument.

68 Michael McConnell is the lawyer in question. Sam Levin, "New Law Clinic Handles Religious Liberty Cases," *Stanford Magazine*, https://stanford.io/3zfLs7K. The brief listed McConnell first and also included Steffen N. Johnson, Patricia A. Dean, Andrew T. Karron, and John C. Massaro.

69 Brief for the Becket Fund for Religious Liberty as Amicus Curiae in support of petitioners. *Mitchell v. Helms*, 1999 WL 638630 (US) (USAmicus.Brief,1999). The anti-Catholic Know Nothing party actually took over state politics there, but as Green points out, "As Professor Ray Billington indicated in his seminal study of antebellum nativism, the Know Nothings were relatively ineffective in enacting anti-Catholic legislation, even in those states where they briefly held clear majorities." Green, "Blaming Blaine," 126.

70 See "Isaac Backus, 1775 Resolution to the Massachusetts Assembly," in *The Founders' Constitution*, Vol. 5: *Amendment I (Religion)*, Document 21, Univ. of Chicago Press, http://press-pubs.uchicago.edu/founders/documents/amendI_religions21.html.

71 Carol Gerwin, "The AntiAid Amendment," *CommonWealth*, Jan. 1, 1999, https://bit.ly/3OdbTzl.

72 *State ex rel. Weiss v. District Board of School District No. 8 of City of Edgerton*, 76 Wis. 177, 44 N.W. 967, 980 (1890) (Cassoday concurring). Many American Catholics during the 1870s *wanted* the compelled support principle, even if the church hierarchy would have preferred public money. When the Ohio Constitutional Convention in 1873 was considering removing the compelled support clause, one Catholic delegate rose to oppose the move, saying the amendment, "was presented without the cognizance, and urged without the indorsement of a single Catholic of this Convention, other than its author. . . . I do not believe even a minority in numbers of Catholics want such change, or any special privilege under law or Constitution." Mr. Jackson, Mar. 25, 1874, *Journal of the Constitutional Convention of the State of Ohio*, 1873–74, Vol. 2, pt. III, https://bit.ly/3Mu0Xwe.

73 Ginni Thomas, "Justice Thomas Opens Up on Life, Faith, and His Interracial Marriage," *Daily Signal*, Jan. 7, 2018, https://dailysign.al/392sEyh. Yes, this was an interview with his wife. | 74 Ibid.

75 "2018 Commencement Speaker Clarence Thomas' Catholic Faith Illuminated in New Film," Christendom College, Feb. 20, 2020, https://bit.ly/3Lt4xGO. The college itself was unapologetically Catholic as well, according to the "Catholic Identity" page on its website, https://www.christendom.edu/about/catholic-identity/.

76 *Mitchell v. Helms*, 530 US 793, 912–13 (2000).

77 140 S. Ct, 2259. Roberts's hedge was also a dig at the state: "We agree with the Department that the historical record is 'complex.'" Ibid. He muddied what were clear waters.

78 Ibid. Roberts also cited two law review articles, one that begins by discussing Thomas's argument.

79 *Espinoza v. Montana Department of Revenue*, https://www.oyez.org/cases/2019/18-1195, 39:05.

80 Ibid., 52:55. This history is all wrong, incidentally.

81 Brief of the Cato Institute as Amicus Curiae Supporting Petitioners, *Espinoza v. Montana Department of Revenue*, 2019 WL 4568206. "Article X, § 6 of Montana's constitution—the state's Blaine Amendment, a provision that many states passed in the late 19th century during a rash of anti-Catholic sentiment—forbids the appropriation or expenditure of any public funds, directly or indirectly, for 'sectarian' (that is, religious) purposes." https://bit.ly/3OKgyJN.

82 See Brief for Pioneer Institute, Inc., as Amicus Curiae in Support of Petitioners, in *Espinoza v. Montana Department of Revenue*, 2019 WL 4512938 (US), v (US,2019), citing its own publication: Cornelius Chapman, "The Know-Nothing Amendments: Barriers to School Choice in Massachusetts," white paper (Boston: Pioneer Institute, 2009). The Pioneer Institute, based in Massachusetts, is funded by Koch money. Annual reports show David Koch to have been one of the biggest funders lately and a funder going back to the founding. For instance, the 2017 report (31) shows David Koch in the top category, $100,000+ donors with three foundations, https://pioneerinstitute.org/annual-reports/.

83 140 S. Ct., 2260.

84 Roberts attended Notre Dame Elementary, then La Lumiere School, "a small but affluent and academically rigorous Roman Catholic boarding school in La Porte, Indiana." Kavanaugh and Gorsuch attended Georgetown Prep, a Jesuit boys' college prep school. Thomas attended St. Pius X Catholic High School in Savannah and then transferred to a Catholic boarding school that trained students for the priesthood; he then began college at Conception Seminary College before transferring to a fourth Catholic school, College of the Holy Cross. Alito appears to have attended public school, at which his parents taught; unclear on where he went below high school; he and his family are very Catholic and worshipped at Our Lady of the Blessed Sacrament Roman Catholic Church in Roseland, NJ, for decades.

15: RELIGIOUS FREEDOM AND SEGREGATION ACADEMIES

1 Bob Jones Sr., "Is Segregation Scriptural?" (Greenville, SC: Bob Jones Univ., 1960). Originally a sermon given as a radio address on WMUU, on Apr. 17, 1960, it was later published in pamphlet form.

2 See Heather McGhee, *The Sum of Us: What Racism Costs Everyone and How We Can Prosper Together* (London: Profile, 2021), (e.g., 25 for cement). See also Rose Hackman, "Swimming While Black: The Legacy of Segregated Public Pools Lives On," *The Guardian*, Aug. 4, 2015, https://bit.ly/37K5z2J.

3 The Supreme Court even upheld this leasing-to-segregationists workaround in 1971. *Palmer v. Thompson*, 403 US 217 (1971).

4 *Brown* was actually a series of arguments and decisions, and desegregation cases stretched into the 1990s until the Supreme Court, under Rehnquist, began hacking away at *Brown*'s protections and legacy.

5 Chris Ford, Stephenie Johnson, and Lisette Partelow, "The Racist Origins of Private School Vouchers," Center for American Progress, July 12, 2017, https://ampr.gs/3vpQE6J.

6 *Griffin v. School Board*, 377 US 218 (1964).

7 Todd G. Shields and Angie Maxwell, *The Long Southern Strategy: How Chasing White Voters in the South Changed American Politics* (New York: Oxford Univ. Press, 2019); Joseph A. Aistrup, *The Southern Strategy Revisited: Republican Top-Down Advancement in the South* (Lexington: Univ. Press of Kentucky, 2021); see also Angie Maxwell, "What We Get Wrong about the Southern Strategy," *Washington Post*, June 26, 2019, https://wapo.st/3MpyCqi.

8 Rick Perlstein, "Exclusive: Lee Atwater's Infamous 1981 Interview on the Southern Strategy," *The Nation*, Nov. 13, 2012, https://bit.ly/3MtqMME.

9 Joseph Crespino, *In Search of Another Country: Mississippi and the Conservative Counterrevolution* (Princeton, NJ: Princeton Univ. Press, 2021), 173. Here, Crespino is writing specifically of the 1964 Civil Rights Act.

10 Rose Friedman and Milton Friedman, *Free to Choose: A Personal Statement* (New York: Houghton Mifflin Harcourt, 1990), 164.

11 Crespino, *In Search of Another Country*, 226.

12 See, e.g., S.Res.806, "A resolution defending the free exercise of religion,"116th Congress (2019-2020) , https://bit.ly/3lWOaa8; Mike Lee, "Senate Conservatives Ask Appropriators to Hold the Line on Life Protections," press release, May 21, 2019, https://bit.ly/39iD3W5.

13 Chas Danner, "GOP Senator Cindy Hyde-Smith Made 'Public Hanging' Joke," *New York Magazine*, Nov. 11, 2018, https://nymag.com/intelligencer/2018/11/gop-senator-cindy-hyde-smith-made-public-hanging-joke.html.

14 Roger Wicker, "Wicker, Hyde-Smith Promote National School Choice Week," press release, Jan. 25, 2021, https://bit.ly/3KsxscO.

15 Ashton Pittman, "Hyde-Smith Attended All-White 'Seg Academy' to Avoid Integration," *Jackson Free Press*, Nov. 23, 2018, https://bit.ly/39cUreP.

16 Robert Luckett, "From Council Schools to Today's Fight for Public Ed," *Jackson Free Press*, Feb. 15, 2017, https://bit.ly/3NToeIt.

17 *Alexander v. Holmes County Board of Education*, 396 US 19 (1969).

18 Crespino, *In Search of Another Country*, 228.

19 Sarah Carr, "In Southern Towns, 'Segregation Academies' Are Still Going Strong," *The Atlantic*, Dec. 13, 2012, https://bit.ly/3ktpEwB.

20 Olatunde C. Johnson, *The Story of Bob Jones University v. United States: Race, Religion, and Congress' Extraordinary Acquiescence*, Statutory Interpretation Stories, William Eskridge, Philip P. Frickey, and Elizabeth Garrett, eds. (St. Paul, MN: Foundation Press, 2010), Columbia Law School Public Law and Legal Theory Working Paper No. 10-229 (2010), https://scholarship.law.columbia.edu/faculty_scholarship/2523, citing David Nevin and Robert E. Bills, *The Schools That Fear Built: Segregationist Academies in the South* (Washington, DC: Acropolis Books, 1976), 14, 25.

21 Crespino, *In Search of Another Country*, 237–48.

22 "Governor of Mississippi Backs Private Schools," *New York Times*, Jan. 4, 1970, 78, https://nyti.ms/3y6ftGF.

23 *In Search of Another Country*, Crespino, 237–48.

24 Anthea Butler, *White Evangelical Racism: The Politics of Morality in America* (Chapel Hill: Univ. of North Carolina Press, 2021), 140.

25 See, e.g., The Academy Stories, www.TheAcademyStories.com.

26 Ellen Ann Fentress, "White Churches Involved at Every Step," *The Academy Stories,* https://bit.ly/3PYO13Y. Fentress is the editor of this site.

27 Lynn Watkins, "Seg Academy: My Memories," Academy Stories, accessed Nov. 26, 2021, https://www.theacademystories.com/post/5-songs-that-make-me-really-happy.

28 Crespino, *In Search of Another Country*, 248. | **29** Ibid. | **30** Ibid., 249.

31 See *Green v. Kennedy*, 309 F. Supp. 1127 (D.D.C 1970); *Coffey v. State Educational Finance Commission*, 296 F. Supp. 1389 (D. Miss. 1969).

32 Johnson, *The Story of Bob Jones University v. United States*, 6. These were announcements. IRS News Releases (July 10, 1970), No. 1052 (July 19, 1970), 7 CCH 1980 Stan. Fed. Tax. Rep. ¶¶ 6790, 6814. The rules would take longer. IRS Rev. Rul. 71-447. 41. IRS Rev. Proc. 72-54, 2 C.B. 834 (1972).

33 See, e.g., Butler, *White Evangelical Racism*, 68–73. | **34** Crespino, *In Search of Another Country*, 237.

35 For instance, the racist Virginia voucher system used in Prince Edward County did not extend to religious schools. The Milwaukee voucher program was expanded to include religious schools in 1995.

36 *Lemon v. Kurtzman*, 403 US 602 (1971.)

37 Adam Liptak, "Alton T. Lemon, Civil Rights Activist, Dies at 84," *New York Times*, May 25, 2013, https://www.nytimes.com/2013/05/25/us/alton-t-lemon-civil-rights-activist-dies-at-84.html.

38 403 US 602 at 608.

39 *Lemon v. Kurtzman*, 403 US 602, 644 n1 (1971) (concurring). More specifically, Lemon argued: "The nonpublic school system in Pennsylvania is a white school system" with "a few token (middle-class) black students. The non-Catholic church-related schools are virtually 100% white. The Catholic parochial school system has a larger percentage of black pupils, but it is segregated. The only figure that is known at this time is the percentage applicable to Catholic schools inside the City of Philadelphia, which is understood to be 6%. This must be measured against a Negro enrollment of 59% in the Philadelphia public schools." Brief for Appellants, *Lemon v. Kurtzman*, 403 US 602, 1970 WL 116871 (US), 49–50.

40 Though at oral argument there was rather a long exchange about funding a hypothetical playground at a hypothetical religious school, *Lemon v. Kurtzman*, Oyez, www.oyez.org/cases/1970/89, oral argument at 1:58:30.

41 *Lemon v. Kurtzman*, 403 US 602, 627–28 (1971) (Douglas concurring).

42 Jones, "Is Segregation Scriptural?"

43 The school was a family business. Bob Jones senior founded "the world's most unusual university" in 1927 and ran it until 1948, when Bob Jones Jr. took it over, and then Bob Jones III in 1971. *Bob Jones University v. Simon*, 416 US 725, 734 (1974); Johnson, *The Story of Bob Jones University v. United States*, 11.

44 *Bob Jones University v. Connally*, 341 F. Supp. 277, 278–79 (D.S.C. 1971), rev'd, 472 F.2d 903 (4th Cir. 1973).

45 Brief for the Petitioner, *Bob Jones University v. Shultz*, 1973 WL 172321 (US), 8.

46 By litigation, more than 5,000 students from kindergarten to grad school. Johnson, *The Story of Bob Jones University v. United States*, 11.

47 Bob Jones Univ. fundraising letter, Dec. 9, 1970. In *Bob Jones Univ. v. Simon*, 416 US 725 (1974) Appendix, 60-62, 62. In the Gale database, *Making of Modern Law: US Supreme Court Records and Briefs, 1832–1978*.

48 Letter, Bob Jones Univ. to District Director of the IRS, Dec. 30, 1970, in Appendix to the *Bob Jones Univ. v. Simon*, 416 US 725 (1974) 56–60. In the Gale database, *Making of Modern Law: US Supreme Court Records and Briefs, 1832–1978*. | **49** Ibid., undated statement. Appendix, 63.

50 However, the attorneys representing BJU also represented the Amish in the Yoder case and argued for state aid to religious schools in the case Alton Lemon brought. See "William B. Ball," Oyez, accessed Oct. 6, 2021, www.oyez.org/advocates/william_b_ball.

51 The Goldsboro Christian School in Goldsboro, North Carolina, was consolidated with the Bob Jones University case. That school was segregated because its god had "separated mankind into various nations and races" and so that such separation "should be preserved in the fear of the Lord." Johnson, *The Story of Bob Jones University v. United States*, 10. A few years after the Supreme Court decision, the preachers who ran the school expelled the homecoming queen—who had the delightful last name of Outlaw—two months before graduation for modeling swimsuits in a mall department store, labeling her a "bad influence." Associated Press, "School Is Ordered to Readmit Girl Who Modeled Swimsuits." *New York Times*, Mar.14, 1987, https://nyti.ms/3MGpDSq.

52 Johnson, *The Story of Bob Jones University v. United States,* 12–13.

53 *Bob Jones Univ. v. United States*, 461 US 574, 580 n2 (1983).

54 Butler, *White Evangelical Racism*, 66–69.

55 *Bob Jones Univ. v. Connally*, 341 F. Supp. 277, 278–79 (D.S.C. 1971), rev'd, 472 F.2d 903 (4th Cir. 1973),

56 Johnson, *The Story of Bob Jones University v. United States*, 2, tells the fuller story of interplay of *Brown*, the Civil Rights Act of 1964, and the various IRS regulations at play.

57 *Runyon v. McCrary*, 427 US 160 (1976).

58 *Bob Jones Univ. v. United States*, 461 US 574, 604 (1983).

59 *Bob Jones Univ. v. United States*, 461 US 574, 603 (1983)(emphasis added).

60 Ibid., 603–4. | **61** Ibid., 622.

62 Crespino, *In Search of Another Country*, 256.

63 Billings got his start because he was "alarmed by plans to revoke the tax-exempt status of private schools, many of them Christian," so he "formed the National Christian Action Coalition, packed his belongings in a trailer and hit the road with his wife to preach against what he viewed as a godless humanism dominating American life," wrote the *New York Times* in his obituary. "Robert J. Billings Is Dead at 68; Helped Form the Moral Majority," June 1, 1995, D21, https://nyti.ms/3ONB64b. Billings cofounded that powerful coalition with Paul Weyrich and was executive director of Jerry Falwell's Moral Majority, then the religious advisor to Reagan's 1980 presidential campaign. After that, he worked in the Department of Education for Reagan as "Mr. Conservative." "Robert Billings, Religious Activist and Moral Majority Co-founder," *The Virginian-Pilot*, June 1, 1995, https://bit.ly/39iiwkp. Billings later served in Reagan's Department of Education, for a time alongside Clarence Thomas, who became an assistant secretary of education in 1981. Crespino, *In Search of Another Country*, 256.

64 Johnson, *The Story of Bob Jones University v. United States*, 16, citing Department of the Treasury News Release, "Treasury Establishes New Tax-Exempt Policy," Jan. 8, 1982. Reagan himself had the DOJ switch its position in the case, to support Bob Jones Univ. The court appointed William Coleman to step in and argue the case.

65 For an explanation of the political and legal calculus, see James Forman Jr., "The Rise and Fall of School Vouchers: A Story of Religion, Race, and Politics," *University of California, Los Angeles, Law Review* 54 (2007), 547–604 (2007), https://scholarship.law.georgetown.edu/facpub/77.

66 Clint Bolick, *Voucher Wars: Waging the Legal Battle over School Choice* (Washington, DC: Cato Inst., 2003), 109–12.

67 Forman, "The Rise and Fall of School Vouchers: A Story of Religion, Race, and Politics."

68 James Bock, "NAACP Opposes School Vouchers, State Takeover of Failing Systems," *Baltimore Sun*, July 17, 1997, https://bit.ly/3Lqz2gs.

69 Stephanie Saul, "Public Money Finds Back Door to Private Schools," *New York Times*, May 21, 2012, https://nyti.ms/3LxpOz5. The study showed that after two years, enrollment in the metro counties where the private schools were located increased by 0.3%. "A Failed Experiment: Georgia Tax Credit Scholarships for Private Schools," *Southern Education Foundation* (2011), https://files.eric.ed.gov/fulltext/ED535565.pdf.

70 "A Failed Experiment," 15. The report concluded that "instead of providing the state's neediest children trapped in low performing public schools with new, affordable opportunities for a good education," neo-vouchers "publicly finance[d] the private education of relatively well-to-do students, many of whom are already in private schools," 59–60.

71 According to 2014 numbers. Edgar Mendez, "75% of Voucher Applicants Already Attend Private School," *Milwaukee Journal Sentinel*, May 20, 2014, https://bit.ly/3Mz9oGA.

72 160 of 163 schools. "163 private schools register for Wisconsin Parental Choice Program," press release, Wisconsin Department of Public Instruction, Jan. 31, 2017, https://bit.ly/3xtZQ9x.

73 Richard D. Kahlenberg, Halley Potter, and Kimberly Quick, "Why Private School Vouchers Could Exacerbate School Segregation," *The Century Foundation*, Dec. 19, 2016, https://bit.ly/38Sf2W1; William J. Mathis and Kevin G. Welner, "Do Choice Policies Segregate Schools?," National Education Policy Center at the Univ. of Colorado Boulder, Mar. 2016, https://bit.ly/3x7HpYj; Halley Potter, "Do Private School Vouchers Pose a Threat to Integration?," *The Century Foundation*, Mar. 21, 2017, https://tcf.org/content/report/private-school-vouchers-pose-threat-integration/; Osamudia R. James, "Opt-Out Education: School Choice as Racial Subordination," *Iowa Law Review* 99 (2014), 1083, https://bit.ly/3kjehHP.

74 Nicole Flatow, "Louisiana's Voucher Program Is Making Segregation Worse, Justice Department Finds," ThinkProgress, Aug. 26, 2013, https://bit.ly/3MxCWEk.

75 *Brumfield v. Dodd*, NO. 71-1316 (E.D. La. Jan. 30, 2013) U.S. Memo in support of motion for further relief, 1, 5 https://bit.ly/3ONBCPF .

76 In the states with deeply racist histories—South Carolina, for instance—it's worse. Kahlenberg, Potter, and Quick, "Why Private School Vouchers Could Exacerbate School Segregation."

77 Sean F. Reardon and John T. Yun, "Private School Racial Enrollments and Segregation," Civil Rights Project, Harvard Univ., June 26, 2002, 8, https://bit.ly/3y1hZxy.

78 See "Dispelling the Myth of 'School Choice,'" Freedom from Religion Foundation, https://ffrf.org/faq/state-church/item/22744-voucherfaq.

79 See Jarvis DeBerry, "Louisiana Lawmaker Needs Lesson in Religious Freedom," NOLA.com, July 8, 2012, https://bit.ly/3y16dU8; Alice Dowty, "Hodges Now Leery of Jindal Reform," *Livingston Parish News*, June 29, 2012, https://bit.ly/3OD6xy6.

80 *Zelman v. Simmons-Harris*, 536 US 639, 703 (2002) (Souter dissenting).

81 *Zelman v. Simmons-Harris*, 536 US 639 (2002).

82 *Zelman v. Simmons-Harris*, 536 US, 653 (Rehnquist, majority opinion).
83 Crespino, *In Search of Another Country*, 226.

16: RELIGIOUS FREEDOM AND "PROMOTING THE GENERAL WELFARE"

1 Erwin Chemerinsky, "Giving People a License to Discriminate Because of Their Religious Beliefs," *Los Angeles Times*, June 17, 2021, https://lat.ms/3h9TZyE.
2 *Reynolds v. United States*, 98 US 145 (1878).
3 Antonin Scalia, *Scalia Speaks: Reflections on Law, Faith, and Life Well Lived* (New York: Crown, 2017), 333–41, 336; Bruce Allen Murphy, *Scalia: A Court of One* (New York: Simon & Schuster, 2015), 231. See also Rosen, *Supreme Court*, 198.
4 This quote describes the three nuns who opened a branch in Nantes. Abbé A. Leroy, *History of the Little Sisters of the Poor* (London: Burns, Oates & Washbourne, 1906), https://archive.org/details/littlesisterspoo00unknuoft, 64.
5 Jessie's Place required anyone it helped to attend and later tithe to the Church of the Highlands, Alabama's biggest church. Greg Garrison, "Does Shelter Require Homeless Women to Attend Megachurch and Tithe?," AL.com., Oct. 20, 2017, https://bit.ly/3tf6lw8. Jessie's Place was operated by the Jimmie Hale Mission. Tony Cooper, who was executive director, explained, "We are a Christian ministry. Tithing is just a part of our Christian walk. We're trying to get them to exercise the discipline of giving back to God what's his. We charge them nothing. It's not like we're trying to get their money. The tithe does not go to us." There are far worse examples. Criminal, even. See "Church Leaders Charged in Forced Labor of Homeless People," FOX 5 San Diego, Sept. 10, 2019, https://bit.ly/3NUcJAx.
6 Cheryl Corley, "Illinois, Catholic Agencies at Odds Over Gay Adoptions," NPR, July 5, 2011, https://n.pr/3y2xd5A.
7 Deborah Yetter, "Baptist Group Refuses Kentucky State Contract to Provide Care for Abused, Neglected Kids," *Louisville Courier Journal*, May 6, 2021, https://bit.ly/38y1Ll8.
8 Laurie Goodstein, "Bishops Say Rules on Gay Parents Limit Freedom of Religion," *New York Times*, Dec. 28, 2011, https://nyti.ms/3Nk8r5I. See also Manya A. Brachear, "Catholic Charities of Rockford Ends Foster Care, Adoption Services," *Chicago Tribune*, May 26, 2011, archived at https://bit.ly/3sZeMM3.
9 Declaration of Cynthia Figueroa, Philadelphia DHS Commissioner, paragraphs 15–18, https://bit.ly/3LqAmzW.
10 Specifically, Catholic Social Services would not certify otherwise eligible same-sex couples as prospective foster parents and wouldn't conduct home studies with same-sex couples as part of the couple's adoption application. *Fulton v. City of Philadelphia*, 320 F. Supp. 3d 661, 672 (E.D. Pa. 2018), https://bit.ly/3J5wJyb.
11 *Sharonell Fulton et al. v. City of Philadelphia et al., May 2020*, https://bit.ly/3atzVr0. Amato reported to his board president, Bishop John McIntyre, and the bishop reported to the Archbishop, who was Charles Chaput at the time this all happened. Ibid., 204.
12 Catholic Social Services of Philadelphia, "Our Catholic Identity," https://bit.ly/3OLJelK.
13 Ibid. "In all our efforts on behalf of the poor and hungry, homeless and neglected, disabled and disadvantaged members of our society, we endeavor to incorporate our work into the healing *and saving mission* of Jesus the Christ."
14 James Amato essentially ran Catholic Social Services, and he reported to his board president, Bishop John McIntyre. The bishop reported to Archbishop Charles Chaput. Chaput retired, but Catholic Social Services had already asked the Supreme Court to take the case by then. *Sharonell Fulton et al. v. City of Philadelphia et al., May 2020, 204*, https://bit.ly/3OLJelK.
15 In a speech to Roman Catholic seminarians entitled "Facing the Future with Hope and Joy," which was later published, Chaput said, "Not naming the real problem for what it is, a pattern of predatory homosexuality and a failure to weed that out from Church life, is an act of self-delusion," https://bit.ly/3EVk8fS.
16 See, e.g., Gwendolyn N. Bright, *Grand Jury Report on the Sexual Abuse of Minors by Clergy (2005)*, (Darby, PA: Diane Publishing, 2011), https://bit.ly/3vTCKZB; Renee Cardwell Hughes, ed., *Final Grand Jury Report on the Sexual Abuse of Minors by Clergy (2011)*, (Darby, PA: Diane Publishing, n.d.), https://bit.ly/3vrGK4D. The 2005 report noted that the "successful cover-up of the abuse resulted in the expiration of the statute of limitations" so that none of the "rapist priests" or their protectors could be charged. The grand jury released the 2011 report because, five years later, "not much has changed." It explained, "The rapist priests we accused were well known to the secretary of clergy, but he cloaked their conduct and put them in place to do it again. The procedures implemented by the Archdiocese to help victims are in fact designed to help the abusers, and the Archdiocese itself. Worst of all, apparent abusers remain on duty in the Archdiocese, today, with open access to new young prey." Between 1961 and 2003, John Krol and Anthony Bevilacqua were archbishops first, then cardinals. Both were repeatedly named and implicated for their roles in the cover-ups. These investigations led to the first conviction of a Catholic Church official, Msgr. William Lynn, for covering up the abuse.
17 Joel Mathis, "Archbishop Chaput's War on Obama Is Bad for Philadelphia," *Philadelphia Magazine*, Mar. 26, 2012, https://bit.ly/3tk2HRD.
18 In his acceptance speech, he argued that America's "common moral heritage was the First Commandment, 'I am the Lord your God; you will not have foreign gods before me,'" a claim that wrongly conflates morality and Christianity, a claim I debunked in *The Founding Myth*. "Receiving Canterbury Medal, Archbishop Chaput Warns of Religious Freedom Loss," Catholic News Agency, May 7, 2009, https://bit.ly/3aC0SJ7.
19 Mark J. Stern, "The Supreme Court May Give Foster Care Agencies a Right to Refuse Same-sex Couples," *Slate*, Feb. 24, 2020, https://bit.ly/3J1wNiE.

20 Freedom from Religion Foundation, "FFRF: Supreme Court's Fulton Decision Is a Mixed Bag," press release, June 17, 2021, https://bit.ly/3Lt49YV.

21 Why take the case? If this was going to be a punt that permitted discrimination, why get involved in the first place? There's no mandatory right to appeal to the Supreme Court in such cases. So why? Well, it was taken before the 2020 election. It was actually argued on election day. So at least four justices wanted to accept the case when Ruth Bader Ginsburg was still on the court, before the talk of court reform exploded after McConnell stole another Supreme Court seat. I think this talk and these proposals influenced the court. Which is all the more reason to keep up the talk and pressure.

22 OAR 471-30-038(3), *Black v. Employment Division, Department of Human Resources*, 301 Or. 221, 223, 721 P.2d 451, 452 (1986).

23 Brief Amicus Curiae of Professor Eugene Volokh in Support of Neither Party, *Sharonell Fulton et al. v. City of Philadelphia et al.*, 2020 WL 3078491 (US), 25, https://bit.ly/3I0WH4A.

24 Rob Boston, "A Texas Theocrat Was Convinced That the 2020 Election Was Going to Be Stolen. You Won't Believe What He Did Next," May 9, 2022, Americans United, https://www.au.org/the-latest/articles/hot-ze-election-fraud; Patrick Svitek, "Steve Hotze Asked Texas Gov. Greg Abbott to Order Rioters to Be Killed," *Texas Tribune*, July 3, 2020, https://www.texastribune.org/2020/07/03/steve-hotze-texas-greg-abbott-rioters/.

25 See U.S. Food and Drug Administration, "Warning Letter: Health and Wellness Center International One, L.L.C. dba Hotze Vitamins," Dec. 2, 2020, https://bit.ly/3I0yxav.

26 Technically, Hotze sued on behalf of his management company, Briarwood Management, which runs the companies and employs their employees. Hotze Declaration in Amended Brief in Support of Motion for Summary Judgment and Permanent Injunction, 4:18-cv-00824 #90, http://files.eqcf.org/cases/418-cv-00824-90/, 33.

27 See, e.g., Manny Fernandez, "In Weaponized Courts, Judge Who Halted Affordable Care Act Is a Conservative Favorite," *New York Times*, Dec. 15, 2018, https://nyti.ms/3xnRksV.

28 *Bear Creek Bible Church and Braidwood Management v. Equal Employment Opportunity Commission*, Civil Action 4:18-cv-00824-O, (N.D. Tex. Nov. 1, 2021), https://bit.ly/3mhezjg.

29 Ibid., 45–50. The full docket of the case is interesting because some of Hotze and the church's briefing was done before the *Fulton v. Philadelphia* decision and some after. Comparing the arguments, you can see how excited the Crusaders were about the new case. The docket is publicly available here: https://bit.ly/3koIghj. Compare, for instance, entries 73 and 90.

30 Nick Fish, Twitter post, https://bit.ly/3OKcr0r.

31 Mike Konczal, "The Conservative Myth of a Social Safety Net Built on Charity," *The Atlantic*, Mar. 24, 2014, https://bit.ly/3OVaoH8.

32 Peter Montgomery, "Religious Right to Romney: Safety Net Un-Biblical," Right Wing Watch, Feb. 3, 2012, https://www.rightwingwatch.org/post/religious-right-to-romney-safety-net-un-biblical/.

33 Jerry Falwell, *America Can Be Saved!* (Murfreesboro, TN: Sword of the Lord, 1979), 52–53.

34 Clare Kindall, "Symposium: The First Amendment Does Not Require Governments to Contract with Parties Who Do Not Comply with Neutral, Generally Applicable Rules," SCOTUSblog, Oct. 29, 2020, https://bit.ly/3634Ubf.

17: WHAT'S NEXT?

1 U.S. Commission on Civil Rights, "Peaceful Coexistence: Reconciling Nondiscrimination Principles with Civil Liberties," Briefing Report, (Sept. 2016, https://www.usccr.gov/pubs/Peaceful-Coexistence-09-07-16.PDF.

2 *McCreary County, Ky. v. American Civil Liberties Union of Ky.*, 545 US 844, 882 (2005) (concurring).

3 Ronald Brownstein, "The Supreme Court Is Colliding With a Less-Religious America," *The Atlantic*, Dec. 3, 2020, https://bit.ly/3vS5qlP. Ira Lupu quoted.

4 This is the ritual circumcision ceremony known as metzitzah b'peh. The clinical term for this Orthodox Jewish practice is "direct orogenital suction."

5 Justin W. Moyer and Julie Z. Weil, "Lawsuits Challenge D.C. Law Allowing Kids to Get Vaccines without Parental Permission," *Washington Post*, July 18, 2021, https://wapo.st/3I4vS0F; Debbie Truong, "Parents Take Aim at D.C. Law That Lets Minors Get Vaccinated without Permission," NPR, July 19, 2021, https://n.pr/3rpyO22.

6 Complaint, *Resurrection School et al v. Gordon et al*, Case #1:20-cv-01016 (Oct. 22, 2020) US District Court for the Western District of Michigan, paragraph 22, https://bit.ly/3Kwcx8t.

7 Agence France-Presse in Vatican City, "Pope Says Anti-maskers Stuck in 'Their Own Little World of Interests,'" *The Guardian*, Nov. 23, 2020, https://bit.ly/3pUJaoY.

8 Marci A. Hamilton, *God vs. the Gavel: The Perils of Extreme Religious Liberty*, rev. ed. (New York: Cambridge Univ. Press, 2014), 72. "Roughly 30 states plus the District of Columbia now have exemptions for religious parents from the medical neglect laws."

9 Marci A. Hamilton, "The Time Has Come to Overrule Wisconsin v. Yoder," Casetext, Mar. 17, 2014, https://casetext.com/analysis/the-time-has-come-to-overrule-wisconsin-v-yoder.

10 *Pierce v. Society of Sisters*, 268 US 510, 535 (1925).

11 *Hosanna-Tabor Evangelical Lutheran Church and School v. Equal Employment Opportunity Commission*, 565 US 171, 199 (2012).

12 H.R. Rep. No. 485 part 2, 101st Cong., 2d Sess. 76-77 (1990). See also 29 C.F.R. Pt. 1630, App. § 1630.16(a), see *Equal Employment Opportunity Commission v. Hosanna-Tabor Evangelical Lutheran Church and School*, 597 F.3d 769, 777 (6th Cir. 2010).

13 597 F.3d at 781.

14 The *New York Times* editorial board noticed this tactic. Though it didn't quite connect the dots: "In his opinion for the unanimous court, Chief Justice John Roberts Jr. seems to minimize the scope of the ruling by avoiding 'a rigid formula for deciding when an employee qualifies as a minister' and by not saying how the exception would apply in other circumstances." Editorial Board, "The Ministerial Exception," *New York Times,* Jan. 12, 2012, https://nyti.ms/312A7ZM.

15 Susan Candiotti and Chris Welch, "A Litany of 'Thou Shalt Nots': Catholic Teachers Challenge Morality Clause," CNN, May 31, 2014, https://cnn.it/3xmmZMD.

16 *Our Lady of Guadalupe School v. Morrissey-Berru*, 140 S. Ct. 2049 (2020).

17 "Trump Administration's Church Bailouts Cost Taxpayers $6–10 Billion, American Atheists Reveals," American Atheists, July 6, 2020, https://bit.ly/3MBwTP3.

18 *Bostock v. Clayton County*, 140 S. Ct. 1731, 1741 (2020). | 19 Ibid., 1737. | 20 Ibid., 1754.

21 *Bear Creek Bible Church and Braidwood Management v. Equal Employment Opportunity Commission*, Civil Action 4:18-cv-00824-O, 1 (N.D. Tex. Nov. 1, 2021).

22 *Roman Catholic Diocese of Brooklyn v. Cuomo*, 592 U.S. ___ (2020) (per curiam); *High Plains Harvest Church v. Polis*, 592 U.S. ___ (2020); *Tandon v. Newsom*, 141 S. Ct. 1294 (2021). Brought by Liberty Counsel, First Liberty, and First Liberty, respectively.

23 *Fulton v. City of Philadelphia*, No. 19-123 (US Jun. 17, 2021).

24 *Shurtleff v. Boston*, No. 20-1800 (U.S. May 2, 2022), Camp Constitution, "Camp Constitution Expansion," archived at https://campconstitution.net/camp-constitution-expansion/.

25 *Shurtleff v. City of Boston*, Dckt 20-1800 (brought by Liberty Counsel); *Carson v. Makin*, Dckt 20-1088 (brought by the Institute for Justice); *Kennedy v. Bremerton School District*, Dckt 20-418 (brought by First Liberty Institute); *303 Creative LLC v. Elenis*, Dckt 21-476 (brought by Alliance Defending Freedom). In this last case, the court granted cert on the free speech question only, but we shall see.

26 Of course, the court will decide some cases in favor of minority religions, and some minority religions will get swept in with Christianity's wins. The Crusading justices are conservative ideologues, but not stupid. But they're not putting minority religions atop the hierarchy or giving them a blanket opt-out to laws. In fact, I expect at some point in the future to see some privileges extended to minorities, almost certainly the result of criticism like that contained in this book. I expect it because these are not judges guided by principle, and politicians see how much retrogression they can get away with imposing.

27 See, e.g., *Carson v. Makin*, Oyez, www.oyez.org/cases/2021/20-1088. Oral argument audio, Justice Kagan statement at 00:04:00 and 01:46:55.

28 Jay Wexler, *Our Non-Christian Nation: How Atheists, Satanists, Pagans, and Others Are Demanding Their Rightful Place in Public Life* (Stanford, CA: Stanford Univ. Press, 2019).

29 "America's Changing Religious Landscape," *Pew Research Center,* May 12, 2015, www.pewforum.org/2015/05/12/americas-changing-religious-landscape/; Jack Jenkins, "'Nones' Now as Big as Evangelicals, Catholics in the US," *Religion News Service,* Mar. 21, 2019, https://bit.ly/3H1Bqck.

30 "Memorial and Remonstrance against Religious Assessments, [ca. 20 June] 1785," Founders Online, National Archives, https://founders.archives.gov/documents/Madison/01-08-02-0163.

31 One scholar has referred to this as "insulation from evidence," or, perhaps more precisely, "insulated from revision in light of evidence." Brian Leiter, *Why Tolerate Religion?* (Princeton, NJ: Princeton Univ. Press, 2013), 34, 40.

32 *Thomas v. Review Board, Indiana Employment Security Division*, 450 US 707 (1981).

33 Or, to take a less cerebral example, people who are struggling to get reliable childcare, and are fired because they are repeatedly absent or late as a result, are denied benefits. But people who repeatedly miss work because of their god have a right to such benefits. For a particularly poignant example, see *Nyaboga v. Evangelical Lutheran Good Samaritan Society*, No. A11-2067, 2012 WL 3641017, at *2 (Minn. Ct. App. Aug. 27, 2012).

34 Memorandum Order, *United States v. Chansley* (1:21-cr-00003), District Court, District of Columbia by Judge Royce C. Lamberth, Feb. 3, 2021, https://bit.ly/37SwiKb. See also Nicole Chavez and Christina Carrega, "'QAnon Shaman' Rioter Will Eat Organic Food, While Most Prisons and Jails Have Reputation for Serving Food That Is Unhealthy," CNN, Feb. 9, 2021, https://cnn.it/3Q5qn63.

35 *United States v. Seeger*, 380 US 163 (1965); *Welsh v. United States*, 398 US 333 (1970); *Gillette v. United States*, 401 US 437 (1971).

36 Daniel Carroll, delegate from Maryland to the First Congress, Annals of Congress, House of Representatives, 1st Congress, 1st Session, Aug. 15, 1789, 757–58, https://bit.ly/3vNHb8k.

37 James Madison, Annals of Congress, House of Representatives, 1st Congress, 1st Session 440-51 (June 8, 1789) House Debate. See also *The Founders' Constitution* Vol. 5, *Amendment I (Speech and Press)*, Document 14 (Chicago: Univ. of Chicago Press), http://press-pubs.uchicago.edu/founders/documents/amendI_speechs14.html.

38 These numbers are not reliable, and the military rarely publishes data about the religious makeup of its force. They lump the nones as "Other/Unclassified/Unknown." Kristy N. Kamarck, *Diversity, Inclusion, and Equal Opportunity in the Armed Services: Background and Issues for Congress* (Washington, DC: Congressional Research

Service, 2019), https://fas.org/sgp/crs/natsec/R44321.pdf. The Military Association of Atheists and Freethinkers has been using FOIA to compile data for a decade, http://militaryatheists.org/demographics/.

39 Tony Perkins, "Atheist Chaplains: Seeing Isn't Believing!" *Patriot Post*, July 25, 2013, https://bit.ly/39o7UBa.

40 "Religious Support and Internal Advisement," Army Techniques Publication No. 1-05.04, Mar. 23, 2017, 1–8, https://fas.org/irp/doddir/army/atp1-05-04.pdf.

41 See, e.g., *United States v. Isham*, 48 M.J. 603 (N.M.Ct.Crim.App. 1998).

42 Joseph B. Topinka and Matthew W. Caspari, "Legal Overview of Confidentiality and Reporting of Military Behavioral Health Records," in E. C. Ritchie, ed., *Forensic and Ethical Issues in Military Behavioral Health* (Office of the Surgeon General, Dept. of the Army, U.S.A., and the U.S. Army Medical Dept. Center and School, Fort Sam Houston, TX), 13–19, https://bit.ly/3MCavFl.

43 James Dao and Dan Frosch, "Military Rules Said to Hinder Therapy," *New York Times*, Dec. 7, 2009, https://nyti.ms/3ogco1r.

44 See, e.g., the Central Florida Freethought Community's activism in this arena, ably led by Jocelyn and David Williamson. Central Florida Freethought Community, "Invocations We've Given in Central FL," https://www.cflfreethought.org/invocations.

45 Complaint, Exhibit B, in *Barker v. Conroy*. 282 F. Supp. 3d 346 (D.D.C. 2017), https://bit.ly/3Obu5cn.

46 "The Satanic Temple Celebrates First Satanic Monument on Public Property," Associated Press, July 19, 2021, https://bit.ly/3MVag9a.

47 Michelle Margolis makes this argument in *From Politics to the Pews: How Partisanship and the Political Environment Shape Religious Identity* (Chicago: Univ. of Chicago Press, 2018); Sam Perry and Phil Gorski make this argument in *The Flag and the Cross: White Christian Nationalism and the Threat to American Democracy* (New York: Oxford Univ. Press, 2022).

48 Julie O'Donoghue, "Louisiana AG Jeff Landry Advises His Employees on How to Circumvent School COVID-19 Restrictions," *Louisiana Illuminator*, Aug. 3, 2021, https://bit.ly/3tq87ee.

49 Antonio Planas, "Brother and Sister Banned from High School for Not Wearing Masks," NBC News, Aug. 26, 2021, https://nbcnews.to/3z0FXtl.

50 Elisha Fieldstadt, "Ohio Lawmaker Refuses to Wear Mask Because He Says It Dishonors God," NBC News, May 6, 2020, https://nbcnews.to/3EXlExW.

51 "As a Christian pastor, theology professor and former seminary president, I will need someone to explain to me why wearing a face mask in a pandemic is at odds with being created in the image of God," wrote James Emery White in response to Landry. James Emery White, "About Those Religious Exemptions," *Church and Culture*, Aug. 26, 2021, https://bit.ly/3FSrzUs.

CONCLUSION

1 Leslie Griffin, "Symposium: Religions' Wins Are Losses," SCOTUSblog, Aug. 4, 2020, https://www.scotusblog.com/2020/08/symposium-religions-wins-are-losses/.

2 John Gramlich, "How Trump Compares with Other Recent Presidents in Appointing Federal Judges," Pew Research Center, Jan. 13, 2021, https://pewrsr.ch/3tMO7BB. The Senate confirmed three Trump nominees to the Supreme Court, 54 Trump nominees to the Circuit Courts, and 174 Trump nominees to the District Courts. The numbers are slightly jumbled because, for instance, four of the District Court nominees were nominated a few months later to Circuit Court positions. Barrett was nominated and confirmed to the Seventh Circuit and then months later to the Supreme Court.

3 "*Fiat justitia, ruat caelum*," Merriam-Webster.com, accessed May 29, 2021, https://bit.ly/3OWd07J.

4 *Reynolds v. United States*, 98 US 145 (1878).

5 Georg Strack, "The Sermon of Urban II in Clermont and the Tradition of Papal Oratory," *Medieval Sermon Studies* 56 (2012), 33, 35, https://bit.ly/3aIujJH.

6 Edward Peters, *The First Crusade: The Chronicle of Fulcher of Chartres and Other Source Materials* (Philadelphia: Univ. of Pennsylvania Press, 1971), 53. Robin W. Winks et. al., *A History of Civilization: Prehistory to the Present* (Englewood Cliffs, NJ: Prentice Hall, 1992), 239.

7 Amy Coney Barrett, "Associate Professor Amy Coney Barrett, Diploma Ceremony Address," Notre Dame Law School, Commencement Programs, May 2006, 13, https://scholarship.law.nd.edu/commencement_programs/13. | 8 Isaiah 2:2–4.

Index